The Fourth Civilization

The Fourth Civilization

Technology, Ethics, and Society

VOLUME ONE

RICHARD J. SUTCLIFFE

RESOURCE *Publications* • Eugene, Oregon

THE FOURTH CIVILIZATION
Technology, Ethics, and Society, Volume One

Copyright © 2024 Richard J. Sutcliffe. All rights reserved. Except for brief quotations in critical publications or reviews, no part of this book may be reproduced in any manner without prior written permission from the publisher. Write: Permissions, Wipf and Stock Publishers, 199 W. 8th Ave., Suite 3, Eugene, OR 97401.

Resource Publications
An Imprint of Wipf and Stock Publishers
199 W. 8th Ave., Suite 3
Eugene, OR 97401

www.wipfandstock.com

PAPERBACK ISBN: 979-8-3852-2681-8
HARDCOVER ISBN: 979-8-3852-2682-5
EBOOK ISBN: 979-8-3852-2683-2

11/26/24

Scripture quotations marked (NIV) are taken from the Holy Bible, New International Version®, NIV®. Copyright © 1973, 1978, 1984, 2011 by Biblica, Inc.™ Used by permission of Zondervan. All rights reserved worldwide. www.zondervan.com. The "NIV" and "New International Version" are trademarks registered in the United States Patent and Trademark Office by Biblica, Inc.™

Scripture quotations marked (ESV) are from the ESV® Bible (The Holy Bible, English Standard Version®), © 2001 by Crossway, a publishing ministry of Good News Publishers. Used by permission. All rights reserved. The ESV text may not be quoted in any publication made available to the public by a Creative Commons license. The ESV may not be translated in whole or in part into any other language.

To my dearest wife Joyce, now enjoying heaven,
Our sons Nathan and Joel,
Our daughters-in law Charlene and Jen,
and
Our seven wonderful Sutcliffe Grandchildren

Contents

Acknowledgments	ix
Introduction	xi
Preface	xix

Part One | Laying The Groundwork

1	History and Technology	3
2	The Foundations of Science and Technology	67
3	Basic Concepts in the Theory of Ethics	145

Part Two | Four Wavefronts On A Sea Of Change

4	The Information Revolution	221
5	Robotics and the Second Industrial Revolution	298
6	The Intelligence Revolution	342
7	The Biospace Revolution	387

Bibliography	459

Acknowledgments

EVERY WRITER OWES A debt to others who have gone before. Some of those whose influence may be detected here are: Carl Henry, C.S. Lewis, John Warwick Montgomery, Francis Shaeffer, Eric Drexler, Edward O. Wilson, the contributors to and editors of such publications as Analog and Popular Science, Henry Morris, Isaac Asimov, and a host of others—some mentioned in the reading list, and others not.

Much of the original version of this manuscript was typed by Miss Nancy Tiffin, a student of Trinity Western University. Portions have also been read and commented on by Dr. John Klassen, now retired Professor of History at TWU, and much encouragement for work of this type has been provided by the (now retired) academic dean and vice-president of TWU, Dr. Ken Davis—the epitome of a Christian scholar and gentleman to all who know him, and by Glen Van Brummelen, a Mathematics Historian who uncovered the true history of the decimal point, and Dean of the TWU Science faculty during the time this fifth edition was prepared.

In addition, the efforts of various reviewers of the earlier versions are greatly appreciated. Not only did they correct numerous errors, but also pointed out many places where the writing was unclear, jumped too hastily to conclusions, or obscurely stated the points being made. It was heartening to see several of them drawn into the discussion sufficiently to argue specific points all over the draft pages. If other readers receive this book in the same spirit, it will have been a success, even if nearly everyone disagrees with nearly everything in it.

On a more personal note, my late wife Joyce, and my two sons, Nathan and Joel, also suffered patiently through some neglect when the final draft of the first edition was being prepared, and I deeply appreciate their encouragement to go on, even at times when the task seemed too great.

Introduction

Purpose

THIS BOOK IS INTENDED to stimulate its readers to think about the ethical and societal consequences of some of the technology that they use already, or that may be about to become important. It attempts to lay a foundation for the study of such issues in a fashion that integrates history, ethics, and religious beliefs with technique.

It has been clear to many people for some time that fundamental social changes are taking place as a result of the introduction of new and sophisticated technologies. Most discussions of this concentrate on the transitions themselves, but this book is an attempt to outline what will become the chief operating assumptions of society if and when the turmoil of transition is largely past. One of these assumptions is that far more of its citizens will need a basis for ethical decision-making and, as a consequence, will need to have considered such issues before they face them as decision-makers. Another is that specialization will be replaced by integration.

Thus, this book is idea- rather than data-oriented. This may cause some difficulty for its readers, for such discussions are no longer common. However, its thesis is that they will become both necessary and routine, and the book can therefore be viewed as an attempt to practice what it preaches—to be a part of the New Renaissance literature and to inspire its readers to become New Renaissance people.

Likewise, the vocabulary level is at a higher level than that often used in books intended for either university or general audiences. This is deliberate and is intended not simply to expand the readers' word list, but to require them to work at the book, rather than skim it.

INTRODUCTION

The idea is not merely to discuss difficult issues at a level accessible to second and third-year students, but to provide some experiences that will serve as a means of helping decision-makers think about the broad consequences of high technology and begin to culturally relate their decision-making so that it is not done in a vacuum.

On the other hand, some of the factual material, for instance relating to history, ethical schools, and specific scientific material and technologies is patently not in-depth, but mere overview. Specialists in any of the many disciplines discussed herein are welcome therefore to view such treatments as superficial, but doing otherwise would increase the size of this work many times over and defeat the integrative purpose altogether.

Audience

The original intention was to direct this book to technically literate students of science, computing, engineering, and/or technology. In the case of technical schools or institutes, such students would normally be in their second term or second year. If university students, they would be in their third or fourth year. However, since the only prerequisite for the study of the topics here is the willingness to think, students in all other disciplines and the public as a whole ought also to find this work of interest. Indeed, what is being encouraged here is not just a tentative crossover by arts, humanities, or science students, so that they peek gingerly into the other's territory. Rather, the readers are being asked to move towards radical integrations of the hitherto separate compartments of their lives and thinking.

In any case, the audience consists of potential professionals or technicians who need a foundation for making decisions with ethical and societal consequences. Since another of the assumptions being made here is that the term "professional" will aptly describe most workers in the next civilization, this is a broad audience indeed.

Warning To Students

In the author's classes, you usually get higher marks for arguing against him and his textbook than simply agreeing with him. It depends on how well your arguments are supported and presented. This may or may not be true in a course you are taking from someone else, so be cautious.

INTRODUCTION

Organization

The book consists of three major parts and a concluding section.

PART I lays the groundwork with a brief consideration of the historical and foundational perspectives in technological and societal change, and attempts to provide an understanding of the basis for ethical thinking. Here, the case is made that history, technology, and ethical decision-making are linked. They must be studied together because they necessarily act together and are used together.

PART II concentrates on describing major recent and current technological changes and makes some extrapolations and speculations about the future. It deals with the major trends and forces that are shaping the new civilization. Some of the notions here are pushed rather far; this is done intentionally to highlight the potential dangers of taking certain technologies to their ultimate conclusions. Readers are invited to decide for themselves whether some of the suggested future technologies are possible or even plausible but to keep in mind that many things considered to be neither by past generations are now a fact. Indeed some of the forecasts made in the earliest editions of this work are now partially or completely fulfilled and have been edited from future tense to past tense.

PART III deals with technological issues relating to society and certain of its key institutions. The potential responses of those involved in law, government, business, education, and religion are considered in detail.

Part IV concentrates on individuals and their lives in the new society, and also constitutes the concluding chapter. It represents an attempt to collect the fragments of the closing days of the industrial age and suggest some ways in which they can be integrated into the next civilization.

Each chapter, and some additional sections, is introduced with a "set piece." These are seminar conversations among a small class of university students taking a course based on this book. In keeping with an old tradition in Philosophy, these dialogues feature a regular cast of characters along with a few visitors.

The regulars include:

Dorcas—a New Testament-era figure who is innocent of modern history and technology,

INTRODUCTION

Ellen Westlake—a modern feminist skeptic, law student, and radical socialist,

Nellie Hacker—a computing student with an impatient desire for truth,

Johanna Lud—a sensitive sculptor and poet whose secret passion is to smash all machines, and

Alicia—whose real identity is hidden behind a microphone and speaker until later in the book.

Their arguments are moderated by the *Professor*—a somewhat bemused individual whose function it is to keep its participants on track.
Frequent guests are:

Lucas Dominic—a powerfully built, precocious local high school student, and

Eider, Mara—from Earths with different histories, technologies, and societies than ours.

Mother Goose makes a cameo appearance, at least in part to assure the reader that all these characters are fictional.

For the 2024 edition, some discussions are revisited or renewed as the characters participate in a reunion in the same venue.

These set pieces cover a wide range of topics but are more specific than the chapter material and quite informal. The idea is to provoke (engage, startle) the reader to think about at least a few of the issues before settling into a somewhat more systematic consideration. Even the main body of each chapter is written somewhat more conversationally than most books at this level because a formal style would mitigate against achieving the goals of the book.

To facilitate additional discussion by the readers, questions at the end of each chapter ask for a more detailed consideration of points made in the chapter or connected with it. Some of these may suggest major projects All of this will be found under the heading of "Further Discussion," rather than "Exercises"—a slight but deliberate blurring of the textbook mystique. No answer key is provided, and in the actual classes based on this book, the author does not offer more than a low average final grade to students who merely parrot his views. In classroom debates, he expects students to undertake a defense of views not their own and offer critiques of those they hold. Engagement, rather than uniformity of views, is the optimal outcome. After all, few people change their views on

INTRODUCTION

topics important to them as a consequence of an argument with someone else. But perhaps engagement can at least lead to self-examination.

A modest bibliography of articles and books accessible to students at these levels and to casual readers is provided in an Appendix.

Instructors making use of this book may feel free to condense material that is very familiar to their students, depending on their backgrounds. It is not recommended that any chapters be left out in entirety; rather, selected ones should be supplemented with related materials according to student interests.

Content

In another departure from modern dogma, the book is not sanitized of religious thought and ideas; but these are an integral part of it, where such references are appropriate. A discussion of ethical issues in the Western version of modern civilization would be hopelessly incomplete if shorn of any reference to the Judeo-Christian influence that shaped this culture's institutions over the centuries. Chapter 11, on the role of religion in society, is critical to the book, and is presented with the hope that it adds some insights that are usually missing in modern works.

Again, the material here is *not* presented at what is usually termed "scholarly depth," and this will disturb some traditionalists. This book attempts breadth, partly as a countervail to industrial age specialization, and partly because of the belief that breadth will be a prerequisite for every citizen of the Fourth Civilization. This is a controversial assumption, and as reviewers have already indicated, each chapter is separately vulnerable to criticism for that lack of scholarly depth by the specialists in the topic of that chapter. The fact that most such specialist reviewers also thought the content of other chapters to be profound may be an indication that the book has achieved the necessary breadth in a limited number of pages without becoming overly superficial.

Because of the interdisciplinary and survey nature of this work, there is little here for which startling originality can be claimed. Even portions of the Metalibrary concept have been thought of and partially implemented by several others (using different names, such as "hypermedia" and the "world wide web") since the first draft of this manuscript was created. Only the name is original. Others have taken the "meta" concept further, applying it to the Metaverse, a term that can mean either the virtual world in its entirety or a simulation of a real or imaginary world.

The models for personhood in the context of education and religion provided in Chapters 10 and 11 represent modest attempts to improve on many previous abstractions of similar types. The model for ethical theories presented in Chapter 3 is a modification of that devised by Carl Henry, and the framework for the creation/evolution debate is largely to be found in the works of the protagonists themselves.

What may be original is the assembly of material from so many disciplines into a single book, and the call for a new integration of it all—even a prediction that it must be so integrated. The term "new Renaissance" to describe some of the opening years of the Fourth Civilization has, not, to the author's knowledge, been used previously by others before this author coined it about 1980, and his examination of the prospects for a new reformation of religion may also be unique. Likewise the term "Metalibrary" is the author's own, with the prefix and noun "Meta" as used by others appearing decades later.

However, even though the author owes obvious debts to many others, herein will not be found the usual assembly of quotations in support of the book's theses. Except in the section on creation and evolution, where the protagonists present their cases, the discussions are based partly on reading, and partly on experience and observation. That is, while this book necessarily exists as part of many far larger streams of thought and literature, the reader is asked to evaluate its content for itself, not for the weight of quotations the author could have assembled to add force to its arguments.

One early reviewer commented (apparently negatively) that this book mixes descriptive and evaluative comments. This may not be conventional wisdom today, but one of its major premises is that all description is necessarily to some extent evaluative. The students's task is not to separate the two but to assume that every statement, having been filtered through the maker's worldview, assumes some evaluation in its making, and requires more for its understanding. This is true of every book, even when the works of others are referenced, and especially when they are quoted, for such apparent support for the author's theses masks the fact that all such references have been filtered by the one selecting them, and cannot be taken merely at face value out of their entire context. Even bibliographies reflect such selection; there are hundreds of additional books that could have been a part of every such list. In this case, they represent a

INTRODUCTION

few possible starting points for further exploration. Any instructor using this book for a course will have another such reading list, and its intersection with the one here may be rather small. In addition, the assignments point out many of the controversial issues by inviting the reader to refute either the author's contentions or those of the sources cited.

Thus, some parts are polemical, because some issues are more important than others, and they become major theses of the book by being argued. Other topics are "only" described, but in such description, there are numerous assumptions. It is when the assumptions are less obvious that there may be the most danger in blithely and uncritically accepting them; one need be much less concerned in this respect with the controversial. The reader should therefore take to heart a warning that the contents of this book are presented by the author as a true expression of individual belief and sum of experience. The words "mere opinion" may be used to dismiss the entire work, but this pejorative is itself overworked and therefore conveys little meaningful information.

Related Literature

Many books have been written to explain technology, particularly since the 1970s, and there have recently been some specific works on ethical issues related to business or computing, but the author knows of no directly competing book. Again, the assumption here is that such interdisciplinary and integrative studies will become routine in the Fourth Civilization; that such a blend is therefore essential to understanding the society now emerging. No doubt this will eventually become just one in a long list of similar books, and many of them will surely improve on the treatment given the themes here.

Preface

I OFFER THIS BOOK with the typically Canadian hope that it will assist in the pulling together of diverse threads and that it will promote peace and unity between peoples of different national and cultural backgrounds, and having differing worldviews.—Aldergrove, 1988 08 03

Comments on the 1998 Revision

This book was initially commissioned by a commercial publisher and had reached the stage of advertising when two successive events killed the commercial project.

First, some members of the editing staff raised objections about (a) the Christian orientation of the writing, and (b) the "Science-Fiction" aspects of some of the predictions—most notably those of the Metalibrary and PIEA, the fall of the Soviet Union, conflict in the Balkans, and the reunification of the Germanies. No apology is needed for the former; there are plenty of books with other biases editors don't mind publishing; at least this one has its predispositions openly displayed. As for most of the latter, I can only say that time has proved or is proving me correct.

Second, the would-be publisher was bought out by a huge conglomerate, closed, and all the copyrights returned to the respective authors. Thus, apart from its use as a course book at Trinity Western University in the early 1990s, the materials languished on the shelf for nearly a decade.

A lot has happened in ten years, and the minor changes in this text are too numerous to list. Perhaps more interesting is what remains the same. The main thesis of the book, its logical organization, and its conclusions remain unchanged. If anything, the support in actual events is stronger than ever, and my conviction of the necessity for a comprehensive integration of knowledge with other aspects of what makes us

PREFACE

human has increased. Of course, some forecasts had to be switched to the past tense. Others may be by the next edition.

Meanwhile, many students have suffered through the use of this book, and so have conference attendees and others who have heard portions of it expounded, so there have been new critics, and almost all of them have forced me to make changes. Perhaps the most important of these is an extensive re-writing of the last three chapters, where much material has been added. Some that were removed at the request of the publisher are back in, some scientific and other errors introduced by the publisher's overzealous copy editor removed, and certain of the discussions now have a more obvious Christian bias. Readers are even more encouraged to disagree. Teachers of this material are encouraged to have students present those disagreements to the class and to hold formal debates on some of the issues raised. The courses based on this book at Trinity Western University employ outside speakers, an intersection with interdisciplinary courses offered by other departments, debates, and student presentations to ensure other views are considered.

This time, let me express the additional hope that the book will provoke my fellow workers in the scientific community to a comprehensive dialogue among all the disciplines of the modern university, and in particular with my fellow Christian intellectuals.—Bradner, 1998 11 03, revised 2000 08 06, and 2002 06 30

Further Comments on the 2000 WWW revisions

The Summer of 2000 saw the decision to put the entire book on the World Wide Web as shareware. This was done for two reasons. First, conventional publishers seemed little interested. Mainstream houses do not publish much with Christian content, and Christian houses lack expertise in technical areas. Neither are interested in interdisciplinary tomes. Second, it's time to practice what I've preached for years. The Metalibrary is being formed and this book might as well be an early part of it. Besides, my programming text has sold better in self-published form on the Internet than it ever did with a conventional publisher, and my fiction also became available there this year. Since this text gave rise to the fiction, it seems appropriate it be web-ified as well. More extensive revisions may be undertaken in two years, and input is welcomed.

PREFACE

In the course of preparation for the web, a few typos were removed and an index was prepared. The latter work provoked other minor changes and clarifications, especially in newer material. The reader might notice some inconsistencies in spelling, the use of parentheses, and the use of hyphens in compound adjectives. These arise because the original publisher edited away Canadian spellings and I have not thought it practical to restore them, but the newer material is mostly spelled Canadian, eh?—Bradner, 2000 08 06

Comments on the 2002 revisions

The text underwent careful editing, changes back to consistent Canadian orthography, and saw numerous clarifications and updatings, perhaps several thousand changes in all. Some arguments were sharpened, and a small amount of outdated material was removed. Interestingly, most of the book has continued to stand the test of time well. One of my worries, that in a sufficiently advanced technological society, individuals could too easily gather into their hands the means of mass destruction, has proven all too prescient with the September 11, 2001, World Trade Center attacks.

Indeed, this concern provoked my excursion into fiction, where I explore the ideas of this book in the context of an alternate society, one with different priorities and problems. Many of the characters who conduct the dialogues have made their way into this fiction, some of it already published, some yet to appear. For this edition, I owe a special and large debt to I.K. Romero, who undertook to read and comment on the entire text and who discovered numerous small flaws that had escaped all previous editors.—Bradner, 2002 07 10

Comments on the 2024 Edition

Twenty years using this book have passed with only minor corrections made to the content for the fourth edition in 2004, ones that seemed not to need a comment here. The surprise is that more than 90 percent of the material is still as relevant as when written and the book has only one new subsection added to the original table of contents. In particular, apart from minor updates and additions, the section on artificial intelligence is substantively unchanged. Several classes have used the material in the intervening years, but it has become dated, especially as more of its predictions, once thought bold (if not fantastic as some would-be editors claimed), have long since materialized in whole or part. One of the more important, found several times in the author's technology column The Northern Spy but only slightly mentioned previously here, was that far from the Internet creating a global village of mutual understanding, cooperation, and even love as many technological optimists were boldly forecasting, it would instead exacerbate differences, stoke old hatreds, and empower extremists. In many of the arenas examined herein that scenario has not only materialized, it has become a defining characteristic of 2024 society.

The spreading of lies, the acceptance of misinformation, the mistrust of science and government—all have escalated in more recent years, and are some of the issues expanded upon in these revisions. As predicted, bringing people closer together via instant communication only enabled haters to congregate and reinforce each other against those who were hated of old. Lies, racism, sexism, and ethnic and political hatreds pervade modern life.

The sideways spinoff of what was here called the Metalibrary long before the word "Internet" was coined and the World Wide Web created, into what some now refer to as the Metaverse also gets a mention. The author's term was about universal information and its access; the latter is said to be about constructing and experiencing one's virtual reality—a quintessential isolating behavior in an era where profound social, political, and economic cooperation is more needed than ever before.

So there is much to talk about—new bibliographic sources to mention, new technology and societal directions to consider, and new political, military, health, and ethical crises to dissect.

However, many of the predictive parts, some written in the 1980s, especially those dealing directly with information and artificial intelligence, have merely been altered from future tense to past tense, others only modestly elaborated or somewhat reworded, but not substantially changed.

It is worth observing once again that the discussions here on the historical studies, the philosophy of science, epistemology in general, and moral philosophy in particular, are not intended to convey a professional analysis of each discipline, but a working summary intended to be generally applicative and practical rather than specifically academic and theoretical. Professionals in most of those fields will therefore find

PREFACE

the approach here to be incomplete, perhaps simplistic, but they should consider the intended audience—not their graduate students, but undergraduates in computing and other sciences who need broader perspectives beyond their subject area. Thorough integration at a high level to the satisfaction of all disciplines would require numerous volumes, fragment rather than integrate the narrative, have no appeal to the intended audience, and therefore be unusable for everybody.

Moreover, in light of events of the 2020s, the optimism of previous editions has been muted in this fifth edition, for the forces of racism, sexism, willful ignorance, intolerance, hatred, brutality, and war have increased rather than decreased in power thus far, partly or wholly because a smaller percentage of people possess anything resembling a fixed moral/ethical compass, but perhaps more because one could expect fragmentation to be exacerbated in the death throes of a fragmented age. The real question then may be not so much what shape the Fourth Civilization will take, but whether there will be anything left to become the fourth once the third has fully imploded.

Students in a Trinity Western University course were given a draft of the new edition for the fall 2022 semester, and that has provoked more additions and revisions, including a thorough spelling and grammar check. So have events of the past two years. Several thousand minor changes were made, and a few discussions expanded.

One of the most obvious changes for this fifth edition is a radical reorganization and a very significant update of the bibliography. Previously, each chapter had its list of works relevant to that chapter. However, the topics herein are all so connected, that such a strategy became impossible to manage coherently, making some important works difficult to assign to one chapter and producing excess duplication. For this edition therefore, all the works directly consulted, plus a few not yet in the author's possession but whose online descriptions seem interesting and relevant have been combined into a single listing in the end matter. Some works have been deleted, references to classics updated to reflect reprints and/or subsequent editions, and numerous newer volumes added to the list. The result is far from comprehensive. Whereas there were few textbooks at the intersection of technology, ethics, and society when the then soon-to-be-defunct Charles Merrill Publishing commissioned the first edition of this book in the 1980s, there are far too many to list today. Serious students of the subject will find it easy to locate many more relevant works.

PREFACE

Another important change is that the publisher's binding restrictions require the content to be split into two volumes, each encompassing two of the four sections.

It seems likely this edition will be published by a house located in the United States. Thus, the orthography and punctuation have, sadly, reverted to American.—Bradner and Langley, 2024 08 30

PART ONE

Laying The Groundwork

CHAPTER 1

History and Technology

THE JOURNEY TO ENLIGHTENMENT *begins on the ivy-covered campus of the Memorial University of the Sciences, the Humanities, Education, Arts, and Technology (MUSHEAT), a private West Coast Liberal Arts University whose lacrosse teams once terrified the league with their battle cry of "Eat Mush."*

In a curiously self-referential twist, the MUSHEAT computing science department offers a course based on this very text. The time is variable, with most of the conversation recorded here in 1985 taking place around the year 2000, but with a few edited clarifications or inserted comments made by some characters at periodic informal reunions lasting more than the following two decades (anachronistically permitting later revisions, where necessary, to catch up with a forecasted or anticipated future that had morphed into an actual past, or taken on a new aspect in the light of events). A very few insertions were offered by children of some of the initial characters when they took the course more recently, in one case, by a student whose mother and father were both among the initial participants. For clarity and (in)consistency, those comments are, in the latest edition, attributed to their parents—with their permission, of course.

As the first session opens, the Professor, Nellie Hacker, and Ellen Westlake are sitting at a table in a small seminar room. As the first edition is written, some fifteen years before these seminars, Nellie is depicted as a senior student in computer science, and Ellen is finishing law school at a nearby larger university part-time while working as an organizer for HUBRIS (the Hoteliers' United Bouncers and Roustabouts Industrial Society).

PART ONE | LAYING THE GROUNDWORK

She is taking this course nearer her home for transfer credit. A third student, Alicia Copland, is not present in the room but communicates with the other participants remotely by microphone and speaker, though not video. There are several empty seats reserved for late enrollees who could not make it to the first class and will view recordings to catch up. Before each class, all students enrolled in the seminar were required to read the appropriate material in this text, though initially not these dialogues, for that degree of self-referentialism induces logical contradictions that would imperil either their completeness (and possibly their very existence) or else their consistency, both contraindicated given their engagement to play their roles both throughout this textbook and also in the author's novels of the Timestream.

Professor: Well, what did you think of the chapter on history and technology?

Nellie: I'm still not sure why we ought to be concerned with history at all. I thought this was a course on technology and related ethical and social issues.

Ellen: History is meaningless except as a record of the struggle of workers to master their destinies in the face of oppression.

Nellie: It seems to me that people are a lot better off under good old Western-style capitalism than they ever were under Marxist dictatorships.

Professor: Alicia, how about something from you to keep us on track?

Alicia: (from the speaker) Good afternoon, Professor. Thank you for allowing me to participate in the discussions. Could I suggest that advances in technology are the driving force behind historical events?

Ellen: That's true, but eventually the workers must and will control the technology and create history themselves.

Nellie: Haven't you heard, Ellen? Marxism is dead; we're at the end of history, and liberal democracy has triumphed. There are no Soviets anymore and the current communists are state capitalist dictators.

Ellen: We will not be at the end of history until the mass of workers control the means of production.

Alicia: In the past, most technology-driven historical watersheds centered on just a few individuals, or even a single person, rather than on the actions of a large number of people.

HISTORY AND TECHNOLOGY

At this point the door opens, and another participant enters, taking one of the empty seats.

Professor: Let me introduce a new member of our group. I have borrowed Dorcas, also known as Tabitha, from the first century A.D.—specifically from the book of Acts Chapter Nine.

Ellen: (startled) How did you do that?

Nellie: (chuckling) Better not to ask, Ellen. Anything can (and usually does) happen in the Professor's seminars. Hello, Dorcas.

General introductions follow, in which it is revealed that Dorcas' specialty is the study of history.

Professor: Alicia, I believe you mentioned the link between technology and historical events.

Alicia: Yes, and I was about to illustrate. Tell me, Nellie, why did David defeat Goliath?

Nellie: (hesitantly) Because David trusted in God?

Dorcas: You sound like you're only saying that because you think it's what the Professor would like to hear.

Nellie: (sharply) Well, you surely agree.

Dorcas: Of course. But David also used a higher technology than Goliath. A spear carrier like the Philistine had no chance against a high-speed projectile. David knew that and used it to his advantage. Why do you think the bow and arrow were invented?

Alicia: Quite so. Now Ellen, why did the Germans lose the Battle of Britain? They were numerically superior in the air.

Ellen: Fascists always lose, eventually.

Nellie: You've missed the point. The British had radar and the Nazis didn't; right, Alicia?

Alicia: Close enough. The Germans had the technology but failed to deploy it. Further illustrations, please.

Nellie: English long-bowmen in the day of King Richard made armor obsolete by being able to penetrate it from a distance.

Dorcas: Alexander took Tyre because he had better siege equipment than the Babylonians who had tried and failed before him. He could

5

PART ONE | LAYING THE GROUNDWORK

not have carried on his campaign against Egypt and Persia with a hostile city at his back. His success at Tyre encouraged him to go on as far as India.

Nellie: Enough on war, already. What of the plow, the steam engine, internal combustion, numerous medical advances, the vacuum tube and transistor, the computer, and the smartphone? In their way, each of these altered subsequent history. All were initially the work of one or a very small number of people.

Professor: Shall we regard Alicia's proposition as proven, and consider the converse?

Ellen: When society is ready for a technology, it gets invented? History drives technology at least as much as the other way around. We get the inventions the workers need and deserve.

Nellie: You're right about that. There are numerous examples of the simultaneous independent discovery of ideas in mathematics when the time was appropriate. Calculus and non-Euclidean geometry are two examples.

Dorcas: The system of Roman roads and aqueducts was as much a response to the need for better services to growing cities and the requirement for better communications as a driving force behind the spread of the Roman version of civilization.

Nellie: Edison set out quite deliberately to invent the light bulb. He was meeting a known need.

Dorcas: It's been re-invented? How interesting.

Alicia: Who is to say that the automobile so much shaped modern society as its invention was necessitated by the direction society was already taking? Better transportation was necessary to hold more spread-out cultures together.

Dorcas: Which came first, the worm, or the dirt?

Alicia: I think that lost something in the translation, Dorcas. Now, identify the critical technological advances that have most influenced the course of civilization.

Nellie: The gathering and storing of seed.

Dorcas: The domestication of animals. The plow. The idea that people could gather in one place and make the land give them what they wanted rather than having to go out and find their food. Agriculture made communities and towns possible and efficiencies on the farm allowed some community members to be released from food gathering to become scholars and teachers . . .

Ellen: (interrupting) . . . and oppressors such as kings . . .

Nellie: (cutting her off) . . . not to mention communist dictators, economists, lawyers, and greedy union leaders.

Professor: Order, please. Next stage?

Ellen: Easy enough. You liberate the animals by building machines to do the work. Massive population shifts take place. Capitalists take advantage of the naivety of the migrating farm workers to enslave them to the new machines and a new round of . . .

Nellie: . . . oppression begins. Yes, we know. And, what about modern sanitation, medicine, and all the consumer goodies that became available to the "masses" during the industrial age? Face it, Ellen. People are better off now than they were before it began. Besides, those oppressed industrial workers were starving in squalor in the countryside, and as bad as those urban conditions were, the cities were an improvement.

Professor: I'm going to have to wear a striped shirt to class to keep the two of you under control.

Alicia: If I may finish, the high technology of automated machinery, computers, video, communications, transportation, and medicine is creating a new revolution with as profound a set of changes as any time in the past.

Professor: If society and technology drive each other, what are the catalysts?

Dorcas: People.

Nellie: Do you mean society as a whole?

Dorcas: No, but particular individuals with a great vision who almost single-handedly changed the course of history.

Professor: Examples, please.

Dorcas: Alexander, Julius Caesar, Plato . . .

Nellie: Galileo, Newton, Einstein . . .

PART ONE | LAYING THE GROUNDWORK

Ellen: Marx, Lenin, Stalin . . .

Nellie: (clasping her head in her hands in exasperation) Oh, my God.

Dorcas: (matter-of-factly) Jesus Christ was the greatest revolutionary of them all.

Ellen: There's no evidence he even existed. If you ask me . . .

Nellie: What rot; we didn't. Do you believe Tiberius Caesar existed?

Ellen: Of course.

Nellie: Why?

Ellen: (hesitantly) Well, the testimony of historians, of course.

Nellie: But the testimony of contemporary historians for the life of Christ is much more consistent, was written at a date closer to the events, has far more documentary evidence, and therefore is much more likely to be authentic than that for Tiberius.

Professor: You have a point, but I think a little research might soften that view somewhat, Nellie. This is a good place to intervene and ask how a historian "knows" anything. Dorcas is the expert here.

Dorcas: A good historian gathers many accounts of events, sifts and compares them, and publishes what seems to be a factual account based on the weight of evidence.

Nellie: But, what about the inaccuracies and deceptions?

Dorcas: Some do embellish and deceive, but a good historian tells it as it was, and attempts to provide reasons why people behaved as they did, keeping the personal ideology at a minimum.

Professor: (looking at the wall clock) Good definition, but I'm afraid our time has elapsed for this week. I'll have a little thousand-word essay from each of you on this topic.

He gathers his books and leaves. As he does so, Nellie and Ellen begin a new discussion that the closing door cuts off.

Nellie: You see, Ellen—history is facts—just the facts.

Ellen: No, that's not true; the winners get to write history. Interpretations become the facts. If one generation sees things with a different perspective, history itself changes, because we create our own worlds, and this is certainly true of the historical ones. In the long run, it is not the original facts that matter, but how the masses are conditioned to interpret . . .

1.1 The Art and Science of History

Students often think of history as a simple listing of events, names, and dates. However, an understanding of events also requires knowing something of both the motivations influencing the people who made those events happen, and of the methods by which the results were achieved. In particular, the history of every society is intertwined on the one hand with its technological development, and on the other with the moral and ethical principles upon which the society is built. This book is concerned with all three concepts (history, technology, and ethics) and the relationships among them.

One goal of the study of history is attempting to look ahead as well as back, for by understanding the past and present one gains keys to the future. For instance, even though the technology that will influence the society of the future is very different from that which shaped historical events, there is still much to be learned by examining the past. It is possible to see how societies have already responded to (or developed from) radical technological changes, and thus to suggest how current trends might shape the future. To assist in this, a brief examination of the nature of historical studies is in order.

> There is a flow to history and culture. This flow is rooted in and has its wellspring in the thoughts of people. People are unique in the inner life of the mind—what they are in their thought world determines how they act. This is true of their value systems and it is true of their creativity, true of their corporate actions, such as political decisions, and it is true of their personal lives. The results of their thought flow through their fingers or from their tongues into the external world. This is true of Michelangelo's chisel, and it is true of the dictator's sword.—the late Francis Schaeffer in *How Should We Then Live*

What Does a Historian Do?

A historian is more than simply a collector of facts about the past or present. In some ways, the "doing of history" is not unlike that of science, for in both disciplines it is well understood that a collection of data, however vast, does not become useful information until it is organized and interpreted. Like a courtroom judge who must sift through often conflicting eyewitness reports to discover the truth of events, the historian must reconcile accounts of the events under study that are often in sharp disagreement.

There are various reasons for the contradictions that arise even between eyewitness accounts of the same event. For instance, suppose two people standing at the roadside witness a traffic accident from different angles, each noticing aspects that the other does not. The first witness observes a car stop at an intersection and another car attempt to pass on the left, whereupon the stopped car suddenly makes a left turn and is struck broadside by the passing car. Everyone in both vehicles is killed and little is evident about the cause of the accident from the tangled wreckage. This witness is convinced that the driver of the passing car is at fault for attempting to pass when it was not safe to do so. The second witness, however, sees the accident from the front and to the left of the flow of traffic instead of from the right side and behind as does the first. She observed that the stopped car had a right-turn signal on when the moving car attempted to pass on the left. To her, the accident is the fault of the driver who signaled to turn one way and did the opposite.

Yet, despite knowledge of the misleading turn signal, the coroner who examines the bodies comes to agree with the first witness. She once barely avoided a similar accident by reacting quickly on the brake pedal to a slight movement of the leading driver's arm. Wondering why the following driver did not pick up such a clue despite the false signal, she tests the body of the passing car's driver and finds the blood alcohol content to be four times the legal limit. She has little doubt about where most of the blame lies.

Previous experiences, the time of day, road conditions, lighting, the amount of time spent watching, racial and sexual prejudice, and what a witness expected to see all might also color the reports that a court hears. Each person takes the stand sworn to tell the whole truth, but even if all do exactly that to the best of their abilities, there will still be disagreements and contradictions.

Moreover, knowledge arrived at in such a manner should never be equated with absolute truth. It may have a sufficiently high probability of being close enough to the truth to settle blame or guilt in a courtroom, even when the required standard is to be "beyond any reasonable doubt," but the door must be allowed to remain open for new evidence on which to base an appeal to overturn the initial ruling

Likewise, when considering historical events, it is necessary to take into account such things as nationalism, the pride of winners, the shame of losers, and the tendency of reporters and historians to support a particular academic theory, political or religious faction, or an individual historical figure. As a result of such biases, the accounts of world events reaching a later historian will diverge even more than those of the traffic accident in the example above. Add in the passage of hundreds or thousands of years and the perils of assigning credibility to third or fourth-hand copies of originals—each possibility embellished with the copyist's ideas—and it may become difficult to sift original contemporary fact from later revisions or myths.

What is more, historians have usually concentrated on the few outstanding figures who were at the center of events—the kings, queens, generals, politicians, academics, technologists, and other acknowledged movers and shakers. Where there were sources available from minority groups or common citizens, these were often too fragmentary (or too voluminous) to shed much light on the larger events that shaped the time under study. This is changing as computers allow such material to be assembled and sifted to get a broader or more everyday perspective on events.

Establishing the facts carefully and scientifically using the same kind of evidence weighing employed in a courtroom is the first task of a historian. The accuracy of newly discovered accounts must be assessed by checking them against other documents (perhaps describing related events) whose reliability is already accepted. The personality, motives, level of education, and knowledge of the account's author must also be taken into consideration.

For instance, in a society that attaches great importance to the mythology of a variety of gods and goddesses, the appearance of a comet or the conjunction of two planets might be viewed as a clash between the gods, with a simultaneous war here on Earth regarded as related. The tendency to explain the world in such terms is called *mythopoesis*. Likewise, the majoritarian expression of events in their original context might obfuscate competing minority accounts or altogether prevent them even from reaching, much less being considered by succeeding generations. Although later historians might well have the opposite view of what was the more important, they may be left with very little useful material with which to work.

Biblical interpretation is a good case in point, for while the intended message and general principles may be timeless, the milieu in which they are illustrated (including the then-current language, culture, beliefs, political events, and other contextual factors) all play into a full understanding of what is being said, and it is not legitimate exegesis of any document to either (a) speculate on contextual particulars without hard evidence, or (b) to insert modern theories, values, or beliefs into the contextual interpretation. The idea that only the latest interpretative theories and practices are correct and that the ancient commentators did not understand their own society or documents is one C.S. Lewis termed the "fallacy of the modern."

Of course, it is no more valid to give credence only to ancient authorities, and none to more recent ones. Supposed facts, evidence, and past interpretations of both must be weighed when creating a narrative of history.

To sum up, the practice of the discipline of history is more than a mechanical sifting of facts and weighing of evidence, and the results must be more than a mere narrative of human actions. History must also serve as an explanation of actions and events in their own cultural and technological context, and it must at least attempt to explain the possible motivations of the people involved. The facts alone (who, what, and when), however carefully verified, only slightly engage the mind in the study of history. The how (including the technology) and why (ethical and other motivations) capture one's interest at a much deeper level, for it is in the explaining of these two that one gains a useful understanding of events and the ability to apply what has been learned to new situations.

This is the art of history—to place events within a context that tells something about the people and ideas that moved the events in the first place, and that were in turn changed by the events after they took place. Events involve real flesh and blood human beings, and if one is to understand the forces that move societies, one must understand the people who shape those forces and are shaped by them.

History seeks to explain societal and individual experiences and to integrate opinions, motivations, causes, actions, reactions, and effects into a comprehensive view of people in the context of their whole society. For instance, on the one hand, history must take into account the technologies that may have influenced events or that developed as a result of events. On the other hand, it must also take into consideration the moral/ethical (and other) human motivations of the actors.

Interpreting History

The historian must also produce a narrative that can convey to others the comprehensive picture created by sifting the collected materials. Thus the scholar must be able to write clearly and effectively. It is important to realize, however, that the result does not gain some canonical status ("truth") merely because it has been published—all accounts of history are filtered through their authors' views about the world, people, their motivations, and the meaning of historical events.

At the most radical extreme are those who ignore or dismiss the evidence of history and write their own. For instance, some deny that the holocaust of millions of Jews in the Second World War ever took place, claim that the Southern U.S. slavery of blacks was good for them, say that the 911 destruction was a false flag operation engineered by American intelligence agencies for nefarious purposes, that Donald Trump won the presidential election of 2020, that there never was a moon landing, that the COVID pandemic was a hoax, or that the 2022 Russian invasion and destruction of Ukraine was a mere policing action. Evidence, no matter its weight, is irrelevant to people with a sufficiently biased view, and would-be dictators count on this. The implied racism, suspicions, willful ignorance, or hatred demonstrated by such pseudo-histories has such incendiary potential that it strains the ability of society to guarantee universal free speech, for it raises the specter of the true history being repeated.

In like manner, the old-fashioned Marxist views history as the unfolding of a class struggle between the poor masses and the wealthy (capitalist) elite: history moves toward an inevitable climax wherein the mass of workers will control all wealth and its means of production. Historical writing done within the framework of this worldview interprets the period under study in terms of such clashes because that worldview requires a class struggle to permeate its interpretations of everything. Such alternate accounts may reinterpret what all other historians have said about events to the point where they become unrecognizable. This reinterpretation is both acceptable and morally right to the Marxist historian. In such ideologies, the truth of past events is variable and must serve doctrine, for it alone is fixed. The Marxist believes that worldview creates history, and the account generated by such a historian necessarily conforms to that worldview. Note, however, that this is only one example of reading modern beliefs and values into a past that has left us no evidence of their existence during the time under study.

It is one thing to do this when writing novels based in an improbable past, or an alternate history, for in such cases there is an explicit invitation extended by the author and accepted by the reader to suspend disbelief to enjoy "what if" entertainment. It is difficult enough to give credence to the supposed world built by a purported historical romance novelist writing about, say, a strong female lead character in a period during which it would have been all but impossible for such a person to have existed. It is quite another matter to do it for a purported factual account of actual history.

The main character in George Orwell's anti-totalitarian novel *1984* is employed by the government to change old magazine and newspaper reports of party officials' speeches so that they will conform to current party policy. His fictional "Ministry of Information" is engaged not in securing and publishing factual material, but in ensuring that the record of history is altered to fit the current policies of the ruling party. Truth attaches to party doctrine, not to mere facts. Every dictatorship must do something similar to create a fictional veil of ongoing legitimacy. It is thus, for instance, that Russia's Putin created a narrative of Ukraine (or portions thereof) as an indivisible part of, and in rebellion against Mother Russia to justify invading and annexing all or portions of that country. The Chinese Communist imperialists are engaged in the same practice to justify annexing Taiwan and making the South China Sea its exclusive property.

Likewise, the iconic "Circumlocution Office" in Charles Dickens's *Little Dorrit* exists only to ensure that society cannot change, for instance by adopting any new technology, thus preserving the status quo for all having a comfortable government sinecure—a parody to be sure, but with a large element of descriptive truth for almost any government system gone stale and devoid of ideas.

Such considerations are relevant in the study of all literature, not just the historical. The deconstructionists hold that no body of writing has any inherent meaning, even if one was intended by the author. For them, meaning is created and attached solely by the reader, and such activity is unique and relative to each individual, not absolute. It is also common to read as well as write present values into works of the past, or to criticize (or even ban) them for not promoting political and social views held to be correct in modern times. Thus the works and thinking of past writers are often dismissed as irrelevant rather than studied for understanding. Historical figures once deemed great for their positive body of work become so excoriated for social views deemed today to be unacceptable that they come to be vilified, even erased from modern historical accounts.

While these are extreme examples, they force us to recognize that accounts of the past always come to us filtered through a worldview that includes some theory of what history was, or in the modern school of thought, ought to have been. Even when applied to the same body of data, this filtering process may produce very different results, depending on who does the filtering.

The view of some Greek philosophers—one that has had periods of popularity ever since—was quite different. In this view, history was not an expression of political dogma, but an eternal repetition in cycles of the same kinds of events. Perhaps something could be learned from those events, but perhaps not. What was certain was that if Rome burned Carthage, enslaved its peoples, and poured salt on its arable land, the same thing one day would inevitably be done to them by another people and that their conquerors in turn would also ultimately meet destruction.

There would be another Plato to deliver the messages of another Socrates; kingdoms would become democracies which when fully corrupt would lapse into dictatorship; and their dictators would in turn proclaim themselves kings and begin the cycle of government anew. Time and history had no beginning, no purpose, and no end—it just was. One could not rely on the gods to escape the cycle; one could but be subject to the fates' or the gods' whims. In this view, no real explanation for history is possible, for in the long run, inexplicable forces shape events—forces that are beyond the scope and knowledge of mere human beings. Taking this mythopoeic notion to its extreme, one could well conclude that there is little humankind can do in the face of events but continue a fateful existence as bit players on an unknown stage before an unknowable audience. Some today embrace such a view, supposing our existence ephemeral—a mere simulation or game running on a cosmic machine.

The observation about the repetition of government styles cannot be denied entirely, for such cycles may be seen to some extent in modern times and societies as well. For instance, in the first half of this century, both Russia and Germany went from imperial monarchy to democracy, into dictatorship, and back out again, and by 2022 Russia had reverted to a closed, brutal dictatorship. Moreover, it is legitimate to ask whether democracy contains within itself the seeds of its destruction. Democracy assumes that people will act in the best interests of the common good, but its laws must reflect that they often instead act selfishly or malevolently and require restraint. As bureaucracy and regulations grow, and selfish demands increase, some may come to believe that a period of dictatorship or monarchy is necessary to salvage order out of what they see as growing chaos.

Any governing regime has its opponents, some of whom may entertain violent overthrow of the current authorities. An unforeseen side effect of the information society's enabling technology is the provision of means for such people to contact each other and organize their efforts—an effect seen in Washington, D.C. on 2020 01 06 with the attempt to overthrow democracy in the United States by installing the losing candidate as President in defiance of the actual vote. In previous times coordinating such an event would not have been nearly as easy.

A few thinkers have taken the idea of the predictability of history further, wondering if it may become possible to develop systematic descriptions of trends in history and society so that events can not only be forecast but also be managed by taking "corrective" measures. One of the most popular of all science fiction future histories was Asimov's *Foundation* psychohistory series, whose premise was that just such a detailed analysis and prediction was possible, even throughout millennia.

However, while some insist that complete scientific descriptions of history are both possible and necessary, others claim that no definitive explanation for history is possible or needed. In the last hundred years or so, "scientific" views of history have become increasingly popular, for humanity as a statistical whole is thought of as being subject to analysis and prediction. In this thinking, once the motivations of the masses could be measured and tabulated, their response to economic or technological stimuli could be accurately predicted. Appropriate technology and education could then be adapted to engineer and control the desired society. Such theories are popular among both political rightists and leftists, neither of whom seem to realize that they are both advocating the same kind of society—a sort of "scientific totalitarianism" or "technocratic dictatorship."

Finally, it is worthwhile to consider a Judeo-Christian perspective on the subject. The possibility of some thematic repetition as history progresses is not completely ruled out by these historians, though they regard history as much more than a record of purposeless recycling of events with no beginning and no end. Both Jews and Christians hold that the world and its peoples had a definite beginning and a purpose (to serve the Creator). The Bible chronicles events after creation: the rebellion and falling away from God by the first human beings, a new start after the worldwide catastrophe of the flood, the promise of a Messiah given to the nation of Israel, and the provision of the law to set that nation apart as an inheritance for God. The Christian scriptures add that the law intentionally demonstrated the impossibility of pleasing God through an imposed morality. Perfection was required to reach God's heaven but could not be manufactured, only received from God as a gift by faith. They detail the coming of Jesus Christ as the promised Messiah to usher in a new covenant with God based on his grace alone. Christians look forward to a return of Christ for judgment and reward, and a final culmination of the Earth, its peoples, and their histories.

Thus, both Judaism and Christianity claim a comprehensive view of history as a definite progression. In the latter, the sequence of history is centered on the cross, but both root all their claims in a series of historical events. These events are potentially verifiable by the same means applied to other occurrences. Although this text will not present a detailed history of Western religions or discuss in other than general terms how their institutions have directly affected the events of Western nations, it is important to make two points:

First, whatever one thinks of the Judeo-Christian religions, one cannot underestimate the effect that they have had on Western culture and ethics, the law, and government in particular. Ideas derived from the Bible can be found at the heart of much that is held critical to modern Western law, particularly in matters of human rights. The influence upon these nations' governing documents, laws, and jurisprudence is particularly potent.

Second, in the latter part of the twentieth century, religious influences were to some extent becoming more prominent in Western culture after at least a century of decline during which secular statism and agnostic humanism had largely replaced Judeo-Christian thinking as "religious" forces. For a few decades, such phrases as "born again" once more appeared in the headlines of newspapers and magazines; prominent

PART ONE | LAYING THE GROUNDWORK

religious leaders sought public office, and the morality of politicians came to be scrutinized publicly by a press newly sensitized to the deep interest of the public in such matters.

Membership in theologically conservative organizations that were both socially and politically active grew rapidly. Even though these were numerically offset to a degree by the continuing exodus from the more liberal mainline groups, the net result was higher visibility for religion in North America. In this context, it is not surprising that religious views of history, technology, and ethical issues would once again be regarded as legitimate topics for scholarly study, and debates once thought conceded are now being rejoined. All this activity has interesting side effects, for as Naisbitt (*Megatrends*) pointed out "evangelical publishers now account for a third of domestic book sales." The work of religious artists has also become an important factor in the music market.

However, this took a different turn after 2000 when the majority of professed evangelical Christians, at least in the United States, came to hitch their theology and lend their time and energy to promoting a particular brand of right-wing nationalistic politics while eschewing what they ought logically see as the more Biblical mandates of seeking the redemption of individuals through the Gospel, and that if they must expend energy forging political alliances, doing so with a focus on social justice.

Meanwhile, there was for a time a broad resurgence of interest in other forms of spirituality, including various reinterpretations the so-called "New Age" movement has placed on some traditional Eastern religions that have made such ideas marketable in the West.

This increase of interest in religion following the end of the industrial age might be seen in a broader context as part of a reaction against the perceived "hardness" of the science and technology that dominated the recent past. A revived epistemological view was often heard—that one can indeed know things to be true in ways other than exclusively through the scientific method.

The desire to have structure during a time of change may also be a factor, especially in formerly Communist countries where people seeking stability often found religious leaders to be more credible than political ones. There was also a new desire to assert the importance of people over things, or at least to promote a "high-touch" aspect of society to balance the "high-tech." Thus, not only did Christianity appear to enjoy at least nominal revival, but so did many forms of religion, philosophy, and mysticism.

However, the more recent alignment of many professing American Christians and some churches with specific political parties to advance what they perceive as a necessary religious agenda by political means has erased any goodwill that might have previously existed, either between the religious and non-religious, or between religious hardliners and their more liberal counterparts. Given the kind of heat generated over such differences, one can easily suppose that North America's histories yet to be written of present times will cast Christians as scapegoats. One might also ask why political means to achieve their social goals should be used when Christ himself eschewed such.

It is worth observing that both these trends were more pronounced in the United States than in Canada, for there the controlling paradigms had been for some time decidedly anti-religious. It would hurt a Canadian political candidate who made an issue of her religion, and religious lobby groups have minimal to no influence on politicians or the courts in this country.

The opposite may have become more the norm. In 2018 Canada's Supreme Court considered a case where two accrediting bodies denied Trinity Western University's application to certify its proposed law school because TWU's code of conduct required its community members to agree to Biblical standards of moral behavior around sexuality and marriage. The court ruled seven to two that, though the denials did infringe on the university's freedom of religion, the infringement was justified to protect the public interest, which no longer supported such restrictions because diversity values had become more important to the general public. In effect, this meant that the Charter of Rights and Freedoms, and hence the body of law in its entirety, meant whatever the Supreme Court determined was in the center of current public opinion on the issue at hand—a potentially dangerous precedent for any minorities in future as public opinion will surely shift in as yet unforeseen directions.

Yet another turn of events has visited widespread disdain and revulsion upon some old mainline denominations. In Canada, Ireland, and France in particular, credible accusations of neglect and abuse linked to increased rates of disease and death have been made of now defunct residential schools, homes for unwed mothers, and/or parishes once run and staffed by churches and their religious orders. For many people, scant to no interest in religious affiliation has been supplanted by disdain, horror, and demands for reparations. Despite that the Pope eventually apologized for the role played by the Catholic Church in Canada's residential schools, these reputations cannot be repaired in the foreseeable future. Indeed, in much of Europe, religion was already in ill repute, and this has deepened that sentiment.

In summary, though earlier editions of this book noted a revival of interest in religion, this trend in many countries has since reversed to the point of backlash, and this could have a strong influence on the people and societies of the coming age.

Conclusion

It should distress no one that there are conflicting views of history, its interpretation, or even the facts themselves. The important lesson is that each person is part of a culture and has a view of the world through which all knowledge (including that of history), is filtered. One who appreciates this lesson and has a clear perception of both their personal worldview and cultural surroundings gains a better understanding of both the events of history and of a place in them, as well as the ability to engage in debate about their meaning in an informed way. Here again is Francis Schaeffer on the subject:

> People have presuppositions, and they will live more consistently based on these presuppositions than even they themselves realize. By *presuppositions* we mean the basic way an individual looks at life, his basic worldview, the grid through which he sees the world. Presuppositions rest upon that which a person considers to be the truth of what exists. People's presuppositions lay a grid for all they bring forth into the external world. Their presuppositions also provide the basis for their values and therefore the basis for their decisions.
> "As a man thinketh, so is he," is really most profound. An individual is not just the product of the forces around him. He has a mind, an inner world. Then, having thought, a person can bring forth actions into the external world and thus influence it.—*How Should We Then Live*

Placing history in a larger context is very much a theme of this book, for throughout, events, technology, and ethical issues are discussed relative to one another. An important thesis here is that ideas, actions, and people are inseparable, and many disciplines of human thought regarded as distinct are part of a tapestry. Because of this larger context, the title of this chapter could have been expressed in terms of sociology rather than history. Use of the latter word reflects a need to place the discussions in a continuum of time, for the major concern in this book will be that of the mutual influence of ethical and social issues, of technology, and of both internal and external events over time. This continuum will also be evidenced in the attempts made in several chapters to peer into the future.

1.2 The First Four Phases of Civilization

A more detailed history of the world's peoples would surely refine the four broad divisions suggested here into many subdivisions, with excellent arguments about why all were necessary and important. However, more than one book would be needed to complete that task. It cannot be done here

Furthermore, one goal of this book is to take the moral, social, and technological pulse of the Fourth Civilization, which is just well underway. Any speculations on a possible fifth will be minimal and most such will be left for other works.

Finally, the reader should note that it is not the intention to suggest the four phases or levels of civilization outlined here are necessarily experienced in chronological order, nor is any intrinsic or value rating being given. Rather they are presented as levels of technological sophistication, efficiency for income generation, and fraction of the total population involved in the characteristic pursuit in that phase. Also, in any given region or culture, loss of an enabling technology is always possible due to war or natural disaster. Moreover, if the Biblical account of the first man and woman is to be taken seriously, they lived in a unique environment that could be seen as a hybrid between the first two. Last, at a given level of technological sophistication, a society could remain stable for a long time, and the same is true of transition periods.

The First Civilization—The Hunter-Gatherers

The simplest (though not necessarily the earliest) type of society has little need for organization. People who live by hunting animals and gathering edible plants wherever they find them require a large expanse of territory just to keep each individual alive. Consequently, such hunter-gatherers move about, following the weather and food availability. Family groupings are small; life is short and brutal, and sophisticated medical care does not exist. There is little store of knowledge apart from what parents pass to their children, and anyone who does have the time to invent the wheel has little chance to inform anyone else, let alone to market it. Ethics and the practice of religion are personal, and cultural matters including language may be highly localized.

The highest technologies in a hunter-gatherer society consist of fire for cooking and protection, simple throwing or clubbing instruments for hunting or defense, and clothing manufactured from animal products. There might be some metalworking, animal domestication, and possibly the use of wheels. People may band together in extended families (tribes) of up to a few hundred with a common language, limited trade, and some broad knowledge of traditional or legendary history and geography. Such tribes may eventually establish fairly complex social structures.

The most highly developed society of this type was probably that of the North American First Nations before the arrival of the European settlers. Theirs was a society with low population density and primitive technology but with well-developed social and economic structures, including continent-wide trading routes. Yet, they found themselves unable to meet the challenge presented by the arrival of the expansion-minded European colonialists. They could not compete effectively with the European technology (wagons, guns, and iron tools), and retreated before the better-organized and equipped invaders. They also suffered from a lack of immunity to diseases like smallpox, polio, mumps, scarlet fever, whooping cough, and viruses, and from the slaughter of buffalo herds. In many jurisdictions, their children were taken, supposedly to be educated and acculturated into European ways of thinking, but the residential schools set up for this form of cultural destruction were ill-run, the poorly treated and fed children became more subject to disease, and many died as their elders experienced the near destruction of their civilization.

Hunter-gatherers must expend most of their total working energy on feeding and defending themselves (though they may have some leisure time). They lack the resources to support very many non-food-producing members such as teachers, lawyers, scholars, city dwellers, and perhaps even their elderly. As a result, such societies gain technology slowly and may remain nearly static over many centuries.

HISTORY AND TECHNOLOGY

The Second Civilization—The Agriculturalists

As an intermediate stage before the second level of civilization begins, some people domesticate animals and become nomads, with a wider geographical range and a somewhat expanded social complexity. Whether this step takes place before or after the domestication of plants, it transforms hunting from a solitary, weary pilgrimage to a community experience. The key discovery needed to make the actual transition to an agricultural civilization is that it is more economical to save seeds from desirable plants and grow them systematically in suitable fixed locations than to go out and find them wherever they happen to have sprouted on their own. The same can be said of food animals. Raising them in a confined location close to a fixed community is far more effective than trying to hunt them. If a single technology can be pointed to as the most important factor in developing an agrarian economy, it is the use of the plow, though arguments could also be advanced for earlier innovations such as the sickle or the flail.

Farming provides a powerful motivation for further invention because the more one's arm can be augmented by tools, the more land that can be put under cultivation, and the more wealth generated by each person. Wheeled carts, animal-drawn plows, and increasingly complex planting, husbanding, and harvesting techniques become highly prized as do the skills of the artisans who craft appropriate tools. People discover how to breed both plants and animals to increase their yield and usefulness, and once a family can produce more than it can eat, trade expands and service settlements become towns, then cities. Metal tools replace stone implements, and the economic advantages motivate a switch from copper and iron to brass. and eventually to steel in the search for stronger plows and other tools.

Agriculture provides a basis for supporting large numbers of non-food-producing populations. Some manage to acquire wealth by using specialized knowledge rather than by producing food, and a class structure grows. Scholars and students can be supported, as can artists, musicians, and theatrical players, for the growing upper class will desire pursuits in which to take their leisure. Once information can be communicated to others in written form, it can also be transmitted to the next generation. The amount of knowledge then increases greatly, and philosophy, mathematics, and other academic disciplines find a place in society.

PART ONE | LAYING THE GROUNDWORK

At the same time, armies can be outfitted for adventures in other lands, and societies grow far beyond the bounds of single families, cities, or even regions. Technological know-how is also turned to the production of decorative jewelry. Gold, silver, and gemstones may also become more important. The needs of cities also drive invention in both architecture and the design of water and transportation systems. Ambitious empire builders must both construct and maintain roads and find ways of ruling the oceans. They must also codify systems of law and apply them at least deliberately even if not always uniformly. Religious practice may also become organized and standardized and its institutions grow in power and size along with the society, at times forming alliances with the state to maintain stability, or even taking over some of its functions.

None of this progress is without cost to the ordinary person, for daily food production life in an agrarian society demands steady, heavy labor and is more complex than in a hunter-gatherer culture, though the food supply is more likely to be consistent. There are more and broader civil obligations to meet, including taxes, conscription, and dealing with government bureaucracy. Farmers have their lives ruled entirely by the land, the weather, and the state; they are not free to take a day or two off after a successful hunt. That is, the gains in security achieved through larger networks of mutual obligation are partially offset by losses of individual freedom for some. This is particularly true if farmers are members of an empire-building society since the wealth generated by their work must support large armies. In such a case, farmers may be virtual slaves to land they often do not own.

The largest and most successful such society in the ancient world was the Roman Empire. Centered on the Mediterranean Sea, it dominated Europe, Asia Minor, the Middle East, and Northern Africa for centuries. Its capital city, Rome, grew to a population of over a million people, a level not reached again after its decline until the 1930s. When the empire fell, the Roman system of roads deteriorated and communications and transportation suffered to the point that no other power could grow to dominate in quite the same way. Because many such links were lost, a great deal of knowledge was not transmitted to succeeding generations, and progress toward the next stage of civilization stalled for centuries. Instead, nations rose and developed localized languages, customs, and technologies.

During this time one group that successfully straddled the first two civilizations was the Mongols whose base was initially nomadic, but who conquered and ruled a settled empire stretching across much of Asia and part of Europe.

European empires were based on oceangoing communication, and these were centered on such trade routes as proved strategic for their time. Venice and Genoa came to dominate the Mediterranean, and afterward, Portugal and Spain ruled the South Atlantic. Later still, the British, French, and Dutch joined Portugal and Spain in roaming the world's oceans in search of food, preservatives, subject peoples, claimable land to colonize, and goods to trade. As a result, advances in technology centered around shipbuilding and military applications. The widespread use of gunpowder, particularly for ship-mounted guns, increased the ability to kill large numbers of people in a short time. This changed the nature of warfare dramatically but had little direct effect on society itself. In such encounters, those nations prevailed that took the trouble to train their midshipmen in trigonometry and seamanship and to require their munitions suppliers to mix gunpowder uniformly. Countries with inferior military education and technology gradually lost both territory and influence.

The increase in the number of foundries, the continuous search for better metals, and the increasing use of small machines set the stage for the advent of the next society. It was Britain that carried the trade-centered empire to global proportions more successfully than any other nation, and it was there in the eighteenth century that the critical mass of technology first became sufficient to take the next step.

The Third Civilization—Industrialists

The harnessing of the steam engine to factory-based machines for the production of textiles in the north of England and English-ruled Ireland started the next major series of changes. Known as the Industrial Revolution, because of the rapid conversion to the new technologies, this period was characterized by a large-scale transfer of people from rural to urban life, as they gave up farm laboring and cottage industries for work in the new factories, and farms themselves became mechanized, thus needing far fewer workers. This urbanization became more dramatic with time. The trend spread, first to Europe, then to North America, and subsequently to other parts of the world, even though in some places it was not accompanied by a sufficient increase in jobs to keep the new city population at work, resulting in extensive urban poverty.

PART ONE | LAYING THE GROUNDWORK

Profile On . . . A Changing Society

The latter part of the industrial age saw a dramatic decline in the proportion of the population involved in farming—the principal occupation of the agricultural society. As time passes, fewer people grow food for an ever-expanding total population. As the chart below shows, farm families had become an all-but-invisible 2 percent of the U.S. population by 1987, beyond which time it stabilized just under that level.

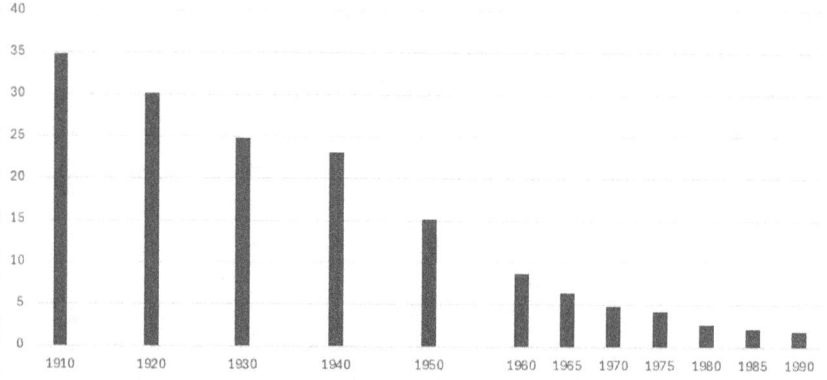

Figure 1.1 U.S. Farm Population as a Percent of Total Population
Source: United States Department of Agriculture

Workers, at first little better off as virtual slaves in urban slums than they were in rural poverty, gradually became consumers of the goods they produced and their standard of living began a rapid and almost unbroken rise that continued through the twentieth century. As the list of factory-produced goods lengthened, machines were also revolutionizing mining and later farming. For the first time, a society became possible in which the majority of people did not have to live at a subsistence level, expending nearly all their energy just to stay alive.

Technological breakthroughs continued at a rapid pace through this time and these have put lasting marks upon the nations that made them. In the latter part of the twentieth century (as in Roman times, but on a larger scale) national borders became less important in the face of transportation and communications technologies that were capable of bypassing such barriers. No one people can for long keep secret or monopolize any given technology, and there was an increasing sense that the world is one interdependent and integrated place, at least economically.

As we shall see, however, the cultural, religious, and political trends were the opposite—toward more disagreement and fragmentation.

The typical person in an industrial society is better off materially than at any time in history, having more education, longer life, better medicine, faster personal transportation, more consumer goods, and better communications facilities than ever before. To be sure, new technologies have, as usual, been used to cause death and destruction on a wider scale in the past century than in any previous one, but despite this, there has been a continuous increase in the productivity of an average worker. This increased production has been accompanied by ongoing urbanization and consumerism, and a greatly increased food supply.

Moreover, leisure time is available to the workers for the first time in history. Whole new industries have been spawned by this development, and tourism is not only a big business, but in many places, it is the largest business of all. Indeed, as the wealth one person can produce has increased, the percentage of people working in non-goods-producing service industries has risen dramatically. This trend, too, could no doubt continue, even in the absence of new dramatic changes in production technologies.

The initial upheavals of the Industrial Revolution saw vast numbers of people attempting to improve their economic conditions by leaving the land and moving to the city. The Western world has long since gone through this phase, but in some parts of the world, such movements are still underway, though the pace is faster and the time frame shorter. Many of those who moved simultaneously severed their connections with organized religion. The institutionalized church had begun to lose its authority in any case, for it insisted upon the teachings of traditional authorities to explain the physical world and its workings long after these had been undermined by the influence of the philosophies associated with modern science.

Some religious leaders came to believe that the idea of an infinite, unchanging God with absolute moral standards could be extrapolated to lend a similar absolutism concerning the physical world. Religious traditions, whether liturgical, governmental, or scientific, were invested with the weight of divine authority, becoming as unchangeable as God. Knowledge was not an incomplete and inexhaustible aspect of an infinite God. Instead, it was finite and complete. The Bible (and by association God) came to be seen by many as a limited creation of the institutional church. What was created by humans could eventually be seen as flawed, and then discarded. At the same time, the increasing availability of consumer goods helped to promote a materialism that separated people from the spiritual roots of traditional morality.

Meanwhile, the rising intellectual class was quick to seek new interpretations and draw different conclusions in ethical and moral arenas that religion had once claimed for its own. Thus, the success of the Industrial Revolution also spawned new ideologies to compete with Judeo-Christian teachings for the hearts and minds of the modern Western peoples. People came to place their religious-like faith in the philosophies of science (scientism), reason (rationalism), progress (progressivism), the state (statism), or humankind (humanism) as the measure and end of all things. Many discarded ideas like the worship of God as creator and sustainer of the universe and likewise dispensed with the social aspects of religion. Over time, religion ceased to be part of the glue that held society together. Simultaneously, the abundance of wealth and the newfound ability to indulge in consumption tended to replace the concepts of duty and interdependence with the notions of self-actualization and autonomy epitomized initially by the "yuppie" phenomenon of the 1980s, but that eventually became mainstream.

This is not to say that traditional religion (or social values) have altogether vanished from everyday life, for they made somewhat of a comeback in later years, which by the 2010s in the United States had resulted in an odd alloy of assorted political issues with at least a form of religion—one that previous generations had reserved for social causes—an unequal marriage that bodes little good for either. On the other hand, in the rest of the Western World, religion had so little influence by this time that such a mix was not possible. On the third hand, in Muslim dominated countries, the two were always linked and have become more closely tied than ever. And on the fourth, in the rising giant that is China, loyalty to the state is paramount, so any potential competitors for that loyalty, whatever they may be called, are rigidly suppressed. The same became true of 2022 Russia, where any deviation from Vladimir Putin's messaging on his invasion of Ukraine was ruthlessly suppressed, and even the Russian Orthodox Church signed on to vigorous support of his version of statism.

On the whole, though, religion came to have much less influence on intellectuals or the leading institutions in Western society in the Industrial Age, and this fact alone would set off the last century-and-a-half as unique among all periods of history.

Some hail the decline of traditional religious influence and the rise of individualism, citing a beneficial increase in freedom for the human mind from such changes. Others note that the simultaneous fragmentation of the culture tends to make society more difficult to maintain as a working entity. Still others worry about the track record modern humans have using technology in the absence of religious influence. Life and the Earth itself are at risk from nuclear weapons on the one hand, and from widespread pollution on the other. Moreover, the last century saw the most devastating wars in all human history, as well as political and economic exploitation on a larger scale than ever. It has also seen deliberate mass killings in the pursuit of racial, religious, and political motives, ones that dwarf the most ambitious pogroms of earlier centuries. Given the rise of political movements focused on revenge against perceived enemies rather than sound governance for the benefit of all, there is little reason to suppose that the twenty-first century will be any different.

The machine age brought unparalleled prosperity to those who own or serve the machines and can buy the goods they make, but it has also brought the world to the brink of destruction by some of the same technology. Thus, while one could judge from material evidence that the human race is better off, such a judgment cannot be unqualified. Material goods have not in the past been regarded as the chief measure of the value of the human spirit, and it seems unlikely the machine age could be looked back upon as an idyllic or utopian time.

Meanwhile, there have been striking new developments that have already brought even more radical changes, and bode more dramatic ones yet. It is a commonplace observation by now that critical mass in certain technologies has been reached, and a whole new kind of civilization has already arrived.

The Fourth Civilization—The Information Brokers

This transition is also characterized by many social changes, some representing continuations of long-established trends. Others may be due to reactions against what some see as the excesses of the industrial age. For example, society is gradually embracing a set of changing attitudes and new technologies that are concerned with the environment in which people live and the quality of life. "High touch" sometimes balances "high tech." There has been some increased interest in ethics, morality, religion, and the disciplines of thought and study that relate more to people than things, the consequences of which will be considered later in the text. On the other hand, certain new technologies can be cited as formative for the next mature phase of civilization. For convenience, they are here grouped into four major categories, and these provide the chapter divisions for the next section of the text.

The first, and most characteristic, is the rapid development of computer-based data systems toward the goal of universal information availability. Anyone who wants to learn the facts of a subject can find the desired material and do so without leaving home. This will have a profound impact on political systems, education, most institutions, and the use of media, much of it new. Along with this can be cited improvements in communications and transportation. Not only are people able to travel farther and faster than ever, but they can exchange information with anyone else easily and inexpensively. New communication methods are also causing dramatic changes in the conduct of business. In all, the consequences of freer information flow are greater and farther reaching than those caused by Gutenberg's invention of the printing press.

It is also worthwhile to note that such universal availability of information means that little or none of it is likely to be lost, however difficult the social aspects of the transition to the next civilization may prove. The redundancy of information storage makes it easier to ensure that what is available to one generation will remain for the next. Of course, the next generation may not interpret or use a given piece of information in the same way, because values (including spiritual ones) are much harder to transmit than facts.

Moreover, much of the "information" residing on the Internet is not curated. It may be "true" in the mind of whoever posted it, but lacking any real-world supporting data to validate it. Consequently, seekers can as easily find misinformation to support whatever they choose to believe, regardless of whether it is rooted in reality, imagination, or fabrication. This is not an observation of a shift in human behavior, merely one that the citation of facts is insufficient to change entrenched attitudes or beliefs in unfacts, and this is easily seen when one examines attitudes towards members of other so-called races, members of other nationalities or political parties, or persons of other socio-economic classes. Prejudice is not based on reason, but on unreason, not on informed minds, but on willful ignorance and acceptance of falsehoods, with the Internet used to lend it pseudo validity. The very existence of COVID deniers, conspiracy theorists, election deniers, and other believers in non-facts provides cases in point—the Internet enables such small groups of non-truthers to congregate in echo chambers where they feed each other group thinking while denying or ignoring the real world fact in favor of fantasy.

The next aspect of technological change characterizing the Fourth Civilization is the culmination of the second Industrial Revolution. Jobs continue their recent rapid shift away from the smokestack industries and into service industries, and this shift has accelerated. The most revolutionary aspect of this has been the introduction of robots to replace people on assembly lines. But that is only the beginning. They may also replace truck, bus, train, and taxi drivers, pilots, ship crews, warehouse workers, tellers, cashiers, and other retail workers, plus a host of others, including making inroads into professional practice such as health care. The result could be the reversal of many aspects of the first industrial revolution—from the workers' point of view, the most radical change of all. Would the end of work be utopia or dystopia?

A third that is often cited is the further development of computer-based or artificial intelligence (AI). Combined with developments in robotics, this could further mechanize certain aspects of decision-making, managerial, and other professional-level workers such as accountants, lawyers, teachers, real estate agents, surgeons, and the like. This is the third, or intellectual, phase of the transfer of human tasks to machines (First came manual labor, then skilled craftsmanship and repetitious jobs, and eventually some brainwork.) Whether a machine employed in such tasks will ever be said to *understand* either the issues or the decision is another matter. The chief consequence of such a move could be yet another dramatic change in the way many individuals make their living and a consequent re-ordering of the social fabric.

The fourth group of formative technologies has to do with life itself—the most fundamental of all issues, and the one to which study and some understanding has come the latest in human history. A developing understanding of the genetic code implies the ability to manipulate life forms, engineer them for specific uses, prolong human life far beyond the present limits, and solve medical problems that have resisted all previous efforts. The development of RNA vaccines is a related example—they obviate the need to inject dead or disabled viruses to teach the immune system, and are therefore potentially safer, pending the necessary and inevitable assessment of ingredient side effects in each case.

In addition, how people live is being given increasing attention. In the Fourth Civilization, such things as air, soil, and water may all be re-engineered for human benefit, rather than treated simply as expendable raw material for factories. There could also be an increasing focus on technologies for food production, on developing new habitats in places people have not lived before, and on enhancing the quality of life in other than simply material ways.

Since much of the dramatic change in all four of these characteristics is due to the development of high-technology devices, many based on microprocessor equipment, the invention of the computer in the late 1940s looms as the most significant single technological advance responsible for ushering in the new civilization.

Details on the effects of these formative technologies will be left to the appropriate specific sections. Perhaps this summary will assist the reader to begin considering what kinds of societal change these new trends in technology may cause, even before reading a more detailed analysis (and speculation) later in the book.

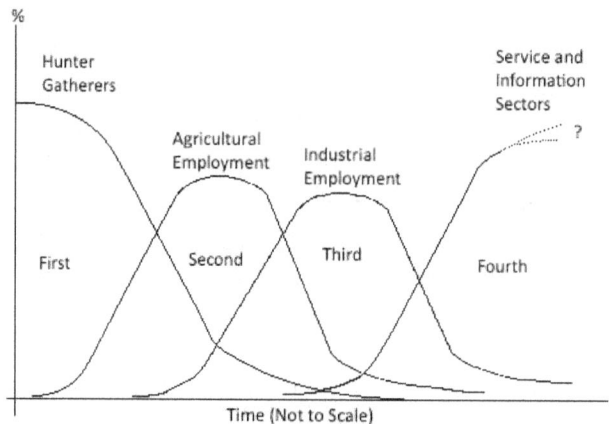

Figure 1.2 The Four Civilizations in Overview

The chart above gives a simplistic summary of the four civilizations insofar as employment is concerned. The true story is more complicated, and it should not be thought that some "inevitable advance of the cycles" is being presented. The latter two transitions needed to take place only once among human societies; sufficient communication had by then been established to ensure that the effects would spread throughout the world. The availability of instant information (and misinformation) immensely complicates any such analysis as has been sketched here. Many more people have knowledge of the most recent technologies and are prepared to attempt skipping the intermediate development others went through to get to that point. Thus, the path through the four stages, while presented as characteristic, can only properly describe the first time it happened; the experiences of nations trying to catch up must be very different. To put it another way, the wheel had to be re-invented from scratch many times, but barring a complete collapse of modern civilization, computing technology does not.

A different view of the four civilizations can be seen by observing that the hunter-gatherers acted for the most part alone or in small groups, and had little flexibility to make changes in their lifestyle or culture. The agrarians had more flexibility, though they too tended to remain in the same occupation their entire lives. An industrial society is centered around organizations more than individuals, but there is greater flexibility and ability to change than in the other two. An information-oriented society could return us to a more individualistic orientation, but there is more flexibility and freedom for both individuals and organizations. The tension between flexible and inflexible organizational structures and between collectivizing and individualizing trends will be important themes throughout this book.

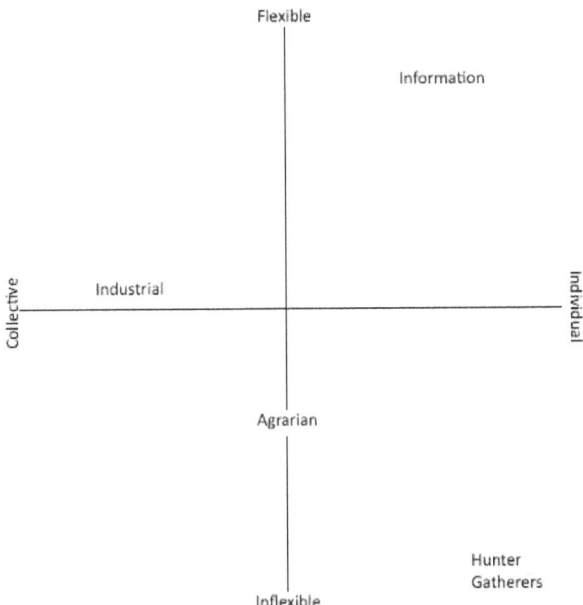

Figure 1.3 The Four Civilizations: An Organizational Paradigm

PART ONE | LAYING THE GROUNDWORK

1.3 History and Technology

The last section presented an overview of the four main phases of civilization. It is also useful to follow several threads of specific technological development through these phases and to indicate the effects they have had on society. In later chapters attempts will be made to follow some threads forward to determine what their future development could be. The topics in this section have been chosen for discussion because of their universal importance in all cultural change, because they strongly impact behavior (and thus tend to generate many basic ethical questions), and because they are particularly important in understanding the Fourth Civilization.

Technology and Food

Increases in food production efficiency have been closely associated with great societal transformations in the past. The transition from hunter-gatherer to agricultural society depends entirely upon the recognition that food can be obtained more efficiently through effective management of limited land areas (farms and ranches). Later, rapid improvements in food production must take place simultaneously with a nation's industrial revolution, for while one group of machines lures workers to the city, another must make it possible for the land to allow them to leave.

Food production is fundamental to the existence of any organized social group. A nation whose people are starving can play no leading role on the world stage, and its very existence will be threatened if the food shortage is prolonged. When changes occur in soil fertility due to poor land management, climatic alterations, or the devastations of war, a people may find itself on the move in search of new land, or becoming absorbed by another group as refugees. They may simply starve to death, or they may go to war against their neighbors to seize their food.

Particularly fertile land may have so many wars fought because of it that it becomes unusable, for its farmers abandon it to the ravages of the fighting, and topsoil with no crop to anchor it may blow away. Also, fertile land tends to be concentrated in great river valleys and deltas, so some nations have much more than others. Consequently, in times of peace, food-producing nations will trade in great volume with goods manufacturers from other countries, and the establishment of food trade routes and transportation facilities becomes critical.

Through the mid to late industrial stage, whenever food was abundant, populations increased exponentially. However, the amount of arable land does not often increase; it may decrease with overcropping, poor management, and desertification. Therefore, the development of technology that enables more food to be grown on a given piece of land has always been critical both to social stability and progress to the next phase of civilization.

From stone knives, bone spears, arrows, and cutting and cleaning implements of hunter-gatherers, to the plow, sickle, and horse-drawn combine to the modern collection of tractor-powered machinery, there have been steady improvements in techniques of food production. Today there is also a wide variety of fertilizers, pesticides, fungicides, and other chemicals employed in growing food, and both milk and beef cattle are fed an increasingly artificial diet to squeeze the last gram of cream or hamburger from each animal.

At one point during a period of slow change in food production techniques, Thomas Malthus (1766–1834) became convinced that the population would always tend to grow faster than the food supply. He was pessimistic that this could have any other result than mass starvation. The fact that the world's food supply supports far more people than Malthus thought possible is due to two factors: First, for a considerable time, the more sparsely populated Americas absorbed large numbers of Europeans, and even today their vast cereal-growing lands provide food in great quantity for countries that have not been able to grow their own. Second, technology has provided more and better varieties of food animals and cereal grains, and this has had a particular impact in places like India, which now produces a far larger proportion of its food than previously. Indeed, subsidies to farmers in Europe and the United States had, even by the mid-1980s (and the trend continued), produced such a food surplus as to suggest modern famines may be more the result of a failure of political will to feed everyone than of any actual food shortage. Today, more people are fed by fewer people working less land than a century ago, and this trend too shows no sign of slowing.

These developments do not imply that Malthus was entirely wrong; they merely postpone the inevitable shortage of arable land to the future. After all, at any given level of food technology, there is an absolute upper limit to the population the planet can support. Yet, it can never be assumed at a given time that the upper limit of all possible food production technologies has been reached.

Technological optimists are convinced that the ability to produce food will continue to keep pace with (or be only just behind) population growth. They also observe that factors like urbanization mean that more people live in a context where having children confers little advantage (unlike on a farm) and assume that reduced birth rates will eventually stabilize the total population. Indeed this has already happened in many countries. They also note that much food is spoiled, eaten by insects or rats while in storage, poorly distributed, or wasted, and that ameliorating these problems alone would ensure plenty.

Pessimists are ready to forecast imminent mass starvation. They believe the world's population will pass (or has passed) the ability to provide food long before it stabilizes, and that global warming will remove more land from food production than it adds. Whatever the case, the transition to and progress of the next civilization will require the food problem to be faced and resolved continuously. War is another detriment to food production, especially if a country on the receiving end of aggression is a regional or global breadbasket. Because food is a fundamental need, its provision is closely related to many other areas, and it will be necessary to return to aspects of this issue at several later points.

Technology and Energy

Primitive societies were little concerned with this class of problems. A warm fire sufficed (where this had been discovered), and people walked unawares over future Middle Eastern, Canadian, and Alaskan oil fields, the Athabaskan oil sands, the British and Australian coal deposits, the Colorado shales, and the Texas gas and oil deposits. Later, human labor (including slaves), animals, wind, and water were the power sources of the agricultural age. Additional forms of energy were necessary to provide the enhanced lifestyle of both farmers and seafarers, for their ambitions to tame their environments had grown beyond the ability of mere human strength to fulfill them.

The industrial age required vastly more energy than had ever previously been consumed. England became a leader partly because she sat on a mountain of coal, and there was no reluctance to saturate the land and air with soot and smoke in the name of progress. Today, natural gas and oil have proven cleaner and more convenient, but all three continue to be used at an ever-increasing rate, and all are problematic for the climate because of their Carbon Dioxide combustion byproduct. These fuels, plus water power, nuclear fission, and alternative energy sources are used to generate electricity for industry and homes.

The advent of the information age has greatly increased the total need for energy, for there are more people with higher expectations for a lifestyle of abundance than ever. More goods than ever need to be produced, and even if all people were to work in offices while the factories were operated solely by robots, manufacturing would still require increasing amounts of energy. So do computing devices. Indeed, cryptocurrency mining alone uses more energy than some countries.

New sources will eventually be required as old ones are exhausted, and there will be proponents of a variety of replacement energy technologies, including hydro, solar, geothermal, tidal, and nuclear fusion. The "high touch" culture—with its concern over the quality of life—demands safe, clean, and renewable energy sources, and therefore some of the old ones will eventually pass out of common use long before the resources on which they are based become depleted.

For example, the switch from internal combustion to electricity for vehicles will greatly reduce the demand for petroleum products. However, cleanliness and safety both carry price tags. No matter how great the desire for both, there is a point beyond which further progress toward such goals is uneconomic. If the perceived cost of a power source—in monetary, energy, or human terms—exceeds the expected return, it will not be used. In North America, this had, for example, happened for nuclear power by the mid-1980s, though subsequent political and economic developments could change or redirect this decision, especially if the potentially much cleaner nuclear fusion plants are ever built in scale. Yet another issue is that the world at present lacks sufficient electrical generating capacity to dispense with petroleum fuels on the road, the rails, and in the air for the foreseeable future.

Moreover, as Putin's invasion of Ukraine in 2022 highlighted, Europe had by then allowed itself to become utterly dependent on Russia for much of its gas and oil, giving the latter an economic club with which to blackmail its customers to add to its threat of nuclear devastation should any nation attempt direct intervention.

Every civilization requires energy—and the advanced need more than the earlier, witness the rolling blackouts that routinely afflict many third-world nations. Neither are energy-guzzling North American mega markets like Texas and California or the European Union exempt. Per capita energy consumption throughout the world will surely continue to increase for many more years, so technologies that provide it will continue to be critical.

Technology and The Environment

At the hunter-gatherer stage, the environment determines the available technology, and to a great extent, cultural responses to that technology. People with no access to copper will not have a bronze age, and those who live in a favorable climate with plenty of game may never be motivated to become farmers. If fish are available, people take their food from the water. If neighbors have desirable products, they may either go to war and take what they want, or develop trade. The technology used to overcome the environment is limited to clothing, shelter, and simple hunting tools.

To a great extent, the environment determines the technology of an agricultural society as well. Soils and climates can support some crops but not others. Grapes cannot be grown in the far north, nor wheat in a rainforest. River valleys may be fertile but are subject to destructive flooding. However, during this phase, there is a gradual increase in the stock of tools designed to allow farmers to overcome environmental limitations—whether they are for planting and harvest, or for pumping water from the land to stay productive in a flood plain.

The industrial age, with its great faith that humankind could master all through machinery, saw an about-face in the relationship between man and the environment. Technology became a tool to overcome and exploit the Earth, rather than a means to steward and better live on it. Pollution was not merely accepted, it was pointed to with pride as a visible sign of great progress—the smell of money. It was only realized very late in this period that no life can survive on a poisoned planet.

Each society must live in its environment and manage it appropriately to ensure survival. The hunter who killed all game within hunting range had to relocate, and so did the farmer who exhausted the soil's nourishment through poor cropping practices. The industrial age has seen the greatest impact on the environment, with dramatic changes to the land, the forest, the air, and even space around the planet.

A continuation of these uncontrolled changes to the environment on the scale seen in the industrial age could eventually render the Earth uninhabitable. If the greenhouse effect caused the climate to warm sufficiently to melt the polar ice, many large cities would vanish under the oceans, and much of southern North America could become a hot desert. If temperatures go the opposite way, other areas would disappear under sheets of ice. If acids from the burning of coal and oil continue to pour down upon crops and forests all plant life could die. If the rest of the Amazon rainforest is cut and burned for short-term subsistence farming, atmospheric oxygen levels could drop and carbon dioxide increase, both substantially. The enterprising pessimist may choose from these and many other bleak futures. The entire Earth is involved, so it would be difficult for its multiplied billions to secure new living quarters if the current ones become uninhabitable.

In the information age, new possibilities exist to make informed choices concerning the environment and to manage the quality of air, water, soil, and climate. The knowledge that a problem exists and the techniques to solve that problem can be communicated and implemented rapidly throughout the world. Of course, the will to make the necessary changes and pay for them is less easily transmitted, and the effects would take considerable time to manifest. This situation also illustrates how using one technology may eventually require that another be developed to repair side effects from the first—a theme that will be discussed further in Chapter 7. Suffice it to conclude for now that a major task for the citizens of the Fourth Civilization will be to learn how to live with the environment and manage it well.

Technology and Health

The systematic practice of medicine is a late development in human history. The earliest physicians had little knowledge of anatomy and none about the causes of disease. They relied on what would today be termed "folk remedies" for their cures. For instance, a common technique for centuries was "bleeding" the patient to let out supposedly diseased blood, a practice now known to be harmful in most circumstances. The Romans maintained a staff of army doctors whose anatomical knowledge and surgical skills became quite advanced, but their work had little application to the common citizen, who was at constant risk of death from disease and such simple-to-solve problems as appendicitis. Disease theory developed in the eighteenth and nineteenth centuries and such practices as sterilizing surgical instruments, quarantining sick patients, wearing masks during respiratory pandemics, and eliminating unsanitary conditions made important contributions to increasing life span.

Some of the most important advances in modern medicine were the development of vaccines and antibiotics. Diseases such as smallpox, polio, typhus, flu, yellow fever, mumps, diphtheria, and tuberculosis that once killed millions of people, have now been eliminated or have had their effects greatly reduced (though TB is still problematic in some parts of the world, and the SARS-CoV-2 virus killed millions and did lasting damage to many more in the early 2020s). Continuing improvements in sanitation, particularly in Western cities where sewage is enclosed instead of running in the streets, have also contributed to an increased chance of surviving childhood and beyond.

The use of antibiotics, coupled with the later development of hormone treatments for birth control (the "pill") had a profound effect on sexual practices after the mid-1950s. Many people had already abandoned religious notions of the eternal consequences of promiscuity. Now, they were also freed from such temporal consequences as pregnancy and sexually transmitted diseases. As a result, the public perception of morality was redefined to fit the new freedoms and sex came to be marketed as recreation instead of being seen as part of the previous social, religious, and moral contract of monogamous marriage. Whether the private behavior of people changed as consistently as the public view of it is more difficult to assess. Both those who were fundamentally committed to the old moral standards and those who had never followed them no doubt acted as they always had. Others followed public opinion and adopted a new lifestyle because the general perception of what constituted normal behavior was now the opposite of what it had been.

Of course, the medical story of the early 1990s was the failure of technology to provide fast cures for the new venereal diseases of herpes and AIDS, and the consequent abandonment of some aspects of the sexual revolution, at least for the time being (and at least in public). Moreover, by the end of that decade, several strains of bacteria had become resistant to antibacterial drugs, leaving researchers scrambling for replacements as infection rates notched upwards.

One could use the sexual revolution and its effects to argue that modern medicine hurt both morality and religion. However, one could as easily blame modern communication and transportation technology, claiming that by being in touch with other societies and their values, the people of the West first came to take a relative view of both, then simply discard them altogether.

The COVID pandemic from late 2019 brought new frontiers and challenges to modern medicine. On the one hand, new means to create viral antibodies were developed that used a portion of the virus' RNA to teach the human body how to make effective antibodies to the virus without requiring dead or disabled whole virus particles—a vaccination strategy that could, in theory, be safer than the older methods. However, the political-religious climate had by that time become sensitized by conspiracy theorists, promoters of quack cures, plus anti-government and anti-science activists, so that control measures authorities attempted to emplace were treated with deep suspicion and outright defiance in some quarters.

Were there people who reacted to the vaccine ingredients? Of course. Whatever the vaccine contents or substrate ingredients, there will always be some people allergic or susceptible to an adverse medical reaction. As for the bizarre "cures" some swore by, a person could promote drinking water to cure the disease. Since most people recover, an appearance of effectiveness would result sufficient to activate false claims of a cure.

It did not help that in some jurisdictions, bars were given preferential treatment over Church gatherings by officials who gave the appearance of acting in ignorance of what churches were and did. Others in the highly individualized society campaigned for freedom, personal choice, and the liberty to do as they pleased, in disregard of any implicit social contract to do others they contacted no harm by their actions.

Consequently, tried and proven health measures such as mask and vaccine mandates, travel limitations, and restrictions on gatherings were labeled by some as limitations to fundamental freedoms. In juvenile displays of ignorance and selfishness, health workers and officials became targets for intimidation, threats, and violence.

Paradoxically, medical practice itself has its roots not just in the desire for survival, but also in the ethical impulse. There have always been strong moral (and often religious) convictions associated with the development and provision of medical facilities for the masses of people who have not previously had them. This behavior—not so much one of self-interest, but of compassion—had previously been at the heart of medical missions and humanitarian aid to undeveloped nations, disaster relief, and universal medical care in the industrialized world and elsewhere.

Health and government officials may not have realized how much those values had eroded, even when the financial obligations shifted from charities to the state.

The practice of medicine has also meant the average age to which people in all nations may expect to live is higher than it has been in modern history, and there is a better opportunity than ever for an individual to survive serious disorders such as cancers, brain tumors, and heart diseases. However, longer life spans mean more people, thus exacerbating food and housing supply difficulties. In addition, medical services are still not well distributed, and accessibility remains a problem in many parts of the world. Improvements in medical technology shift the balance of population (to the young at first, and then to the old). They also tie up expensive resources in facilities and trained people, costing more money, and affecting what can be spent on other things.

That is, changes in medical practice have wide repercussions in the entire society in which the new techniques are employed. Such interconnections of medicine with society and public policy are well expressed by an important principle of interdependence that applies to many other aspects of social interactions as well:

It is impossible to do one thing.

The modern challenges to medicine, if met, will cause new and dramatic changes in the ways people live, in how many of them live, and in how long they live. Some of these changes will be considered in a later chapter.

Technology and Warfare

The first stone tool developed for clubbing an animal could also be used for hitting its inventor's neighbors over the head and taking their food. Bow and arrow or spear could hunt both animals and men. Carts could carry produce to market, men to war, or captured enemies back to slavery. Black powder could clear stumps or fire cannonballs. Ships could carry trade goods or an invading army, and simple machines could pump water or become battering rams.

The same technology that produced tractors also built tanks. That which made airplane passenger and mail service possible also created aerial warfare and firebombing. The telephone lines by which one "reaches out and touches" far-away relatives also carry military orders. Satellites can either transmit communications over previously sealed borders, or spy on the enemy living there. Nuclear energy is used to produce power, radioactive medicines, and unlock the secrets of matter itself, yet destroy the world in a few hours. Chemistry can produce healing medicines or develop the tools for warfare to kill millions.

Every technology has the potential to improve the living conditions of human beings or to harm them. Some complain bitterly because devices made for peaceful use are twisted into weapons of war. Others point to civilian spin-offs of military technology as sufficient justification to pursue the arts of making war.

Human history presents an unbroken record of nation coveting nation, of peoples hating peoples, and of the endless making of war to such destructive ambitions. Whether caused by shortages of food or land, envy over another's prosperity, racial, ethnic, or religious hatred, the desire to seize land and resources, or competition over trade routes, there have always been wars. Those involved have always sought out and used the highest available technology for killing the enemy. A nation that lost one war due to inferior technology, if allowed to survive, could always rebuild, create new weapons, and try again. That is:

It is impossible to fight one battle.

More generally, no inventor or technological innovator in any field can ever foresee the consequences for either peace or war of a particular idea or device. All technology has consequences for society and the subsequent development of new technologies. This leads to other statements of the principle of interdependence:

It is impossible to have one idea.

It is impossible to invent one thing.

This version could be made more general than these specific (and individually useful) statements as follows:

PART ONE | LAYING THE GROUNDWORK

It is impossible to think one thing.

In nuclear weaponry, humankind now has the technology that could not only kill every person in the world but also sterilize it of life altogether. Since wars normally result in the highest available technology being used, the task facing humanity today is nothing less than the elimination of war altogether, for the human race cannot survive a new global conflict. With the fall of the Soviet Union, and the collapse of its military apparatus, the potential for superpower warfare had greatly diminished, but the probability remains high that those same weapons will find themselves one day in the hands of others with more hatred and fewer scruples. At the same time, because the war industry is an important factor in the economies of many nations, survival will also mean social, and economic change. The fundamental urge to survive will also mean that the new civilization will be different in its view of humankind and of the appropriate use of technology and the popular ethics of war will change to reflect the price of war.

This is why Western nations failed to come to the substantive aid of Ukraine with troops in the face of the unprovoked Russian invasion and massacres of civilians in 2022. Their leaders were intimidated by the explicit threats of Russian dictator Putin to unleash devastating nuclear strikes, and they quailed at the MAD prospect (Mutual Assured Destruction).

Profile On . . . Decisions and War

A Few fateful decisions affecting World War II

Decision: In the late 1930s, the Nazis, motivated by racial hatred, decided to persecute the Jews. Scientists and engineers from all over Germany (including Albert Einstein) were forced to resign from their positions. Many left the country. Those who remained were eventually murdered.

Consequence: Allied nations received an influx of highly intelligent and well-trained experts in the very fields critical to the development of technologies needed to win the ensuing war. Einstein was influential in the decision to develop the atomic bomb.

Decision: On September 29, 1938, Britain's Neville Chamberlain abandoned his promises to Czechoslovakia and agreed to Hitler's demand that he be allowed to annex large portions of the country. Hitler falsely promised that he had no more territorial ambitions.

Consequence: Other parts of Czechoslovakia were annexed by her other neighbors. Germany not only seized the remainder, but Hitler, emboldened by what he saw as a weakness in Britain and France, invaded Poland as well, the action that triggered war.

Decision: In June of 1940, Nazi Air Marshal Göring launched the Battle of Britain, bombing major population centers to demoralize the British citizenry.

Consequence: Her industrial capacity was nearly untouched, so Britain continued manufacturing airplanes that proved superior to the German ones, inflicting heavy losses on the Luftwaffe, and eventually forcing the Germans to accept defeat in the air.

Decision: In June of 1941, Hitler decided to break his secret pact with Stalin, and ordered his army to invade Russia.

Consequences:

1. Cold winters, long supply lines, and the Russian army brought the Germans to a halt within sight of Moscow. As the Germans were pushed back, the misadventure weakened the German army, forcing Hitler to fight on two fronts.

2. Blaming his generals for the defeat, Hitler dismissed them and assumed personal command—a task that proved beyond his ability.

Decisions: Despite steadily worsening relations with the Japanese, the United States military command decided to ignore the early December 1941 warnings of an Imperial fleet mobilization in the Pacific. Meanwhile, the Admiral of the Japanese fleet failed to convince his political superiors that attacking the United States would be a catastrophic military error.

Consequences: Japan surprised the American fleet at anchor in Pearl Harbor on December 7, 1941. Much of the U.S. Pacific force was destroyed in the sneak attack, and Japan had a free hand to expand its empire throughout the South Pacific for the next two years. To this day, some claim (with no credible evidence) that this was a deliberate ploy by high U.S. officials to gain public approval for entering the war. And, in the end, attacking the United States was indeed a catastrophic error.

Decision: In August of 1945, the Japanese government decided to ignore American warnings about their new and destructive weapon.

Consequence: Reasoning that the cost in lives would be much greater if an invasion of Japan were to be launched, the U.S. dropped atomic bombs on Hiroshima and Nagasaki. The war ended but at the cost of much of the population of both cities.

Technology, Transportation, and Communication

The ability to maintain a nation of any size is as closely tied to the availability of fast and efficient means of transportation and communication as it is to the provision of sufficient food. Indeed, as previously observed, these two are closely linked, for the food problem is one of transportation as well as one of production. A carbon tax on fuel, even if rebated to low-income families to appear both environmentally sound and net zero, still raises the price of the food and clothing that consume most of the budget of those same families.

With every advance in the ability to move goods and people about or to transmit messages over larger distances, the effective size of the world shrinks and the potential size of nations (or empires) grows. The converse is true as well. For example, when the roads deteriorated after the fall of Rome, European peoples established more localized nationalities. Not until centuries later did the resulting nations build empires once again.

Over the last century, barriers of distance (for developed countries) have for all practical purposes ceased to exist. This does not necessarily mean the world will eventually become a single nation politically, though it is in some senses already one economically. It must be remembered that familiarity breeds contempt, and enhanced communication and transportation facilitate killing one's traditional enemies as much as they foster understanding of them. There never has been any realistic prospect of permanent peace on the planet, nor of a global village being established.

Meanwhile, the computerization of transport has allowed supply chains to become far more efficient than at any previous time in history, thus reducing the need for inventory storage both before and after manufacturing. The downside to this, as both COVID and the Ukraine war revealed, is that the more optimized a supply chain, the more fragile and least amenable it is to rapid change.

Standard of Living

There can be little doubt that people are for the most part better off in the material sense today than at any time in human history. Many of the poor are not as poor as they once were, and the world could probably feed all its people (for a while) if the political will existed to do so.

In Western nations, even the lower middle classes are wealthy beyond the dreams of ancient peoples. Typical citizens own or control their living space, can buy any kind of basic food (and many luxuries), and have several modern appliances (stove, refrigerator, washer, dryer, central heating) that do more work than a houseful of slaves or servants. Moreover, their leisure time is abundant, and entertainment industries are big business. There are inequities of course, for even in wealthy nations, the gap between the rich and the poor is becoming greater all the time, and there are rapidly growing numbers of homeless people even in the most prosperous cities, as inflation and scarcity drive up housing costs. There is also still an economic and technological chasm between the rich and poor nations. However, there can be no doubt that technology has improved almost everyone's standard of living, and few would care to return to the days of poor nutrition, no medical care, high infant mortality, and a thirty-year average life span.

Where are these trends leading? There are two very different views of the possible future, and the contrast between them illustrates the difficulties involved in attempts to look ahead.

The first is to suppose that if the standard of living continues to rise, there would eventually be no practical difference between the rich and the poor, for beyond a certain point the actual amount of wealth is more a means of keeping score than it is an indication of class differences. This is the most idealistic and optimistic view. It must be tempered by the observation that such progress has not in the past led to classless societies. It is much easier to imagine that there will merely come to be new definitions of class than that there will be no class differences at all.

A second is to suggest that continued growth will inevitably result in collapse. The more emphasis put on material goods, the less regard there would be for people, straining the bonds of society. Such concepts as duty could break down as people isolate themselves, become laws-unto-themselves, and live for their pleasure without regard for others. Moral consensus could vanish. Having lost the glue that holds it together, society could dissolve into chaos. This is the most pessimistic view.

Those who hold to cyclical views of history might subscribe to one of the bleaker two scenarios, whereas those who hold to some purposeful view of history may believe that society will remain cohesive even if both material goods and war-making abilities increase without limit. The true course of future history is likely to contain some elements of both.

In any event, production efficiency for material goods cannot continue to raise the general standard of living without at some point causing profound changes to the way people view and use consumer goods. Just what these changes might be is unknown, though some possibilities will be considered later.

In addition, many now unknowable technologies and events will affect the future. The generation of the 1940s might have forecast changes due to, say, television, for it had been in the making for some time, and the example of radio was available. It would have been impossible to predict the effects of computers, however, for their ascendency was due to then unforeseeable technical breakthroughs. Each generation of new technology contains such elements—ones that would seem magical to people twenty years earlier. By their very nature, aspects of tomorrow's standard techniques that are magic today are unknowable. What is more, wars, revolutions, stock market crashes, terrorist attacks, other monetary crises, shortages in commodities (such as oil or its putative replacements), supply chain fractures, nuclear disasters, new trade patterns, changes in consumer preferences, political and religious scandals, and other factors, also shape the society to come, determining what behavior and attitudes are acceptable, what technologies will be pursued and used, and what ethical standards will be followed, created, or discarded.

Moreover, one can never underestimate the power of general disappointment with and the desire to distance from the perceived failure or irrelevance of the values and activities of a previous generation. There is every reason to believe that this perception has become pronounced and that sharp shifts in the dominant worldview may be in the offing, with even more dramatic consequences for society and the technology it uses.

Summary

New technology has always had profound social effects. Moreover, technologies are not only linked to social change but to each other. The pursuit of a given technological change necessarily causes societal change, engenders new technologies and—in typical feedback fashion—alters the seminal technology itself. It would be well to restate the principle of interdependence once again:

> It is impossible to change only one thing.

Finally, because of its central importance to the present and the future, it is necessary to consider the specific development of computing technology. For this, a separate section is warranted.

1.4 A Brief History of Computing

People have long recognized the competitive advantages that could be realized by having available more efficient data storage and greater computational capacity. From counting on fingers to making marks on the walls of caves to the invention of picture numbers to the modern check or banknote, to digital currencies, there has been a steady progression away from directly manipulating the objects that computations describe and toward the use of abstractions to represent the originals. Mechanical devices played an important part in this progression. More than one culture has come up with the idea of placing beads on a string (the abacus). In some places, these are still the preferred calculating devices after several thousand years. A skilled operator can calculate the cost of a large number of purchases on an abacus much faster than most people can enter the data into a calculator.

Some who have studied the ancient British monument known as Stonehenge concluded that it was an enormous calculating device for making astronomical predictions. Other monuments left by the Babylonians, South and Central American Indians, and South Sea Islanders may have had similar purposes. The Scottish mathematician John Napier (1550–1617) devised Napier's Bones and published tables of logarithms intended to simplify tedious arithmetic computations. These led directly to the wooden or bamboo slide rule, known and loved by many student generations before the development of inexpensive electronic calculators.

To the French mathematician and theologian Blaise Pascal (1623–1662) goes the honor of inventing the first mechanical adding machine (1642). It was based on a system of gears similar to those in an automobile odometer and was used for computing taxes. However, parts for the device could not be manufactured with sufficient precision to make it practical, and it never became widely used. About thirty years later, the famous German mathematician and co-inventor (with Newton) of calculus, Gottfried Wilhelm von Leibniz (1646–1716), made a similar but more reliable machine that could not only add and subtract but also multiply, divide, and calculate square roots. Many people improved calculating machines over the next century, and by 1900 they had an important place in government and commerce. But as late as the mid-1960s electromechanical versions of these calculators had thousands of moving parts, could do only basic four-function arithmetic, weighed thirty pounds, and took up half a desktop.

Meanwhile, another idea important to the modern computer was emerging—that of the stored program or instruction sequence. This idea arose in connection with the development of automatic looms by the French inventor Joseph Marie Jacquard (1752–1854). First shown at the 1801 Paris Exhibition, these looms used a collection of punched metal cards to control the weaving process. The machine, with variations, is still used today, though it is now no longer controlled by punched paper cards or tapes, but by direct connection to a computer.

The first computer—a machine combining computational ability with stored programs—was designed by the British mathematician Charles Babbage (1792–1871). He worked on his "Difference Engine" for about eleven years before abandoning the project. Later, he designed a much more ambitious "Analytical Engine" that was intended to be an algebraic analog of Jacquard's loom. Although Babbage even had a programmer for the engine (Lord Byron's daughter, Ada Augusta, the Countess of Lovelace), this machine was never constructed in his lifetime. Its concepts were not realized until 1944 when the Mark I computer was developed in the United States.

By this time, the punched paper medium had become standardized through the work of Herman Hollerith. He devised a card data storage and sorting system for the U.S. Census Bureau, which was first employed in the 1890 census. Hollerith left the bureau six years later to form his own company, the name of which was changed to International Business Machines (IBM) in 1924.

Meanwhile, vacuum-tube technology had developed to the point where an electronic computer could be manufactured. The first of these were the British code-breaking devices Colossus Mark I and Colossus Mark II built in 1943 and 1944 for the British intelligence service at

Bletchley Park. The latter attained speeds not matched by other computers for a decade. When the war was over, these machines were dismantled and their parts sold as surplus, for no one realized they could have application to civilian life.

At about the same time, the groundwork of researchers in the United States came to fruition in the construction of the Electronic Numerical Integrator and Calculator (ENIAC) by J. P. Eckert and J. W. Mauchly at the University of Pennsylvania. This machine, which contained over 18,000 vacuum tubes, filled a room six meters by twelve meters and was used principally by military ordnance engineers to compute shell trajectories. In subsequent years, many similar computers were developed in various research facilities in the United States and Britain. Such devices, which generally were limited to basic arithmetic, required a large staff to operate, occupied vast areas of floor space, and consumed enormous quantities of electricity.

Eckert and Mauchly were also responsible for the first commercial computer, the Universal Automatic Computer (UNIVAC), which they manufactured after leaving the university. Their company was eventually incorporated into Sperry (later merged with Burroughs to become UNISYS), which manufactured large industrial computers for many years. Today, those early vacuum-tube monsters are referred to as "first-generation computers," and the machines that were their successors were called "mainframes."

The transistor, developed by Bell Labs in late 1947, and its improvement during the early 1950s, was designed to replace the vacuum tube, reducing both electrical consumption and heat production. This led to the miniaturization of many electronic devices, and the size of typical computers shrank considerably, even as their power increased. Transistorized machines built between 1959 and 1965 formed the second generation of computers.

Prices were still in the hundreds of thousands to millions of dollars, however, and such machines were generally seen at first only in headquarters of large research and government organizations. Even by the mid-1960s, not all universities had even one computer, and those that did often regarded them as exclusive toys for their mathematicians and research scientists. There were occasional courses at the fourth-year level, but freshman introductions to computer science had not yet become popular.

PART ONE | LAYING THE GROUNDWORK

The invention of the integrated circuit dramatically changed things in the computing world. The first result was another, even more significant size reduction, for what once took up several floors of a large building now occupied a small box. The first of these third-generation computers was the IBM System 360, which was introduced in 1964 and quickly became popular among large businesses and universities. This size reduction also resulted in the first "pocket" calculators, which appeared on the market in the early 1970s. Even at the initial price of several hundred dollars, these put into the hands of the average person more computing power than the first UNIVAC possessed. New models proliferated so rapidly and so many new features were incorporated into the pocket calculator that one company decided to have a chip designed that would allow it to program new functions to reduce the time required to bring a new model to market.

The chip, made by Intel Corporation, and called the 4004, gave way to the 8008, and then to the 8080 and 8080A. The latter became the backbone of the new small-computer industry, as numerous companies developed kits and fully assembled computers. In its later incarnations by Zilog as the Z-80 and other descendants, such as the 808x, 8048x, Pentium, and subsequent CPU chips, this invention lives on in millions of microcomputers. Not long after the 8080 became a commercial reality, Motorola developed the 6800 chip, which had the advantage to programmers of being cheaper and somewhat easier to work with than the 8080. It, too, became popular for a time, but soon gave way to other designs.

At about the same time the Z-80 was developed, the 6501 and 6502 chips were derived from the 6800 as low-cost industrial process controllers. In 1976, the 6502 was also used to build a small computer, this one entirely contained on a single board. It was called the Apple, and Apple Computer Corporation went on to sell millions of the original Apple computer and its descendants, then various iterations of the Macintosh computer, its market value eventually surpassing that of all other corporations in history in the process, and becoming the major source for nearly every important advance in small computer technology for decades.

In 1977, Radio Shack joined the competition with its Z-80-based machines. In Europe, the equivalent popularizing role was played by Commodore (a Canadian company) and by Sinclair (a British firm). A few years later, IBM came into this market with the 8088-based PC. The mere presence of the giant changed the whole market for a time, with most other manufacturers seeking to make machines compatible with those of IBM. Eventually, some of these "clone" makers, such as Compaq, became a larger presence in the market than IBM itself. By the late 1990s, the machines generating the most attention were capable of storing more and manipulating larger numbers than anything previously seen in the microcomputer market. They were also capable of handling processing requirements of the graphics user interface (GUI) first realized in the Xerox Star, Apple Lisa, and Macintosh, then in Commodore's Amiga and Atari machines.

Integration of circuits had now reached the point where millions of components were being crammed into a single chip. Between 1987 and 1991, major new commitments were made by Apple with the Motorola 68030 and 68040-based Macintosh models and by IBM with their OS/2 machines. With the latter, IBM also followed Apple's lead into graphics-oriented software, helping to ensure this style of interface a continuing acceptance in the marketplace. Graphics user interfaces were also adopted by the makers of scientific workstations such as those made by Sun Microsystems, and were being attached to other machines running the UNIX operating system.

In the early 1990s, Microsoft, already the dominant manufacturer of operating systems for Intel 80x86 chips and of applications for both these and Macintosh platforms, began to market a GUI called Windows that was a rough copy of the Macintosh Operating System. The courts ruled, however, that it was not a close enough imitation to fall under copyright law, and Windows (in various flavors) gradually became dominant on Intel-based machines (sometimes later called "Wintel" systems).

By 1995, Apple had formed partnerships with Motorola and IBM to develop new microprocessor technology and was already marketing machines based on the new PowerPC RISC chip, while IBM was porting its operating systems to the new chip as well. The two were readying new operating systems and preparing specifications for a common hardware platform on which to run them. Apple had licensed its operating system and the first Macintosh clones were appearing on the market—some from very well-known consumer companies such as Motorola. Microcomputers had become powerful enough that the minicomputer category had been all but crowded out of the market on price/performance considerations.

By 2002 Microsoft had moved through Windows 95, 98, and NT to Windows 2000 (ME). The world had also seen the demise of OS/2, and the migration of the MacOS to a new UNIX-based OS (NextStep, later rebuilt and renamed OS X) developed by Steve Jobs—the once ousted co-founder of Apple. At the same time, Apple had transitioned to the RISC-based G4 PowerPC chip and was offering machines whose raw processing power would once have placed them in the supercomputer category, Meanwhile, in its lower-priced line, Apple had made computers into fashion statements, an innovation others were also quick to copy.

However, by 2009 the PowerPC line of chips had reached its maximum potential for laptops, for IBM was reluctant to manufacture low-heat versions, being more interested in the server market where heat was not considered an issue, so Apple switched to Intel chips for several years, then again in 2020, chaffing at its dependence on an Intel that was by now having manufacturing issues, Apple brought out machines using "M" chips of their design and took over the industry lead in speed and efficiency. This spurred Intel and others to improve their existing lines, and by 2024 the various types of CPU and graphics controller chips competed on nearly a level playing field, and with better performance at each iteration.

While much of the marketing activity and most headlines focused on the microcomputer segment of the industry, larger machines had undergone startling changes also. Fourth-generation supercomputers could be used in situations where calculation complexity or data quantity was so great as to be beyond the ability of ordinary mainframe devices. These machines are used by governments, the military, and academic research institutions. Newer generations of computers are on drawing boards, and many new developments will continue filtering down to become the consumer-oriented devices of the future. At the same time, however, desktop computers, with their ever-faster chips and larger memories, were encroaching on application domains once thought to belong only to supercomputers, and laptops routinely gained processing power unimagined a decade earlier.

At the opposite end of the scale, pocket-sized computing devices had also become important. These ranged from the DOS or Windows-based miniaturized version of the desktop sibling to the specialized personal time and communications organizer (Personal Digital Assistant or PDA). Also called (by this author for a not-yet invented version) the Personal Intelligence Enhancement Appliance (PIEA), these devices boast handwriting recognition, wireless communications abilities, sophisticated time management, and health monitoring functions. Apple's

Newton was a key initial player and innovator in this market, the 3Com/Palm Pilot dominated for a time, then Apple changed the game three times with the iPhone, which initiated a whole new "smartphone" category of communication product, the iPad, which likewise founded a smaller-than-laptop category of computer, and the Apple Watch, which interacted with and complemented others of the corporation's devices. All were imitated at both the high and economy end of the price scale, but by 2022 Apple owned the premium product sector of computing-like devices.

For most future applications, microprocessor-based computing devices will have sufficient power to suit the majority of individual, academic, and business uses. They are inexpensive, easy to link (network) for sharing other resources (storage devices and printers), and they run languages and other programs similar in design to those once employed on mainframe computers. Much development work (particularly in programming and publishing) is being done with microcomputers and tablets in view. It was safe to predict in earlier editions of this book that descendants of these machines are the ones most people would be referring to when they spoke about computers in the future, and this has certainly transpired.

Larger machines will also continue to grow and change (though their numbers will not), as will organizations depending on them. Moreover, fully capable computers of the future will be as different from those of today as these are from ones of the late 1940s. They will be much smaller, faster, and with greater storage capacity. They will be integrated with video and communications technology to give immediate access to worldwide databases. They will become even easier to use, and the need to offer university-level courses in their operation has long since ceased, for the pocket devices in particular have long since become common adjuncts to ordinary life. The word "appliance" was often used to describe the future of computers, and does reasonably apply to smartphones (though these are far from the PIEA as envisioned in this author's fiction) but it would be better to include tablets, laptops, and other microcomputers in the tool category.

> Computers are not toasters. They're compound sliding mitre saws. (R. Sutcliffe in The Northern Spy, November 2008, referenced at https://www.thenorthernspy.com/spyslaws.htm)

So broad and diverse have the applications of electronic processors become that "computer" seems a misnomer, for the machines in which such devices are embedded spend little time calculating, and much more finding, organizing, preparing, and communicating data. In this respect, the Internet, especially the portion known as the World Wide Web (WWW) has become a kind of prototype for the universal distributed library of the future, and all organizations are dependent on their connectivity.

Computers have already profoundly changed many of society's institutions (business, banking, education, libraries). They will have even greater effects on institutions in the future. They have also raised or caused new ethical issues, and these will need to be addressed in the interests of social stability. In addition, developments in computing have affected or given rise to other new products and methods in a variety of fields, further demonstrating the interdependence of ideas, society, and technology.

There are microprocessors in radios, televisions, cameras, appliances, automobiles, toys, and games. Entertainment and telecommunications industries are heavily dependent on new electronic technologies. Computers themselves are directly attached to research instruments that gather and interpret data in basic physics, chemistry, and biology experiments. The resulting changes and advances in scientific research have also caused profound effects on society and its institutions. They have resulted in new social and ethical questions being raised, whose very asking could not have been anticipated in the industrial age. These include issues relating to software copyright, data integrity, genetic engineering, artificial intelligence, comprehensive displacement of human workers (including professionals) by robots, how to live in and manage an information-based society, and how to repair and reverse the extensive damage wrought by the industrial age.

Technical trends and possible social and ethical consequences will be examined and extrapolated in more detail in later sections of the book. It is at least possible to conclude at this point that the advent of the Fourth Civilization (aka "the information age") is owed more to the modern computer than to any other single invention of the late industrial period.

1.5 Forecasting the Future

It has already been observed that events constituting history are understood in the context of both motivation and technology over a time continuum. Similar considerations apply to attempting to predict the future—that is, forecasting what might yet happen to society as a result of current and new technology and people's motivations.

On the one hand, the flow of events perceived to date may usefully be projected forward, if this is done in a reasonable fashion that takes into account the most likely results of said flow.

On the other, few modern-day forecasters can claim the authority of Biblical prophets, who correctly predicted events in complex detail (and sometimes names) decades or centuries ahead of time. Today's forecasters rely on extrapolating ahead the trends of the recent past, rather than on Divine revelation. Therefore, all such modern attempts at long-term prophecy will fail, at least in part, for they cannot take into account the human-unforeseeable watershed events and decisions that result from creative departures from tradition, and that change a society and its technology quickly and dramatically. Nor can they foresee wars and their fallout for both "winners" (if such exist) and losers (everyone?).

Who could have forecast the uses of electricity, the internal combustion engine, or atomic energy, even ten years before their discovery? Who can take into account the serendipitous discoveries of ten years from now, or the result of, say, a narrow election win or loss on the people governed? Who knows exactly how today's decisions and discoveries will change the course of society a year, much less decades, from now? Because of such uncertainty, all forecasting implies considerable speculation, even when it appears to be a straightforward extrapolation. Indeed, given the recent history of political and technological change, assuming that things will continue according to current trends may be the most unreliable speculation of all. Any one of the alternative futures proposed by today's forecasters may indeed come to pass—or none may.

Speculation about the future is necessary for progress, for scientific, technological, economic, and political breakthroughs are all impossible without the application of a lively imagination to possibilities no one else has seen. Noted speculator and science fiction writer Arthur C. Clarke (*Prophets of the Future*) has this comment on qualifications for a successful predictor of the future:

PART ONE | LAYING THE GROUNDWORK

I would now go so far as to say that only readers or writers of science-fiction are really competent to discuss the possibilities of the future. This claim may produce indignation, especially among second-rate scientists who sometimes make fun of science-fiction (I have never known a first-rate one to do so—and I know several who write it). But the simple fact is that anyone with sufficient imagination to assess the future realistically would, inevitably, be attracted to this form of literature. I do not for a moment suggest that more than one per cent of science-fiction readers would be reliable prophets; but I do suggest that almost a hundred percent of reliable prophets will be science-fiction readers—or writers.

Some expect a day when forecasting at least the broad outlines of future society (and perhaps many details) will become possible—even commonplace. Perhaps the best-known fiction with this theme is Isaac Asimov's own Foundation series. It would also be foolish to assume that a technique for predicting future history could be developed without the forecasters becoming the managers of that history, influencing critical events to make the outcome better—at least in their own eyes.

This book also deals with many speculations about the future. Most are attempts to determine which outcomes of technology are likely, based on historical experience and existing trends. That is, this work is more concerned with extrapolation than it is with speculation. However, some things are new or are yet at the research stage, and it is difficult to make predictions with any degree of confidence. This difficulty has not stopped others from publishing their ideas, and there now exists a rich literature on future scenarios, aspects of which will be discussed in more detail later (along with new ones).

Visions of the Future

One of the earliest classics in the field was Jacques Ellul's *The Technological Society*, published in 1965. Ellul had a clear vision of some of the tragic aspects of the technological revolution. He saw society losing what had made it truly human, blundering rapidly down unexplored paths, following guides competent in narrow technical fields but in little else. Ellul was not afraid of technology but felt that its material promises were empty, that society's faith had come to be in progress for its own sake, and apart from a higher standard of living, there was little for the human spirit to celebrate in the new age. Although his comments were made in the context of the old industrial age and its failures, many others have expressed similar views of the information age since that time.

One of these is Theodore Roszak, long a critic of the goals of artificial intelligence research, whose 1986 book *The Cult of Information* is subtitled *The Folklore of Computers and the True Art of Thinking*. Roszak castigated many other modern writers as members of an unthinking cult who have made "information" into what he called a "godword." He desired to re-establish a clear distinction between what machines do when they process data, and what human beings do when they think—a distinction that he felt had been incorrectly blurred by others. Here was Roszak's view of some of the technological optimists:

> We might almost believe, from their simplistic formulation of the information economy, that we will all soon be living on a diet of floppy disks and walking streets paved with microchips.

The most optimistic views of the future came from such as Alan Toffler (*The Third Wave*), John Naisbitt (*Megatrends*), Grant Fjermedal (*The Tomorrow Makers*), Harry Stine (*The Hopeful Future*) and Eric Drexler (*Engines of Creation*). All of these were willing to foresee many new and better potential worlds resulting from current and projected technologies. A society of plenty, the colonization of space, near immortality, and the removal of class barriers are among the predictions that these and other writers made. They are in a long line of philosophers who believe that *Progress* is an inevitable upward flow in the state of human affairs.

Indeed, from the late 19th century *Progress* became a quasi-personalized idea—as have Gaia, Nature, Evolution, Love, and Justice—invested with qualities that resemble those of deity. Things would always get better, wars were only "mistakes" in the flow of progress, and technological solutions would always be found to all problems.

It is not hard to find some data to support such optimism. After all, much of what was science fiction in the 1950s is now a reality. Space flight, cancer cures, information utilities, nuclear power, robots, personal computers, and many other once-fanciful ideas are now taken for granted. Of course, far more of the old predictions have yet to be fulfilled, and perhaps never will be, but the most optimistic in the scientific and technical community often seem to believe that a permanent utopian civilization is within the very grasp of humankind.

PART ONE | LAYING THE GROUNDWORK

Profile On ... A technological optimist

G. Harry Stine (1928–1997) was well-known among readers of futurist publications for his unabashed confidence in the future. The selection below, from *The Hopeful Future*, is typical of those who believe in Progress to solve problems through new technology. The chapter title for the section from which this is taken is *Enough Energy for Everybody to Do Everything*.

> The human race will never run out of energy or suffer from an energy shortage.
> As Caoanda observed, we're surrounded by energy. In the past when human beings faced the possibility of exhausting or exceeding available energy supplies, thereby creating an "energy crisis," they discovered new energy resources and learned how to use them. Each time, we worked our way out of an energy crisis by developing new energy sources and technologies. If the trends are reliable—and there's no reason to suppose they're not—we'll also work our way out of the current energy crisis...
> Forecasts about limits to growth are based on specific energy resources and have assumed no future technical developments. Technology defines resources. Waterwheels made water into an energy resource. Steam engines did so for coal. Internal combustion engines did the same for oil.
> At the time forecasts about an energy crisis are made, inventors are already quietly developing the new technology that will develop new energy sources within twenty-five years and, within fifty years or less, will completely displace the older energy technology.
> Current technologists completely miss when they forecast how we'll work our way out of an energy crisis. For various reasons, they discount or neglect to consider the role that new technology will play in less than twenty-five years.
> Technologists prefer to improve familiar technology by a fraction of a percent than to gamble on a major improvement from unfamiliar technology. They manage to make marginal improvements in old technology just before it is made obsolete by new technology.

The reader can judge for herself how well this prophecy has succeeded in the decades since.

On the other hand, there is a rich popular literature on apocalyptic visions of the future—forecasts of imminent disaster. These see little or no hope for humanity or the Earth. If it does not perish in a nuclear holocaust, everyone on it will starve to death when all arable land has turned to desert due to global warming or been poisoned by industry. Perhaps all will freeze when air pollution becomes dense enough to block the sun and lower the temperature, or die of heat when the "greenhouse effect" increases it instead. Alternatively, life could all dissolve in acid rain, perish from hard solar radiation when the ozone layer disappears, or even be annihilated when a superior race of aliens passes by and we meet its disapproval. Not a year goes by without a forecast of global economic collapse, nuclear conflict, or the provision by some would-be prophet supplying a date on which Jesus Christ will return and God is supposed to end the world, despite the Bible specifically stating that date cannot be known.

No conclusive evidence can be cited for any of these extreme scenarios. The kind of future expected may depend more on the predictor's personality than on the analysis of today's trends. The optimistic technologist says there is hope for a bright future; thoughtful philosophers worry that humanity has lost more than gained; and the doomsayers have given up all hope. Amid this uncertainty and contradiction, others have tried to find spiritual answers to difficult questions. Some have turned to mystical claims that meditation can bring on a new order; others to the Biblical answer that God the creator alone determines the fate of the universe. Some may see such a refocusing as another manifestation of the tension and balance between the high touch and the high tech. It may be regarded as part of a struggle for liberation of the human spirit from the perceived bonds of the machine age. It may be a holding position while people await more definitive data from the scientific community, in which their absolute long-term faith resides.

Others place their faith in political solutions, to the point where it becomes impossible for them to believe or accept that their favored messiah-like candidate for office lost the election when (s)he was so "obviously" the only one who could rescue the Capitol, the State or Province, the nation, the corporation, or society in general, from the depredations inflicted by the "others." The latter may have a similar view of the former.

The actual near future will likely fall somewhere between utopia and apocalypse. New and existing technologies need to be examined both for their potential to improve the human condition, and for their potential to cause harm—an exercise seldom undertaken to date, in part because of the rush to market, in part because such sober analysis is unwanted in a politically charged atmosphere, and in part because those qualified to do the work rarely seek public office because they are fully embedded in the real world.

Part two of this book concentrates on the various technological revolutions and the direct effects they may have on society, and part three focuses on the roles of certain major institutions. It is worth noting, however, that if any modern-day seers (including the author of this book) knew what the future would bring, there would be far more money to be made in the stock market than there would be in writing books predicting potential tomorrows.

1.6 Summary and Further Discussion

Summary

There are a variety of views about the meaning of history and whether it is a purposeful and controlled unfolding, or a series of fated cycles. To be useful, accounts of history must be interpreted in a flow from the past through the present. With some care, its lessons might be usefully extrapolated to forecast the future. History is influenced strongly by the motivations of the people who make it, and by the technology that they use. Its events in turn shape ideas and technology for the next generation. Its meaning is strongly influenced by those who write it.

Although many divisions in history can be identified, those useful to this text are:

- Hunter-gatherer (the First Civilization)
- Agricultural (the Second Civilization)
- Industrial (the Third Civilization)
- Information (the Fourth Civilization)

Many nations are now well into the fourth phase, and the transition is being accompanied by broad changes in society and technology, as well as by a lively new interest in ethical issues.

Specific examples of the historical development of certain technologies include:

- Technology and food
- Technology and health

- Technology and warfare
- Technology and transportation
- Technology and communication
- Technology and standard of living

The brief history of modern computing indicates how this particular technology has developed and become a powerful influence on society. Much of this text is concerned with such mutual influences, and many of these will be developed further in later sections.

Research and Discussion Questions

1. If you are reading an account of some event in the past, what clues could you look for in the narrative to determine how factual it is? In particular, how does a falsehood or exaggeration distinguish itself from the truth? How does a mythical account distinguish itself from a historical one? How could you spot possible distortions designed to favor the author's political, religious, or economic theories, or biases?

2. What are some of the external sources to which one could turn in an attempt to verify a historian's account? Describe as many as you can think of, and comment on their value.

3. Consider Caesar Tiberius and Jesus Christ. Do library research to find out which of these two has more complete and reliable documentary evidence to verify the historical accuracy of the main events of their lives (this could be a rather extensive research project). Now also comment on the extent to which such evidence is accepted by scholars and/or by the population in general.

4. What effect, if any, did the invention of the printing press have on the industrial revolution? On society in general?

5. This chapter speaks much about the interplay of motivations (especially ethics), technology, and the events of history. From your knowledge and research, provide examples of important historical events that hinged on (a) a specific application of technology; and (b) a moral/ethical or political decision by a key player in the event.

6. Which do you think is more nearly correct: that societies develop in the way they do because of technological advances, or that

technological advances take place because the society in which they are made is ready for them?

7. What were some of the effects on family life due to the industrial revolution?

8. If you (a product of the industrial/early information age) were suddenly thrust into a hunter-gatherer society to make your way with no technological help, what would you do to survive?

9. If the plough is the key invention for the agricultural society, and the computer for the information society, what can be said of the industrial society in this respect? Is there a single piece of technology that can characterize the whole age? If so, what is it? If not, why not?

10. Write a history of the automobile, focusing on its effects on the economy and society of the Western world.

11. Write an account of the effects of television on Western society.

12. Write an account of the effects of computers on Western society.

13. Some material in the chapter focuses on particular turning points in history. Try to imagine how the world's history would have been altered if certain events had not occurred. Write down what the major differences in today's society and technology would be if:

   a. the Romans had built a practical steam engine from Hero's model. Could an industrial revolution have taken place in A.D. 100?

   b. the Mayans and Incas had both discovered the wheel and begun to use animal-drawn carts centuries before the Spanish arrived. (i.e. What if the Europeans had met a civilization as much or more advanced than their own?)

   c. half the munitions factories built in the United States before the Civil War had been in the South, instead of (virtually) all in the North **or** the South had followed up at either of the battles of Bull Run, pursued the defeated Union army, and taken the undefended city of Washington, D.C.

   d. England had been overwhelmed by Germany in the Battle of Britain.

   e. Lee Harvey Oswald had missed, and John F. Kennedy had lived to be re-elected.

f. Hewlett-Packard had bought and killed what became the Apple computer that Steve Jobs and Steve Wozniak tried to sell them.

g. Donald Trump had either (i) been defeated by Hillary Clinton, or (ii) defeated Joe Biden (iii) repeat this for the 2024 election, i.e. suppose its results were reversed.

h. Either (i) Vladimir Putin had never invaded Ukraine, or (ii) NATO had intervened with troops, closing Ukrainian air space, and sent a fleet to the Black Sea to blockade Russian efforts there.

i. Canada had been able to build new oil pipelines to the United States and the West Coast and an LNG exporting plant (or two) before the 2022 energy crisis.

j. Brian Boru had survived the Battle of Clontarf in 1014 and lived to establish a strong, unified, and enduring monarchy in Ireland. (See the author's Alternate History Fiction Science Fiction featured at https://www.arjaybooks.com

14. The text mentions some turning points in World War II. What were some others?

15. What is the importance of studying history for our present-day society? for the future?

16. There have been many who have attempted to prophesy the future. Look up one or two of these from (i) before 1990 (ii) between 1990 and 2005 and (iii) between 2005 and 2020 and assess the extent to which they succeeded or failed.

17. Try to obtain one of the supermarket "tab's" annual issue of psychics' prophesies for the ensuing year. Describe these and say how many came true during the following year.

18. The Western notion of prophecy comes largely from the Bible.

    a. What does the word "prophet" mean in the Biblical context?

    b. Make a list of at least twenty prophesies, both the making and fulfilling of which are recorded in the Bible.

    c. Make a list of at least twenty Biblical prophesies that do not appear to have been fulfilled as yet.

PART ONE | LAYING THE GROUNDWORK

19. Write your prophecy for the next ten years of technology.

20. Look up the Gutenberg project. Who is it named after? What are its goals, and why was/is it important (or not)?

21. The text attempts to formulate a principle of interdependence. Explain this, and try to reformulate it in other words.

22. Make a list of the ten most important turning points in history and explain why each was so important.

23. Make a list of the ten most important current problems that could be turning points in an account of our history written in the future.

24. Look up the term "mythopoesis." Explain it in the historical context. Now consider the craft of writing (i) historical fiction (ii) "futuristic" fiction (iii) alternate history fiction. How do the authors of one or more of these genres employ myth to explain or critique the society in which you live and work or study?

25. In particular, choose a science fiction author and either discuss the "world" the author has fictionally built as the stage for his/her story or specifically discuss the cause-and-effect issues around the technology available to the characters and how it influences the world in which they fictionally live. NOTE: To be called "*Science* Fiction," science and technology must be an essential plot element, a character as it were, without which there would be no story.

CHAPTER 2

The Foundations of Science and Technology

The professor and Dorcas arrive slightly late for the seminar and discover Nellie and Ellen berating each other over political issues. The other chairs are empty, but two additional students follow the professor into the room.

Professor: Ah, off to a good start, I see. Well, if I can tear you from your conversation for a few moments, I would like to introduce two new participants.

Nellie: Sorry.

Professor: (turning first to a tall, thin-looking woman with a gaunt face). This is Johanna Lud. She teaches poetry and sculpture classes at the local community college. Johanna, meet Nellie Hacker, a computer science major here at the University. And, in the other corner, I present Ellen Westlake, a fourth-year law student, campus president at her school of the Young Socialists, and a union organizer in real life. Like you, Johanna, she is taking our course for transfer credit to her college.

(Turning next to a powerfully built but somewhat ill-at-ease young man on his left) And, a special visitor, Mr. Lucas Dominic. Lucas is a local high school student, and somewhat of a prodigy. He works part-time as a research assistant in our university physics labs and has special permission to take two courses each semester from us. I

PART ONE | LAYING THE GROUNDWORK

asked him to drop in on one or two of these seminars because of his special interest in some of the topics.

Johanna: (sourly) My dean said I had to take this course to graduate.

Ellen: Welcome to the club.

Nellie: What's the problem? Surely a teacher is interested in ethics, society, and technology.

Johanna: (taking a chair) Bingo on the first two, dearie, but what this world needs is fewer machines, not more.

Lucas: (also sitting down) Everyone depends on science and technology. There's no way to avoid it.

Johanna: We'd be better off returning to simpler ways.

Nellie: Would you give up modern medicine?

Ellen: Why should we?

Nellie: There's a lot of high-tech in the drugs and machines that save your life when you need it.

Johanna: But we don't know what goes into vaccines, for instance, so we should have the freedom to refuse them, not be coerced by the government to risk life and health.

Lucas: That's nuts. Vaccines save lives. Without modern medicine, the average Joe or Jane would be a dead duck by the age of thirty.

Johanna: I don't have any objection to medicines when they're necessary, but in general we ought to use what helps people to be themselves, to be productive and to relate to others. People ought to be people, not servants of machines, of government, the pharmaceutical companies, or the rest of high-tech.

Ellen: It's the relationships between people that make society possible and that creates the state. All for one, and one for all.

Johanna: (glaring at her) Actually, dearie, I'm not too wild about statism either. Too much centralized control takes away an individual's freedom.

Nellie: That's for sure!

Ellen: But, you can't avoid some dealings with government.

THE FOUNDATIONS OF SCIENCE AND TECHNOLOGY

Johanna: True, but individual liberty is too important to be forever giving more powers to the state.

Ellen: The state is the people and the people are the state. They exercise their collective and universal will through the organs of the state.

Nellie: Yeah, right. In your system, everyone has the same will all right, but it's imposed by the party doctrine writers of the day. Orwell, here we come!

Lucas: Getting back to the topic—you also can't avoid benefiting from technology—it makes everyone's life better.

Johanna: Name an example.

Lucas: Nellie did—medicine.

Johanna: No, I mean of machines benefiting me.

Lucas: (pulling out a cell phone) Got one of these?

(Johanna starts to say something, thinks better of it and defers, somewhat red-faced.)

Lucas: Thought so. You do use a phone.

Johanna: (annoyed) Of course. It's essential when you need to contact people.

Nellie: So, you depend on the available technology.

Johanna: Only when I have to.

Lucas: Which is a lot more than you realize. Computers run those telephones, monitor transportation and control hospitals and doctors' offices. There are even electronics in most household appliances.

Johanna: I know all that; I just don't put the blind faith in technology and science that you seem to.

Dorcas: And, what is wrong with faith?

Lucas: Scientists don't need faith. They work based on logic and empirical evidence alone.

Dorcas: Your version of "Man is the measure of all things"?

Lucas: Exactly.

Ellen: Everyone has faith in something—you in science, me in the working class, Johanna in herself and her art, Dorcas in God, and Nellie . . .

Johanna: (looking askance at Dorcas) Oh, surely no one believes in God anymore!

Lucas: (reflectively) My guardian does.

Johanna: But you don't . . . or do you?

Lucas: I'm not sure for myself, but "God" is a hypothesis that a scientist can do without.

Nellie: (hesitantly) That may be true in a sense, but religion and science or faith and reason don't overlap anyway, so does it really matter?

Dorcas: Very much so. For one thing, the methods of the historian, which are not unlike those of your modern scientists, can be used to weigh the historical evidence for the claims of Christianity. Surely you moderns don't deny that Christ rose from the dead—I have seen him myself.

Johanna: Hallucination. Lock the girl up.

Nellie: The professor borrowed Dorcas from the first century. She really means it.

Lucas: It doesn't matter. Whether the Bible is true or not isn't relevant to science, for science does not need faith.

Johanna: Now, just a minute, young man. Ellen's right. Everyone has faith, has a "god" if you will. You believe in the scientific method as the way to knowledge, but others discover things in different ways.

Lucas: (stubbornly) If it can't be verified scientifically, it isn't knowledge at all.

Nellie: An E. O. Wilson fan? Don't you think that's overstating it a bit, Lucas? After all, what about art and poetry; what about economics and political science?

Lucas: (leaning forward) As to the former, whatever they represent, it isn't knowledge; and as to the latter, they are just opinions.

Johanna: For a young kid, you're a pretty opinionated snob yourself, aren't you?

Nellie: (leaning back laughing and pointing her finger at Johanna) Ad hominem! Ad hominem!

Dorcas: What do you mean by "opinion"?

Lucas: Those are the things you can believe by yourself without it mattering to anyone else.

Dorcas: Such as?

Lucas: Such as whether God exists.

Johanna: No, you can't include that. I don't believe in a personal god myself, but its existence is either a fact or a myth, so some people are right and others are wrong. Moreover, since people behave differently depending on their religious beliefs, those beliefs do matter to others. Someone who believes their god orders them to fly airplanes into buildings is a threat to us all.

Lucas: Yeah, well someone who won't get a necessary vaccine and gives a disease to a person who then dies oughta be charged with criminal negligence causing death and given a nice long vacation with free room and board at government expense. Opinion and knowledge don't mix. What do you think about the textbook we have to read for this course?

Johanna: Terrible.

Lucas: An opinion.

Dorcas: No, what she said is a true statement about her reaction to the book. That reaction is as much "knowledge" as the scientific kind.

Lucas: But, such reactions are different for every person. Science is always the same, so it's more useful. It's factual, not opinion.

Alicia: Perhaps you could define science, Lucas.

Lucas: Science involves the search for truth by using the human senses. We gather empirical data, interpret it according to the best available evidence and publish the results for others to examine, criticize, or duplicate.

Johanna: What about when you're wrong?

Lucas: All scientific theory is subject to later reinterpretation in the light of new evidence.

Ellen: So scientific truth changes?

Nellie: Not so fast, Ellen. Understanding improves as knowledge increases. Science is always an approximation of truth.

PART ONE | LAYING THE GROUNDWORK

Ellen: It sounds to me like scientific knowledge is nothing more than the current consensus of workers in a given field.

Professor: Ellen has a good point there, though she has overstated it by that "nothing more than." The consensus of informed people in a given field is not a concept unique to science but also exists in law, history, and mathematics.

Johanna: The problem with this young man's interpretation is that he confines knowledge to the results of using the scientific method. Science tells us how things work, but it says nothing about the ultimate meaning of life. Moreover, no machine can ever do that.

Ellen: Life has no meaning. It just is.

Lucas: Well, you certainly can't use science to prove the existence of God.

Dorcas: Can you disprove his existence?

Lucas: No, but that's exactly my point. If it's not possible to utterly disprove a hypothesis, then it isn't possible to prove it either, so it's not science.

Dorcas: Not only is the existence of the creator God absolutely true, but He has also revealed Himself, first in His word, and then by His Son Jesus, who authenticated His claims to be God by the working of His power. There's a historical record.

Lucas: I don't trust historical records. If something cannot be personally proven by observation or logic it is not science.

Dorcas: It does not follow that it isn't true.

Nellie: In fact, there's a mathematical theorem that says that no finite logical system is complete enough to prove everything that happens to be true without also being able to contradictions, and vice-versa. You get completeness or consistency, but never both.

Johanna: Well, I'd have to take your word for that, but I'm convinced there's a lot more to knowledge than the scientific.

Nellie: (intently, and ignoring her) Wait a minute Lucas, what about evolution? Is it true?

Lucas: (more cautiously) Most scientists say it is.

Nellie: Hah! By the criteria you have just given, evolution is not science either. You can't observe it happening, verify it by repeatable experiments, or prove it ever happened. Its supposed driving mechanisms of mutation and natural selection both destroy information. So, their position is inconsistent.

Lucas: (looking uncomfortable) Perhaps so.

Ellen: Some of what scientists call knowledge is a consensus of their views and is subject to change. It can be made to appear to be even more of a consensus if everybody in the field quotes each other regularly.

Nellie: Like the author of this book says: "If I quote you, and you quote me, who is any the wiser"?

Johanna: Did the author say that, or did you?

Nellie: Perhaps we are quoting each other.

Alicia: (Interrupting) Professor, the time is up.

Professor: Ah, yes. The two points of contention are whether technology is beneficial or not and whether faith and scientific empiricism are exclusive or not. I think we have a good handle on the issues. For next week, I'll want a two-thousand-word essay taking one side of either of these two debates. Work it out properly, with no personal attacks, and provide a good bibliography.

He gathers his books preparing to leave, but Ellen and Johanna exit ahead of him, grumbling over the assignment and the unfairness of being required by their respective schools to take the course. As they leave, a final snippet of conversation is heard.

Professor: (to Nellie and Lucas) Sounds like the two of you get on well.

Nellie: Yeah, Lucas. You're all right. Don't let those two faze you. Johanna can be just as rude as Ellen.

Lucas: (flushed and embarrassed) Thanks, well ... I've known you for a while, and you're o.k. too, Nellie, that is, for a girl.

Nellie: What!

Any more progress toward a lasting friendship was here cut off from the narrator's hearing and the readers' eyes by the closing of the door.

PART ONE | LAYING THE GROUNDWORK

2.1 The Kinds of Knowing

Logos

One of the most important philosophical questions has to do with the meaning of "knowing" (epistemology). That is, what does one mean by such statements as "I know this is true," or "We hold these truths to be self-evident"? The answer to meaning questions like these depends very much on culture, discipline, and the thought system of the one who is the alleged "knower," for there are a variety of ways to regard this concept.

In the tradition represented by certain of the ancient Greek philosophers such as Plato, and as later reinterpreted by such as Rene Descartes (16th century), the highest and most reliable form of knowing was the most abstract (including the mathematical), for knowing is equated with the result of reasoning.

True ideas, once appropriated from the realm of the divine and put into the transmittable form of words by logical argument and rhetoric, were termed "logos"—(literally a "word" but carries with it an element of both the spiritual and what moderns would call the "logical" or "reasonable"). Taken to extremes, the science of this kind of philosophy consists of logic alone and logic judges everything else, including the physical world. What cannot be brought into this realm is either uninteresting or suspect.

For instance, in this view, the god who created the universe was not just unknown, but unknowable, unless he would deign someday to send to mortals a logos (word) to reveal himself—a task that John assured them had been fulfilled in Christ (John 1).

An example of this kind of knowing is the statement "Two plus two equals four." The truth of this statement seems to depend on universal ideas independent of language or the notation in which they are written and so this truth is considered knowable absolutely (within the context of the usual counting numbers). This is true regardless of whether it is written that way, or $2 + 2 = 4$ or $II + II = IV$, or deux + deux = quatre or $10 + 10 = 100$ (base 2).

Such knowing also includes modes of reasoning such as:
All women are mortal.
Nellie Hacker is a woman.
Therefore, Nellie Hacker is mortal.

The conclusion is held with confidence (given the premises) because the rule for such a logical process (this one is a syllogism called modus ponens) is regarded as infallible.

Logic is important in itself, and its study is a worthy prerequisite for every discipline, for all scholars need to be able to think clearly and correctly. However, taken to extremes, one could claim there is no truth but logic alone, and it judges everything else, including the physical world. In this view, anything else is at best uninteresting, perhaps suspect, and may not be considered knowledge at all. In the most radical view, applications of the pure science of thinking to the mechanics of the physical world, including the development of science and technology, are unimportant, even beneath the notice of the philosopher. Knowledge is thought of as an end in itself rather than a means to generate applications or artifacts. Why should the Greek thinkers have built steam engines? Did it not suffice to demonstrate their theoretical possibility?

Empiricism

Another kind of knowing is derived from experience, or, as Aristotle would have said, from the substance a thing has (including its potential properties) rather than from its abstract form. That is, this kind of knowing is practical, not just theoretical. Such is the knowledge derived when the scientific method is applied to the physical world.

One could also express this in terms of data and information. Data consists of the raw facts of a matter, so far as these can be ascertained; information is the meaning attributed to those facts by some community of appropriately informed experts.

- That Canada has a $2.1 trillion debt on a gross domestic product of $2.1 trillion might be a fact; whether one should conclude that the country is on the verge of bankruptcy, and what to do about it, are matters of interpretation. After all, the United States, a country with only nine times the population, has a $34 trillion debt on a gross domestic product of $24.4 trillion. [2022 figures]

- That a political leader has been pursuing secretaries sexually may be factual; whether anything can, should, or will be done about the matter is a consequence of interpretation within a value system, including the values and agendas of political priorities.

- The fossils dug from the earth provide a factual record of dead organisms; the meaning of that record depends on its interpretation, for no human alive has seen the creatures who left those bones. This is true to an extent of all history, the more so if sufficiently removed from the present.

This (empirical) kind of knowledge depends utterly on the ability to gather and interpret evidence from the physical world. It also depends on the ability to give meaning to that data and communicate that meaning reliably to other people. That is, the data and the consensus on the information it conveys, together constitute "knowledge" in this realm.

It is important to realize that the consensus of experts that is at some point called "knowledge," is always in process and may be wrong. Indeed, "knowledge shifts" are not at all uncommon. A theory might be taught as a universally accepted fact for many years, only to be later (and perhaps suddenly) replaced by a contradictory one. However, as long as one realizes that what is called knowledge in this data/information sense is both an approximation and a moving consensus, it is still possible for those involved in a particular field to say they "know" a lot of things. With considerable refinement, this is the knowledge model used in the sciences today.

While modern scientific thought has roots in the rationalism of ancient Greece, it owes its current form to modifications made first by Renaissance humanists and later by the materialists and logical positivists of the nineteenth century. The sphere of modern science is the systematizable, the organizable, the empirically investigatable, and the repeatably demonstrable. It is not always possible to tell what belongs in this sphere, nor is it always possible to induce knowledge of absolute truth from instances investigated by the senses. (Because stones fall to the ground more quickly than feathers does not mean that it is the inherent nature of heavy objects to fall faster than light ones.)

Thus, there must always be an element of doubt, approximation, and incompleteness to science. Karl Popper believed such doubt expressed the very essence of the scientific method: "It must be possible for an empirical scientific system to be refuted by experience" (*The Logic of Scientific Discovery*). Absolute verification was not the issue to Popper, but potential falsifiability by empirical means was. Scientific results could be thought of in terms of probabilities of truth, but this was the best knowledge a scientist could have.

It is important to note, however, that doubt implied by potential falsifiability does not question, much less deny the existence of the reality being investigated. Rather, what is to be doubted is that the currently accepted descriptions of that reality constitute the final and most accurate possible description of the subject.

Extremes of Empiricism (1)—Positivism

Some of its most radical philosophers have taken empiricism to other conclusions. They have held that the experience of the human senses suffices to describe the entire knowable universe. For them, the supernatural is specifically defined out of existence, as is everything not approachable with the standard methodology of science. In short, if it is not scientific, it cannot be knowledge. That is, while such moderns do not disdain practical applications of their intellectual achievements, some have scorned anything not achieved through a particular type of mental discipline.

Extremes of Empiricism (2)—Deconstructionism

In a departure from the classic Greek reverence for knowing as a pure abstraction, knowledge is sometimes today held to be almost entirely experiential—to the point that material phenomena are held to exist only as they are perceived. For example, some philosophies of physics have held that should a tree fall in a deserted location, and there is no observer to witness it, not only is there no sound, but the tree continues to exist in both fallen and not-fallen states until an observer comes along to trigger it into one or the other condition. Should a century go by meanwhile, the second state could exist in an instant, complete with old, decayed wood as soon as the first traveler passed that way. That is, human observation is not only necessary to give the physical world meaning; it creates the physical reality to observe—the very existence of an objective reality is radically doubted; no verifiable or absolute truth exists; and its place is taken by whatever a person perceives to be the case or wants to be the case.

Empiricism and Practical Science

Whether they believe experience describes real-world phenomena (most practicing lab scientists), or that observations create the events they purport to describe (some theoreticians), there is still a general belief among scientists that all data is acquired through the senses, and becomes knowledge only as it is filtered by the intellect. This approach is useful, provided everyone involved realizes the relative truths it produces are determined by specific intellectual filters, with not all views equally valued or listened to in the process. Every society has certain dominant, ruling, or control paradigms that set its intellectual agenda and provide it with its characteristic way of looking at the world. When these reigning paradigms undergo a shift, some old "knowledge" ceases to exist, and other things come to be placed among the "known" (The false becomes true, and vice-versa.)

- Scholars once "knew" that the earth was the center of the universe; today they "know" otherwise. (The idea that they once believed the Earth was flat is, however, fictional.)
- Intellectuals once "knew" that God created the world, but most today say they "know" it came about by chance, evolution, and natural processes.
- Most people "know" that COVID-19 is real and that vaccines and mask mandates worked to combat it, but some "know" there is a hidden science telling them the existence of the virus is a fake, and the health measures were only undertaken as a conspiracy to exert absolute government control over the population. The odd thing about this and other "secret" conspiracies is that they know about it. How, if it is so secret?

There is another problem with taking radical doubt too far. Is the proposition "nothing is real" itself real? David Stowe (*Popper and After: Four Modern Irrationalists*) makes the following points about this approach to knowing:

1. It implies that human knowledge has not been increasing—a proposition that is at variance with experience.
2. It implies that all the potentially unlimited number of worldviews are equally valid, and so every kind of physical law or theory is equally as improbable as, say, a logical self-contradiction. Thus knowledge is impossible. This, says Stowe, is irrational, and neither can nor does provide a working philosophy for scientists.

However, the scientific method does depend on the idea that knowledge gained by the application of the senses has to have its truth content measured by reliable standards and that its acceptance depends upon informed judgements. For example, the statement "objects released in air fall to the Earth's surface" is universally attested as true by the experience of every human being. The statement "the sun will rise tomorrow," is very nearly in the same category. However, most people must accept "the Earth is an oblate spheroid" based on evidence gathered by others, for they have no means of performing the relevant experiments. Some therefore feel free to believe the Earth is flat, or hollow, or the center of the universe, and that other claims are due to deceptive conspiracies. Likewise, only a few can verify that "naphthalene has a molecular weight of 228.30." That is, the reliability of many knowledge statements is subject to human judgment. Yet, they all imply that there is an objective reality to judge. Other factors also influence the truth value of statements made from empirical evidence; these will be discussed in more detail in later sections.

The Contrast with Other Fields

The arts and the humanities of the Western World, by contrast, are based on a more subjective tradition. Their heritage is culturally characterized by a strong Judeo-Christian influence (as redefined by the Reformation thinkers) and influenced to a somewhat lesser extent by materialism. Though humankind is still given a central place in modern Western versions of these philosophies (most notably in the humanities), humans are not regarded as mere observers, evolving by chance and whim in a purely mechanistic universe. Rather, humanity is part of a whole that is greater than the human mind or senses can comprehend and may therefore obtain and use that which may legitimately be termed "knowledge" quite apart from experience as an observer in the scientific sense of the word. An artist, musician, or writer (fiction or non-fiction) also uses reality filters to make a statement about the world and a personal response to it, but these filters are not identical to those of the research scientist, though they are of a comparable kind.

In this tradition, there is a tendency to view the material world as a limited and incomplete or even flawed manifestation of realities that go beyond physical perceptions of the physical universe. This is certainly true among religious thinkers, though such a view is found in other disciplines as well. For instance, modern art and music—perhaps in partial reaction to the success of the sciences—have both moved away from interpretations and depictions of the physical world and have come to concentrate either on representing the emotions of the artist or on releasing raw emotions from the audience. In common with the deconstructionists of the written literary work, these practitioners have moved to the notion that there is no reality in their work apart from the experience of responding to it. Thus, their connection with the physical world has diminished even as the threshold of artistic activity needed to release the raw emotions of the audience has increased.

It is important to realize that a statement such as "this is the best piece of writing (art, music) of the year" is a true observation of the speaker's interaction with the work. Even if no other person agrees, the statement is no less true in the individual sense. That is, some knowledge can be highly personalized. Even the box office success of a work is not a statement of absolute merit. Rather, it is the aggregate of many such instances of personalized knowledge, or to use the common term, of "taste."

Statements about the past can also be problematic, for the more distant events are in time, the less that can be definitively said about them, because repeatable experimentation is generally unavailable, data is thin, its descriptions are filtered through the presuppositions of the writer of the history, and it is interpreted through the bias filters of its readers.

Intellectual Multiculturalism

C. P. Snow in a 1959 lecture later published as *The Two Cultures*, postulated there had come to be a division of intellectual activities into two distinct categories, with scientists in one, and almost everyone else in the other. Snow detected deep and sometimes bitter animosities between the two groups. Each had its view of what constituted knowledge, how it is obtained, and what are the ethics of applying it. What is worse, the depth of division between the two camps was directly proportional to the sophistication of the technology developed by the one, and to the despair of the other that it will never have the power to control that technology. Some people could travel in both circles, but they almost had to become different persons when they moved from one culture to the other.

Some fourteen years later, Jacques Ellul (*The Technological Society*) expressed a more comprehensive view of the situation. He saw the technological mindset (if not strictly the scientific one) becoming overwhelmingly powerful, sweeping all other forms of thought away—becoming not just dominant, but the only way of thinking. Technique (i.e., efficient method) was in his view irresistible. Every task or discipline has a most efficient technique that eventually emerges, develops fully, and destroys anything of lesser efficiency. All humanity will ultimately be caught up in a kind of amorphous technological totalitarianism extending over every aspect of life—one that cannot be avoided because of its claim to maximal efficiency.

Meanwhile, a group of intellectuals known as deconstructionists promoted a radical rejection of the idea that objective truth and meaning even exist. They claimed both were missing even in a written text because only at the experience of interaction with the text was meaning generated in the reader and because this could never be shown to be universal, the text had no meaning in itself, even if one was intended by the author.

What antinomians did for the study of morality, deconstructionists, in general, did to epistemology (the theory of knowledge); for them, nothing could be legitimately described as known.

With despair over the perceived dominance of technique reinforced by the parallel deconstruction of truth itself, many intellectuals were left viewing humankind as shorn of purpose, hope, and values—its very humanity simultaneously deconstructed of meaning and sold for a technical lentil stew.

Attempts to liberate technique by construing it within a framework of meaning—such as Schuurman's 1972 book *Technology and the Future*—underscored the feeling among philosophers that the technological boat had set sail for destinations unknown and left both them and the human spirit stranded forlorn on the shore.

Indeed, by the mid-1980s, Allen Bloom (*The Closing of the American Mind*) could lament that the battle seemed lost. In their obsession with technology, he believed that Americans had entirely lost sight of the humanities, especially of philosophy, even of logical thinking. For Bloom, philosophy had become a voice crying in an academic wilderness: no one was interested in hearing it, and none were qualifying themselves to do so. Even science had given way to the demands of the marketplace, relinquishing its claim to be a pure discipline. He recommended returning students to the rigor of classical Greek thinking as an antidote to the sloppiness he detected in modern approaches to knowledge. His critics in turn have not been certain that Bloom's criticisms are valid, or whether any such return is possible. (The sharpest opponents of an important role for philosophy in education claim it is irrelevant to economic reality, adds no understanding of the physical world, and thus is not worth studying.)

In like manner, Charles Sykes (*Profscam*) claimed that the university had become captive to professorial vested interests, neither doing research nor teaching very well, and offering a form of education that had little value for any but foreign students. A spate of similar books joined the attack on the relevancy of the university enterprise in the eighties and early nineties.

Noted Biologist and philosopher of science E.O. Wilson (1929–2021) took his views in a different direction, advocating for a resurgence of logical positivism, a philosophical approach that radically denies the existence of any knowledge not derived through strictly empirical (scientific) methods. Nothing else could be said to be "known." Of course, adopting this view would deepen the divide between Science and all other disciplines far beyond what was perceived by Snow and Ellul. For a fuller discussion, see the final chapter.

In later years, as high technology became easier to use, artists and writers embraced computers as a means to their ends and became among their most enthusiastic and demanding users. It is interesting to ask whether this phenomenon is a refutation of Snow, a vindication of Ellul, a further point of lament for Bloom, *et al*, or something else altogether.

It is also worthwhile to observe that an atmosphere of despair is unstable, for it presents opportunities for new infusions of hope into the mix, sometimes from unexpected directions. This observation could explain the increase in interest in spiritual answers being given to the truth and meaning questions by the end of the twentieth century.

However, the following quarter century has seen that wave wash out on a shore of indifference, to be replaced by political activism fueled in part by a radicalized parody of evangelicalism in the United States, and by angst over immigration both there and in Europe. Far from technology uniting the world as a global village, it has enabled anger, suspicion, hatred, and radical activism on a scale never before seen.

As noted in Chapter 1, some optimists see no loss at all in becoming an overwhelmingly technically oriented society, for there are manifest benefits to many technologies. Still, doubts and questions remain—are there no other valid ways of "knowing" other than by science? Must not empirical (scientific) sense-based knowledge forever remain an approximation or interpretation of a reality that cannot be known absolutely? Finally, is a technological society rich or poor in human values?

Belief

Another knowledge model is that of a belief widely, sincerely and reasonably held. Beliefs rest on some evidence for the thing believed does have an empirical aspect. However, most people use "belief" in a different way than they do "knowledge." Things "believed in" are generally considered to be less secure in their foundations, and perhaps less widely held to be true than things said to be "known." That is, a small group's (or one person's) certitude that something is true, based on what others might regard as incomplete evidence, is termed a belief, while a more widespread consensus about something is more likely to be termed knowledge. Of course, a belief, however widespread, is not necessarily true just because it is sincerely or widely held—it could be sincerely wrong in all the holders. On the other hand, scientific knowledge is not always true either—it is occasionally shown to be wrong after having been defended as absolutely true for a protracted time. One could even argue that all knowledge is based on degrees of belief and acceptance.

The adherents of some religions, Christians included, would add yet another term, "faith," by which they would mean absolute knowledge derived through a gift of God's revelation. Faith is knowledge that does not lose certainty because it lacks universal consensus or current empirical evidence. The idea is that God exists and knows all; humanity finds truth by paying attention to what God has revealed. As John asserts: "In the beginning was the logos, and the logos was with God, and the logos was God." *John(1:1)* He goes on in the same vein in an attempt to convince literate Greek readers that the otherwise unknowable God had now sent a revelation of Himself in Jesus Christ and thus had become personally knowable.

In addition, much information about the universe God has made can also be found by a sufficiently careful examination—this is sometimes expressed as "thinking God's thoughts after Him," or "knowing God by his works." In the faith context, absolute knowledge is external to the human race—it is revealed rather than being discovered or invented. Thus, empirical knowledge (of things discovered or invented) cannot in this view be relied upon, for nothing can be known with the certainty of the things revealed. Neither science nor belief are therefore qualified to judge such knowledge; they are simply tools to enhance it.

In this theory of knowledge, there is no *a priori* conflict between the absolutes affirmed by faith in God's revelation and the approximations obtained by the senses (scientific). However, conflict does exist in practice for two reasons.

First, there is the tendency for institutions to develop around the holders of faith. Such institutions then demand faith affirmation for their pronouncements, and these may touch upon empirical matters rather than on the revelation allegedly being safeguarded. Individuals find it far easier than do institutions to be simultaneously affirmers of the faith and seekers of empirical knowledge. Organizations can sometimes officially adhere to statements on matters peripheral to the original faith long after most of their (still faithful) members have abandoned those statements.

The second reason for conflict between faith and empiricism is that members of the scientific community often reject faith affirmation as inherently abhorrent, regardless of whether such matters fall within their sphere of competence and training, and even though they affirm faith in and build institutions around a set of philosophical presuppositions relating to the accepted epistemology of science.

One could summarize these difficulties by saying:

> Religion attempts to answer questions about ultimate meaning; these and not the detailed workings of the physical world are its territory. That is, its theologians stray when they pronounce upon physics as much as do the philosophers of science when they speak concerning the meaning of the universe.

Opinion

The last kind of knowing to be considered here is called "opinion." This is regarded as having the weakest claim upon the term "knowledge," and is also the hardest to define. Opinion is commonly thought to consist of positions privately and personally held to be true, and that can be maintained without reference either to facts or to the effect of the opinion upon other people. Determining whether a statement falls into the category of opinion is extremely difficult. To disparage a statement by another, one may say: "That's just your opinion." There often seems little rebuttal from such a judgement, for it appears to rest on the democratic notion that all personal views are of equal value and equally likely to be true as they are to be false (or neither). Statements such as "it's too cold," "that was a good book," "God exists," and "killing is bad" could all be disparaged as "mere" opinions.

However, the first two of these are true statements about the speaker's reality—they are matters of taste, rather than of opinion in the casual sense of the word. The third is a statement of faith, and the fourth is about moral objects. These last two statements are surely more than private opinions, for they cannot be privately held or acted upon, but are by very nature about relationships, for to act on them is to affect others.

If one tries to define an opinion as a claim about knowledge of which the speaker is unsure (e.g., "I think the bum is guilty.") then the statement is not directly connected to an external reality, however strongly stated. However, a statement of doubtful knowledge of truth is eventually resolvable as to its truth or falsity, so it is related to facts and is not just an entirely personal and private reality. What is more, people act on their views, so what are called opinions do affect other people, and their truth or falsity therefore matters.

For instance, a person who believed COVID was a hoax and vaccines and masks merely means of control by political conspirators, and who contracted and spread the disease could cause another person's death. Such an "opinion" is more of a semi-religious or political belief. It not only denies reality but has serious potential consequences, perhaps including the possibility of being charged with criminal negligence causing death.

Likewise, a lawyer who persists in bringing lawsuits before a judge, say, over a client's claims of a fraudulent election, but has no evidence to offer other than said client's opinion, risks being disbarred for wasting the courts' time with frivolous actions.

There may not be anything left for this category—what are called opinions are either another kind of knowing or else are meaningless (as far as determining potential truth value is concerned).

PART ONE | LAYING THE GROUNDWORK

Summary

It would be far beyond the purpose of this book to analyze the shades of meaning of the "knowledge-terms" in any greater depth, or to present all the arguments concerning their correct use. Those interested should consult a good text on epistemology and one on systematic theology. Instead, in this chapter, a further examination of the notion of scientific knowledge will be undertaken. A comparison with other disciplines will be suggested that may shed light on how scientific ideas develop and on the relationship between science and technology. Consideration will be given to the role of science and technology in the development of society, and certain technology categories will be looked at with a view to their potential impact on the future.

2.2 The Nature of Scientific Enquiry

One characteristic of humankind by which it distinguishes itself from all other life forms is an insatiable curiosity about the workings of the universe. Societal conditions have not always allowed this curiosity to be indulged; many practical pursuits require wealth and freedom from manual labour and these are not available for everyone. Theoretical pursuits also demand toleration of investigators whose entire exercise may be mental, and whose results may mean little to the average person or even the economy. The systematization of such work gives rise both to technology (or technique, as it might better be called) and to science. These are not the same thing, despite being closely linked in all cultures, and the purpose of this section is to give careful consideration to both, to see how they are related, and to investigate some of the scientific and technological influences on society.

Science

First, consider science, the more theoretical of the two. The fundamental premise of any discipline that is to call itself scientific is this:

> The universe that is the object of a scientific study is sufficiently orderly to be in some sense measurable, testable, and at least potentially predictable.

Radical doubters notwithstanding, the doing of science seems to require at least the perception of a systematic reality to have something that it can be about. It is often a simple matter to distinguish disciplines of a scientific type from those of most other kinds. For instance, the creation of music, painting, sculpture, and the writing of poetry or novels are not generally regarded as scientific activities. These pursuits may have rigid rules for some aspects, but they need not always, for their practitioners are supposed to be free to present ideas and impressions without being bound by anything called reality.

Even a novelist wanting to lure readers into a fictional story must create sufficient realism that the reader is not turned off by fundamental flaws. The action must be at least possible given the premises, the character's responses to situations must be believable, and the world in which they live both internally consistent and in reasonable agreement with known or potential science and technology. A writer of alternate history science fiction, for instance, must build a complete world that could plausibly stem from a decision point or nexus of known history in a manner that allows the reader to suspend disbelief for a time without encountering jarring impossibilities. A reader can also be turned off by gratuitous explicit content that serves no function for advancing the plot.

It is also possible, though more difficult, to distinguish science from the humanities (philosophy, languages, literature, etc.), and from the studies of society (sociology, anthropology, psychology, economics, etc.). In the latter group in particular, attempts are often made to apply scientific methods, but this is not always entirely successful. After all, it is not known whether human behavior is predictable in the same manner as that of things under scientific study are assumed to be (except, perhaps, in the large, that is, statistically). Although it is methodology (and not results) that determines whether a discipline is scientific, the method of science assumes an element of predictability, and it is not until at least some work is complete that one knows whether this factor is present. A discipline may use the methods of science on the assumption that they are appropriate, but it is only as those methods produce reproducible results that practitioners can gain confidence that they are indeed "doing science," and not something else.

It is easy to *assume* that scientific methods do or ought to apply to a given field of study. It is more difficult to discover how to make them apply (which is partly a matter of technique). It is harder still to demonstrate that the assumption was correct and the phenomenon being studied can be demonstrated by the methods being used to be predictable. Finally, if some orderly pattern is discovered, these techniques may shed no light on the source of the perceived order (or lack thereof).

The Case of Mathematics

The case of the discipline of mathematics is particularly interesting, for its philosophers can take one of two extreme (but not necessarily entirely mutually exclusive) views:

- that mathematical ideas are entirely theoretical and speculative, with no necessary connection to the physical world, or
- that mathematics describes things with a prior existence.

That is, do mathematical ideas come into being the first time someone thinks about them (created by thought), or are they pre-existent (already manifest in the universe) and only being discovered as time goes on? For example, the equation $ax^2 + bx + c = 0$ (a, b, c are real numbers with a > 0) can be solved for x (even if the solutions are complex numbers) by use of the quadratic formula.

$$x = \frac{-b \pm \sqrt{b^2 - 4ac}}{2a}$$

Figure 2.1 The Quadratic Formula

Did the quadratic formula only exist when a human being first conceived of it, or has it always been inherent in the concept of numbers and merely had to be noticed?

Although some will hold out for the absolute truth of one or the other of these two positions, mathematics has both aspects, for while the entities it discusses are on the one hand mental ones, these ideas do on the other hand have some relationship to the physical universe. Their pre-existence could be argued:

- The concept of number is universal and pre-existent. God has always existed in three persons, for example. However, the numerals employed for the communication notation used by humans to express this idea are cultural inventions, not universal truths. Thus, the ideas contained in the assertion that (something) equals four are inherent in the concept of number, and are not inventions. However, the notation in which the idea has been written is an artifact, for rather than "two" or "2," one could use "deux" or "II" or "10" (base two notation) without changing the meaning.

- The same is true of the meaning of the quadratic formula on the one hand, and any particular way of writing it on the other.

- The use of base ten numerals like 4645 to express the idea of 4000+600+40+5 is probably due to the vast majority of humans having ten fingers with which to begin learning how to count. There is no a priori reason why one should not use a system founded on a base of two, three, eight, sixteen, or some other number. Indeed, one does use base twelve (dozens and/or gross) to measure quantities of eggs, buns, or hours, base sixty to measure degrees, minutes, and seconds, and bases two or sixteen inside computers. Base eight (octal) has fallen out of common use.

- Pythagoras' Theorem on right triangles is true regardless of how it is written out, and it unfailingly categorizes triangles as right triangles or not regardless of what any observer may think or how that observer might write the general concept and a specific result. It is true even if you call the things "left triangles."

- Likewise, the interesting observation that the number 1961 reads the same right-side-up or upside-down is entirely a construct of the notation; it has no universal truth in itself. On the other hand, the idea of symmetry that this example illustrates is universal and can be found wherever some object can be rotated or flipped onto a copy of itself.

- In the same vein, the numeral 1001 not only has several such symmetries, but could represent the number one more than a thousand if in base ten, the number one less than ten in base two, and the number one more than the cube of twelve if in base twelve, namely one thousand seven hundred twenty-nine, that is, the smallest number that can be written as the sum of two cubes in two different ways.

- In a broader sense, this idea is illustrated by the universal notion of complementarity found in such pairs of opposite ideas as: left/right, up/down, right/wrong, and good/evil—all of which exist independent of the language and script used to describe them.

- Similar arguments can be made, not just for number theory, but for statistics, topology, algebra, analysis, discrete mathematics, graph theory, calculus, transfinite numbers, the various geometries, and set theory. Although some of these ideas have appeared on the human scene recently, the very rationality of their interconnectedness argues that they are in some manner inherent and inevitable (part of objective reality) and that they will certainly be discovered once one thinks long and deeply enough.

Who Can Understand Mathematics?

The difficulties in understanding the nature of mathematical statements are compounded by the fact that in all but the simplest cases one must *be* a mathematician to perform its mental experiments. A grade ten student in remedial (general) mathematics once said to the author: "I know everything there is to know about mathematics already; why should I have to take this course"? The sad fact was that he barely had acquaintance with the multiplication of fractions and had never heard of the sub-fields of mathematics mentioned above, much less of computational geometry, complex analysis, relativity, probability, combinatorics, statistics, <insert several more>, or any of their applications—the chasm of his ignorance was unbridgeable as there was no mutually understood language in which to communicate the ideas.

That is, in this realm "truth" can only get *informed* consent—can only be understood—if one has sufficient training and experience in mathematical thinking to qualify as a member of the consensus. Not just anyone can comment meaningfully on mathematics, for to grapple substantively with its ideas requires special knowledge and experience. Even among highly qualified mathematicians, embarrassing errors take place. For instance, a proof for a widely accepted theorem is sometimes later shown to be incorrect and either a new proof must be supplied, or the theorem may be shown to be false after all. In one celebrated case in the 60's and 70's a graph theory result was purported to have been proven in published papers by three successive writers, and all three proofs were subsequently shown to be incorrect. When this author, flush with the excitement of having discovered that the third attempt was likewise incorrect, mentioned to a member of his thesis committee having read the papers in question, he was quickly deflated by the return comment; "I suppose you noticed the obvious error in his reasoning."

One could summarize by saying that whether mathematical truths are created or discovered by mathematicians, they certainly cannot be discerned apart from the collective experience, training, and beliefs of the mathematical community, and this is not unlike the situation in the scientific community and some other disciplines. Specialized training is often required to comprehend some ideas.

That is, acceptance of mathematical and scientific results by most people, even those trained in another branch of the discipline, requires some degree of acceptance of the consensus of the specifically expert members of the community. This consensus, because it is an interpretation, is not necessarily *absolutely* true. For example, no matter how much a mathematical model for the first few seconds of the existence of the universe may be consistent with present-day scientific observations, acceptance of the model as factual is a leap into faith, one that is comparable to that held by others in an all-powerful creator having made everything in six literal days. To what extent can we assume that scientific methods and the conclusions therefrom are valid and applicable when investigating matters of the distant past?

Is Mathematics Certain?

By the latter part of the nineteenth century, logicians were well aware that the standard methods of logic employed at the time led to fundamental contradictions. For instance, consider the definition:

> The barber of Seville shaves all the men of the city who do not shave themselves.

or, similarly:

> S is the set of all sets that do not include themselves.

Or, again:

> The following statement is false.
> The previous statement is false.

Now does the barber shave himself or not? Unless one sneakily attempts to escape the logical trap by positing that the barber is a woman, a machine, or an alien, either answer leads to a contradiction. Is S a member of S or not? Can either of the last pair of statements be true (or false)? The existence of such contradictions introduces an uncertainty into mathematical logic itself, not just into the correctness of a portion of its consensus. That this uncertainty could not in *any way* be resolved was shown in 1931 by Kurt Gödel when he proved that no finite set of axioms used to describe a mathematical system could prove both the consistency and completeness of the system.

Consider, for example, the natural numbers:
$\mathbf{N} = \{0, 1, 2, 3, 4, \ldots\}$.

Gödel showed that, on the one hand, any set of axioms (rules) that could be used to prove all true statements about these numbers would necessarily be inconsistent (lead to contradictions like the one above). On the other hand, if the set of axioms is consistent (no contradictions possible) it could never be sufficiently complete to derive all statements about the system that were known to be true. As Douglas Hofstadter puts it: "In short, Gödel showed that provability is a weaker notion than truth, no matter what axiomatic system is involved." (Hofstadter, p. 19)

> As far as the laws of mathematics refer to reality, they are not certain; and as far as they are certain, they do not refer to reality.
> —*Albert Einstein*

That is, unless one is willing to use logical tools known to be unreliable (potentially inconsistent), there are always truths about the number system that cannot be proven.

The same principle applies to computing, for one equivalent to Gödel's theorem (the undecidability of the halting problem) demonstrates that no machine can be built using finite logical systems that can process all problems, or even determine ahead of time whether they will be successful in the attempt. Simply put, not everything knowable is computable. That is, human beings can know more than finite logical machines, no matter how elaborate those machines may be.

In a similar vein, it is not possible to prove with the rules of human logic that God exists (or that he does not). His existence may be strongly *inferred or supported* from evidence, but not *proven* in a logical or a priori sense. See additional comments on the feasibility or infeasibility of hard (human equivalent) artificial intelligence in a later chapter.

Comparing Other Disciplines to Science

This concept of uncertainty applies to science as well because Gödel's Theorem applies to *all* finite logical systems, not just to the mathematical ones. Science must also deal with the uncertainty that the closer something is observed the more the very act of observation changes the thing being examined, and so the less accurate the observations become.

Yet, the entrance of such uncertainties into the scientific realm does not create the difficulties for its practitioners that it might for theoreticians. After all, a researcher in some other part of the world with similar equipment needs only to be able to duplicate a reported experiment and obtain essentially the same experimental results within a reasonable margin of error. For science, duplicatable results are the important thing, even where there is no agreement about the interpretation (meaning) of the results.

Indeed, questions about *ultimate* meaning are not really on the agenda of science, and scientists who speak of them are no longer talking about their specialties, but about those of others. The Nobel prize-winning physicist who goes on the talk show circuit to proclaim the non-existence of God is no more qualified to speak on that subject than is a theologian to declaim on gravitational field theory or to interpret chromatography and NMR results.

Also, the diverse intellectual pursuits, such as theology, art, poetry, philosophy, languages, sociology, psychology, mathematics, and so on, while methodologically different, are organized disciplines in the same sense as the various sciences. Each such field of study constitutes a recognized body of knowledge with its own rules, practitioners, and special methods of interpretation. One distinguishes a scientific discipline from any others precisely through its intellectual methodology, the rules for which serve both to define what is science and to determine what are its appropriate fields of study.

The Scientific Method

A typical short-form elaboration of the scientific method in five steps goes something like this:

1. Observe the universe in question, collecting raw descriptive data.
2. Analyze the data, systematizing and interpreting it.
3. Synthesize a theory (formulate a hypothesis) to explain the data, or develop a model to illustrate it (i.e., create a mental abstraction of the presumed physical reality).

4. Test the theory or model rigorously (trying to disprove it) under as many variant conditions as possible to determine the degree of correspondence between the abstraction and the physical universe.

5. Modify the theory or model and re-test it until it agrees with all known relevant phenomena. If a universal consensus is reached on a particular theory it might be promoted to the status of a "law."

This process might be summarized by saying that science is a search for true descriptions of the world by making logical inferences drawn from empirical data. Although this description of the scientific method would probably be accepted (with variations) as a working definition by the vast majority of those who term themselves scientists, one must realize that it is only an approximation of what science is. Some cautions must be added to properly explain it.

First, applying the method implicitly assumes the hypothesis is testable. Some are, some are not. Strictly speaking, the latter are not scientific, for something that cannot be tested can neither be refuted nor validated.

Second, taking a narrow view of this process would exclude mathematics—a discipline that attempts to produce its results by logic alone. Yet mathematics not only provides the language, structure, and tools for systematic investigation, but it also has reasons of its own to be applied to the real world. Mathematics is therefore inextricably intertwined with all scientific disciplines. Not only can no science exist without the language of mathematics to analyze and describe its investigations, but also the boundaries between applied mathematics and science are vague.

The term "mathematical sciences" has therefore become common today, and few people are unhappy with the tendency to regard these disciplines as more a science than an art. That this acceptance somewhat undermines the working definition of science given above is of little practical importance to most scientists, for an exact definition of the field's overall scope has little effect on their work.

Third, whether mathematics is included or not, the definition given has one potential drawback: the tendency of some to regard scientific knowledge as the exclusive form of knowing and to specifically exclude from the "knowable" category any results obtained by other methods. This philosophy, called logical positivism, asserts that logic combined with the empirical methods of science forms the *only possible* way to "know" anything. It rejects the conclusions of other methods of enquiry as irrelevant—as not being knowledge.

While this view was widely held in the nineteenth and early twentieth centuries, and some still try to defend it today, it has lost much of its popularity among philosophers. It is now realized that scientists do not operate exclusively within the empirical methods given above. On the contrary, as John Ziman remarks, "they tend to look for, and find, in Nature little more than they believe to be there, and yet they construct airier theoretical systems than their actual observations warrant." (Klemke, p. 35) This may overstate the case somewhat, but it leads to an important observation regarding the "doing" of science.

Scientists work within a worldview.

That is, like everyone else, a scientist brings to the work at hand a framework of ideas about how things ought or seem to work, a set of preconceptions about why the world behaves the way it does and a collection of goals that are regarded as desirable to achieve. All the scientist's work is done within the context of such a worldview—it influences every decision and every step of investigation and analysis. Because of this, theory tends to come before the collection of data and not as a result of it. Consequently, data is often collected under the influence of the theory that is supposed to explain it, and researchers are naturally inclined to reject data that does not fit. This process is not dishonest in any way; rather, it is human nature to observe and interpret the world in terms of what one already knows or believes about it. A shared community worldview also lends consistency to the voice of science as it speaks to matters of public concern.

Fourth, consensus in a community (scientific or otherwise) can be remarkably broad, monolithic, and resistant to change. Unfortunately, this consistency can sometimes hamper objective investigation and make truth harder to approximate. Important insights and discoveries in any field often come about because the worldview expands or changes to allow people to see things in a new way. Those who make this breakthrough may have a difficult time convincing anyone else to listen because a changed worldview is necessary for people to re-examine matters considered settled.

Such "new views" are common in the artistic world. Each generation reflects its worldview in its artistic creations and may fail to communicate with the previous generation through these forms. Rock music, for instance, expresses a direct connection with one's emotions, a raw "me-ism" that can be incomprehensible to those who do not share its context. Indeed, it could be argued that it is not the nature of some music to be comprehended—that both its medium and message are entirely emotional.

Examples of paradigm shifts from the history of science include Galileo's interpretations of evidence to support a heliocentric model of the solar system, the periodicity of the elements, atomic theory, radioactivity, Einstein's theories of relativity, and quantum mechanics. All were ultimately accepted by the scientific community, but each had difficulty at first due to the radical change in worldview required to comprehend the new model. That the latter two have inconsistencies that have not yet been reconciled suggests there is room for re-interpretation of data or refinement of the theories.

This explanation is not intended to suggest, as some "new-age" philosophers do, that a new way of looking at things (a new model or paradigm) changes or becomes the underlying reality, a sort of ultimate "man is the measure of all things." Rather, it is to point out that the practice of science does not quite conform to the view of its philosophy as expressed solely in the step-by-step scientific method. Scientists do assume an underlying reality, but they interpret or filter that reality, so their results partially depend on the nature of those filters.

Fifth, the results of scientific enquiry are always approximations, subject to reinterpretation in the light of new data that may be more exact, be collected differently, or be interpreted through a different lens. There is also the possibility that new data will overthrow a fraud, a hoax, or a conclusion derived more from wishful thinking than from careful reasoning. For instance, a technician being asked to do radioactive dating of some sample might ask the supplier what range of dates are acceptable, and might not report any test results that fall far outside this range. The non-conforming results are thought to be spurious. But, what if there is another view that explains them all as part of a consistent data set? The very necessity of verifiability for scientific theories implies their potential for refutability with new data or interpretations, and this is a good thing, for once we assume we already know everything about some phenomenon, we close ourselves off from learning more.

Another complication arises from the fact that some scientific workers engage in the building of highly speculative theories with little or no connection to actual data. This habit is particularly widespread among astronomers and others with an interest in the origins and mechanics of the universe as a whole (i.e., cosmologists). Such speculation is healthy because it tends to open up many new lines for investigation. Scientists must speculate if they are to make any progress at all, for otherwise they will generate no hypotheses and be unable to learn anything. However, this necessity of practice does illustrate that the boundaries between science and the more speculative or metaphysical disciplines are not quite as sharp as may sometimes be believed.

The Role of Consensus

These observations on the imprecise aspects of science lead back once again to the example of its ally, mathematics, for a better idea of what science is, if it is not just pure logic combined with rigid experimentalism. As mentioned before, mathematics relies on a community consensus of what is "true"—one that is not infallible, but that is at least a reliable determinant of what things are part of the discipline and of what constitutes a properly derived result.

The existence of this peer consensus is not entirely unlike that of the high-diving or figure-skating judge who holds up a scorecard after each performance. The consensus of the group (i.e., the average scores) becomes the final judgement on the dive. The determination of what constitutes good science or good mathematics takes more people and a longer time (perhaps generations), but is nonetheless the result of a community examination over time of the work in question, and is a consensus of its value. It is even possible to quantify this agreement somewhat by counting the number of times a paper or book is cited positively in the bibliographies of later works—the higher the number (in reputable journals), the more firm the consensus of worth. Because the majority of published "research" papers are never once cited by anyone, those that are cited many times quickly distinguish themselves from the others.

Looked at in this way, science loses none of its empiricism, precision, or status—but it is seen as one among many consensual ways of agreeing about the way the universe appears to work. On the other hand, this view does cause science to lose some of the mystique and exclusivity that it has built up during its 150-year ascendancy over other thinking modes in the West, for this perspective places it in a continuum of disciplines, blurring the edges between it and other concepts of truth-seeking to some extent.

Other Considerations

The methods of science are also important in a variety of fields, (such as government or economics) where facts need to be gathered and interpreted for the benefit of the decision-making process. Scientific techniques can be invaluable in discovering "what is going on." Of course, subsequent decisions will always depend in part on prior values and consequent evaluations not provided by the fact-gathering process alone.

For instance, as the costs of techniques soar, decisions have to be made about what research to fund and develop, and what to delay or drop altogether. How much goes to AIDS, COVID-19, or other anti-viral research, how much to computing, how much to developing new fields, to transportation, to the environment, and so on? Such decisions raise political, economic, and ethical questions that scientific investigation cannot by itself answer. Moreover, there is no particular reason to believe that the conclusion about what *should* be done, when reached by a scientist, is *a priori* any better or any more logical than the conclusion reached by a politician, or by the general public about what they want done. Indeed, if a scientist takes pride in the belief that only empirical methods produce knowledge and everything else is erroneous or irrelevant, then the resulting rejection of other thought processes, disciplines, and people is more likely to produce bad decisions than good ones. Knowledge, thinking, decisions, and their consequences are interrelated. Science provides one of many methods of thinking and obtaining knowledge; it is most effective when integrated with others as well. That is;

It is impractical to think one way.

One must conclude, therefore, that the logical positivists, in seeking to exalt the scientific method as the only road to knowledge, actually restricted its domain and made it less useful than it should have been. In short, it is precisely the appropriate integration with other ways of thinking that makes scientific methods generally applicable and practical. Such applications of science and the relationship between science and technology are the subject of a later section of this chapter. The next section is devoted to placing the theory-making of science into the larger context of a broader thinking mode.

2.3 The Role of Abstraction

Among the activities of scientists, the forming and manipulating of scientific theories is important enough to warrant a discussion of its own. Theory formation is considered by some to be such a unique undertaking that it is the province of a privileged few and has no parallels in other endeavors. However, like the scientific method as a whole, theory formation is an example of a broader and relatively common activity whose exercise is necessary for all citizens in a sufficiently complex society. Indeed, the ability to propose theories may be one necessity for the formation of such a society in the first place.

What is an abstraction?

The Western Judeo-Christian religious tradition holds that God is capable of holding in his thoughts all the details of the fine structure of the universe simultaneously. This limitless knowledge and creative energy brought the physical universe into being in the first place and its ongoing expenditure holds it together. Although not all agree that God even exists, much less is omniscient and all-powerful in this sense, no one seriously believes it possible for any human being to achieve such a universal awareness. Even mundane and ordinary objects (a chair, a tree, a cow, one human cell) are sufficiently complex to make such a comprehensive understanding impossible. It has been centuries since a single human being could have even a passing acquaintance with the knowledge of all available disciplines, and it is now no longer possible for any person to comprehend the whole of any single discipline. Neither is it correct to assume that everything knowable about a given discipline has already been discovered, or ever will be.

Fortunately, it is not necessary to have such comprehensive knowledge about something to make appropriate use of it. One can enjoy a car ride without knowing how to drive. It is not necessary to be able to build an automobile to drive one, and not required that the workers building it be able to design it. The designers need not be able to produce the metals and plastics from which it is made. None of these must know how to refine the petroleum products required to run it. Road designers, builders, and mechanics occupy related specialties, and so do the legislators, salespeople, auto company executives, parts manufacturers, insurance adjusters, repair specialists, and many others.

Each of these has different priorities for what they must know about the automobile. For each, there is an *essential* subset or extract of detail taken from all that is available to comprehend about the subject. Each views an automobile by focusing only on the details essential to a particular role and needs only a cursory acquaintance with the specifics of importance to others.

A similar process is at work in the formation of theories by scientists (and others). Here, it is clearly understood that no object can be comprehended in every detail down to the sub-atomic. It is the concentration on essentials and the exclusion of detail that makes understanding manageable, or even possible. Such a process gives a researcher an intellectual handle on the subject that would be impossible if knowing everything was deemed to be the only adequate kind of knowledge. It is therefore possible to conceive of or use something by knowing an appropriate and sufficient subset of its properties. In this light, consider the following definition:

> Abstraction is the process of excluding or digesting details to concentrate on essentials.

One aspect of abstraction is deciding which properties are the essentials to the task at hand, and which are details that can be ignored. This decision very much depends on the community within which the abstraction takes place, for to be useful, an abstraction, like a logos, must not only be comprehended, it must be communicated. If only one person understands it, but cannot transmit its essence to another, an abstraction has no practical value. Thus, the kinds of abstractions that come to be widely accepted depend on the level of knowledge and education of the community for which they are intended. For instance, a solar-system-like model for explaining atomic structure is sufficient for those who are not equipped to grasp the finer points of probability and quantum mechanics, but quite inadequate for researchers at the frontier of knowledge in the field. Likewise, there are a variety of models for explaining the workings of a modern economy, and these vary in complexity and usefulness depending on whose understanding is being addressed. The needs of most citizens are quite different from those of a politician making a decision, or those of a professional economist summarizing available information for that decision. Likewise, a child's concept of mathematics: "She got more than I did" or the teenager declaiming "I know everything there is to know about mathematics" may seem adequate to the one expressing it, but is far from satisfying the researcher in advanced graph theory, hyperbolic geometry, or the modeling of laminar flows, ocean temperatures, or flows through complex networks.

Other Abstractions

This process of attempting to explain a myriad of details through an abstraction of certain broad outlines or essentials is not confined to the sciences or even to the academic disciplines that attempt to use the scientific method. Numerous examples are possible from other fields:

- Words and numerals are symbolic abstractions of specific number ideas.
- A chart or graph is an abstraction of data or relationships into pictorial form, to allow them to be visualized, and therefore understood from a different perspective.
- A computer program is an abstraction of a problem solution into a specially devised symbolic language (notation) that could itself be termed an extended algebra.
- A language (including a computing notation) is an abstraction designed to communicate other abstractions. It could be termed a meta-abstraction. There are even meta-languages whose purpose is to describe either the syntax or semantics of languages.
- Whenever someone learns a skill, a trade, or a sport, the necessary activities and actions are abstracted from the task details. Performing the skills becomes automatic, and they can be exercised without thinking about the details. Experienced hockey players know instinctively the best place on the ice to advance their team's play or prevent the other team's.
- The manufacturing/transportation/wholesaling/retailing supply chain is an abstraction that allows people to buy goods without having to make their own.
- All job specialization is a type of abstraction that frees people from excess complication, allows them to concentrate on a small number

of useful skills themselves, and to deal with most of the necessities of life via other specialists in a similarly abstract manner.

- Money, whether expressed as precious metal, coin, paper, cheque, or electronically, is an abstraction for the wealth and activities of nations, corporations, and individuals. More fundamentally it is an agreed-upon abstraction for the value of one's work.
- A representative democratic state is an abstraction that allows individual input into the governing process without having to consider every detail of every person's stand on every issue.
- The Judeo-Christian understanding of God is an abstraction for one who is too complex ever to know entirely.

Thus, far from being the province of academics alone, abstraction is a process fundamental to human activity. The totality of the abstractions used by a culture (including those of language) is an important measure of its complexity. The most sophisticated abstractions are those that allow people to perform complex tasks without much thought. For instance, the graphical interface found on modern computers allows the user to perform very complicated tasks with a minimum of effort (at a higher level of abstraction) by comparison with the textual interface found on old-fashioned machines. Indeed, all computers are multipurpose tools for high-level problem-solving—they enable people to create abstractions for analyzing and manipulating data while avoiding dealing with detail personally.

Likewise, most industrial machines (and even bicycles) have to be operated abstractly—at a level of unconscious skill, for so long as the details must still be thought about, the task cannot be performed efficiently, if at all. (If you have to think in detail about what you are doing, you fall off your bicycle or cut off a finger with a trimming machine.)

While one could criticize the process of abstraction over many levels as removing people from "real" understanding, it is precisely such distancing that gives abstractions their power. It is not necessary to understand how cheese is made to enjoy it. Neither is it a prerequisite to know how to assemble or program a computer to make productive use of it for such tasks as word processing, accounting, or data analysis.

These examples illustrate that abstractions are the most powerful when they are far removed from the thing being abstracted; when they have been refined to the point that they can be usefully automatically employed by most people. This is not easy to achieve. More than a hundred million lines of sophisticated programming code might, for instance, go into creating a word processor to perform its tasks of manipulating the expression of writers' thoughts in words.

Other Names for the Process

So important and pervasive is the process of abstraction that it has a variety of specialized names arising from different disciplines and from the terminology adopted by the various people who have considered or at least utilized aspects of this activity. Some of these equivalent terms are mentioned here because they are of importance in later chapters.

A *digest* is a summary of that portion of data deemed by the one making the digest to be the most essential. It is an attempt to filter the data, removing the non-essential, redundant, or irrelevant. For instance, data reported from experiments are nearly always digested from the entire set obtained; this is necessary for brevity and clarity.

A *Model* is a representation of something in a more concrete or accessible form than the original. It may be also used of a scale model for some proposed project. The term conveys the idea of explaining or showing complex entities using more easily understood analogies. (i.e., ones for which there are believed to be adequate understandable abstractions already). The term *modeling* may be used by scientists to describe the process of theory formation.

Theory formation is an attempt to abstract into some simple statement the workings of the subject under study. This term tends to be less concrete than modeling, for a theory is an attempt to define rather than to model, though in practice the distinction may sometimes blur.

A *paradigm* is also a way of looking at a subject by way of analogy or example. It too is a model, but this term is used in a broader sense to describe abstractions of considerable importance or size (a collection of related abstractions). One example is the evolutionary paradigm, within which there are many specific models for origins. Another is the Marxists' class struggle, to which idea they bend all aspects of their political science and economics.

A *meme* is a (perhaps indirectly perceived) transmittable idea that is the basis of a social movement or a political philosophy. Its spread through a population can be thought of similarly to that of infection because it is the nature of a meme to induce the desire to proselytize. A meme can be benevolent (e.g., the ideals of democracy), fatal to their holders (e.g., the suicide cult beliefs) or fatal to others (e.g., Naziism, Stalinism, Putinism, religious hatred, racism, misogyny).

A *worldview* is a complete set of philosophic or religious presuppositions within which paradigms and individual abstractions are formed. It incorporates the total way in which a person does abstractions (thinks) about the real world and generally finds its expression within the communities of which the person is a member. It encompasses the complete set of memes that a person possesses and spreads. One may speak, for example, of a scientific worldview, of a Christian one, of a liberal one, or, say, of an American, British, Mexican, French, Chinese, German, Ukrainian, Russian, or Canadian one. Within each of these are numerous specific views of parts of the world.

Some media employ word pictures and figures of speech to evoke a much broader point (poetry is like this; so are many portions of the Bible). Other media use visuals to convey a broader message (television commercials). In both cases, a more subtle form of abstraction is used to transmit ideas related to or suggested by the formal communication.

The mention of some abstraction term, theory, title, or worldview name, evokes in the hearer a vision of a collection of related beliefs, views, or typical activities. That evoked image will invariably be to some degree inadequate or incorrect, especially if the hearer is not a part of the community that devised or is described by the abstraction. When such a misconception takes place, it is often because the hearer already holds to popularly believed ideas about the group in question, in which case the hearer's own (mistaken) abstraction is called a *stereotype*.

Thus such words as "fundamentalist," "immigrant," "liberal," "leftist," "right winger," "Christian," "legalist," "unbeliever," "racist," "abuser," and many others, especially ones uttered as pejoratives, will generate in the hearer a collection of related impressions whose semantic meaning depends on what that person already has abstracted under the term in question. This is not to suggest that the deconstructionists are correct and that no message has an absolute semantic; it is only to observe that communication requires agreement on the meaning of the abstractions being used. Likewise, the communication medium is at least part of the message. Ideas pictured are hotter than ones spoken, which are hotter in turn than those texted or posted, which are hotter than those written in books like this one. The hotter a medium the more robust the message being communicated.

Plants and animals do not make abstractions; this is a uniquely human activity. Abstractions make thinking and communicating possible. They make it feasible to understand the world and its processes, whether by science or otherwise. They make it possible to make, to build, to specialize, and to cooperate. They are therefore the essential building blocks, not of science alone, but of human civilization itself. This section concludes with an attempt to abstract itself (despite the dangers of generating the contradictions inherent in any self-referentialism):

> Abstractions are never the "real" thing, and therein lies both their power and their usefulness.
>
> Abstractions are intellectual creations; they are not discoveries.
>
> Abstractions are approximate and relative perceptions or descriptions, not precise or absolute.
>
> Agreement on the contextual meaning of abstractions is necessary for effective communication of ideas.

Before looking at how the making of abstractions bears on the meaning of science, it is instructive to consider also the relationship between theory and practice.

2.4 Science, Technology, and Technique

The Relationship Between Science and Technology

One way of defining what is meant by "technology" is to view it as the handmaiden and child of the doing of science—as the practical adjunct to theory. In this popular view, science serves as the tool to discover the rules by which the universe operates, and technology provides the payback for all the investigative work. This way of looking at the relationship between science and technology has elements of truth but can be misleading. It is one thing to create a model to explain, say, electromagnetism. It is quite another to use the theory to make a product like a radio, a television, a computer, a heart monitor, or a gene editor. The kind of thinking that goes into applying the principles worked out by scientists to the making of physical products is quite different from that which goes into discovering such principles in the first place.

This can easily be seen when one realizes that science is essentially an inductive and theoretical process, wherein one examines many actual instances in the real world of some assumed underlying order and attempts to find a general structure that in some sense explains those instances. The development of technology, on the other hand, involves a deductive or tool-making mentality, by which one derives or builds specific applications of general principles. Perhaps the simplest way to distinguish between the two is to say that science is concerned with *why* things work, whereas technology is concerned with *how* to make something work, that is, how to *do* something.

The fundamental motivating factors are also very different. Pure science can be driven by the desire to know, or by intellectual passion, and requires very little more. The motivation may be pure curiosity; it may be a desire to "think God's thoughts after him," or it may be to "become like God, knowing all," or anything between. As in mathematics, pure science may have an inner cry to be applied (the cry may come from a funding agency), but the researcher need not be personally interested in such aspects. Work in basic science can be done for the same reason that climbers scale Mt. Everest—the challenge is simply there.

On the other hand, the drive to build tools (technology) comes from the need for better and more efficient ways to get things done (*contra* Charles Dickens' Circumlocution Office in the novel *Little Dorrit* whose purpose was to ensure that nothing would be found out and nothing could be done). People innovate to better feed themselves, to defend themselves from attack, to become more effective aggressors, or to gain some other competitive advantage. They build higher, faster, wider, cheaper, and more beautifully than the last person and what they have built fulfills a need and may increase their wealth. They may even do it to help other people achieve their full potential, or because they believe that God ought to be honored in the full use of their talents to benefit others. They may not even be able to articulate reasons why they apply and build, except to say they enjoy tinkering.

One other difference between the two should be noted, and that has to do with methodology. Since technology is required even in the absence of scientific knowledge, it often uses trial-and-error methods. For instance, it is difficult to predict what the physical properties of an alloy will be just by knowing those of the metals to be mixed. The constant search for lighter, stronger, or more ductile alloys cannot wait for science to provide a working model to explain what will happen when a given collection of metals is mixed in specified proportions, for such a theory is a long way behind the need. Rather, metallurgists mix different combinations and then test the properties of the alloys they produce. They may use only general rules of thumb (heuristics) based on experience and not require a unifying theory. This process may lack pure theoretical beauty, but it gets the job done, and that is what technology is for.

Because many of the technological advances of this century have depended on science, it is easy to forget that the creation of tools goes on independently of science—even (to a great extent) in its absence. Moreover, each set of tools or machines has the potential, when once manufactured, to enable the building of others of a higher order—and to do this even before the first set is fully utilized. Yet, the industrial age has seen a phenomenally successful partnership between research science and engineering, and to a considerable extent, the nature and goals of science have come to be dictated as much by needs for new technologies as by curiosity. Pure science has become woven up with its applications and the two can no longer be completely separated. Indeed, it may no longer be accurate to distinguish pure science from applied science, because the separation only sometimes exists in practice. Nowhere is this relationship more evident than in the technology parks adjacent to many universities. Perhaps the best known of these is the Silicon Valley area of California, which owes its existence to nearby Stanford University and the many professors and former students who successfully turn their knowledge into products and cash for advances in computing. The same thing has taken place in biochemistry, where academics are racing to turn a profit by transforming their research into marketable pharmaceuticals, gene therapies, anti-aging treatments, and vaccines. There are endless examples in computing science. AI, anyone?

The U. S. space program generated large numbers of commercial spin-offs to the consumer market. These technologies were developed initially for conditions of zero gravity, extreme temperature, high stress, and limited mass or size, and had ultrahigh reliability requirements, but quickly found uses in more mundane environments. In more recent times, the space industry itself has become privatized, with the American government purchasing rides for people and supplies to orbit, and numerous satellites launched on behalf of enterprising telecommunication ventures.

All technical advances in these fields (computing, biochemistry, space) have had consequences for a wide range of marketable products. The same comment can be made for military technologies, for the entire aerospace industry has grown as it has largely because of the impetus provided by the needs of two world wars, many smaller ones since, and the expectation of more to come. The observation can be repeated for almost any research or technology. Pure research and pure invention do not exist alone and entirely to themselves. Each inevitably affects the other and reflects onto itself. Answers generate both products and new questions. Here, the interdependence principle could be stated:

> There are no such things as pure theories or pure applications.

Technology in its Own Right

However, the relationship between science and technology goes far beyond the fact that one is inductive and creates abstractions and the other is deductive and generates concrete results, for science as it is now known is only a few centuries old, whereas technology has been around at least since the first person thought of throwing a stone. It is not hard to argue that technology gave birth to science by providing a critical mass of industrial tools and complex processes that could only be understood and carried to the next step of their development by inventing the exacting analytical technique called science. Viewed in this way, science could be regarded as a tool of technology rather than the other way around.

If the definition of technology is broadened in the manner of Jacques Ellul to include all systematic techniques—all searches for the most efficient way of doing—then the scientific method itself is an example of a technique. As a technique, it is subject to being studied for its own sake, and to being modified to become more efficient. Seen in this light, scientific enquiries take place under the control of one out of many possible techniques of thinking. They do not so much generate products from theory as they apply a practical methodology themselves. This concept is even more evident when one considers that scientific investigations themselves almost always require tools other than simply a particular instantiation of the mental discipline that is the scientific method.

Whether the device is the mass spectrometer, gas chromatograph, or NMR of the chemist, the meson machine of the physicist, or the computerized microscope employed by the molecular biologist to view activity at the cellular level, or CRISPR to edit genetic structures, there is always a level of co-requisite technology without which the particular science cannot be performed. Indeed, it becomes increasingly difficult to speak of the science without the technology that is required to do its investigations. Moreover, there may well be more efficient techniques to pursue a given line of enquiry. There may even be a better way to do what is now called science as a whole. Techniques that are hoped for but not yet known may not exist, but the point is that it cannot be proven that modern science is or uses the most efficient possible technique of its kind for a particular instantiation of the general method.

Furthermore, just as science and technology drive each other, and their modern versions could scarcely exist without each other, each technological advance drives new ones. That is, just as no scientific discovery is without its implications for technology (and vice versa), the same is true of new products and techniques themselves—none exists alone or is without a broader influence. Some examples include:

- The development of reliable pumps made it possible to mine the deep seams of coal underlying much of Britain, one of the prerequisites for the industrial revolution.
- The burning of coal eventually forced the creation of scrubbing technology for cleaning emissions.
- The development of steel made possible a wide range of machinery, instruments, and consumer goods that could not have been foreseen by those who made the first alloys of iron and carbon.
- The World War II German rocket program led directly to today's ICBMs and space exploration technology.
- Radio led to television, and the demands of both led to communication satellites.
- The growing complexity of telephone systems required automatic switching systems that were eventually computerized.
- The modern microcomputer was made possible by several inventions, most notably the vacuum tube, transistor, and integrated

circuit. It in turn has spawned new products, disciplines, and whole industries.

- The COVID-19 pandemic drove research into RNA-style vaccines.
- A rapidly aging population has too many people needing support in their declining years for the smaller proportion of its wage earners to do so, and this is partly driving research into anti-aging techniques.
- That same demographic shift means there are insufficient people of working age for the jobs available. This and cost considerations drive robotization in many job sectors.
- Global warming is melting polar ice at a rate that will submerge many coastal cities and dramatically change the location and distribution of arable land unless new technology is found to slow the process or ameliorate its effects.

Examples of this sort of thing could be multiplied for product development alone; they lead to two more statements of the interdependence principle:

It is impossible to discover one thing
and
It is impossible to make one thing.

The observation that one invention drives another explains why in the long run the overall growth of technology is exponential, even though any one application eventually reaches natural limits, sometimes relatively quickly. Consider transportation technology, for instance, and its progression through walking, riding, sailing, driving, and flying, to space travel by rocket. Each of these on its own imposes a natural upper limit on speed, but the need to travel farther and faster spurs the development of new transportation technologies. The theoretical limit on propulsion-driven speed is some substantial fraction of the speed of light, but the most optimistic science fiction writers take it for granted as a necessary plot element that a new technique of transportation (warp speed or wormholes?) will eventually be developed to get around this barrier. More conservative voices assert that this is impossible, and that does seem to be true for theoretical and practical reasons. However, such voices have been heard before—the horseless carriage, the airplane, the moon rocket, and the personal computer were all impossible until they were invented. These examples may serve to illustrate an important fact of both science and technology that may be termed the incompleteness principle. It applies to all knowers except the all-knowing God.

> For any field of study or application, it is either impossible to know everything, or it is impossible to know when everything is known.

or, to put it another way

> No body of knowledge can ever be known to be complete, and no technology can be known to be the most efficient possible.

Technique

Broadening the notion of technology to view the scientific method as one in a spectrum of techniques has other consequences. If technique is the search for efficient methods as well as for efficient devices, then one may suppose that virtually every discipline has techniques better suited to that field than to others. This supposition leads to further insight that the best techniques of management or the study of sociology may resemble scientific techniques, but do not have to correspond to them very closely. One then ceases to expect that all technique must be of the scientific kind, for efficiency is surely related to the context of specific fields, rather than deriving solely from universal theoretical considerations. Thus, it makes sense to speak separately of techniques of economics, politics, management, advertising, communicating, teaching, mathematics, science, and clear thinking (logic). One can also suppose that such techniques will lead to more efficient methodologies in each of these areas, without having to apply the label "scientific" to them.

Jacques Ellul observed that every field of human endeavor can be assumed to be subject to the search for technique. As techniques develop, he observed, they do so in the most efficient manner available, reducing the number of choices for method, and tending to become rigid and authoritarian, admitting of no exceptions because of the claim to be the most efficient. He saw the result of this progression of technique to be an amorphous totalitarian society with no individual choice (everyone would of necessity always do things the most efficient way). However, there was a factor that Ellul did not in his pessimism consider—the incompleteness principle. What if some other path were followed from the start? Could not a different "most efficient" point have been reached? How could anyone know that such a point had been reached?

It is not possible to know when the ultimate efficiency possible has been achieved in any field. It may be reached for a given technique applied in a particular way, but there may be other techniques with vastly different results. The high technology explosion in so many fields simultaneously illustrates this better than any theory. The view of the 1950s, like that of the 1890s, was that certain ultimate goals for both scientific knowledge and technological efficiency were close at hand. Such a view cannot any longer be sustained. It is being replaced by a more open-ended thinking that does not suppose that any state of equilibrium (in the sense of an ultimate technique) must ever be reached in either product development or in the potential application of technique—even to the sciences.

To put this concept another way, suppose humankind was indeed created in the image of an omniscient and transcendent God. The process of learning may still be at the stage of the infant who makes piles of someone else's blocks and then knocks them over. Children naturally believe that they know everything, and are constantly amazed to discover that they do not. The principle of incompleteness is worth restating in these new terms:

> No technique can ever be known to be ultimate, the best possible or universally applicable in any or all situations and cultures. All are open-ended.

Summary

The popular conception is that science discovers and technology subsequently applies, but the dependency of the two may be as much the reverse. Technique (efficient methodology) encompasses both science (one technique) and what is commonly called technology or engineering (efficient product development). It is also incorrect to assume that at any given time the most efficient methods have been discovered—or even that a technique for doing something either is or can be optimized.

These insights assist in more properly placing science and technology within a spectrum of related human activities, demythologizing them

THE FOUNDATIONS OF SCIENCE AND TECHNOLOGY

to an extent, and partly removing the notion that technique irresistibly and inevitably progresses to all-encompassing and dignity-destroying final goals from which further progress is impossible. They lead to a more open-ended and continually changing scenario for the future. They also lead to a more realistic view of the practice and practitioners of science and technological development.

Profile on . . . Society and Technology

The Telephone and . . .

What is it for? March 10, 1876: Alexander Graham Bell becomes the first person to transmit speech electrically. The powerful telegraph companies, seeing no business applications, refuse to have anything to do with the "electrical toy." Even its inventors seemed at first not to know what to do with the new machine.

A new occupation: Early telephone subscribers were connected to one another's lines by central operators. Since they could (and usually did) listen to the conversations, operators became powerful and important in their communities, for telephone exchanges were the primary information clearinghouses.

Women and the telephone company: Early operators were usually well-educated single women with a status comparable to school teachers. They were well cared for, but generally required to leave upon marriage and few entered management. However, the sheer size of this workforce contributed to greater acceptance of women working outside the home.

Depersonalization: As exchanges grew in large cities, it was no longer possible for operators to know their customers. They became detached and impersonal handlers of routine switching chores, many of which were ultimately taken over by automated machinery. Today, even the operator's voice is synthesized.

An information medium: The early practice of transmitting concerts and sermons to homes and hospitals became the forerunner of similar entertainment via radio and television. It was no longer necessary to go to an event to experience the pleasure of having attended.

Business practice: Once in use, the telephone was not seen as a social medium, but as a tool for conducting business. For instance, installed at resorts, it allowed workers to keep in touch with their offices. Cell phones allow instant communication almost anywhere. Large businesses can be cohesive, and small ones can compete. Smartphones allow many tasks to be performed on the run or at the beach. The tradeoff is that one is never away from the office.

Urban development: The suburbs and the upper floors of high buildings were not practical as locations for doing business before the telephone. It has contributed to the growth of cities both upward and outward.

Old technologies obsoleted: Fax, and the later telegraph, which peaked in the late 1920s, and again in the mid-forties, was followed by teletype from the 1960s, but all such electromagnetic communication means declined steadily once telephone and its offshoots became electronic. Today, the use of the telephone and its sibling, the Internet continues to grow rapidly even as the amount of first-class mail declines and those electromagnetic precursors have all but vanished. Do modern students even know what typewriters, key-punch machines, tape recorders, or cassette players were?

Better services: The telephone permitted the creation of efficient emergency services over large areas. Medical aid, firefighting, and policing all improved dramatically because of the ability to communicate requests for help quickly.

Crime: The telephone enabled new forms of crime. Prostitutes became call girls. Obscene, spam, and scam calls became ubiquitous problems. Gambling networks became more widespread. Wiretapping became both a new kind of crime and a new method of law enforcement. All translated seamlessly to and greatly multiplied in number and scope with the advent of the Internet, and will even more as AI techniques become more widely used.

Environmental issues: From very early on, complaints were often heard that wires, poles, and towers were disfiguring the countryside. Today, disposable cell phones, the multiplicity of cell towers from numerous competing networks, and the vast quantities of electricity consumed to empower always-on, always-present communication can all be thought of as polluting in different ways.

It changes social behavior: If two people are speaking and a third enters the room, the newcomer must wait for the chance to talk. If instead the third calls on the pocket telephone, most people cannot ignore the demand and will drop whatever they are doing to answer immediately.

THE FOUNDATIONS OF SCIENCE AND TECHNOLOGY

Major Issues

Both it and the Internet are difficult to cost and regulate fairly.

1. How is a fair rate for service determined? Flat fees give businesses and other high-volume users a quantity discount, causing home users to subsidize them. On the other hand, metering local calls requires more equipment and raises the rates for everyone.
2. How are costs and fees split properly between long-distance and local service? This became especially hard to determine when two or more companies are involved and is impossible with the worldwide ubiquity of the Internet.
3. Should telephone and internet service be monopolies to ensure the greatest efficiency and uniformity of service? Or should they be competitive, to ensure the lowest prices?
4. Should either service be closely regulated as an essential public utility, or should free competition be allowed? Which is most in the public interest?
5. In either case, should they be government-owned or private?
6. Should all long-distance directory service calls be free? Credit bureaus were heavy users of this service, reasoning that a phone listing is an indicator of creditworthiness. These are commercial operations, and initially paid nothing to use this service—one reason why it is not now free. But the same comments can be made for search engines, which are only viable by being simultaneously an advertising medium.

The telephone and the Internet change society.

1. They are instruments for socializing and organizing people (the latter often not to good effect).
2. They shrink space and time, making rapid communications with remote places as effective as those next door.
3. "Mail order shopping" transferred first to the telephone, then to the Internet. "Let your fingers do the walking" was not simply an advertising slogan, but a new way of living, one that eventually evolved

to render many brick-and-mortar stores unable to compete with electronic ones, which are now the largest of all retailers.

4. Paper mail became deprecated as "snail mail," was largely replaced for personal, business, and junk purposes by e-mail, but the next generation of users came to prefer Facebook, then Twitter, (X) and other social media platforms for instant communication that became more and more concise until it came to resemble snappy sound bites more than thoughtful communication.

5. The Internet and the social media it hosts became the means of forming cliques of like-minded people and enabled them to direct collective hatred at those they thought different—whether for skin color, language, ethnic group, sex, national origin, class, political stripe, age, or any other distinguishing characteristic they chose to dislike-often for reasons that made no sense.

6. They also enabled new types of fraud.

Electric and electronic communication spawns new technologies:

1. Demand for long-distance and transatlantic service gave rise to copper wire, undersea cables, microwave transmission, optical cable, and satellite transponders.

2. Demand for new services saw the development of multi-purpose video phones, improved facsimile service, head and wrist wearable phones, marriages of phone and cable providers, and entertainment streaming over the Internet (threatening to obsolete local broadcasts of both TV and radio).

3. The pandemic necessitated the widespread adoption of video conferencing and remote classrooms, spurring the sales of and improvements to microphones, web cameras, and multiple versions of software to enable virtual presence.

Telephony and the Internet empower the individual.

1. They are sophisticated, but anyone can operate them (yet another example of a useful abstraction).

2. They create mobility, allowing people to find, apply for, and even perform jobs or attend school at remote locations.

3. They provide access to information that is either stored in distant computing systems or spread about the Internet cloud amorphously.
4. They do not even begin to guarantee that everyone will get along with everyone else. Indeed they tend to do the opposite—facilitate divisions and hatred
5. For better or for worse, the telephone, its descendants, and internet systems carrying social media guarantee that:

> Everyone is connected to everyone else.

2.5 Science and Technology—Practice and Practitioners

It is important to realize that even as science and engineering are disciplines (techniques) like any other, their practitioners are people. They are therefore subject to the same failings of jealousy, narrow-mindedness, pride, error, and even fraud as those in any other field. Since this is a book on issues, a brief discussion of some of the problems in the practice of science and the pursuit of technology is in order.

Worldview and Scientific Debates

First, consider how pride and narrow views give rise to debates and disagreements even in what are regarded as exact sciences. As has already been pointed out, no scientist or engineer works independently of an internal metaphysical framework or worldview or of the community consensus and contextual system within which they work. Every step in the application of any technique (including the scientific one) demands that judgements be made, and these can at best be only relatively objective.

Cultural and global worldviews are non-unique concepts, so individuals see things differently. If the internal thinking framework of any two scientists or engineers (or any two people at all) were identical, one of them would be redundant. For instance, if a reader agrees with everything that is said in this book, then clearly the author is unnecessary to that person except as a reinforcing echo chamber. The non-uniqueness of worldviews and therefore thought patterns is part of why different people choose different specialties for study and work in the first place. It also means that two specialists in the same field may place entirely different interpretations on the same set of data, may expound on varying or even contradictory theories, or develop quite different products or applications from the same theoretical base.

Indeed, the divergence may begin sooner in the process. Any one of the putative researcher's Dean, Vice-Provost of Research, or granting agency, may kill the application to do it as without merit in their eyes. Later, the decision to accept or reject certain data (or to seek it in the first place) is not necessarily scientific or logical—rejection may occur when the data fails to "fit" the preconceptions of the researcher. Armed with competing theories and possibly differing data, two factions of the scientific community may seek to line up institutional and individual support, particularly among the so-called scientific celebrities. If the question is actually (or appears to be) decidable, one side (or some third party differing from both) can eventually emerge from the ensuing debate as temporary victor. In short, even science is not entirely free of politics.

Some of the most controversial discussions take place when the issue is not decidable, for either intrinsic or extrinsic reasons. If the problem is extrinsic, such as the lack of technology for testing purposes, there is still hope for an eventual solution. One of the best modern examples is relativity theory, many facets of which were not at first amenable to investigation in the physical sense. As the years passed, new techniques permitted experiments not previously possible, and the general theory of relativity came to be universally accepted as experimental results matched theory—with the caveat that it is not at this writing completely reconciled to quantum mechanics, which also appears to be sound.

However, if the undecidability is due to intrinsic reasons, that is, the theory itself is of a metaphysical or otherwise unprovable nature, then debates will rage indefinitely. There are no definitive and universally acceptable ways to answer non-scientific questions through the use of science, whether or not it happens to be scientists asking the questions.

Questions About Origins

This will certainly be the case when the two sides are arguing, say, about events that took place in the Earth's past. It is impossible to prove or disprove in any absolute sense many assertions concerning prehistoric times. Indeed, even historians do not always agree on the facts concerning recent events, much less on their interpretation, so one should not expect agreement on questions of prehistoric ones. This is particularly true where questions of the origin of the universe are concerned, and multiple generations of scientists have adopted quite different cosmological models, defended them, and taught them as fact, only to have theirs replaced at a later date. The confidence of the scientific modeler rises if the model correctly predicts things that were not used to build the model, but the inability to test its main premises experimentally means that in such cases, this confidence will always be partly of the faith kind. There is no safer prediction about the future of scientific theories than that some or all portions of the widely accepted big-bang model of the universe's origin will eventually be re-tooled or replaced altogether. In such cases, the new model must be able to explain everything that the old one could, as well as resolve at least some of its inconsistencies and failures.

One could object that acceptance of any strictly mechanistic model for origins, especially one acknowledged to be incomplete and temporary, is of such a different degree than faith in a creator God that the two are not comparable. Some find this objection attractive, but its analysis may be superficial, for it does not take into account the level at which belief systems operate.

Is it a particular mechanism or the necessity to explain origins mechanistically that is the subject of faith? The former may be a holding position pending suitable confirmation of detail and possible modification; the latter might in some cases represent a fundamental and non-negotiable philosophical position. If that which is believed in is a universe presupposed to be mechanistic and without an intelligent planner, then the mechanism currently accepted is mere window dressing for a deeper faith—one that insists on a materialistic explanation for origins, irrespective of evidence. At this level, the two faiths (in a creator God, or natural origins) would be indistinguishable, though they appear different when considering specific details (such as mechanism) rather than the broad presuppositions behind them. The motivation of an affirmer of beliefs is as telling as the details of the belief held.

Evolutionary biology provides a second (related) example of an issue that is not entirely decidable for intrinsic reasons. Conclusions about the biological past will always be tentative, describing what might have or could have happened, with backing from empirical evidence resting on interpretations of data more than on the data itself. Even the evidence gained by comparing the genetic material of organisms catalogues relationships descriptively rather than historically and sheds no light on whether they came about by chance or by design. It is easy to confidently

PART ONE | LAYING THE GROUNDWORK

assume that new discoveries will lend support to a current theory of biological evolution. Some such discoveries may well be made, but different confidences might claim their own supporting evidence.

It is important to note that in both cases, it is not the discussion of specific mechanisms that could have a metaphysical flavor (though it may). To see if that aspect is present, one must enquire deeper and determine whether the individual is *a priori* committed to philosophical presuppositions demanding specific categories of interpretations for origins and life and cannot conceive of alternatives. Such a prior determination is likely to be the case for most people for whom such questions are important. That is, if a person self-describes as a "creationist" or "evolutionist," as a "believer" or an "atheist," their commitment to a philosophical position would at least inform, if not drive their scientific thought and investigations. It is here, and not in the work the person does that the question of metaphysics arises.

Debates over such subjects tend to take place from the poles of said presuppositions, not on any middle ground, or even on the relative merits of specific investigative results. By contrast, the majority of the population, who have little or no professional stake in such debates, might quietly adopt a metaphysical accommodation that assents to aspects of both extremes without attempting to resolve or even be concerned about what others see as inherent contradictions. This is of course also true of many political debates.

For further discussion of the radically differing views on the subject of creation and evolution, the reader is referred to Chapter 11 and is advised concerning the many websites where such matters are argued that she may wish to investigate their metaphysical presuppositions, should they be disclosed.

Questions Requiring the Use of Models

Similar situations can also arise if the objects under study are too small or too fast to observe directly or so large, long-lasting, and slow to change that insufficient observations can be made over any reasonable period, so they can only be described by reference to a model for their behavior (e.g., the wave/particle nature of light, the nature and actions of subatomic particles, quantum theory/relativity, the open/closed/finite/infinite nature of the universe). In such cases, competing theories or models sometimes arise to explain the same phenomena and it may be that the two (or more) sides forget they are arguing not about science, but about interpretations, and therefore at least possibly, about metaphysics. Indeed, modern physics can occasionally be almost as much concerned with philosophy as it is with physical reality (a questionable term when speaking of models to explain observations) and sometimes has difficulty attaching meanings to the terms it employs to describe the phenomena it investigates. The world that is ordinarily seen by people in the everyday sense is not always obviously related to the one seen and modeled by a scientist, an example of the fact that models for the physical do not convey the totality of the thing itself, however useful as abstractions those models may be for presenting summary pictures of the currently accepted consensus on how to explain the phenomenon in question.

The Case of Theology

Another example of the non-uniqueness of worldviews can be seen in the answers various people would give to the question: "Is theology a science, or is it entirely metaphysical"? This may seem like an obsolete question to ask, for the majority view among educated people today would almost certainly be that theology has no connection with science whatsoever. However, this is a new consensus, for just as mathematics was historically Queen of the Arts, so theology was Queen of the Sciences. To the practitioner, theology is the systematic study of a body of factual information—which being revealed by the deity, is no less reliable than if derived from a microscope slide. The receipt of this information from another (instead of by personal observation) is not regarded as a problem, given what is regarded as well-attested source reliability. Theologians observe that people in all fields accept a great deal of information as factual in much the same way; the logic of so doing is not different, though the nature of the source is. For example, no scientist verifies the entire body of prerequisite knowledge before carrying on with the next experiment. To do so would be considered absurd. Thus, the study of God may begin with a faith affirmation, but it continues with a partially empirical, scientific, and therefore fallible study called theology—one that differs in subject matter but shares some methodology (technique) with other sciences.

To any modern scientist who fully trusts empiricism, perhaps even leans toward logical positivism, such a definition of theology as akin to science would be objectionable. Some may believe that unless data can be personally verified (assuming they have the equipment and funding), it is unacceptable. At least perhaps we should agree that unless a theory is at least potentially falsifiable by empirical means it is not scientific.

One might also observe that since in death the senses are left behind, empirical methods cannot be extended across the gulf of the grave, even if one believes in life after death. The methods of history and related disciplines may play into this discussion, but in these the evidence itself, not just the interpretation of it, may be selectively disputed, especially if the event is far enough in the past. Likewise, the social sciences, in general, may use statistical methods to test social models, but some involved in scientific bench research may question whether this is sufficient to call any of these "science."

To take a more personal example, one may accept documentary (and other) evidence that one's great-grandparents existed, though never having met them. The evidence is compelling, though not strictly the result of repeatable experiments. It is easier to dispute the validity of documentation for events and people further in the past, particularly if others' interpretation of those events does not accord with one's preferred worldview. Thus, some accept the Bible or another religious work as a historically accurate document collection describing the actions of God in history, while others selectively dismiss all or portions of such works as myth or fabrication. If even the evidence of history can be so disputed, there is certainly no way to personally use science to verify or falsify claims about the existence of God.

From a historical point of view, this thinking is rather new. Scientists such as Kepler, Bacon, Newton, Boyle, Fleming, Maxwell, Faraday, Joule, Davy, Pasteur, Kelvin, Pascal, and a long list of others of past centuries "did" science because of their deep-seated belief that they could discover more about God by unfolding the nature of the universe that he had created. Indeed, few of the originators and builders of what has become today's science would be comfortable with the philosophical orientation of their heirs. Their worldview was significantly different from that of the moderns. Though they might rejoice at the progress made in the fields they began, they would probably consider the move to a materialist metaphysical basis to be costly.

Of course, one could object that an appeal to the theological views of past scientists is invalid, regardless of how popular these views were—after all, they were a product of a cultural worldview. The objection is valid, but the same objection can be applied to any appeal to the uniformity of worldview and metaphysics of today's scientific world. Consensus in any age, including the present, is not in itself evidence of absolute truth. Moreover, the modern scientific community recognizes the greatness of the science that was done in the past, even though it was accomplished within a very different metaphysical framework. Why then do points of difference among today's scientists (especially concerning religious ideas and interpretations) result in so much hostility and acrimony? Even today, excellent science can legitimately arise from within the framework of a minority worldview. One could even argue that it must do so, to achieve the paradigm shifts that are required to make great breakthroughs. Moreover, religions that speak of a life beyond death generally hold that some senses can be used there. Thus, the argument that God's existence can never be verified or falsified is not yet proven, for one must presumably die in the empirical world to learn the answer.

The kind of peer pressure and search for consensus discussed here can have another and more subtle effect. Academics are rightly conscious of the need for their work to stand on the shoulders of those who have gone before, and so they adorn their reports with quotations from others to lend their own conclusions support. If such quoting is done with due respect to the whole context of the original, it is not only correct but to some extent necessary. However, there is always the possibility that the mutual respect of a small number of workers in a field may generate circular quotations of one another and these may create an impression of far greater authority than what exists. As Nellie Hacker said in the seminar: "If I quote you, and you quote me, who is any the wiser"?

These issues will be picked up again in a later chapter with a more detailed consideration of the creation/evolution debate—in some ways a classic clash of worldviews. For now, it suffices to make the point that the human element in science removes some of its reputed precision, exactness, and reproducibility to the theoretical realm. In practice, things don't happen in quite as orderly a way as they are supposed to.

PART ONE | LAYING THE GROUNDWORK

Publish or Perish

Another pressure on the practitioners of science is caused by the need for them to prove themselves by getting some results accepted for publication in recognized journals. A book placed with a reputable publisher counts for even more, and two books may even be worth a promotion. In the case of technology-driven research, working prototypes, patents, and production models determine success.

Part of the reason for this is the tenure system used by the universities where most North American scientists do their work. Following the research that leads to a doctoral thesis (duly defended before peers) and the degree that is accepted at graduation, the new academic seeks to become attached to the faculty of a reputable university. If successful, a probationary appointment is given that may be renewed for up to four or five years. At that time the candidate's research output is measured by the number of books and papers published. If the level is deemed acceptable, a permanent contract (tenure) is offered; if it is not, and a second review a year later offers nothing better, the unfortunate would-be professor is instead terminated. Teaching ability may not be a significant issue in the process.

In most cases, denial of tenure status at one university ends the research career entirely because a second chance at another institution is unlikely to be given. The (now ex-) academic can either find a position in industry, teach at a community college or high school or chalk the degree up to experience and find another line of work. For those who do become a part of the academic system, a continued high paper production level is required for consideration of promotion from assistant to associate to full professor, and even more importantly, for acquiring research grants from governments and private foundations.

There are several consequences of this system that are not very positive.

First, this practice fails to take into account that research in some areas is much more difficult than in others, takes far more time, costs more, and requires many more co-researchers to produce meaningful new results. There is, therefore, pressure to stay away from such fields and concentrate on those where some answers can be obtained quickly. This increases the volume of research papers but reduces the likelihood that any one of them will be memorable. It is questionable whether anyone reads the majority of such reports once the journal editor is finished with them and officially puts them into print. As the majority are never cited by anyone else, it seems likely many are never read either.

Second, it fails to take into account that some papers are more publishable than others because they are trendier. A mediocre work on a subject that happens to be of current interest is much more likely to be published than a better work in a more obscure area. For instance, it would be much easier to publish work on AIDS, COVID, superconductivity, electric vehicles, climate change, gender identity, or fusion, than on tuberculosis, polio, the properties of naphthalene, traditional family dynamics, or internal combustion engine efficiency. It is all but impossible to publish a substantial critique of a majority interpretation on an important issue. There is nothing either morally wrong or deceitful about this; it is just the human side of science showing through. This kind of bias causes fads to be accentuated even more, but also can dilute the overall quality of the work, and may stifle creativity.

Third, it fails to take into account that money and influence often speak more loudly than other voices. Senior faculty can pressure their more junior compatriots into their fields and away from innovative ideas because they control tenure and promotion committees. Women, blacks, aboriginals, and those who attempt to cross religious or cultural boundaries can be systematically kept out of the system. Funding agencies, particularly those under government control, can cut off grants for political or military reasons and thus can channel research according to their desires. The result is that free and open enquiry is reduced and so is creativity. The progress of new and innovative work must wait for the rare junior researcher not only to become senior (and a funding referee) but manage meanwhile to retain her creative spark. In the meantime, most research will be done in teams with agendas defined by others. The risk of funding individuals is often seen as too great, no matter how talented they may be.

Again, none of this is unique to science, for the dead hand of bureaucracy reaches everywhere. Such problems are characteristic of any institution; that they would eventually reach the scientific community was a foregone conclusion. For example, the old Soviet Union produced more university-trained scientists and engineers per capita than any other nation at the time. Yet, it struggled to catch up to the United States in the quality of basic research and technology. Why? Because the Soviet Union was also run by the largest bureaucracy on earth, gaining approval for a scientific project was far more difficult than in North America. By the time the research had been allowed, the results may already have been in an American journal By the time a technological development was permitted, it might have been cheaper to buy it in a New York surplus store than to build one from scratch.

An old story with many variations illustrates the difficulty of developing new technology in countries operated like the former Soviet Union.

> Noted Russian engineer Ivan Fedorvich arrives in Fort Langley, British Columbia, to visit his old friend and correspondent Stan Barker. Upon arrival at his house, Dr. Barker expresses interest in his visitor's watch. Fedorvich's face lights up as he tells him it is not just a wristwatch, but also a computer, radio, data terminal, and television all rolled into one. It has built-in voice recognition, a gigabyte of memory, and even a programmable alarm clock, and a miniature satellite dish in its concave crystal—a veritable triumph of socialist engineering. "And what," says Barker, "is that," pointing to the large suitcase Fedorvich is carrying with considerable difficulty. "Ah," says Fedorvich ruefully, "the Politburo insisted on using Russian batteries."

Finally, and related to these other factors, the pressure to publish at any cost encourages scientists to find quick and easy solutions, to take shortcuts, and to stay with traditional ideas and methodology. The safe and familiar can become so comfortable that the scholarly apparatus begins to substitute for thought. The watchword is "don't rock the boat," and this approach, while it may get papers published, does little to advance science.

Not all is wrong with the academic system, however, or it would not have lasted as long and been as successful as it has. It ensures new work is reviewed by peers on editorial boards before being published, and serves to prevent almost all very bad papers from being published in reputable journals (though there are fake journals in most fields). It creates a sense of community and a kind of apprenticeship for entry into the community, ensuring that new applicants have at least certain minimum qualifications. If the system does promote mediocrity, it also promotes volume, and every bit of knowledge, however small, pushes back the frontiers of human ignorance. Every once in a while, a truly great insight is achieved, and the spin-off benefits from that one-in-ten-thousand paper can be incalculable.

Similar observations can be made about those engaged in technological development, where building the wrong product, targeting it to the wrong market, or attempting to compete with a dominant market player may fail, thus destroying both product and career. Far more devices and methods are created than ever see the marketplace, but the vast amount of activity does guarantee some revolutionary new products are developed, even though some good ones never see the light of day.

Funding Pressures

It has already been remarked that many decisions for both basic research and technological development are made based on grants available from a variety of funding agencies. It is worth observing further that the largest portion of this money tends to come from government, if only because the size of some projects is far too great for any private means. Specifically, many of the projects so funded are likely to be sponsored by the military. Thus, political and military considerations have the largest say in the direction of research, increasing the direct and indirect control of the state over the technology that shapes society. More will be said in a later chapter about the role of the state; the mere observation of its control over the purse strings is sufficient for now. Like some of the other things taken note of in this chapter, it leads to the conclusion that human, political, and economic factors, more than curiosity or actual needs, may often dominate selection and development in the scientific/technological process.

Other Problems

It is also natural that the kinds of pressures indicated above will lead to serious problems from time to time. Thus, science has not been without the occasional scandal caused by fraudulent data, wishful thinking, fanciful conclusions or hoaxes. In the celebrated case of the supposed ape/human "missing link" known as Piltdown Man, a hoax got out of hand, and what was apparently intended as the deception of a single individual continued to delude the entire scientific community for years. In the case of Nebraska Man, another putative missing link, what turned out to be the tooth of an extinct pig had at first an entire fanciful proto-man built around it, complete with a lifestyle to match. On the other side of the same debate, far too much was made of some human-like footprints that appeared in the same strata as those of dinosaurs. Time and due reconsideration led the people involved to withdraw their original suggestions and reclassify the prints.

Likewise the premature publication and overly optimistic reports of "cold fusion" led to the researchers involved being ostracized by their fellows, their work ridiculed, and the phenomena they investigated became off-limit for anyone else to touch. And, occasionally, there are dismissals of researchers who were caught fabricating data to maintain their standing by cultivating a high publication output or plagiarizing material to pass it off as their own.

There is also a speculative aspect to some disciplines, and this too can generate much discussion about very little. In such cases, the mere repetition of speculation by enough of the leaders in the discipline is sufficient to have others accept it as fact. This is a foible of scholarship that must be lived with, for it too is human nature. However, it is one of the most subtle of difficulties to deal with, because the generation that accepts speculation as fact is unlikely to tolerate challenges to that dogma, and it may take a great deal of time to shift the discipline in question to a different view.

All of these instances reveal the human tendency of scientists to see what they expect to see and to continue to do so long after the means is available to correct their misconceptions. Time is the best remedy for such problems. It also helps to have a general determination to test occasionally even the most fundamental and longest-held assumptions, just in case the universal faith in them has been ever so slightly misplaced.

Faith is often placed in people, too, and science, like any other field of interest, has its few celebrities among the many foot-soldiers. This can be a positive thing, for such individuals are usually the ones who have the charisma and public presence to sell the discipline to a sometimes skeptical and demanding public. Celebrities can also mislead, however, particularly when presumed to be experts about all science and are asked to express to the public views on things that are far from their narrow field of expertise.

Thus, for instance, a book by a celebrity scientist on investment strategies, playing golf, or understanding the Bible might sell very well, despite the writer being entirely unqualified in the subject at hand. This is not just a problem with science, but one it shares in common with the entire "star" system so prevalent in North America, and Western culture generally. A realization that the eminent chemist Dr. Zork is plain Ms. Zork outside her field, that a movie, music, or sports star is not necessarily knowledgeable about anything else, and that a popular, charismatic politician may not be an expert on anything but getting and staying elected, would be healthy for all concerned.

Thus, if one is to ask why some study is undertaken, why some product is built, or why some technique is developed, one would not necessarily find the answer within the nature of the discipline but might find it in its societal context. This is true of both the society of specialist practitioners and also of the larger culture from which they come.

In turn, science, technology, and technique change the society in which they develop, and new ideas become feasible when such changes take place, for they enable all members of society to think and act in new ways.

2.6 The Technological Society?

The society of the late industrial and early post-industrial age was in some ways profoundly influenced by a scientific and technological mindset, and less so by other modes of thinking. This influence is seen in the academic world, where terms such as "social science" are applied to disciplines whose claims to be scientific in methodology can be rather tenuous. It is also seen in the wide-scale application of technique to social, political, and business problems, as discussed in a previous section. For a time, it was even fashionable to attach the term "engineer" to occupations with little or no connection to science or technology. Thus, housewives became "domestic engineers," and janitors "custodial engineers." Even the applicability of the more recent term "software engineer" could be questioned.

The high-tech information society will in the long run be more than simply a gloss over or renaming of existing practices, though even such name changes reflect a genuine shift in the collective point of view of society. People are not just using a new vocabulary, they are not just buying the consumer goods that reflect the latest technological advances—they are planning for and assuming a continuing state of such change. This is done in the purchase of household goods, appliances, computing and hand-held electronic devices, and automobiles (including electric ones), the building of houses, offices, and apartments, and in the other ordinary decisions of life. That all such goods will soon be obsolete and thus can be expected to have only a short lifetime, is assumed and planned for. A disposable economy is a necessary by-product of rapid technological change. So is a general familiarization with relatively sophisticated products. Moreover, people tend to trust technology for solutions to such problems as food scarcity, disease, overpopulation, pollution, and energy shortages. As they trust, so they act. When the scientific/technological community has already delivered so much, it is difficult not to assume that it can answer any question, solve any problem, and build any kind of machine.

This has also caused many old barriers to crumble. As high technology has become commercialized, business people, accountants, and economists have been conscripted to work side-by-side with electrical engineers and computer programmers. Indeed, the computer has generated more crossover among academic and other disciplines than C. P. Snow could have imagined in the early 1960s, for both social scientists and writers have been quick to use this tool to enhance their work. In the first years of the computing discipline, most of its theoreticians and practitioners were drawn from other fields (particularly mathematics), and many a university computing department in the early days of its incorporation into the academy was administered by psychologists, philosophers, mathematicians, and economists, rather than by those with doctorates in computing itself, as there were very few of them at the time. Indeed, high-end research papers for ISO standards work and for presentations at prestigious international conferences were, until the 1990s, mostly written by academics whose degrees were in other fields.

University curricula also recognized this crossover and mounted introductory courses in computing, data processing, data science, and technology for non-science majors. Such students eagerly embraced the machine for the benefits it could bring, particularly to word processing, data analysis tasks (especially financial), and personal use for instant communication, social media, and entertainment.

However, this does not yet mean that a technological culture quickly became universal or deep-seated, even for students, whom one would expect to adapt most easily to change, for few of them emerged from their years of education with much understanding of how those machines worked, except in the most vague and general terms. Given that students' general science and mathematics background was and is often very weak upon entry to post-secondary education, such basic concepts as the binary numbering system or simple programming not only caused eyes to glaze over during lectures but generated a firm resolve to avoid any further courses with technological overtones.

This observation returns us to consideration of the levels of abstraction one needs to function in various societal roles. As computing devices became easier to use, they began to be abstracted by most members

THE FOUNDATIONS OF SCIENCE AND TECHNOLOGY

of society as akin to toasters or any other household appliance—understood only on the level of utility. It followed that courses in their use were eliminated from much of the curriculum. After all, who needs a course on how to use a waffle iron? Indeed, as any high technology matures, fewer and fewer people understand it, even though there are many more who use it. Such developments ought to be expected.

There is a difference, however, between the casual use of a high-tech device such as a smartphone for social purposes, or a computer for routine office tasks and the employment of a computer, with multiple complex applications including programming notation compilers, as a sophisticated high-end problem-solving tool. The former is a consumer appliance, the latter the tool of a professional, more akin to a compound articulating mitre saw than to a kettle.

Thus, the term "high-tech information society" must be understood in the context of technology *use*, rather than in that of the search for technique. The latter is the function of experts in each field who are seeking to optimize their work; the former is the province of every member of society. The increasing use of machines doesn't imply a change in the way people think. They may embrace both technological advances and new techniques for the personal benefits and efficiencies they bring, but not because they find the philosophy of science fascinating. For the typical person, changes in thinking and living patterns are caused by new techniques, not the reverse. To put it another way, it is the highest level abstractions (finished products) that most people employ; they are not interested in the detailed work that went into them being made ready for common use. There is, therefore, an extent to which the technological aspect of society is a thin patina over an underlying culture—one that changes more slowly than it appears on the surface. New technology changes the outward appearance of how people live and work in rather short order, but alterations in the way they think may come about on different timelines, or be triggered by unrelated circumstances.

At the intellectual decision-making level, Snow's observations about the two cultures still have validity. Academics can still think their way in their specialties without much regard for either the changing world around them or for what is happening in other specialties pursued farther along the academic hallway. Poets and physicists can speak different languages, and read different books. They need not speak meaningfully to each other. They may pretend each other's work is irrelevant, as if physicists had no imagination or poets could live in primitive communes and use nothing of modern technology. While there has been a "scientification" of many academic disciplines, the embracing of such transplanted techniques remains uneven, even viewed with suspicion by those who consider themselves traditionalists resisting any form of social change, or who even perceive change in the intellectual world as a threat to their way of life or beliefs.

For those outside the academy, such concerns are intensified. The changes and threats are more immediate and personal, involving the way people live and work, indeed whether they can even continue in their current employment, or will soon, like so many others, lose it due to technological change. They see the barons of high technology gaining an ever larger share of the world's total wealth while experiencing their own decline out through the bottom of an ever-diminishing middle class.

Fear of perceived threats fuels the desire for a scapegoat; ill-understood science presents a ready target; instant communication technology the means to spread destructive memes; and the result is an increasing divide between those whose work drives scientific and technological change to their benefit and the general public outside that sphere.

Such suspicions and divisions are potentially dangerous, for they develop into prejudices capable of destabilizing a society. Politicians (and the citizens they govern) cannot make sound decisions about technology they distrust or do not understand. Scientists with little or no education in the arts and humanities cannot express themselves in a way that makes their work accessible and believable to the general public. They may also lack the foundation for making moral/ethical decisions, and take the attitude that science and technology are always socially and ethically neutral, when in fact neither ever is. Kranzberg (*Ethics in an Age of Pervasive Technology*) puts it this way: "Technology is not ethically neutral because it is not only an instrument of human practice but a form of it also; the ethics of technology concerns human technical practice and its normative problems."

Scientists and engineers are called on constantly to make decisions with ethical implications, not only about the way they conduct their work but about how their work is or may be used. Because of this, they need to be ethically informed, and sufficiently articulate to bring issues to the attention of those outside their subculture.

As they communicate with others, they may close some of the interdisciplinary gaps, and simultaneously become more familiar with the relationships science and technology have with society as a whole. To

THE FOUNDATIONS OF SCIENCE AND TECHNOLOGY

the extent that this happens, their techniques can also become the instrument and the object of social and political policies. Eventually, those who do have technological familiarity may demand more power to make decisions. They will need to qualify themselves to be decision-makers to do this. Likewise, politicians will have to gain a greater understanding of technology and its effects or make way for those who have. The wider public will not even struggle with the theory, but simply use its products as tools. Society will continue to change, for there will be more things that people will be able to do with their tools without thinking about them, and the depth of this collection of highly abstracted activities is an important measure of what a civilization is about.

In the longer term, academics might not be as divided as in the past. Their separation into non-overlapping specialties was a response to the need to know enough facts about one field to do useful work in a world suffering from information overload. As this characterization is now irrelevant because of the ready availability of information on any subject at any depth, the barriers between disciplines may have already begun to come down to some extent, for the means to manage information effectively and find it on demand has become universally available. This topic will be revisited in the chapter on the information society, as well as in the one on education.

The Third World

There are more important tensions in the world outside academia because technological benefits continue to be inequitably distributed on a social and geographical basis. The disparity in technology and wealth between the European, North American and white Commonwealth countries on the one hand, and everyone else on the other, may get much worse before it gets any better. This disparity was also the reason that Russia was so interested in absorbing Ukraine's rich industrial east, and made the breadbasket regions to the west a lower priority—at least temporarily.

To be sure, there are hopeful signs of industrialization, agricultural change, and technical education in the third world. Countries such as China sometimes seem capable of jumping directly from primitive agricultural economies into the information age. However, political and social instability through much of Asia, Africa, and South America conspire to limit growth, and most countries in these regions are still pre-industrial or mid-industrial, with limited prospects for rapid improvement. Some nations have even worse problems, including drought, famine, and assorted epidemics that threaten to carry away many of the educated people they have managed to produce. Alternately, that very education often enables people to seek greater prosperity in the (post) industrialized world, thus further impoverishing their native countries.

The poor of the underdeveloped nations have little meaningful interaction with the prosperous West and there seems little immediate prospect of changing things. As long as this situation continues—and especially if it worsens (as it seems likely to do)—there still exists the possibility that another war could engulf the whole globe. Such a conflict has the potential not only to destroy centuries of technological advances but the human race itself. One of the most important technical problems to solve, therefore, is to find ways to bring the benefits of high technology to all peoples of the world in a non-destructive way. However, even if such solutions were found, they would provide no check on the overweening ambitions of ruthless despots in neighboring countries.

Technology and Trade-offs

There is a tendency on the part of those employed in the daily pursuit of new technology to assume that progress is always good. However, the use of any new technology has a variety of consequences, and there are times when trade-offs have to be made between increasing efficiency and utility on the one hand, and negative social and human factors on the other. Among many examples are the following:

- Improvements in railroad equipment that are designed to make trains safer and more efficient may cause the price of freight service to rise, resulting in more shipments being sent via highways. This produces the twin negatives of lower utilization of the now more expensive service, and a higher death rate because highways are much less safe than railways.
- Large amounts of money are spent making the control rooms of nuclear power plants orderly and efficient. However, if the result is a sterile environment, the resulting operator boredom may increase the risk of accidents.

- The introduction of chemicals into meat and other food may make it better tasting and preserve it longer, but at the risk of other health-threatening side effects when the food is consumed.

- A dam built to reduce random flooding and produce large amounts of electricity may be politically advantageous and improve the economy for a time but erase an indigenous heritage site, prevent silt deposition in the delta below, reduce fertility, and increase both net erosion and dependence on imported chemical fertilizers. The flooded and ruined valley will eventually silt up (sometimes rapidly), destroying the utility of the dam. In the long run, there may be little but damage to show for the expense of billions of dollars.

- The replacement of internal combustion engines in automobiles by electric motors may reduce dependence on oil and lower polluting emissions, but if the cost is the building of more electrical plants and the mining of scarce metals to build batteries, the total costs and losses may outweigh the savings and gains.

- Even when technological and economic goals are achieved in the short term, vast megaprojects create correspondingly large capital debts, and these increase both taxes and inflation, possibly in the long run ruining the economy and lowering the standard of living of a whole nation. A default of a large enough country to the international banks could threaten the economy of the entire world.

- The factories and foundries that bring wealth and prosperity may cause acidic rains to fall (perhaps in another country) resulting in deforestation, soil sterility, fish kills, and respiratory illnesses, and increasing the levels of metals such as aluminum or mercury in the human system to dangerous levels.

- The manufacture of dangerous chemicals may be conducted in a distant part of the world, on the soil of another nation. This has the twin advantage of reducing risks at home and creating good jobs in a third-world nation. It has the disadvantage of increasing the risk that untrained personnel will make mistakes that result in the release of the chemicals and cause large numbers of deaths.

- Computers introduced into offices allow employees to do more in less time. This can lead to them wasting some of their time producing more reports that no one reads or being laid off.

- A focus on technology may cause managers to forget that the principal assets of a company in the information age are its people, not its machines. Always-on connectivity tends to make managers act as if they have always-at-work employees. Continued, such attitudes could destroy the enterprise if most leave.

- The high pace of change in the technology marketplace brings customer benefits with new, ever faster and more capable hardware and software, but that very fast pace often leads to flawed products coming to market, fueling customer dissatisfaction, even a general distrust of technology and the people who produce it. In such an atmosphere, it becomes easy to believe that "they are out to get us," that the big technology companies "are ripping us off" and even that devices such as voting machines or vaccines are somehow "rigged" against or threatening to consumers. It then, for instance, becomes a trivial matter to persuade many people to believe that a perfectly fair election has been "stolen" or that a pandemic is a fraud designed to enrich some or shift some of their power to others.

- That same fast pace of change that delivers new and exciting products ensures the rapid obsolescence of functional but now obsoleted previous generations of similar devices, generating mountains of toxic electronic waste.

- Instant, readily available information allows voters to access data on political candidates and elected representatives, potentially making them more informed. It also exposes the flaws of those same politicians, decreasing trust. One of the more obvious flaws in the system is that few (almost no) elected representatives have a scientific or technical background, yet they are called on to make numerous, momentous, possibly history-changing decisions in those very areas. Since ill-informed decisions are almost always bad ones, trust in government is eroded further.

- Technology developed for peaceful purposes can also be used for warfare. In particular, it can be used by terrorists. The results might be more negative than positive.

- Governments are constantly faced with demands for increased social spending. If they fund technological developments instead, they may have to trade off the certainty of short-term social pain for the hope of longer-term prosperity. If they fund both, the resulting inflation might do more harm than any good coming from the spending.

- Resources are limited. Governments and corporations are always faced with choices between development proposals of uncertain benefit, where selecting one project will surely kill the other.

Examples could be multiplied, and many of the discussions later in this book could be mentioned here as well. The point is that one must always question the potential value of a proposed technology—not everything new and appealing is necessarily good or positive, just as not everything old is necessarily obsolete. There is no shortage of new things that can be done; the difficulty is deciding which ones are worth doing more than the others.

Technology and the Average Citizen

As noted above, typical citizens even in technically advanced countries participate only as users of technology. They labour at stores, factories, and menial office jobs, or stand in line for welfare or unemployment checks. Although they are eager consumers (when possible) of technological products, they neither engage in nor necessarily care about the issues important to those who develop the products they consume, and especially not about those dear to academics.

The average North American knows something about how to maintain an automobile or small machine but would greet any conversation about the efficient layout of motherboards, the details of advanced software development, molecular biology, or philosophy with equal parts ignorance and disdain. The toilers in the humanities and social sciences are not understood at all. There is more sympathy, but not much more understanding, for scientists (who are commonly stereotyped as "mad"), perhaps a little of both for engineers. Most people employ technology at the highest level of abstraction, with no care for its scientific basis and very little for how it is produced. Mathematicians are looked at askance, and a computer scientist is regaled with tales of non-functional hardware and software—much as a doctor at a social function would go away knowing about everyone's arthritis.

Of course, the ordinary citizen is the one most affected by changes in technology—for change always creates new jobs and eliminates others. However, the intellectual and material gap between the consumers of high-tech goods, and the creators, sellers, and managers of such products is considerable. What this will mean for decision-making and effective power in the society of the future is not yet clear. Both centralizing trends and individualizing trends need to be considered to make any forecasts. For most people, understanding is not a prerequisite for participation in a machine-oriented society. However, in the new (information-based) society it may become increasingly difficult for many citizens to function at all without a substantial technical background, for most menial and repetitive jobs will be automated.

A continuing widening of the gap between an elite and the general population in wealthy Western countries would be just as destabilizing and potentially dangerous as the same process on the international scene between countries. If only those who can use the new information tools can work in the new civilization (and this is increasingly so) what place is there for anyone else? Can industrialized nations remain stable if this question is not addressed?

Assessing the Situation

Important cautions must be sounded about the uneven distribution of knowledge and technique, but there are some encouraging signs. Modern society is far from static, and some sub-cultures are moving into territories previously occupied by others. Those in poorer countries, and the lower classes of the richer ones generally know (in theory) how to achieve greater wealth. Thus, education and industrialization are actively pursued by the disadvantaged who seek to move up. There are no secrets about how a nation becomes wealthier, and there are no peoples who would willingly choose to retain the short life span and disease-ridden poverty of the agricultural age when a better choice presents itself.

The poorest people of the most impoverished nations will sacrifice anything to send a child to school, for they know that the next generation can be better off. They would also gladly trade their poverty for the problems of the industrial nations. The same upward route exists for the children of the working class and poor of the industrialized nations, and they take it whenever they can, particularly in the sciences.

Meanwhile, the scientific community is pulling out of its intellectual isolation to some extent and beginning to address the ethical questions related to the society its products are creating. Along the way, there could be some measure of reconciliation with its religious and philosophical roots, though the differences here are still severe. Also, the use of computers has increased among artists and writers. This may not yet have removed all the intellectual barriers to their use of technology, but it has reduced some of the emotional ones, and the anti-technology faction has become more muted. It may be the use of this machine more than anything else that gives legitimacy and common currency to the term "high-tech information society."

This book contends that all the peoples and cultures of the world need each other, that technologies (or wars) pursued by one have effects on the others that cannot be ignored, and that it will be less and less possible for any individual, profession, discipline, or nation to act in narrow self-interest without regard for the interests of others. Just as there has come to be a human-machine cooperation (synergy) for the solving of problems which neither can do alone, there needs to be an understanding that all peoples of the earth are crew on the same ship. All peoples have common interests (even if they are unwilling to admit this); they have a common origin and common destinations. These themes will be developed further under several headings throughout the remaining chapters; for the present here is another aphorism:

> Society is maintained on communication and cooperation, and those in turn require acknowledgment and understanding of common ground to achieve common good.

2.7 Summary and Further Discussion

Summary

Philosophers of various times and in various disciplines have different meanings for the term "knowledge." It has meant the result of a particular kind of reasoning process (logic); it is confined by some to the outcome of the scientific method; and it is equated by others to belief or faith. It can also be personal (taste) or opinion, though most (all?) of what is placed in the last category may properly belong in the others. There are a variety of conflicts among the groups that hold these positions, and these divisions arise within and between academic disciplines and among the general population.

As for the scientific method, it relies on the assumption that there is a reliable and potentially predictable underlying reality behind the phenomena being investigated, though the nature of that reality is itself the subject of some dispute. Science is connected to, but cannot be completely identified with technology, for the search for tools and techniques has often been independent of theory, even though the scientific and technical communities have drawn closer in the last century.

If technique is given its broadest possible definition, it may be seen to include the scientific method as one technique. Whether technique is an irresistible force driving society to certain inevitable outcomes depends on whether or not absolute techniques exist—the most efficient possible for a given task—and this is not, in general, knowable.

The term "high-tech information society," which is often taken to imply a monolithic culture, sure of its content and goals, is misleading given the number of parties involved. The disparities between the "haves" and the "have-nots" seem likely to continue for some time to come, both within advanced nations, and between them and the third world. Although technology now has a more profound influence on society than ever before, most people seem content to use its products in everyday life without needing to understand either how they are made, or the science behind them. In many ways, such automatic and unthinking routine uses of technique characterize a civilization, more than (perhaps despite) the way its intellectuals regard the matter.

Research and Discussion Questions

1. To what extent would it be possible to live without any use of modern technology? Backwoods, off the grid entirely self-sufficient? Give your reasons in detail.
2. Write a research paper describing the historical origins and development of the scientific method.
3. Compare and contrast (a) the methods of historical and scientific studies and (b) the modes of thinking in mathematics and science.
4. What is the meaning of the word "knowledge" as it is used in science, mathematics, religion, economics (or some other social science of your choice) and English literature (or another of the humanities)?

THE FOUNDATIONS OF SCIENCE AND TECHNOLOGY

5. Does "knowledge" mean one thing for the disciplines mentioned in question 4, and a different thing for art, music, and sculpture? What about people who are not members of academia—what do they mean by the term?

6. To what extent can the knowledge obtained by the scientific method be regarded as "true" in an absolute sense?

7. Develop further the argument that the academic disciplines are mutually dependent, and cannot exist entirely on their own. Give specific examples.

8. To what extent, and in what ways can the cultural and intellectual elements of Western society function together more purposefully and harmoniously?

9. Which is more probable and why: that technological developments will reduce class distinctions or that they will increase them? Consider both the short and long term. Consider the effects both within a single nation and between nations in various parts of the world.

10. Does the presence of the human element invalidate the claims of Science to be objective? If so, to what extent? If not, why not?

11. To what extent is computing-related technology unifying or further dividing the academic world?

12. Write a defense of the academic tenure system or a detailed proposal for improving it.

13. Expand further upon (or refute) the suggestion in the chapter that there is no such thing as "mere opinion."

14. Are some beliefs more important than others? Why or why not? Consider the issues of both probable truth and probable consequences.

15. Are some beliefs more permissible than others? Why or why not? Weigh freedom of speech against the possibility of some beliefs harming their holders or others. If some are potentially harmful, should they be repressed, and if so, how?

16. Consider the two statements:
    a. "Religious faith and scientific rationalism/empiricism are contradictory and can never be reconciled."
    b. "There is no conflict between true science and true religion."

Attack or defend (or both) one or the other of these two statements.

17. Explore the contention that there is (or may be) a metaphysical element in *any* position on origins. Do you take a middle position or an exclusive one? Why?

18. To what extent are the high-technology, industrial, and agricultural nations of the world mutually dependent? To what extent ought they be?

19. Does the advent of high technology mean that the gaps between the rich and poor nations of the world will widen or narrow? Discuss ways in which technology can be used to narrow such gaps and ways in which national and international policies can be formulated to achieve such goals. Alternately, argue either that nothing can be done or that nothing should be done about this issue.

20. Is it fair to those countries that develop high technology to have them share it with poorer countries? What would be the consequences of not narrowing such gaps?

21. Research some examples of fraud, wishful thinking, research padding, or hoaxes in modern science/technology and report on the significance of such events in the overall progress of science.

22. Develop further the theme that science and technology are very different concepts.

23. Develop further the assertion that pure research is now seldom done apart from associated technological goals. You may wish to take a position contrary to that posed in question 22 and argue that science and technology are just different aspects or stages of the same thing.

24. Expand further on the theme that one technological advance often drives, or even requires others. Use specific examples from the past and suggest more for the future, based on present problems.

25. The text mentioned the assertion of Jacques Ellul that there is an inevitability to the quest for the most efficient techniques—one which tends to sweep aside all other considerations. The author expressed reservations about this, at least in theory. Read Ellul, and then support or attempt to refute his thesis. You could critique the author's

THE FOUNDATIONS OF SCIENCE AND TECHNOLOGY

views, especially if you are his student, but that may be of little interest to anyone otherwise.

26. Alternatively, attack or defend the thesis that even if technique is an irresistible force, it is leading nowhere (i.e., that it has no inherent goal or necessary outcome).

27. Discuss and expand upon the theme that one measure of a civilization is the size of the set of tasks that its citizens can perform without having to think about them (i.e. they are abstracted).

28. Discuss the relative importance of teaching and research tasks for university professors. Do the priorities change if the perspective is that of the professor? the university? the student? the state? society as a whole?

29. Research (a) the acid rain problem, (b) global warming (c) flawed products brought to market, or (d) the lack of scientific or technical background of politicians. What are the economic, social, or political trade-offs involved in finding and implementing a solution to this problem? in doing nothing?

30. A major city built around a navigable inlet with spectacular natural scenery is considering the building of a crossing for the inlet. It could be a bridge, which some say would blight the landscape and create a navigation hazard. It could be a tunnel, which would do neither, but cost 50 percent more. The tunnel would also create more construction jobs, and based on experience, there is less likelihood of accidental deaths during construction. How can this decision best be made?

31. Should people with strong religious beliefs involve themselves in politics, or should there be a rigid separation between the two? Give reasons based on your view on religion and politics, whatever they may be.

32. Pick an issue of importance to you, one on which you have a strong belief of right and wrong. State your position and your reasons. Then analyze the connection between knowing (as you see it) the right, and doing something right as a consequence. That is, how does your knowledge affect your actions?

33. Now, extend the last question. Suppose you are in a position where you hold some power—CEO of a corporation, police officer, judge,

Prime Minister/President/Supreme Glorious Dictator-for-life. To what extent and how should/can you use your authority to require others you lead/supervise/control to do the right as you see it?

34. What role have "futuristic" science fiction stories played in the development of actual technologies imagined by the authors of such stories? What is dystopic fiction, and what cautionary role has that or other fiction had on your thinking about possible or probable futures?

35. Discuss the right and wrong, the should and the must around the issue of freedom of speech. Is such freedom absolute, regardless of content or truth, or should there be legal limitations, and if so what should they restrain or prohibit, and how should such restrictions be enforced? How do you know your beliefs about this issue are true and not just another opinion among many?

CHAPTER 3

Basic Concepts in the Theory of Ethics

As this seminar opens, the Professor is just sitting. Already present in the room are Nellie, Johanna, Dorcas, and Ellen. Alicia's speaker is also in evidence. There are two empty chairs.

Professor: Ah, attendance is at a peak today; I'm glad you all made it because we have a new member of the group to introduce.

Dorcas: Someone from my time?

Professor: (enjoying a little mystery) No, not someone out of time at all. You have heard of the alternate worlds theory?

Ellen: The what?

Nellie: It's a common theme in science fiction, but I suppose you don't read that kind of literature.

Ellen: Sounds like comic books for kids. Aren't we past that stage?

Professor: Alicia, why don't you explain?

Alicia: Certainly, Professor. Such theories hold that our universe is not unique; that other universes exist in parallel to it, and that in those others history has not followed the same track as it has in ours.

Dorcas: Nellie told me yesterday about a man called Hitler. Might there be a universe in which he never was or, from my perspective, never will be born?

Alicia: Most assuredly. Indeed, the Professor and I have identified several such alternate universes already, and Hitler existed only in this one.

Nellie: Are the Physicists right then—every decision ever made down to the particle level creates a new universe parallel to ours in which only minor details differ, so that the number of alternates grows without bound?

Alicia: Apparently not. There seem to be certain historical crisis points, called "nexi" at which the Earth divides in two, and two Earths, each with their own subsequent history, appear where there was only one before. It seems that other decisions are too insignificant, and the worlds created immediately "flow" back together.

Johanna: Are Ellen and I always the only skeptics? This sounds like pure fantasy. What's the point?

Nellie: I think the point is that one of these empty chairs is for someone from an alternate Earth.

Professor: Quite so. (standing) Would you welcome Eider to our class. She is a specialist in medical technology and ethical issues.

Eider now enters and takes a seat after greeting the Professor. There are introductions all around.

Nellie: Are we allowed to talk about what you just told us?

Professor: One question only, then we get on with today's study.

Nellie: Eider, how is your Earth different from ours; I mean, how did it become different? Or, do you know?

Eider: (smiling) That's three questions. Our world is called Meta Earth, or more popularly the Builder's World and it was the first to divide from yours.

Nellie: When?

Eider: When Cain killed Abel, back at the very beginning of things, he was confronted by God with what he had done. He wavered. Should he confess his deed and ask forgiveness, or lie and try to cover up what he had done? My world and yours result from the two different moral decisions—in yours, he became the father of liars and evildoers, and in mine an object lesson for the mercy of God.

BASIC CONCEPTS IN THE THEORY OF ETHICS

At this point, both Ellen and Johanna make disgusted noises, but the Professor quiets them, and Eider continues.

Eider: Things were never as bad there as here, so God never sent a flood to destroy the Earth. Consequently, our society has developed from a completely different base than yours.

Johanna: I don't know where the Professor got you from, dearie, but I've heard enough world-making myths for one day. Let's get on with things.

Nellie: Wait—what technologies do you pursue?

Eider: We have highly developed the arts of healing, of the understanding of the mind, of human behavior and relationships. In our world . . .

Professor: (interrupting) That will do. Nellie, you can grill Eider all you want after class. I just wanted to establish that she came from a society with a different history and set of cultural assumptions than ours. We want to discuss ethics today, and it seemed good to have a different cultural viewpoint represented.

Ellen: (unable to contain herself) If this fairy tale is consistent, it has implications that interest me. Let me go along with it for a moment. A different beginning implies a completely different history. Tell me, was there someone called Jesus Christ in your world?

Eider: No.

Ellen: Aha! That puts the lie to Christianity. You don't deny the existence of what Christians here call sin, do you?

Eider: No.

Ellen: (turning to Dorcas) Don't you see? If the Christian God is real, he would have had to make the same provision for what you call sin in every one of the alternate Earths, and he did not in theirs. Thus, Christ was just a man, an interesting teacher, and nothing more . . .

Eider: (interrupting her) No, he wasn't just a man.

Ellen: But you said . . .

Eider: I said he was not part of the history of our world. I did not say that we were unaware of the history of yours, or of the significance of Christ in that history. We—that is, most of us—hold that his death, though suffered only on one of the Earths, sufficed for salvation on all of them.

PART ONE | LAYING THE GROUNDWORK

Ellen: O bother, another one.

Professor: Back on track, children. We are supposed to be discussing the existence and universality of ethical and moral principles.

Dorcas: I thought we were doing rather well there, myself.

Ellen: Despite this clever little fiction on behalf of the outdated religious fairy tales some of you cling to, I still maintain that moral principles are just convenient rules that a society decides to use because it perceives them to benefit the majority of the controlling members.

Nellie: On the contrary—they are principles built into the very fabric of the universe. We agree to them because we are all capable of discovering them, in the same way that we discover scientific principles.

Johanna: How do you account for the fact that different societies have different moral values?

Eider: In general, they don't.

Ellen: They certainly do. Consider the private ownership of property. In the decadent West, this is upheld as an important principle. In better societies, it is realized that no one can claim ownership over the land or other property, and it is all held in common. Why, this was the case even in your Christian Bible.

Dorcas: But, the phenomenon you have just mentioned is not at all moral or ethical, but a practical application, and only one possible application at that. Moreover, it was practiced in the form you describe only in a single local Church and for a short time.

Ellen: Nonsense. Greed is a principle held dear by most of the capitalist West, and they got it from Christianity.

Nellie: Dorcas is right. The related moral principle could be: "It is good not to be greedy" or, perhaps "You shall not covet." I don't see any problem with agreeing to disagree on how such a moral principle is worked out in political practice—two systems for controlling or regulating greed could be very different on the surface, but both might work well in their cultural context.

Dorcas: Moreover, even if various cultures do decide on different ethical norms, that fact does not mean they are all equally correct. One or more of them could simply be wrong.

BASIC CONCEPTS IN THE THEORY OF ETHICS

Professor: More to the point, what does the word "good" mean in the context you have just used it, Nellie?

Nellie: It means, "morally upright," "correct," "proper and best"...

Johanna: Meaningless words.

Nellie: What?

Johanna: You can't define the concept of goodness in terms of mere synonyms for the word.

Nellie: Why not?

Ellen: Because you have just traded words around; you have not explained the concept in terms of simpler ideas or words. Since you can't do that, the concept of "good" is meaningless. It is a word that has no underlying content except what a given society chooses to assign it.

Dorcas: "Good" is what pleases God—he has not left us ignorant of what things do.

Nellie: Well, I'm not so sure that is all there is to it. Aren't ethical principles by and large just self-evident? Don't people generally have a sense of what is good and evil, that's more or less reliable?

Ellen: Let me illustrate otherwise. Do you agree that it is good to tell the truth?

Nellie: Yes, I do.

Ellen: Very well then. Suppose telling the truth would hurt someone. For instance, suppose someone you loved very much had cancer, and you knew that if that person found out the truth, it would kill her sooner. Would you still tell the truth, or would you lie?

Eider: Let me answer that one. Your example is flawed, Ellen. There is no way to "know" in advance what the effect on the person would be. You cannot say that you know that telling her would result in her death. I have seen this sort of thing many times. The gnawing uncertainty and suspicion is, in my experience, much worse. There is no doubt in my mind that the truth is superior. It has to be told carefully and gently but told nonetheless.

Dorcas: Isn't what you are calling the sense of good and evil just conscience?

PART ONE | LAYING THE GROUNDWORK

Ellen: Whatever you call it, it does not work. By my conscience, nuclear bombs were evil, but some people claim by their conscience that those bombs were good. I organize workers into unions because it is right for them to unite against their oppressors, but some people refuse to join, citing conscience as a reason. Some are just capitalist lackeys, cheapskates, or liars, but not all, so I have to conclude that conscience is inconsistent and therefore unreliable.

Dorcas: But, you are not willing to deny it exists, are you?

Ellen: Too many people think it's there for that. I'll go with the majority to that extent.

Nellie: Generous of a Marxist.

Eider: Conscience was given as the "knowledge of good and evil" at the fall of Adam and Eve, and it has therefore always been flawed, even corrupted. Moreover, even when people know what is the right thing to do, they may still choose to do what is wrong.

Johanna: I think ethics is just a name for doing the best thing in whatever situation you are in.

Nellie: So, how do you know the best thing when you're in the situation? If there are no rules to go by, how do you calculate what's "right" or "good"? It seems to me that situation ethics reduces to "If it feels good, do it."

Dorcas: I have heard students here say "Just do it."

Nellie: Or even "Do it!" without the hesitation of "just."

Lucas: I saw a T-shirt recently that had all those, but it ended with the single word "Do."

Ellen: Yeah, that's not enough. There have to be rules, even if there is no God to make them.

Nellie: Who makes the rules then?

Ellen: What benefits the mass of people as a whole is put into effect as law by their government and this determines the right behavior.

Nellie: How do you decide who the government will be and how does it decide what are the best laws?

Ellen: The strongest and best are fit to lead and to tell others what is morally right. The average person has to be told.

BASIC CONCEPTS IN THE THEORY OF ETHICS

Johanna: But that's statism—totalitarian rule by an elite. You can't decide morals that way; it's the same philosophy Hitler, Mao, and Stalin used, and Putin and Trump use today.

Ellen: Don't change the subject. It's just survival of the fittest. We got here that way, and we have no choice but to continue to go along with evolution toward our destiny.

Dorcas: It is precisely the fact that human beings have an ethical impulse that distinguishes us absolutely from animals. We have a different nature, and part of that nature is the ability to choose between right and wrong.

Nellie: The ethical impulse looks out for others. It is exactly the opposite of "survival of the fittest."

Ellen: Your ethics is a denial of your destiny.

Alicia: Could someone define the word ethics?

Several People at once: Duty!

Nellie: We've read this book, Alicia. After all, we're in it.

Alicia: Very well. Duty to whom?

Johanna: To oneself alone. Everyone's primary duty is self-realization, self-actualization, and self-fulfillment.

Eider: (looking puzzled) You belong to the three self movement? I thought that was Chinese.

Nellie: Wrong modern culture, wrong reference. I'll explain later, Eider.

Ellen: Everyone's duty is to people as a whole; that is to the state. The primary duty is to serve the collective cause and advance its evolution.

Nellie: I'll say it is to people as individuals.

Dorcas: Yes, as Brother Paul says, Christians are to put the interests of others ahead of our own.

Eider: Duty to God. To serve His perfect will. Within that, I agree with Nellie and Dorcas.

Alicia: And, how do you know what your duty is? Where do you find out?

Johanna: You do what is best to maximize pleasure and minimize pain, first for yourself, then for others—in which case, it's the most loving thing that you ought to do.

Ellen: In the ideal state, you obey the collective will of the people in all matters, including ethics.

Nellie: But you don't think much of a democratic state, do you?

Ellen: I don't mind a democracy, it's racist colonialist imperialism disguised as a democracy that I can't stand.

Alicia: And the rest of you?

Eider: Conscience exists and works fairly well, even though it is flawed.

Dorcas: As to what's right and wrong, these are things God has told us in the law and the prophets. There are moral standards that describe Him and tell us how far short we fall of Him. Ultimately, goodness is something only God can give to us because only God has it.

Eider: Not only that but believing in Jesus Christ is how the gift of decreed goodness in God's eyes is given, along with the ability to do what is right.

Ellen: Wait, I have a question for you Christians. What about homosexuality?

Nellie: (indignant) It's wrong, period.

Johanna: Now just a minute. I find the idea unpleasant personally, but who are you to impose your morality on someone else, just because you don't like theirs?

Nellie: The Bible says . . .

Ellen: Who cares what the Bible says? People who are gay or lesbian were born that way; they can't help what they are. If there were a God, she must have made them like that, but in any case, you can't condemn them for being what they are.

Nellie: But . . .

Dorcas: Ellen is right, Nellie—at least about the last part. We are all born sinners, so none of us can condemn anyone else. Some people are more inclined to one sin, some to another. What matters is whether we give in to those inclinations to sin or, with the power of God in us as his people, we resist them.

Nellie: (settling back in her seat) If it is the action of sin and not the inclination to it that the Bible condemns, then it is not being a homosexual that is the problem, because that's just being a sinner, which we all are.

Dorcas: Right. We *are* all the same thing; what we *do* is the subject of ethics.

Ellen: (angrily) I don't accept that distinction.

Professor: (interrupting) Well, we've got the various views of ethics staked out quite nicely. Your assignment for next week is to consider the position with which you most disagree, and write a 2,000-word paper, with references, of course) . . .

Nellie: . . . (gleefully interrupting) ripping the other side to cross-shredded fragments.

Professor: (mildly) Why, no—defending it to the best of your ability.

There is general outrage at this, but the professor insists, and with a sly smile and a slight shrug, packs up, and leaves.

3.1 What is the Study of Ethics?

The first task facing anyone who desires to understand ethical issues is to determine what is the nature of the things being studied. This task does not appear to be as straightforward as it is in some other disciplines. After all, moral objects are not of the same sort as chairs, automobiles, or electric motors. Nor are they of the same sort as planaria, fir trees, water buffalo, harp seals, or even the girl next door. Consequently, the study of moral or ethical ideas must be approached rather differently than the study of physical objects, whether inanimate or animate.

For instance, an automobile can be measured; the relationships between its parts can be described completely, and detailed specifications for building another just like it can be developed. On a less exacting level, the owner of a car can use the senses of sight, touch, and possibly smell to distinguish a particular vehicle from several functionally similar but not identical ones. On yet another level, an automobile can be described in terms of its performance. One might wish to own a car that can stop from 100 km/hr in less than ten seconds, can accelerate to this speed in less than 20 seconds, or uses less than eight liters of gasoline to the hundred kilometers (in some places this would be expressed in miles per gallon), or can accept a battery charge in fewer than ten minutes that is sufficient to drive another 200 km. These performance factors can be tested for and the results published for all to see. Decisions can then be made based on concrete, reproducible, experimental data.

The point is that scientific methods can be employed to describe (in some measurable sense) every physical object and every living thing. Not only can the natural earth and its contents be so described (geology, biology, chemistry, and physics), but so can the products of human invention (engineering and technology)—all this despite the reservations about the nature of reality discussed in Chapter 2.

Some things are relatively less tangible and may nevertheless be physically measurable and therefore open to an exacting study. Consider the color red, for instance. By agreement, people use the word red to describe a particular part of the visible light portion of the electromagnetic spectrum. Someone could object that "redness" might not be perceived by everyone in the same way. However, the mutual agreement means that it is still possible for any person having a standard vision to decide whether or not something is red simply by referring to personal knowledge of this consensus. Everyone has from birth been involved in an indoctrination into a language for describing the properties of the physical world, and in particular, into the meaning and application of the word "red." Likewise, a two-year-old can know what "John Deere green" means, although of course there could be some confusion if he is colorblind.

It is not even necessary to know what an electromagnetic spectrum is to be a part of the consensus that some object has the redness or greenness property. Even though there are many shades and kinds of both, the communication of the idea of these colors does not at all depend on any technical understanding of the ideas. Redness or greenness can, except in cases of color blindness, be communicated accurately, even though the terms are an abstraction of physical properties, and not, in the strictest sense, measurements (although they could be turned into ones by attaching a particular wavelength of visible light to each word). This is true even though it cannot be guaranteed that every person experiencing color does so in the same way.

The difficulty with moral objects—like others that are not physical—is that one cannot often describe them in the same ways as one does the physical ones. If one says that it is "good" to tell the truth, for example, one must ask what is meant by "good." How can one tell when

BASIC CONCEPTS IN THE THEORY OF ETHICS

such a quality as goodness is present, and how does one know whether some actions have more goodness than others—that is, how does one quantify goodness?

Goodness is not a noun that describes a physical object like a chair. It is also a different kind of abstraction than "red," for the latter can be thought of as referring to a measurable physical quality, even if neither directly nor exactly. Color names describe something in the physical world, even if those who use the descriptions do not know or care about the scientific principles underlying the concept. Goodness, on the other hand, may not be physical, but most people do attach detailed meanings to the term. Though a Christian would ascribe the quality of goodness to God alone, many do not point to any person or thing as its origin, yet may aver that it exists.

The study of moral issues is not only different from that of science but also from, say, history, sociology, or economics. In the last three cases, the exact methods of science may not always be applicable, but the practitioners of such disciplines all agree that they are studying *something* tangible. That is, they are certain that factual determinations can be made in these disciplines and that there are objective truths to study or discover, even if the character of such determinations is quite unlike the character of physical objects.

For instance, not all historians would agree that "Nero fiddled while Rome burned," but they would agree that the truth or falsity of this statement is at least theoretically determinable—capable of being decided based on the weight of the testimony of sufficient reliable witnesses. The historian gathers accounts of the incident under study and attempts to weigh these accounts to get at the truth—all the while assuming that there does exist an objective and potentially discoverable truth. The outcome of such a study may not be supported by a repeatable experiment in the same sense as in laboratory science, but the outcome is not regarded as less than "knowledge." Furthermore, historians assume that any similarly competent person can repeat a study of the available evidence and either come to substantially the same conclusions or attempt to achieve some new consensus of what constitutes historical truth. The important concept is the agreement among historians on methodology, evidential content, and (ideally) conclusions. Even where there are disagreements about these, there is no argument that objective historical truth does exist.

Likewise, not all economists would agree ahead of time on whether a tax reduction would decrease the average price of a can of beans, but all would assume that with good and sufficient data, such actions can be studied after the fact and well-founded conclusions drawn as to what the effects have been. That is, economists suppose that they are studying something real in the sense of its being perceivable and measurable, even if they cannot always agree on how to make the measurements or on what the data means—especially before a proposed change.

To summarize, in the scientific disciplines, one gathers first-hand, empirical evidence in a repeatable fashion and evaluates this data to verify or refute a knowledge assertion statement. In several other fields, data of a slightly different type are accumulated and conclusions are drawn based on what seems to be the weight of evidence. Even where the facts are in dispute, there is little doubt that all these disciplines have a factual basis.

The study of moral issues is not as straightforward, for in this case one cannot explain varying views of truth merely by making allowances for imprecision and differences of interpretation. Disagreements go deeper, for it is more difficult to obtain agreement about the nature of moral statements, what they are based on, where they come from, and whether they are well-founded. This difficulty is not lessened even when there is agreement about the content of a statement. For example, several moralists might agree that "Abstinence from sexual relationships outside marriage is good" constitutes a valid moral statement, but each one could have a different reason for saying this. Other moralists might agree that such a statement is deserving of study but would disagree with the content. Still others might deny even that the statement is worth making or has any meaning.

In addition, two moralists might agree on the nature and validity of a factual statement, but act in very different ways as a result because they hold differing views on related moral issues. For example, two people might agree that "the incidence of AIDS is increasing" is a true statement, and even that this fact has moral implications. They might then come to opposite conclusions about how those having this disease should be treated socially. These differing conclusions have to do with the philosophical and religious presuppositions behind their moral reasoning processes, and the extent to which knowledge of the facts, fear, or prejudice enter into their thinking.

Likewise, the two might agree in general with the statement "Waging war is never good," but faced with a war between their respective countries believe in entirely different political narratives concerning the

BASIC CONCEPTS IN THE THEORY OF ETHICS

"goodness" of the particular conflict. See for instance the Russian and Ukrainian versions of what one termed a police action to eliminate Nazism and reduce the risk of potential NATO enemies on its borders, and the other calling it a brutal and unprovoked invasion to seize territory, replete with war crimes amounting to the attempted genocide of an entire nation.

It is easy to make statements about whether an action is right or good, without giving the matter much thought or even being aware of what these two words mean. Are they synonyms or do they have slightly different connotations? Can they be defined in terms of other words that do not have moral/ethical meanings, or is the concept each conveys an irreducible and indefinable idea? Are they (as some claim) such subjective terms that their meaning is private to each individual and not communicable to others?

At this point, it would be valuable to set this discussion aside for a while and attempt your definitions of these two words. (Try it!) Most people find that they can readily produce several additional synonyms to elaborate on the moral concept of goodness. This procedure sets a word in the cultural context of a list of other words with similar or identical meanings.

One teaches children in this manner, first tying a word abstraction to a concrete object, and then enhancing the child's vocabulary by referring new words to the abstractions the child has already learned. For instance, the word "car" could be taught by pointing to the family vehicle. At a later date, if the child questions the word "automobile," the earlier abstraction "car" can be referred to. If this fails, a trip to the garage for another look at the physical object could be in order. At some later time, perhaps in a high-school automotive course, the child will become able to redefine "car" in terms of an assembly of simpler, more fundamental, and repairable parts.

This example makes evident several difficulties in assigning meaning to words with moral content, such as good and right. Here are a few of the more interesting ones:

1. Are "good" and "right" synonyms in the same manner as "car" and "automobile"? That is, if one sets aside varying meanings in other contexts, do they have the same meaning in a moral context?

2. What is the concrete object that can be pointed to define a first word with moral connotations, and so get a handle on the remaining

synonyms? That is if goodness and rightness cannot be found in the garage or on the street, where can they be found?

3. For the more sophisticated inquirer, what are the constituent parts of goodness and rightness into which these complex ideas can be disassembled for more detailed study? Or, are there none—because they are irreducible concepts that cannot be defined in simpler terms?

4. If they do have constituent parts, do those parts sometimes malfunction, as does a headlight or an electronic ignition, and if so can they be replaced or repaired?

Aspects of the last three questions, the most difficult, will be dealt with in this chapter. For the moment, note in connection with the first question that a problem arises because there are many uses for the word "good" that carry the meaning "desirable," "more than satisfactory," or the like. There are similar problems with the word "right." Consider, for instance, the use of the word good in the following statements:

1. World War II was good for the North American economy.
2. Vanadium is a good catalyst.
3. Friendship is good.
4. It is good to tell the truth.
5. It is good to get vaccinated against viral and bacterial infections.

Historians and economists might argue about whether statement one is true as it stands, but they would be comfortable with modifying and qualifying it until they had a version that they could agree was either true or false. The record of their decision would also carry with it a review of the facts or statistics that went into making the decision, as well as a discussion of what were the agreed-upon criteria to place positive or negative interpretations on movements in a nation's economy. With all this in hand, similarly qualified experts who did not participate in the initial decision would have the means to become a part of the consensus (or not) at a later time. However, even if other experts did not agree with the conclusion, they would have little trouble attaching rather specific meanings to the word good as it is used in the initial statement.

Likewise, scientists would also have to qualify and quantify statement two, for it may not be true under all circumstances. Moreover, this assertion is true as it stands only relative to the effectiveness of other catalysts in similar circumstances. It is not even necessary to know exactly what Vanadium is or what catalysts are to realize that meaningful criteria could be established and experiments done to verify the truth of statement two. A person who knows little or nothing about chemistry could imagine a numerical value is attached to this use of the word "good" such as: "A good catalyst shall be defined as one that speeds up the progress of a chemical reaction by a factor of at least 3.14 over what it would be in the absence of said catalyst." In short, there is some general agreement in such cases about what the word "good" will be taken to mean, and disagreements about the meaning will be neither sharp nor divisive but simply indicate that a better definition or a more specific term is needed.

It is much more difficult to say precisely what statements three and four mean, and even harder to determine their validity. There are two groups of questions associated with such statements.

The first questions focus on meaning. What kind of statement is being made? Is it a description of a fact? Is it an expression of the belief of one person or a small group of persons? Is it, on the other hand, the declaration of a generally accepted consensus—that is, a collective decision of society? Does the statement represent the conclusion drawn from some logical thought process by a repeatable method of deductive reasoning from more fundamental principles or assumptions? Or, is it perhaps the announcement of a discovery in a way similar to the determination of facts in other disciplines? That is, has some principle of the moral universe been uncovered that has the same kind of validity as a physical law by being inherent in the reality perceived? Does this mean that there is a moral sense, like that of touch or taste? These questions will be considered in the following sections. For now, note simply that the greatest division among theories of "good" is on whether such ideas are decided upon or discovered.

What exactly does the word *good* mean in the contexts of statements three and four? It seems clear that it means something fundamentally different than in statements one and two, but just what? Does good carry the same meaning in three as it does in four, and would both statements still convey the same idea if one used the word *right* instead?

Finally, consider statement five. How a person would react to it might depend on their background. Someone who has come close to death in their youth from polio, scarlet fever, or mumps, to name a few, would likely be very positive about vaccines, reasoning that they prevented illness and death. Others might have bought into "government wants to control us" conspiracy theories, or exaggerated the known rare bad reactions into a majority, become fearful and consider any new vaccine, however successful, as anything but good.

A second group of concerns focuses on the validity or content of such statements. How does a person determine if statements about moral concepts are true? Even granted that people can reach an understanding or at least an agreement about the meaning of goodness in both statements three and four, how does one determine that friendship or truth-telling belongs in the category of good things? Is there only one good of which all others are aspects, or are there many goods? If many, what happens if two goods conflict? Is it possible to prioritize goods or rights so that such conflicts can be eliminated or at least reduced?

Furthermore, if something is in the category of good, does it also follow that it *should* be pursued—that is, does there exist an imperative that what is good ought to be promoted or done by everyone? (This last question adds a new one to the first group: What do the words "should" and "ought" mean in the context of moral statements?) Finally, who or what authority is authorized to pursue the shoulds, and with what force? That is, if good does imply should, can society or an individual in it legitimately require behavior that ought to be done because it is good? That brings us back to statement five. Governments argued that the proven safety and efficacy of COVID-19 vaccines meant it was right for them to mandate vaccines to engage in certain activities. "Good" became "should." Some were glad of it but others rebelled.

It will come as no great surprise to learn that many books have been written in an attempt to answer these questions. A complete survey of all the schools of thought on each of these points is far beyond the scope of this work, but in the balance of the chapter an attempt will be made to summarize the major positions on these issues. Anyone who considers seriously the specific social and moral/ethical issues raised in this book must at least have some idea what it is that people are doing when they make moral judgements, and how the judgement-making method in question fits in with those of the major schools of philosophy.

Before going on, here are three working definitions:

The study of the meaning and nature of moral statements is called *moral philosophy*.

BASIC CONCEPTS IN THE THEORY OF ETHICS

The study of the content of moral statements to apply them to right and wrong human behavior is called *ethics,* and one who makes statements resulting from such study is termed an *ethicist* or a *moralist.*

Profile on Issues . . .

The Good and the Should—A Few Questions

Once the good and the right are known or believed to be true, what power has it to constrain a course of action? Here are samples of questions that arise in such contexts.

Self-enforcement:

Does the knowledge of good automatically imply a person will do that good? Does failure to do good mean the person did not know the good? Who is responsible for the failure—the one who did not do good, or all those who did not ensure the person fully knew the good? Does it make a difference if "belief" is substituted for "knowledge"?

Who is responsible for a crime—the criminal, society, or no one?

Individuals enforcing the good on others:

Can one individual require a second to do what the first knows or believes to be good?

- May a parent require a child to submit to the parent's beliefs about what is good behavior; to discipline for the opposite?
- Ought a person intervene to prevent another person from being harmed (killed, beaten, robbed, raped, defamed, economically exploited, harassed)?
- Ought a person intervene to prevent another person from self-harm (suicide, reckless driving, using drugs, entering a bad business or social contract, believing wrong or harmful things)?
- If so, ought force be used? To what extent and in which situations?

PART ONE | LAYING THE GROUNDWORK

The State enforcing the good on individuals:

- Must the state enshrine its citizens' moral consensus in law or are there circumstances in which law is above moral consensus? If the latter, does the state have a duty to re-educate its citizens to a new and correct (by its lights) morality?
- May the state require (with what force?) its citizens to submit to (agree to) the political, moral, or religious theories on which it is based? To what extent ought it permit seditious talk? action? To what extent is your answer dependent on one's political or religious affiliations? For instance, if a parent has religious objections to blood transfusions, may the state intervene and force one upon a child to save life?
- Does the state have the right to require a certain religion of all its people? no religion? If in the name of impartiality, the state separates itself from or ignores religion altogether, does this constitute anti-religious discrimination?
- Is the reason for the separation of church and state the prevention of state involvement in the church or church involvement in the state? both?
- May the state legitimately regulate the employment practices, business affairs, or teachings of churches? of church-owned schools? for a church-owned property, building, or business? May it require the hiring of an out-of-work pastor or teacher currently on welfare? May it overrule a church's decisions on whether to admit a member to the church or a student to its school if these decisions conflict with the state's agenda?
- May the state overrule a church on questions of morality, declaring that since a particular behavior is legal, the church contravenes the law and violates individual rights by declaring it to be immoral, and therefore illegally discriminating?
- Does the practice of granting property tax exemptions for churches and income tax deductions for contributions to churches constitute state promotion of religion? what about religious slogans or sayings in a nation's constitution? on its coins?

BASIC CONCEPTS IN THE THEORY OF ETHICS

How closely may the state observe and regulate the economic activities of individuals in the name of promoting the common benefit, detecting cheaters, or ensuring fairness?

- Ought it to keep cross-matched records of all economic dealings to spot income tax cheats?
- Ought it to sell census data to private marketers?
- Ought it to guarantee certain minimum medical protection, dental protection, living accommodations, food, clothing, or wages to its citizens?

Should the state enact laws discriminating against a dominant religious, political, sexual, or ethnic group to redress perceived past inequities giving that group an advantage?

- Should the state fund minority lobby organizations to assist them in pressing their case to the state?
- Do university entrance quotas and faculty recruitment and promotion standards that favor minorities (diversity, equity and inclusion rules) work to the advantage or the detriment of the minority? the majority? the university? society?
- Ought women be front-line combat soldiers? If a draft is in effect, should women be drafted into the army in equal numbers as men?

What punishments may the state legitimately employ against those who break its laws (none, economic, physical, social)?

Specifically, which of the following ought the state be permitted to do:

- require certain actions of its citizens to prevent self-injury, and subsequent economic loss to others and the state (e.g. compulsory seat belts, motorcycle or hockey helmets, or compulsory treatment of drug addicts)?
- censor the advocacy of violence against some group? the promotion of fraudulent schemes to obtain money? the advertising of dangerous goods?
- prohibit the sale or possession of substances (drugs) or objects (handguns, assault rifles, machine guns, swords) deemed dangerous?

- publish the names of convicted criminals in the newspaper?
- confiscate the assets of criminals for state use?
- imprison those convicted of violent crimes? of economic crimes?
- make restitution to the victims of crime?
- require restitution from those convicted of a crime?
- physically punish certain criminals, say, whip a child molester or rapist, or execute a murderer?
- lock a device on the leg of a convicted criminal or parolee to track the person's location?

One State enforcing the good on another State:

May one state intervene with another when the second violates its own citizens' rights according to the laws of the first? by international law? What if the international law is unwritten, or has never been agreed to by the offending nation? Should a nation intervene with (a) economic, (b) political, or (c) military sanctions or direct action (such as an invasion) if a second state:

- invades a third state to capture its resources or to kill its people?
- systematically oppresses a group of its people because of the color of their skin (blacks in South Africa), their religion (Moslems, Jews, and Christians in countries unfriendly to their religion), or their economic political and ethnic background (see Kampuchea, Uganda, Rwanda, Ukraine, other examples)? What if oppression becomes large-scale slaughter?
- kills large numbers of its citizens for protesting state tyranny (students for instance)?
- engages in a methodical economic exploitation of most of its citizens to enrich the rulers and their friends (oligarchs of many times and countries)?
- harbors (encourages and finances) terrorists or criminals (drug dealers, murderers, thieves, fugitives from justice) whose activities are detrimental to other states?
- employs economic and social systems known to be inefficient and harmful to its people?

BASIC CONCEPTS IN THE THEORY OF ETHICS

- is overfishing international waters whose resources are vital to itself?
- uses industrial processes that are polluting the first nation (acid rain, chemicals dumped into border rivers and lakes)?
- subsidizes its industries or otherwise allows them to sell goods in the first nation at prices lower than they can be produced there?

Does God or some other power Intervene?

The oral traditions and scriptures (including the Bible) of several religions record instances of God (or gods) intervening in the affairs of individuals or nations to enforce some good or right action. Does such "higher intervention" still take place? Is there a corresponding outside intervening agency opposing good and favoring evil?

3.2 Moral Philosophy—The Good, the Right, and the Loving

As long as the human race has existed, in all of its societies, there have been codes of moral conduct. For example, a person might be expected to keep a promise or to tell the truth. Indeed, it is difficult to imagine how any society could exist where contract- or promise-keeping was not practiced, or violators and fraudsters not at least reprimanded. Likewise, there have often been some restrictions on sexual relations, as well as on violence to settle disputes. Behavior deemed suitable on some occasions is not on others, and severe violations of a given society's codes always result in organized consequences.

There are four sets of these conventions governing interpersonal behavior. They are religion (including magic and witchcraft), ethics, etiquette (including folkways), and the law. The last two are conventions to enforce behavior patterns, so they are largely derived from the first two, which are collections of beliefs about behavior. Also, the influence of religious ideas on ethics is very strong. In addition, the word "moral," though often used as an unqualified synonym for "ethical," tends to have religious overtones. In this context, the Bible has had a particularly powerful influence on Western civilization and its ethics. It offers an externally referenced explanation of the origin of ethical ideas outside human society by referring to God as defining good. It also offers an internal one, citing the role of conscience.

The very existence of society implies that there is an organized control of the interrelationships among members of the society. Agreements about what constitutes acceptable behavior, (i.e., rules of conduct, morals, and ethics) are the essential glue that holds society together. When these rules are codified and documented, they are called *laws*, and their enforcement may be delegated to authorities such as police, lawyers, and judges. When they are enforced by peer pressure alone, they may be called *etiquette*. Among free peoples, a consensus is necessary on what ought to be the content of law for there to be any practical possibility of enforcing them. Under tyranny, any law deemed desirable by the state—no matter how oppressive—can be maintained by sufficient application of force. Examples of such in this century include those headed by Stalin, Hitler, Mao Zedong, Pol Pot, Idi Amin, "Papa Doc" Duvalier, Vladimir Putin, and a host of other brutal dictators and criminal gangs in all parts of the world.

As long as there have been scholars, people have wondered where ideas of what is good or proper behavior originate. What follows is a classification of answers given to such questions. For purposes of simplification, the categories are larger than those that moral philosophers would usually create. Distinctions are made on the kinds of responses that would be given to questions raised in the last section. The material here is only one (fairly simple) way of summarizing a vast body of literature for non-experts.

To begin with, schools of moral philosophy could be divided into three major groups on the question of where ethical ideas originate.

Group I—Moral/Ethical Laws Are Deduced by Pure Reason

For this group of moral philosophers, ethical statements are obvious, in the sense that logic alone supposedly suffices to determine the contents of moral statements and how they are to be applied. This perspective, the position underlying some of the traditional Greek philosophies, has had a strong influence on Western civilization, particularly in its notion of justice as a high ideal that transcends both law and human behavior.

The fundamental assumption of these philosophers is that all who are sufficiently trained in the art of reason—anyone who proceeds rationally and logically—will arrive at the same moral principles. In this view, ethics is not a product of culture, language, history, or opinion. Rather, to the properly trained mind, moral rightness is thought to be intrinsic to the universe.

Group II—Moral/Ethical Principles are Decided Upon

Others assert that moral questions are decided upon as an act of the will. To this group, a moral principle such as the requirement for truth-telling represents a collective decision of society that such behavior is desirable—a decision that may only partly be the result of some logical thought process. That is, moral laws are not proven like mathematical theorems but are arrived at because society collectively deems them (for whatever reason) to be in the best interests of most of its members. This theory does not so much describe *why* specific principles are agreed upon, what weight each has, or how they ought to be enforced; it merely asserts that this is the process by which they come to be accepted.

Group III—Morals and Ethics are Derived From External Absolutes

This group asserts that moral principles exist independent of the will of any individual, or even that of humanity as a whole. Here, moral principles are deemed universal, either because they are part of the attributes of God, or because they are in some other manner built into the fabric of human existence, or even of the universe. In this view, humans do not so much deduce or decide upon appropriate moral behavior. Rather, they discover or have revealed to them preexisting principles. They then choose whether and how, or not, to apply these.

The Psalms summarize nicely this view that goodness is part of the character of God, flowing by revelation through to human beings.

> The law of the Lord is perfect, reviving the soul.
> The statutes of the Lord are trustworthy, making wise the simple.
> The precepts of the Lord are right, giving joy to the heart
> The commands of the Lord are radiant, giving light to the eyes
> The fear of the Lord is pure, enduring forever.
> The ordinances of the Lord are sure and altogether righteous
> They are more precious than gold, than much pure gold;
> They are sweeter than honey, than honey from the comb.
> By them is your servant warned; in keeping them there is great reward.

—Psalm 19:7–11 (NIV)

Blessed are they whose ways are blameless, who walk according to the law of the Lord.
Blessed are they who keep his statutes and seek him with all their heart.
They do nothing wrong; they walk in his ways.
You have laid down precepts that are to be fully obeyed.
—Psalm 119:1–4 (NIV)

Further Discussion

Within these three large groups, one can further distinguish several positions that depend on what the members of the various schools of philosophy say about how many—if any—universal moral principles exist. One can also make distinctions on whether moral statements are regarded as:

- binding—prescriptive of what should or must be done.
- aspirative—desirable ideals toward which one ought to strive.
- non-binding—descriptive of what people may do, but with no force behind them.
- emotional—expressing the opinion of what someone likes people to do.

The positions taken on these questions also depend heavily on where the philosopher thinks moral ideas originate, so some of these will be considered subheadings under the three main groups. The experienced student of philosophy will have no doubt seen a variety of different classifications of this same material.

3.3 Ethics and Pure Reason—The Legacy of The Greek Philosophers

This section will examine the first of the three views just mentioned—that moral statements originate through a process of reason or logic. In this view, all who are trained in the application of logic must necessarily arrive at the same conclusion about ethical matters. Those in this group agree that moral principles are absolute, for logically derived principles do not change with the majority opinion from one place or time to another, as logic itself is immutable. They also tend to agree that more than one absolute exists. Consider this statement as a simplified representative position of this group:

> Moral statements are absolute because they are arrived at by pure reason. They are related to self-evident virtues, each statement promoting a single virtue. There are no conflicts among these moral statements because they do not overlap.

As mentioned earlier, this was the position to at least a degree of certain Greek philosophers, including Plato and Aristotle. It has also been adhered to in various forms in more modern times, a common modification being the omission of the second sentence or even a recognition that conflicts may indeed exist between the different absolutes.

However, despite the contention that logic alone is sufficient to arrive at ethical statements, the actual conclusions of this group about the number, nature, and priority of ethical principles vary widely.

Plato held that the goal of the rational person was the cultivation of personal virtue (or excellence) and happiness. In his view, such a person knows what is true by pure reason, can control desires, and is capable of both philosophy and command. The ideal ruler in the Platonic state is its best philosopher. Some of the virtues that Plato put forward were temperance, courage, wisdom, and justice. Aristotle, on the other hand, emphasized those of friendship, pride, and moderation.

Today, it is easy to underestimate the importance to these teachers of human reasoning and the spoken word (logos) they used to convey that reasoning by way of argument. The logos of reasoned argument was not just a symbol or even just a conveyor of meaning; it was the very substance of knowledge itself. Logos made reasoned discourse possible; it was, therefore, the very stuff of knowledge; it was what made one truly human. It also had an element of the spiritual, for before it could be conveyed by the rules of discourse, it had to be apprehended from the realm of the divine. The gods revealed ideas, humans conveyed them, and thus an idea became a logos. That is why the English Bible translators sometimes render the Greek word as "logical" and other times as "spiritual."

On the other hand, the interesting thing for a modern reader of Plato and Aristotle is the near-total absence in these philosophies of discussions of right and wrong in the moral sense that these words were used in the Christianized societies that followed. The Greek philosophers did not equate virtue with what has been termed morality in modern culture. Rather, they believed that moral concepts were either self-evident or incidental to the training of the virtuous. Likewise, modern concepts of justice—such as "all are equal before the law"—would have been foreign or perhaps even immoral to Plato. To him, it was entirely correct that there be differing standards for the virtuous philosopher-governor on the one hand and the uneducated masses on the other. Again, it would not be so much, say, truth-telling, that was at issue to Aristotle, but loyalty to one's friends. The long-term goal was the perfection of pure reason in governing the relationship between individuals and the state. Indeed, it would be accurate to say that the advancement of a person's rational life was the ultimate good in these schools.

Issues of right and wrong in ordinary life were in a different and much lesser category than the pursuit of philosophical excellence. Such matters were regarded as being common knowledge, within the reach of ordinary people, and sufficiently self-evident even to the untrained as not to be worthy of detailed rational consideration by a philosopher. Here is a clear separation between common morals, which anyone could understand and apply, and the ethics of virtue, to which only the deep thinker could truly aspire. Once having achieved an understanding of those ethics, they could be justifiably proud of the difference between them and the common person. Indeed such issues as friendship could arise only between good men; one could not be friends with a slave (thought of as a living tool) or a woman (not regarded as rational). To be sure, some taught philosophy to women as well, but this was uncommon. These principles might be summarized in this way:

> Goodness refers to virtue, and rightness to action.

Another illustration of the difference between modern Western ideas and the ideas of some of the ancients can be found in Plato's concept of justice. In his view, the just person *must* fulfill his or her proper role in a state—that of ruler, administrator, or citizen. Each person has a natural position of control or subordination, and any perversion of this is an injustice. No one should ever seek to act outside their just station in life. To propose, therefore, that the same laws should apply to both commoner and king would be illogical, and therefore seditious to the proper order.

As to common morality, Plato believed that there was a moral nature with which the rational person lived in harmony, even though this might often be in contradiction to the conventions or practices of the non-rational person. In this view, morality is part of nature itself; it is not man-made or dependent upon culture or invention in any way. It is part of the natural order, as are male/female distinctions, skin color, and the nature of the elements: water, fire, earth, and air.

In an ethic based on reason, moral laws are supposed to exist apart from convention, culture, or decree. They do not change with time or civilization. They simply are. The task of both the individual and the state respecting such matters is to determine the correct natural order of morality and justice and then to change convention, law, behavior, and legal justice to conform to that right order. In this view, it is not only possible but also probable that the vulgar, uninformed, and irrational masses will have as a conventional morality a code that upon rational examination will prove to be immoral because whatever common opinion may be, true (logical) knowledge cannot be wrong. It is a logos.

Socrates, according to Plato, held that a person who once knew what was good could not choose to do evil, and therefore the acquisition of knowledge through philosophy was sufficient to attain all virtue. Moreover, wrongdoing in anyone's own eyes can never be a voluntary act. Thus, for example, an evil tyrant could neither be happy nor informed.

By the time of Immanuel Kant (the late 18th century), these traditional absolutist views were virtually unchallenged. Kant reformulated them in terms of a law of duty (not love, which is an emotion) that he called the "categorical imperative." Briefly stated, it is this:

> Whatever one does, one must act in a manner that is consistent with wanting that action to become a universal law. The corollary to this is that people are to be treated as ends, not as means to an end.

Kant was so convinced of this law of duty, which he claimed to have formulated by pure reason, that he rejected any admixture of love, compassion, or the pursuit of happiness in governing actions as dangerous corruptions of the Moral Law. He regarded the categorical imperative as the triumph of pure moral reason.

However, there are several flaws to the notion that true morality can only be discovered through pure reason. The first is that the actual law discovered by Kant seems, if it stands alone, to be rather arbitrary. Why not pick some other law, such as "Do what enhances your self-interest"?

It seems apparent that Kant was trying to bring within the sphere of duty (his highest goal) a statement incorporating the Golden Rule of Jesus Christ, "Do unto others as you would have them do unto you." Because of the potent influence of Christianity in the Europe of that era, it was important to Kant that reason appear to achieve the same ethical result as religion. At the same time, Kant believed that he was not merely modifying the Golden Rule but held that even if Christianity did not exist, pure reason would have discovered this principle unaided. Kant believed duty to transcend not only philosophy but also the results produced by the application of the senses (science). By serving duty in accord with the categorical imperative, all true notions of etiquette, morality, and law would be derivable.

In summary, Plato concluded that ethical duty was collectively owed to society or the state. Aristotle stressed friendship, and Kant decreed that the primary imperative was to duty itself. For each, the well-governed state had an obligation to enforce moral laws, putting weight behind the "should" when applied to the "good."

There are five great difficulties with such views of ethics. The first is that if they are valid, all philosophers ought to arrive at the same conclusions about what are the highest principles of moral law, and ought to apply them to ethical conduct in at least very similar ways. That they do not suggest that one needs to seek another source of absolutes than unaided human reason.

The second is the abstractness of the concepts. Such theoretical ideas often seem to have very little practical context. It is not clear how to use such a system to make applications to specific situations to act morally. It is not always clear what is meant by the term "virtue" or what specific qualities ought to be included within its purview. Likewise, it is difficult to agree on what specifics do follow from the categorical imperative. This abstractness is not necessarily a weakness, for the strength of the categorical imperative also lies in its generality, which is achieved precisely because the statement speaks not to the ethics of specific actions but to the moral process by which the ethics of any action is determined. On the other hand, such generality, along with many specifics, was already present in the Bible (and to an extent in other religions) before Kant; his work refocused and summarized Biblical thinking rather than providing a radical departure from it.

The third is that experience also forces one to question the assumption of some absolutists that a sufficiently well-informed person cannot choose to do what is wrong. On a most practical level, this assumption mocks the aching heart of every parent who has taught a child to do right, only to have the child grow up to do evil instead. That this happens, and does so frequently, calls into question the Socratic assumption that adequate knowledge of good alone is sufficient for enforcing good behavior. On a global scale, the increase in all forms of knowledge would presumably carry with it more knowledge of what is good, and this would in turn result in a more moral society. Yet, the last three centuries have seen as much war, tyrannical oppression, brutality, and other evils as have any time in human history, if not more, and it continues.

Indeed, although education became more extensive in scope and application from the latter part of the twentieth century, it has become abundantly clear that knowledge and goodness demonstrably do not increase together. One could argue that it is the absence in the curriculum of the study of virtue that is at fault, but as those who control the schools cannot themselves agree on what, if any, moral principles ought to be inculcated, it appears that this avenue is a dead end.

Fourth, there is a ring of arbitrariness to these philosophers' conclusions. It is easy to imagine coming to a different conclusion than that of Kant's, and indeed modern philosophers no longer do necessarily place the categorical imperative at the top of their list of logical conclusions about morality. Other considerations have become paramount, and other priorities have risen to the fore. This would appear to be a fatal blow to the whole concept that sufficiently trained thinkers will always arrive at the same conclusions about moral philosophy.

Fifth and finally, a Christian must argue that since all aspects of humankind, including the intellect, are fallen and flawed due to sin, we cannot reason perfectly, and therefore cannot come to infallibly correct conclusions about moral principles by unaided reason. In this view, the ability to reason perfectly, as God does, is damaged by the fall, and therefore the process and the conclusions are bound to be wrong (at variance to God's) at least some if not most of the time. Thus, at the end of the day, the Christian discovers at the heart of this theory a mistaken confidence in human reason and so must reject this theory of moral philosophy as fundamentally defective, and even idolatrous. It is also not enough to rescue the morality-as-pure-reason theory to say that humankind is made in the image of God and can therefore perfectly think His thoughts after Him because this weak attempt at a recovery still ignores the fall, so is fatally flawed.

All these considerations and others are the object of many books. They have led modern philosophers to consider many other positions, some of them non-absolutist.

3.4 The Non Absolutist Philosophers—Morals are Decided Upon

Position 1: Moral statements have little or no meaning.

The most extreme position here is occupied by those philosophers who assert that there is no such thing as absolute morality. That is, there are no universal norms on which choices of right or wrong can be based. To this group, called secular antinomians, there are not only no discoverable moral ideas independent of human reasoning but there are also none that can be reasoned out from first principles or axioms—that is, antinomians deny the existence of any such axioms. A few of them may accept the existence of a good god but yet deny that even his revealed principles for human behavior always apply. At the very least, members of this group will assert that such words as good, right, moral, and ethical are all essentially synonyms for some indefinable concept that is common to all these terms but cannot be explained in simpler words. They conclude that such words are therefore meaningless in any practical sense.

Some of these go further, arguing that moral statements are absolutely without meaning because they are not about physical objects and are not therefore verifiable through scientific methods. They also assert that moral statements are not logically deducible from non-moral premises. These thinkers, variously known as logical positivists or materialists, hold that logical argument and the scientific method applied to the material world are the only possible ways to know anything; all else, including moral statements, is rejected as irrelevant. What isn't knowable from the application of the five senses and the filtering of data through the scientific method isn't knowable at all, so it isn't anything.

Despite taking this stand, some might still consider moral statements to be useful, even if they are not verifiable. However, this usefulness would be entirely utilitarian and pragmatic. For example, a speed limit serves the purpose of promoting a valuable kind of order in which fewer people are inconveniently and messily killed. Perhaps, they might argue, moral statements are similar, providing all realize that they have no inherent compelling force of their own but are merely convenient conventions or agreements. That is, etiquette has a use but not morality, because the latter term implies a universalism that the former does not.

In this view, unethical behavior, if there is such a thing, is not wrong because wrong has no fixed meaning. However, some in this camp might concede that if a behavior inconveniences or harms a sufficient number of people, society has a legitimate right to restrain it. This is a democratic view of ethics and one that has some appeal, for right and wrong can be almost anything the majority in society wants them to be. Of course, to say that no absolute wrong has been done seems a cold consolation to the victims of rape, to the families of hostages, to those who have been defrauded, murdered by criminals or zealots of any description, beaten or shot in the course of a crime, abused as children, bombed, tortured, or eliminated by a regime of evil, or to others whose "level of inconvenience" is rather high. However, this view does assert that terms such as "good" have some use, even if they have little or no meaning.

Some antinomians may go even further, holding that the terms "right," "wrong," "good" and "evil" have neither meaning nor practical application. In this extreme view, all people have an absolute right to do whatever they conclude is proper, and there exists no authority that can legitimately restrict this right. All people have the total personal responsibility to assess whatever situations they are in and to act accordingly. To say that an action is wrong is an unwarranted invasion of privacy; no person can legitimately participate in, or even comment upon another's moral decisions. Herein lies the ultimate of freedom: there are no bounds, no chains, and no responsibilities—one is accountable only to oneself. This view is sometimes termed libertarianism, though those who hold to social and political movements bearing that name might have less extreme personal views. Others may adopt the more extreme anti-government view of the anarchist.

It may be worth mentioning that there is a kind of religious antinomian position—namely that Christians, having been saved by, and living under grace, are under no obligation to obey moral laws. This appears to be an unBiblical extension of the idea that grace frees the saved person from obeying the Old Testament ceremonial laws that were given to govern and make the nation of Israel visibly distinct from others. Since most of the moral content of Old Testament law is specifically repeated in the New Testament, this seems a difficult position for someone purporting to be a Christian.

Some would moderate the antinomian view, correctly observing that it does uphold at least one absolute, namely freedom, and perhaps a second—privacy. One might advance the following principle as the major contribution of the antinomians, though adding the second phrase might be a stretch for some:

Always act to maximize your freedom and that of others.

Adopting very much from an antinomian position would make this book either very short or entirely unnecessary. The whole subject of ethics would be quickly disposed of if it were to be neatly defined out of existence. The scientist who denies the existence of reality may still be motivated to study the appearances of phenomena but the person who denies the existence of the moral appears to have no basis to be a moralist. The chief difficulty with all antinomian positions, even in their moderated forms, is that they provide little or no grounds for agreed-upon forms of appropriate social interaction, in particular, none for law. They are, in short, a formula for anarchy rather than for society. If each person is a law alone, then civilization is already dead and those who remain are but its pallbearers. This observation also applies to unions, companies, and other organizations within the larger society that occasionally claim the absolute right to act in the self-interest of their owners or members without any regard for the rest of society. That is, they define good to be what advances their collective power or position, even at the expense of everyone else.

These obvious difficulties lead to another variation on the antinomian theme: although morality is not absolute, it is nonetheless appropriate for the strongest in any given group to create and control society as they see fit. In this view, rules of conduct are arbitrary rather than absolute. Those who are strong must arbitrate codes of behavior for the weak, enforcing behavioral codes through their position of strength. It may be argued further by some that the evident superiority of some human beings gives them both the right and the duty to be the arbiters of morals. Anything else, they could continue, would be an encroachment of the weak upon the strong, and such is not to be borne. There are obvious borrowings here from Plato, even though these would deny his premise that morality is absolute. These views are also compatible with those of the social Darwinists, who hold that human society and ethics are evolving in a process of natural selection that will guarantee the survival of strong people, strong ideas, and strong ethics, as well as ensure the unlamented demise of the weak. That is, since the aspect of progress called evolution is inevitable, the more highly evolved (the strong) need be little concerned with the rest (the weak) as they are doomed to be selected into oblivion.

The problem with theories of this type lies in the determination of who the so-called strong are, and why. As the Nazis showed so graphically, the logical conclusion of any theory that purports to uphold a superman morality is that the supposed superior beings may claim the right—even the obligation—to eradicate those perceived to be lesser beings. After all, their reasoning goes, they are merely helping the inevitable progress of evolution to achieve its predetermined goals, so they are doing right.

The world is not so far removed from the Holocaust that it should forget what such twisted reasoning did to the Jews of Europe during World War II. It is easy to make a political or economic scapegoat of a group of people who, for philosophical reasons, are regarded as lesser beings. Once a group has been intellectually ghettoized (for whatever reason) it takes very little time to decide to physically segregate them as well. It is thus a small step from such a philosophy—which is just a thin mask for religious or racial hatred—to genocide, and it is a step that has been taken many times in history.

There is no reason to suppose that the same thing will not be done many more times. Dictators of all stripes find victimizing some "other" group a handy way to cement their power. For instance, the actions of the Russians in Ukraine after 2022 lend credence to the notion that Putin, their dictator, promulgates to his people a view of Ukrainians similar to what Hitler had of Jews.

However, even if this most extreme conclusion—that the "lesser" beings should be eradicated—is not drawn, but the rules that govern society are entirely arbitrary (because there are no moral absolutes from which to derive them), then it at least seems inevitable that the strongest arbiter will ultimately rule the rest. That is, the expected result of an arbitrary moral code is totalitarianism. Once this situation comes to pass, it does not matter to those ruled by a tyrant whether the tyranny is of the political left or right. It is here, in the arbitrary suppression of the ruled, that Fascism and Communism, having entered the stage on the right and left, meet and shake hands both with the kings of old who claimed a divine right to rule and the strongmen of any time and place who seize and weld power by force.

Other brutal dictators formally holding to neither persuasion, but employing identical methods, have brutally exterminated dissent in their nations, invaded other countries to loot and destroy, annex territory, steal resources, or neutralize neighboring governments whose alliances they claimed constituted a threat. Even in the schoolyard, the only thing motivating a bully is "might makes right."

The cyclical view of history that was popular with some Greek philosophers held that in the decay of the moral principles that brought democracy onto the scene, tyranny became inevitable. To some extent, this theory has support from the historical record, for it can be seen in Greek and Roman times as well as in modern societies. When the glue of moral consensus dissolves, society also disintegrates. It then becomes ripe for a takeover by a tyrant from within or without who can impose a new order. On the other hand, if an imposed order is merely a thin arbitrary veneer masking competing hatreds, the removal of the external force leads at once to anarchy, and this fact was thoroughly demonstrated in Eastern Europe after the Iron Curtain came down and the Soviet Union collapsed.

Taking all this into consideration, the principle of maximizing freedom seems to be the only valuable contribution of the antinomians. Yet this principle contradicts the idea that there are no absolutes, for it is thereby being enshrined as just such an absolute. For this book, it will be assumed that both anarchy and tyranny are unacceptable and that freedom must be tempered, for freedom is not the same thing as license. Because of the undesirable outcomes of antinomianism, there is a strong practical motivation to look elsewhere for meaning in moral and ethical statements.

There are religious reasons to do so as well, for antinomianism expresses a hostile antithesis to any belief in a supreme being having the authority and the character to define what is good and hold creation accountable to do it. Since, for example, Christianity does hold such a position as of fundamental importance, it is impossible to follow Christ and also be an antinomian.

BASIC CONCEPTS IN THE THEORY OF ETHICS

Position 2: Moral statements are a consensus.

The philosophers who hold to this view accept that moral statements are meaningful. They do not believe such expressions to be discoveries of universal principles, but rather to be general decisions about behavior made with the ends in view which that conduct should produce. That is, they concentrate on the results of actions rather than on the actions themselves. Actions that lead to desirable ends are defined to be good; others are less so. Two actions leading to the same end are equal in moral content, even if they appear to be contradictory in themselves. For example, in this view, if the same result can be achieved by lying as by telling the truth, or by killing or saving a life, then the respective courses of action are morally indistinguishable.

Two main groups of philosophers held this view, the hedonists and the utilitarians. The hedonist believes that the chief end of a person's life is the maximizing of pleasure and the minimization of pain. This is a natural consequence of the starting premise, for if only the ends of actions are important and not the actions themselves, one might as well put one's pleasure first and follow that with the pleasure of others if any energy remains.

Some hedonist schools have attempted to define or even quantify the measurement of relative amounts of pleasure for varying numbers of people, but this philosophical position remains at its core self-serving, with little support or concern for the benefit of others. Thus, since moral issues are raised principally to discern what one's relationships and responsibilities to society as a whole ought to be, the hedonist view has little to commend itself in a study of societal issues. Indeed, from the point of view of society at large, it seems to have little to distinguish it in practice from the antinomian. The latter disclaims mutual responsibility for moral behavior because no such thing exists; the former because pleasure supersedes responsibility and is the only worthwhile pursuit. It is difficult to imagine how either can provide a basis for any kind of society—an association of people working and living together to fulfill common goals—because neither motivates being especially concerned about others. They are both anti-social.

Perhaps hedonism's most serious shortcoming is its failure to account for the extreme situation in which the majority of society are sadists whose pleasure is maximized by inflicting pain on others. The consistent hedonist, even if uncomfortable with this situation, would have little choice but to admit that the majority of such sadists would do good by torturing, murdering, or otherwise causing pain for the minority.

In stark contrast to hedonism, the Bible draws entirely the opposite conclusion about pleasing oneself by holding up the example of the Christ:

> "Do nothing out of *selfish ambition* or *vain conceit*, but in *humility* consider others better than yourselves. Each of you should look not only to your own interests, but also to the interests of others. Your attitude should be the same as that of Christ Jesus: Who, being in very nature God, did not consider equality with God something to be grasped, but made himself nothing, taking the very nature of a servant, being made in human likeness. And being found in appearance as a man, he humbled himself and became obedient to death—even death on a cross!"—Philippians 2:5 (NIV)

Moral philosophers who are not hedonists but still hold a consensus view of moral statements may be loosely termed utilitarians. These attempt to develop a philosophy of maximizing good results for the largest number of people, without necessarily using the word pleasure to describe that good. The essence of this view can be summarized by the principle:

Always act to bring the largest benefit to the greatest number of people.

This is also a democratic view, though clearly of a different sort than the one that says there are no good norms. Utilitarianism acknowledges the existence of both legitimate moral statements and a form of mutual responsibility. For this reason, it is a widely accepted popular philosophy, and many people embrace moral principles that they perceive or describe as utilitarian.

However, even the non-hedonist utilitarian has the problem of calculating the relative amounts of good at the ends of their acts to morally justify the acts themselves, and this problem stubbornly resists solution. The person doing the calculation is almost certain to weigh personal benefit most heavily, so the dividing line between hedonists and utilitarians may tend to obscure.

The chief difficulty in this position seems to be that actions are regarded as having no intrinsic value in themselves. An attempt to save a drowning child would not in this view be a good act if it failed. If the would-be rescuer dies in the futile attempt, then far from being a heroine, she is a fool. If she dies, but the child is saved, then the act is at best neutral, depending on how one evaluates the relative worth of the two lives.

There is also very little in this philosophy for the person seeking ultimate meaning to life and its activities, for unless one knows ahead of time what will be the outcome of an action, there is neither motivation to perform it nor to avoid it—yet no philosophy offers a method for predicting the future. Decisions must be made at the time action needs to be taken, but then the consequences are difficult or impossible to foresee. It is then that a person needs to measure whether an action in itself is good, and time is not often available for computing probabilities of possible outcomes and weighing these for potential good results.

Thus, on the one hand, this philosophy has considerable value as a means of attempting to find a justification or condemnation for actions already completed, based on their consequences. On the other hand, it fails as a means of making decisions about the conduct one proposes to undertake—it seems impractical to apply in real situations, even though it sounds good in theory. Moreover, as with antinomianism, both hedonism and utilitarianism conflict with the view that there is a God who can and does dictate absolutes. Thus, the Christian, for instance, must decline to use such theories as a basis for judging actions.

Position 3: The only moral statement is the law of love.

This position holds that the most desirable collective moral decision is to set forth a standard of love for persons (not things) as the single universal ethical imperative. This is an attempt to capture a middle ground between the antinomians (no rules at all) and the legalists (rules for everything), and it seeks to do so by setting forth a single intrinsic good, namely love. All actions are relative to the principle of love; they have otherwise no positive or negative value of their own. The principle might be stated as follows:

Always do the loving thing.

Once again, as in the previous cases, actions are not in themselves good. Instead of having the relative value of actions decided by results (as in utilitarianism), actions are judged by the motivations behind them. No general rules for responses to particular situations can be given because one cannot know in advance what a lovingly motivated response or action will be. Instead, one must wait to be in the situation to decide on the most loving course of action.

Because of its emphasis on doing the loving thing according to the situation, this type of moral philosophy is sometimes called situationism. In such systems, there is no rule book for behavior, and no universal or even general principles by which actions themselves are judged; only motives have values attached to them. This position differs from the ones above in that it holds that there is a universal norm—that of love—but it is similar to utilitarianism in that each action is judged in a manner that attaches no value to the action itself but is essentially pragmatic (but with loving motives replacing good outcomes).

This position is also relativistic, for any other ethical norms are valid only relative to the one universal principle. Indeed, they are only valid if they happen to serve the law of love in a given situation. It is not possible to say that either lying or promise-breaking is bad in itself, for the situationist might decide at some point that lying is the most loving thing in particular circumstances and is therefore good, but not in others, so is in those cases wrong.

Moreover, this strategy is a personal one. Its practitioners concentrate on the person who is to be the object of loving action rather than on abstract ideas of right and wrong actions.

Notice that the corollary to this principle is essentially the same as that of the categorical imperative, even though the motive for stating it is quite different:

> Things are to be used, people are to be loved. Above all, people are never to be used as the means to an end.

The love so expressed could even in some cases be akin to the New Testament concept of agape—the giving of self without respect to merit or expectation of return. It is most particularly not erotic love, which is seen as self-serving rather than truly loving, and it is much more than brotherly love, fraternal affection, or friendship. Therefore, such expressions as "sexual morality" are at least difficult to discuss if not entirely meaningless in such a philosophy, for a sexual act of whatever kind is never thought of as wrong in itself. Morality depends on the motivation of the participants, rather than on the act itself.

Because of the emphasis on the value of persons and because of its claim to be able to resolve apparent conflicts in marginal cases (do the most loving thing), this theory is attractive to many people, whether their moral convictions arise from religious considerations or otherwise. However, this position is not without its difficulties, though they are not as great as some of the ones already examined. The chief problem is that love is ambiguous. If there are no discoverable universal principles—and therefore no outside references from which to obtain a definition—then what is love, and from where or whom does it acquire meaning?

Does love get its meaning from the situations in which the principle is applied? If so, situationists are faced with a circular definition, for love was supposed to be the judge of the situation. How can the term gain its only meaning from the situations for which it is supposed to be the arbiter? Is love an emotion—and is one supposed to "feel" the loving thing in a particular situation? How? And, if so, love may not be a moral idea at all, for emotions differ both with personality and over time. Finally, is giving the love in question in the gift of the giver, and therefore potentially given in his or her self-interest, or is it given in the perceived best interests (by whom?) of the receiver?

There seems to be no means to judge the lovingness of a situation other than by being the one experiencing it. Once a principle becomes so personal that it cannot be the same for two people (or for the same person at two different times or in two different circumstances) it can no longer effectively be communicated at all, and so loses all practical claim to meaning. Thus, if situational experience or emotion alone is the guide for morality, it is not clear how this system differs in any practical way from antinomianism. Additional rules are needed to clarify what love is, how it is to be given, and whether giving it has some other, unstated motivation.

There is no way out of this difficulty, for if there existed any other rules by which one could determine the meaning, timing, and practice of love, then love would not be the only universal norm but would share its position with some other norm. Not only that, but the situationist also seems to have the same problem as the utilitarian in making decisions ahead of time as to the value of actions. Computations must still be done at the worst possible time—when a decision is necessary and action must be taken. Here it is the maximizing of love that must be computed rather than the maximizing of so-called good results, but the effect is not likely to be much different if such approaches are used, for in both systems actions have themselves no moral content and are at best catalysts or conduits for something else.

What is more, it has become common to advocate self-love as the highest or most important form of love. Whenever this becomes so, love-situationism becomes indistinguishable from hedonism.

There is an even more serious problem, namely, the decision to choose this particular single norm. The choice is supposedly not based on the discovery of any more universal principle than love but is a collective decision of society. However, the motivation for this collective choice of love is unclear. Could not something else have been chosen—say hatred? This possibility reveals that there must be some more fundamental principle that leads to the decision to choose love. For example, in the Christian religion love is an attribute of God that is revealed to human beings in the form of the gift of his son to die for sin. This is reciprocated by forgiven believers in him when they comprehensively love God (heart, soul, mind, and strength), and thus love between human beings is also legitimized. "Love your neighbor as yourself" is not the most comprehensive statement of this, but rather, "hold others in higher regard than yourself." Thus, Biblical agape (selfless) love has a context and is part of a hierarchy of activity in which love for God and then others—not simply love in the abstract—are at the top of the pyramid.

Thus, the Bible presents marriage as a type or parable of the relationship between Christ and the Church, a context in which comprehensive, irrevocable, eternal love is freely gifted to each other by two partners tied together permanently. *"Husbands, love your wives, as Christ loved the church and gave himself up for her . . . "*—Ephesians 5:25 (ESV)

Christ, when asked about divorce, quoting from Genesis, taught: *"Have you not read that he who created them from the beginning made them male and female, and said, Therefore a man shall leave his father and his mother and hold fast to his wife, and the two shall become one flesh'? So they are no longer two but one flesh. What therefore God has joined together, let not man separate."*—Matthew 19:4–6 (ESV)

With no authority beyond their choice of norm, the situationists' love, on the other hand, stands alone, and unsupported. In practice, this love is often identified with sexual activity and situationism used to justify complete license in this respect, as if the broader society could not conceivably have any interest in the social or medical consequences.

While it is not quite fair to associate this position exclusively with the so-called sexual revolution, the difficulty it has in dealing with this important and closely related area is a powerful argument that the theory is at least incomplete. Moreover, situationism is sometimes expressed in the slogan "If it feels good, do it," and in this reductionist form, it also becomes indistinguishable from hedonism.

Sexual mores raise yet another problem with situationism. When a pedophile has sexual relations with a child, both parties may feel at the time that the activity is loving. Yet, society persists in regarding such actions as exploitive, harmful to the child, and wrong. Yet it is difficult to see how to reconcile this revulsion with situationism, for if the parties feel right and loving about their actions, on what basis can anyone else condemn those actions from outside the situation? To proscribe pedophilia is to say that the feelings of love at the time of the act are not true love, therefore establishing a higher norm that claims to be able to examine actions themselves for lovingness. This would seem to be an improvement on an ethic based on completely personalized feelings of love and undermines the premise that one can indeed judge what is the loving thing only in a given situation and apart from any border societal context.

Indeed, that society would want to urge any restraint at all on the satisfaction of sexual cravings at any time or place, or with any person, suggests that either other societal norms and/or self-control are being held up alongside love as a parallel value, so that love cannot stand alone.

Christians also have little choice but to reject this moral theory, because they hold that humankind is fallen, and therefore that feelings of love are unreliable at best, and twisted at worst. Moreover, they hold that God who defines what is good does not change, and that therefore moral principles, while they might have to be adapted to apply to a given situation, transcend human experiences and situations. That is, Biblical morality is held to have a universality that goes beyond one's feelings of love at the time of an individual act.

Ethics as a Social Contract

This is another relativistic theory of ethics. Its operating principle and chief contribution are contained in the following:

PART ONE | LAYING THE GROUNDWORK

> Ethics consists of a mutual behavioral agreement between individuals and the society in which they live.

This statement embraces an important value, for it recognizes the dependence of individuals upon society and vice-versa. As has been noted several times, society is a mutuality and its very existence depends upon predictability in the relationships between its members. Here, this concept is acknowledged and ethics is regarded as codifying aspects of the mutually agreed-upon contract. Being a part of society means that individuals have both written and unwritten obligations, both to the culture as a whole and to various individuals. In return, society has an obligation to its members to provide a predictable, orderly framework within which to live and act.

It is also possible to deduce from contractual ethics other principles, for humanity as a whole has an ethical contract (by sharing the habitat) with the global environment—particularly with other living things. Thus, there is an obligation to secure and maintain both the physical and social environment. Again, this could be seen to an extent as Biblical, for it recognizes that Adam was made steward over the garden under the creator, not handed *carte blanche* to exploit it as he pleased.

Thus, the contractual view has great strength, for it seems to give individuals a substantial framework within which to make ethical decisions. Yet this strength is simultaneously a weakness, for it focuses upon the existence of contractual dependence without giving specific guidance about the contents of such contracts. Neither does it contain an intrinsic way to determine the relative importance one ought to attach to different contracts when their obligations conflict.

Not many people will acknowledge themselves to be bound by contracts whose contents are vague or unknown, and for which there is no external enforcement mechanism. Thus, the operating principle has worth but it does not go far enough by itself to be of practical value; it must be combined with one or more other expressions to guide the choice of good actions. In short, at least some of the contracts need to be specified, and this need places all the specific contracts at the same level of importance as the norm of their existence, shading this ethical theory over to a somewhat rules-based system after all. That is, although the notion of dependence is valuable because no one's actions exist entirely unto themselves until an ethical theory can provide specifics, it is inadequate for the whole task of governing behavior.

BASIC CONCEPTS IN THE THEORY OF ETHICS

Contract ethics also shares the weaknesses of all democratic views of right and wrong behavior, for a contract agreed to by a majority may well be unbeneficial or even fatal to a minority. The majority might agree together (a contract) to exterminate all the Jews (or all the Christians, Blacks, Aboriginals, Liberals, Irish, mathematicians, readers of Jane Austin, or people with feet of different sizes) but the mere existence of such an agreement is not sufficient to show that it is right. (Also, having written this, the author realizes he fits in five of these categories he chose more or less at random.) The fact that it is possible to show that there are social contracts that are deleterious to many once again points us to the need for a higher set of norms whereby social contracts may be judged. Moreover, if it does attempt to create a hierarchy of value or importance for contracts, it tacitly admits that there are better, perhaps best contracts, and so begins to become absolutism in the end.

The Judeo-Christian view that has shaped Western civilization does not deny the existence of binding duty contracts but would view them in the context of higher obligations to an Almighty God rather than as just mutually agreed-upon democratic ideals. Indeed, the Bible is replete with examples of covenants that entail behavioral expectations, but these are agreements whose terms are dictated by God Almighty on His terms, and with the full expectation that subsequent human arrangements are not to conflict with one's covenantal obligations to Him.

Summary

Over the last few centuries, a variety of non-absolutist ethical theories have been proposed by philosophers, some of which have become quite popular. On the one hand, the extreme antinomian theories virtually deny the existence of right and wrong; and on the other, the relativistic ones assert that nothing definite can be said about an act itself, for rightness and wrongness depend on other things. Considering the changing views of practical morality, it is uncertain whether these (mostly) relativistic theories actually influence behavior or were simply used to explain and justify whatever a person fully intended to do anyway. Since a lack of guiding principles is inimical to the very existence of society, and since the experience with relativism has not had very positive results, it may be that the future holds a return to some form of absolutism.

PART ONE | LAYING THE GROUNDWORK

Profile On . . . Issues

The Slippery Slope

An argument used by conservatives in all eras goes: "One departure from traditional norms starts a process leading inevitably to complete corruption." This is called a "slippery slope" argument because the premise holds that once society starts down certain paths, it cannot help but slide to the bottom. Moral relativists discount or ignore such arguments, but to illustrate they have at least some validity, consider what might once have been thought a slogan for behavior:

> If is right in God's eyes then do it.

tended to become the allegedly more democratic

> If it seems right in our own eyes, then do it.

Situationism shortened and refocused this, rendering its social slogan:

> If it feels good, do it.

This at least still requires some judgment (about the feelings, not the actions). However, in the late 1990s (at a time when little effort was put into thinking about morality at all) the social slogan became:

> Just do it.

Around the turn of the century, Lucas saw the T-shirt that proclaimed:

> Do!

The outcome of a few decades of the triumph of situationism became antinomianism after all. No wonder we are seeing the return of brutal dictatorships, genocidal wars, anarchy in the streets and a general distrust of government in all its forms. Liberal democracy not only failed to triumph, but its social contract became derelict, its leaders abandoned it for toxic partisan politics, and its citizens not only embraced divisive conspiracy fantasies in its place, but they began to tear it up. Historically, the next stop is either anarchy, a new tyranny, or both. Paradoxically, many professing to be evangelical Christians bought into the explicit political, racial, and sexual hatred fueling this movement, thus putting themselves in the position of advocating the very kinds of injustices their Bible proclaims God forbids and will severely punish.

3.5 Traditional Absolutism

In contrast to those who hold that ethics can be arrived at by human beings alone—either by logical deduction or by mutual agreement—traditional absolutists hold that ethics transcend not only human reasoning and society but humanity itself. In this view, right and wrong are meaningful even without reference to philosophy or culture. That is, moral ideas do not come from the human mind or mutual agreement, but from somewhere else. Philosophers of these schools agree that moral principles are absolutes, but they differ on how such principles are or can be known or discovered. In this section, several such positions are examined. The first is based on the idea that every person knows there at least exist such things as right and wrong.

Position 1: Ethics are discovered by an inner sense that is capable of distinguishing right from wrong.

This widely held view has both great strengths and great weaknesses. Proponents may claim that defenders of pure reason will be at least likely to arrive at similar conclusions because each is directed by the same inner moral sense. They can say something similar about utilitarians and situationists, who (they hold) ought normally to decide that the greatest good or the greatest love is whatever the idealized inner voice universally says it is

Certain of the Eastern mystic and meditative religions have a view of morality that could in some ways be thought of as falling in this absolutist category—even though they do not always directly concern themselves with right and wrong in the same sense as Western philosophies and theologies. Rather, some of them stress being true to one's inner self, a self that is in some sense part of a universal life force or flow of the universe. The inner being is, in effect, a god—or at least part of a god.

Self-examination in the form of meditation, particularly if the physical body can be cast aside or ignored, leads to knowledge of the deity within. A life of peace with all (for all share the life force) is assumed to be the consequence of such knowledge becoming universally experienced at the deepest level.

In one sense, this is an absolutist theory, for it asserts the connection of the inner voice to a universal "all." In another, it is relativistic, for each individual must find the inner voice alone, and no specific and reliable absolutes for moral conduct can be offered by those who have trod the path of enlightenment before, nor is any guidance offered for recognizing when the true self has been discovered, as there is nothing to measure with any confidence in the reliability of the method.

Moreover, it is not actions that are the issue for such mystics but the process of meditation toward self-actualization. If there is a goal, it is the inner experience of a state of harmony rather than a behavior that affects others. Because of the individualistic emphasis and their process orientation, theories like these also became popular in the West, where they were often combined with astrology and spiritism as parts of a New Age religion. It is too soon to judge whether this infusion of mysticism is having a lasting effect on Western thinking and society, or whether it is already a passing fad in a rush to secularism. Note however, that this theory of goodness is directly opposed to the Judeo-Christian one, which holds that God is unique, external to the created order, and is not in some fashion only actualized or instantiated within each person's individual experience through a process such as meditation.

The notion that good can be found through some inner sense—whatever that sense is called—is held as doctrine by many religions, though they disagree on the details. It is also held by secular philosophers, who give other explanations for it. Some of the Greek philosophers were inclined to this view for questions of ordinary right or wrong, for they regarded these concepts as self-evident—matters of common (inner) knowledge, and so not the proper focus of philosophy, which ought rather to be goodness in the sense of virtue. These last concepts were worth putting under the microscope of logic, but everyday morality was too obvious to all, and therefore did not need to be questioned or examined. All people automatically knew about moral rightness; philosophers had more difficult and more interesting concerns to subject to their examination and develop logos.

BASIC CONCEPTS IN THE THEORY OF ETHICS

Likewise, since everyone in society supposedly has this inner voice, a social contract ethics should also be easily constructed. All would desire the same agreement because all have (access to) the same inner knowledge.

The chief point of contention among those who hold this absolutist position has to do with the reliability of this inner knowledge of good and evil. If every human being has such an inner sense and the moral laws detected by the sense are indeed absolute, then everyone should access the same body of knowledge and produce the same results. However, people do not all act in a way consistent with there being a single set of moral imperatives. What can one say about this?

There are at least three answers to this objection. To understand the first, it is necessary to ask once again whether knowledge necessarily results in application. It is easy to see, for example, that the knowledge of scientific principles does not imply even the existence of an application, much less an exclusive or universal one. Two people who know the same theory will not necessarily discover identical or any even applications.

Likewise, people often act contrary to all good advice, common sense, etiquette, and even the law of the land. They can and do contradict other voices; there is every reason to suppose that they could have an inner voice to which they simply refuse to listen. That is, Socrates was wrong—knowing (in some sense) the good does not necessarily imply that a person will do it. Different actions do not mean that the right is not absolute or that it is not known, merely that a person has chosen not to perform it. Putting theory into action requires an act of the will, a decision. That a human being is capable of being willing to do good in agreement with the inner voice implies the capacity for being willing to do the opposite.

It is to make wrong choices less likely that laws are instituted, both to codify a consensus and to mandate sanctions against violators. For the sake of long-term stability then, the law ought to conform to the broad and historical international consensus (many listeners to the inner voice), with such modifications as thought necessary to suit local conditions or emergent technology. Specific issues relating to law will be discussed in Chapter 9; for now, note that a narrow self-interest, whether by one person or one nation, would be unethical according to the standards of this position. That is, it contradicts hedonism.

Second, though the existence of a moral sense has long been widely believed to be true, the notion does have its critics. Those inclined toward moral relativism dismiss the whole idea, saying that no inner sense can exist to detect moral absolutes, for there are none to detect. That is, they would hold that if any voice is being heard, it is either that of the majority custom of society or a product of the imagination.

There is a third answer to the difficulty of actions not following knowledge—a Judeo-Christian one. In this tradition, the inner voice of right and wrong was given by God in the context of the fall from grace into sin. Adam and Eve ate the fruit of the tree of the knowledge of good and evil (i.e., of conscience) because they chose to disobey. However, since through their act, the whole human race fell into sin and out of fellowship with God, conscience could not subsequently be a reliable guide because it too is corrupt. Indeed, no person out of fellowship with God can assume that conscience is trustworthy. Such a one may not even believe there is a voice of conscience, much less act upon it.

Nonreligious proponents of the inner sense idea have a more difficult time with the knowledge/action problem. The best answer may be that bad teaching and some wrong choices corrupt the inner voice and cause it to be more easily ignored, but this answer weakens their position. A critic might then ask, "How do you know that the inner voice is not just collected memories of parents teaching the behavior they wanted"? One response in return is to observe that people seem to be able to apply this sense even to situations they did not face as a child.

A weakness of that response is there are sometimes two contradictory claims to conscience. For example, one person supports nuclear arms as a deterrent against war and a second opposes such weapons altogether. One person advocates funding recombinant DNA or RNA vaccine research and a second considers such work an abomination. Similar contradictory claims of conscience are made for the use of animals in research, in vitro fertilization, abortion, surrogate motherhood, privacy, artificial intelligence research, going to war, and many other contentious actions. In each case, two sides cite the deep conviction of what they say is conscience and cannot understand how an opposing view could be held.

One may try to overcome this problem by claiming that some of the issues cited here are questions of custom, and however dearly held, customs are not morals. Such a reply may be partially correct but still does not explain away all instances of contradictory consciences. Neither is such an explanation likely to be heard by either side of a dispute whose protagonists hear only their own allies' voices, not those of any others, an outcome made more common than ever before by the echo chambers social media platforms provide. An assertion that conscience has become corrupt may help resolve this somewhat, but only if there is something besides conscience by which it in turn can be measured and corrected. Otherwise, there is no logical difference between a corrupt conscience and none at all. Moreover, if there is a point in history before which (or after which) conscience did (or would) not exist, there must at such times also have been (be) other standards by which good and evil could be distinguished (if they can be discriminated).

It is therefore possible to go at least part way toward meeting all but a last and most serious objection to the idea of an inner moral sense: though some point to the Bible for support, its proponents are unable otherwise to prove logically that it even exists. Its secular proponents acknowledge this weakness when they call this theory intuitionism. Yet it nonetheless has the authority of both an extensive tradition and some practicality behind it. The inner voice theory is attractive because it seems to be true in the experience of many people, despite the difficulty in bringing forward logical arguments to demonstrate the existence of this sense. Perhaps most people would concede that there is such a thing as conscience but also agree that it can neither be proven to be reliable nor be regarded as the exclusive source of ethics. Summarizing a modified form of this position:

Everyone has an inner, though possibly flawed, moral sense.

This principle has in its favor the independent belief in it by peoples of widely differing cultures and times. It has against it that conscience is used to justify widely varying and even contradictory actions, and these differences can only be explained in terms of flaws in conscience or by the existence of other absolutes with which conscience coexists or by which conscience is judged.

Position 2: Rules for human conduct are absolute and at least ideally nonconflicting.

The variations within this general group depend on the extent to which human conduct is covered by these rules. Staunch legalists may well have a rule for everything; others might offer far fewer. Some make no claims about the origin of the rules; others are sure that absolute rules can only come from Divine revelation. They may believe that religion is the authority for their moral code and that they must adhere to the code handed down by their god. This group believes that no moral rule can ever be broken without incurring guilt. In religious legalism, the basic set of god-revealed moral laws will often be augmented by a much larger codification of institutional (church) law that is continually being augmented, much as are national laws. The latter ought to have less authority, but when combined with the weight of institutional history, it usually has more. (See, for instance, the Pharisees of the first century and many other religious or church institutions since.)

Legalism in all its forms has a great attraction for many people. Neither philosophy nor conscience is much needed, for the rule custodians are readily available to arbitrate. Furthermore, in many religious versions, fear of a god's punishment (or institutional rejection) for the slightest violation of these codes commands a powerful incentive to obey.

The problem with legalism—and with any other theory that holds that absolute norms do not conflict—is that people nevertheless must sometimes choose between norms. A standard example is that of the spy who is caught and must when questioned either lie or be disloyal. To the classical legalist, this is a choice between evils, and the person who makes the choice is not absolved from guilt by the requirement that the choice is forced. The resulting guilt is real and must be confessed, repented of, and (possibly) atoned for or punished.

Despite this problem, and regardless of the religious overtones, legalist positions have probably been the most popular of traditional absolutist moral theories in Western civilization and have served as the basis for many extensive national codes of law. The chief contribution of rule-based absolutism can be summarized by this statement:

There exist external and absolute rules for moral behavior.

Also of interest here is that rule-based ethical systems are the most vulnerable in times of rapid technological change, for in such transitional periods there are bound to be many novel issues that arise in connection with the development and use of new technology and defy analysis by the old rules and their traditional interpretations. There will be efforts to introduce new rules (such as Internet censorship), but in the period before the rule makers catch up, a kind of moral anarchy may prevail concerning the new techniques. Because this aptly describes today's situation, (the Internet in general, and social media in particular appear ungovernable) the present sociotechnological difficulties serve as an excellent illustration of the difficulties with legalism. These problems suggest another absolutist position.

Position 3: Principles for human conduct are absolute. They exist in a hierarchy wherein the doing of a greater good absolves one from a conflicting choice of a lesser good.

Some of those holding this view would also (like the last group) state that the absolutes in question come only from God. One difference between this position and the last is immediately obvious. In the case where absolute norms come into conflict and a person must choose, no guilt is here attached for breaking the lesser of the norms (provided, of course, that the norm being rejected is indeed the lesser).

Arguments used against Nazi leaders at the Nuremberg war crimes trials after World War II fell into this category. To the claims of Nazis that they killed Jews because of a duty to follow orders, the prosecution replied that there was a higher natural legal order forbidding genocide that made their actions a crime against all humanity, and therefore were punishable even though the defendants had broken no laws of their own country. The court accepted this argument, enshrining in international law the notion that there exists a hierarchy of values that can be used to judge even the law itself and that this is true even if the higher principles have not been formally codified by any country, much less by them all. The same arguments have been used in the prosecution of other war crimes since that time, and no doubt will again be. We could put this as:

> Duty to all humanity is of a higher order than duty to one's country.

There are also overtones here of Plato's concept of an overarching justice that is above law, behavior, and opinion.

Consider also the example of the captured spy cited in the last section. The situation would be interpreted quite differently from this point of view. The hierarchical moralist says that since the good to be done for a just cause is greater if the enemy is deceived than if told the truth, there is no guilt attached to breaking the lesser norm (lying) for the sake of fidelity to the higher (a just cause). Of course, if the spy is supporting the "wrong" cause . . .

Students of the Old Testament might be interested in consulting Joshua 2 for an example of this type. This is the story of Rahab the prostitute who lied to the soldiers of her town of Jericho concerning the spies from Israel, throwing in her lot with the invaders. Despite betraying her city, she gains a high commendation, marries a prince of the realm, and becomes an ancestor to King David, and so also of the promised Messiah. There is more to this than just happening to pick the winning side; she chose the higher good by aligning herself with the forces of God and against those of idolatry, though nothing is said about how she discerned that was the greater cause.

Another very modern-sounding instance of a hierarchy of values in the Bible concerns the issue of surrogate parenthood—not for the mother but for the father. Old Testament law forbade a man from having sexual relations with his brother's wife. However, if an oldest brother should die childless, the next brother was commanded to father his brother's children for him with the widow, so that the dead brother's name would be perpetuated. The issue of family continuance was sufficiently important to override the usual norm, and to do so even though it might cost the younger brother his chance at the inheritance, as he preserved it for those who would be his older brother's legal children.

So important was this obligation to redeem the name, land, and heritage of the heir, that the duty passed to the nearest relative when no brother was available. When Ruth asked Boaz to become her husband and kinsman-redeemer, it was to prioritize perpetuating the name and line of Elimelech over establishing his own. In agreeing to this arrangement, they two also became a part of the line of the Messiah, as David was their direct descendant as well. The account also includes the actions of a closer relative who declined the duty to redeem Elimelech and his property lest it negatively affect his inheritance. Had his father threatened to cut him off if he had anything to do with a Moabitess? Boaz was of sufficient probity, prominence, and security that he could exemplify Godly leadership to his society without fear of consequences.

Workers in countless situations must trade off the values of company loyalty and the pragmatism of profit for professionalism in their work, safety considerations, integrity in business and financial practice, legal requirements, and product quality. Politicians must strike a balance among personal friendships, party loyalties, personal beliefs, and the need to govern a country. Athletes must choose between the value of winning and that of playing an honest game (say, without chemical enhancements). Students may need to trade higher marks and consequent better job potential for similar honesty in their writing and lab reports, for instance, and not engaging others' services or an AI to write something, then claim it as their work. Of course, their professors have AI and other plagiarism detection tools at their disposal, and it is becoming harder to cheat by copying pre-existing materials, even if easier to hire a paper writer or AI who can guarantee a specific grade. The obvious danger in the latter is that lacking specific information on a topic, the AI will fabricate and deliver eloquent nonsense.

Examples can be multiplied—in practice, people do prioritize values. The difficult problem is to create a hierarchy of principles that incorporates, as much as possible, the important insights of the other theories, yet remains absolute.

What can a hierarchical ethicist propose as a suitable ordering of moral duties? Here is one of many possible outlines; this one is based on the discussions of this chapter. The first duty and possibly the second, are Judeo-Christian contributions. Some would omit both, but moralists with a religious background might argue that the first two are the only important part and that the rest depend on them to such an extent that they cannot be neglected. They encapsulate the idea that moral absolutes are not discovered or voted upon, but revealed by God as part of His character. The third one includes duties not previously emphasized in the chapter and does so to recognize the social contract and obligations to people, and also to place humankind in a context of life and even the inanimate environment.

A Possible Ethical Hierarchy

First Principles:

1. Love of God comes before all else, for only in such love can one gain the good virtues and the ability to perform right actions, and only by God's revelation can one discover that there do exist external and absolute rules for moral behavior.

PART ONE | LAYING THE GROUNDWORK

2. Love of other people takes priority over love of self. This is an aspect of revealing the good character of God to others.

The origin of ethical principles:

3. Ethical norms are absolutes that are revealed by God as aspects of His character.

Resolution of conflicts between norms:

4. There is a duty to God, then other people, then oneself; next there is one to animals, then to other living things, and finally to the inanimate world. The latter are aspects of the stewardship God gave at creation.
5. Duty to many people supersedes duty to a few people, yet the many have a duty to protect the few who cannot protect themselves (the poor, the marginalized, the discriminated against, the disadvantaged).
6. It is better to be a whole person than an incomplete person. This is first applied to others, then to oneself.
7. Actions with foreseeable or demonstrable effects weigh more heavily than those with possible or theoretical effects.
8. People are more important than things, even if they are still in development, or otherwise incomplete. Duty is owed to people regardless of whether they are deemed to be completely developed mentally or physically.

New Situations:

9. When it is necessary to derive new ethical norms from the absolute principles because revelation is insufficient and does not cover new situations or technologies, one should adopt the following rules:
    a. Act according to the inner voice (conscience) as generally heard by virtuous people (not necessarily only one's own).
    b. As far as possible, do what is the most loving thing, neither ignoring conventional and prudent wisdom for emotion nor following established customs blindly.

c. Act to maximize the benefit to the largest number of people (this includes their freedom).

d. Remember that each person, including yourself, has a social contract with other people, the biosphere, and the earth.

This is not a complete list, of course, because it reflects only the brief discussions in this chapter, with a few additions. It will do for illustrative purposes and will help in considering various cases later in the book. It should also be noted that after point two the ordering is mainly within the points rather than between them.

Apart from placing love of God and other people first and second (for those who require those points there), this list does not rank the persons or things to which duty is owed, only some of the duties themselves. Thus, one may wish to place duty to family before duty to the next-door neighbor, and duty to one's nation before duty to people in other nations. Placing that hierarchy with this one would add another dimension to the obligations, as well as another set of potential conflicts to be resolved. Such complexities illustrate that the obligations that bind people to other people may be hierarchically ordered to some extent but must be practiced in a multidimensional network, rather than simply in a top-down fashion. Also, the attempt to express duty to humankind within the context of duty to God may be useful but in a rapidly changing society may appear for a time to be inadequate to explain all the details of interpersonal ethical obligation. This problem is not unique to ethical systems whose cultural heritage is religious; ethical responses may grow from various original principles, but the specifics of how they are worked out change as society and its technology do.

Note, however, that duty to one's nation does not imply the latter is intrinsically of greater worth than another nation, and certainly not that one "race" has more value than another. We might expect that cultural differences that usually arise for historical reasons would shape national identities, and this is not necessarily either a bad thing or a good thing, though they can be used to falsely demonize a neighboring people group to justify a land or resource grab war, the most recent of numerous such at this writing being the 2022 invasion of Ukraine by Russia. By contrast, the trivial genetic differences that result in differing skin tones are of no more intrinsic importance than hair or eye color or the length of one's fingernails, and it is difficult to understand why some people make an issue of such matters when from a biological point of view (and a Biblical one) the only race is the human race. People of various skin colors who are raised in the same culture are by far more alike each other than different.

It can readily be seen from this discussion that hierarchical absolutism is not the same as rules-based absolutism. It reflects the complexity of moral choices and attempts to emphasize character rather than simply ritualistic obedience to an established code. That is, it suggests that the making of moral choices is required from without, learned from within, and applied as part of a dynamic growing maturity. This permits the person who believes in a hierarchy of values to adapt rules to situations rather than making them up on the spot and to respond with love without allowing feelings to supersede objective morality.

It is also expressed positively. The person who asks: "What is wrong with what I am doing"? has waited until it is too late to ask and has then asked the wrong question. Rather, this hierarchy suggests that one should ask: "What is best about my possible choices for action"? and then have some measure of the mature character needed to discern or discover the answer. A Christian would do better still by asking: "What good does God want me to do, and how can I please him most by doing it"?

Elements of this list are also reflected in some of the other non-hierarchical or even non-absolutist philosophies, and this serves to illuminate what has been presented in this section. For instance, the situationists' law of love is incorporated by the second and last points, and Kant's categorical imperative is closely tied to several. That ethical norms come from outside individuals or even whole societies is reflected in point three. Reflections of Plato's concepts of duty within the context of the state or society are found in point five, and this item together with the last also includes the notion of a social contract. The idea that a morally educated and informed person has a natural advantage over one who is not is covered in point six.

It also suggests that actions that cause people to build or retain wholeness of mind or body are better than those that do otherwise. The calculation of relative goods is addressed by several points but embodied in a particular fashion in points seven and nine. Point eight asserts the primacy of people over things again and extends it even to the full potential of life for the development of human life. Together with points four and five, it asserts, for example, that an undeveloped, uneducated, or otherwise helpless child is of more importance than, say, money. Point nine recognizes that hierarchical absolutism does not have a rule for every situation and must use every available tool to derive new rules from the old.

One must not suppose that this list agrees in every point with those that all or most hierarchical ethicists would provide, nor that it gives a complete statement of, say, Christian ethics, which, according to Carl Henry (*Christian Personal Ethics*), is best interpreted as hierarchical. Such a comprehensive undertaking would fill a far larger book than this one. However, as indicated, this list does provide a touchstone to important elements of several ethical systems. Although not everyone will agree with it in every respect, it is an attempt to order the contributions of the major ethical theories in a way that incorporates them into a nonlegalistic absolutist position.

Christian Ethics and Legalism

Even by many of its professed supporters, Christian views of ethics have often been legalistic. However, if the Biblical documents (rather than institutional traditions) are taken as defining Christianity, then this religion claims both to explain and to set aside legalism. Those who followed Moses as a nation had a direct and special relationship with God. They were to strive for holiness, not for the sake of formal legalism, but as a witness to all other peoples and nations of the essential good character of God. That they bore His Name was significant; being His people meant being like Him.

New Testament doctrine holds that the Mosaic law was also intended to prove that God's standard (perfection) was too high for any human to achieve unaided. He is too holy to approach except in perfect holiness. In other words, achieving essential goodness through legalism is impossible. On the contrary, argues the New Testament, legalism can only condemn because no person can obey a legal code faultlessly and without guilt. Thus, an entirely different view of access to the goodness of God is required.

The New Testament goes on to proclaim that Christ took all the spiritual punishment required by God the Father for the guilty and repentant sinner upon himself during the physical torment of his crucifixion. Thus, those who believe in him and understand that his death was a personal substitution for them are set free from their guilt. In addition, believers are transformed and made fit for presentation to God by having

Christ's perfect righteousness attributed to them at the same time that their belief in Christ sets them free from their guilt. Thus, for those who receive His grace, the condemnation of an impossible legalism is paid for and at the same time, Christ's real goodness is imputed to the believer. That is, goodness, like love, is a gift from God rather than a personal achievement.

Consequently, Christians do good actions not to gain God's approval, which God has given them without respect to merit, but as acts of gratitude for having already received his free favor. The result is supposed to be a living out of the goodness of the indwelling Spirit of God in practical life and actions. This is possible for the faithful through God's power, despite a natural human inclination to do evil and despite a corrupted conscience. In this view, such a life is the only achievable human good, for goodness is a character attribute of God alone, discovered only by knowing God in a personal way and having God's goodness placed within oneself to live out. Right actions then follow automatically, for they flow from a good heart, and are not a striving to gain favor. To put it another way, God gives his goodness to the believer, and this enables the person in question to do right.

In practice, this view of Christianity has only indirectly affected society. Attempts to codify specific rules for Christian behavior seem invariably to lead to institutions that are to some degree legalistic. These organizations (whether churches or governments) when grown large enough, have exerted much of the religious influence on the culture and laws of the West. Still, Western legal heritage owes much to the direct influence of the Judeo-Christian scriptures, and this is no more evident than in such notions as human rights, which are often incomplete or utterly lacking in places that lack this influence.

This view of Christianity also suggests that although ethics must be practiced in social and institutional contexts, the moral absolutes are expressed personally and individually as the outgrowth of a character directly impacted by that of God's Holy Spirit for His purposes—and not as part of ritual obedience to either the state or a church institution. Indeed, Christ condemned the Pharisees precisely for the error of turning what should have been a matter of character into a set of burdensome external rules that could not be followed even by their promulgators.

> Woe to you, scribes and Pharisees, hypocrites! For you are like whitewashed tombs, which outwardly appear beautiful, but within are full of dead people's bones and all uncleanness. So

you also outwardly appear righteous to others, but within you are full of hypocrisy and lawlessness.—Matthew 23:27–34 (ESV)

Moving On

With the proposed hierarchy, it is time to conclude the subject of ethical theory and turn to more practical matters. From this point forward, theory will not be of foremost concern, but it will underlay many of the discussions in subsequent chapters. To examine actual issues, the author will take the view that rules-based absolutism is both stifling and inadequate; that the non-absolutist positions all inevitably lead one to antinomianism and the destruction of the social fabric, and that only hierarchical absolutism can deal, however imperfectly, with the complexities of life. The hierarchy given here attempts to borrow and incorporate points from other theories and will be used (implicitly or explicitly) to judge ethical problems throughout the rest of this book.

Readers who come to different conclusions on specific points should at least be able to analyze their reasoning and know which moral philosophy they have been following to arrive where they did. Indeed, many of the end-of-chapter questions will demand that they either argue from a contrary view to that of the author or justify their conclusions from an understanding of their ethical framework. The goal is a radical one—to make the reader think. When this material is used in his classes, the author employs formal debates on issues and expects students to be able to argue for positions that they may not hold.

Profile On . . . Issues

Toleration

Introduction: The people who make up a nation may have a variety of ideas and individual beliefs (religious, moral, political, and others). Since, for instance, there are many religions and political parties, such beliefs may contradict each other. In a stable society, there are certain "control beliefs" that characterize the dominant culture, form the basis of normal government policies and laws, are transmitted by its media, and generally present its public face both within the society and to external viewers. Tightly closed societies presuppose that all non-control beliefs ought to be suppressed. More open societies allow a plurality of beliefs some expression, even when these contradict the control beliefs.

> *A Definition:* Toleration is a practice based on the higher value of freedom. It is the deliberate choice not to suppress the expression of beliefs or behavior differing from or disapproved of by the tolerator, except when those pose a threat to life or health.

Is this a moral issue? At the heart of toleration is the belief that other people are moral agents whose freedom to express that moral agency must be respected, even when the beliefs they profess are not given credence. Tolerance is designed to promote freedom, respect for persons, and the education of all who hear or express moral views. It also recognizes that the consequences of intolerance can be catastrophic for society, and is therefore in everyone's utilitarian self-interest to practice it.

Problem: If the control believers use the word "toleration" to imply the dogma that all expressions of belief are equally valid (equally likely to be true), then they will be intolerant of any claim to be right, that is, to know absolute truth or even to place truths or ethics in a hierarchy. Such a view of tolerance may sound very liberal and accepting, but when its absolute is challenged by those who claim on any other grounds to know an absolute right or truth, the narcissism of this pseudo-tolerance causes it to self-destruct, sometimes in spectacular ways. In such cases, those who advocate any moral, religious, or political absolutes may find themselves under severe attack.

Is toleration absolute and unlimited? For the most part, tolerance theoretically cannot be selective and be itself. In practice, it is always exercised over some range of permitted dissent. For instance, if intolerance is one of the things allowed, and that becomes more persuasive than tolerance, the latter may be obliterated. Although not to permit the expression of intolerance seems self-contradictory, tolerance must have some limits or it cannot survive, and will quickly be replaced by some form of intolerance.

Problem: By their dominant position, the control believers in a society are disinclined to tolerate challenges to any of their beliefs. If the control believers are certain of the rightness of their beliefs, those who question these moral, religious, or political absolutes will be at least marginalized, if not ghettoized.

Must all beliefs be tolerated? The holding of beliefs is not strictly in the category of things to which tolerance applies, for there is no way to

BASIC CONCEPTS IN THE THEORY OF ETHICS

know what a person is thinking until those beliefs are communicated. Toleration applies to the expression of beliefs; it makes no demands on an individual for intellectual conformance to the control beliefs.

Ought all expressions of belief to be tolerated? Even some of these are not in the proper category to which toleration applies. For instance, expressions that defame the character of or incite violence against a person or group, or threaten their health or safety, violate the higher value of freedom on which tolerance is based.

Problem: If the control believers are sufficiently dominant and powerful, they may come to define criticism of any of their beliefs as defamation and incitement, and so to be a threat that must be eliminated. This is when intellectual ghettoization becomes first physical segregation and then active persecution.

What are the limits of toleration for non-conforming actions?

1. Acts of violence or those taken in reckless disregard for the life, health, and safety of others restrict the victims' freedom, and must therefore be regulated.

   Problem: A completely passive people is ripe to accept a dictator, or to be invaded by another nation.

2. A state must be at least somewhat intolerant of expressions or actions that threaten its existence.

   Problem: Fear of subversion or invasion can be used to destroy all freedom in a state, or used to publicize an imaginary threat by another nation as a pretext for war.

3. A state may have to restrict the ability of a group or individual to accumulate wealth or power, to avoid threats to the well-being or freedom of others.

   Problem: Some enterprises can only be conducted efficiently (or at all) with large accumulations of capital. Too many restrictions on this results in a lower standard of living for everyone.

4. An organization of workers such as a union or professional association may win the right to bargain working conditions and salaries for its members on behalf of their common collective interest.

Problem: The restriction of freedom inherent in requiring certain people deemed part of the collective to join the union or professional group can, if not handled with due care for tolerance by its leaders, turn into a dictatorship of its own that brooks no dissent from the leaders' positions even on political or social issues unrelated to bargaining.

5. Criminal acts are also presumed to be forbidden by higher principles and are therefore not in the category of tolerable.

    Problem: The greater the freedom, the more scope there is for terrorists and criminals. The more regulations there are to detect such activities, the less freedom there is. Acts that the government in power does not like can be unjustly criminalized.

6. Acts that endanger a person's health or safety may place an economic burden on society. To the extent that this restricts the freedom of others, such acts may have to be regulated.

    Problem: Sufficiently dominant control beliefs may make expressions of competing beliefs a criminal offense (this is how totalitarian rulers maintain power).

3.6 From Theory to Decision—Practical Morality

The focus of this book is not moral/ethical theory in isolation but rather the interplay between high technology and the practical ethics of a society. Some issues of great importance to everyday relationships will not be considered at all in this text, and some that most people would not normally think about become central to these discussions because they relate specifically to science and technology.

Furthermore, it is time to move from theory to practice. It is useful to examine, understand, and even adapt theories of making ethical statements, but if these theories are to have more than abstract value, they must be put to use—in this case by examining a society and trying in part to determine what difference ethical theories make when they are applied in real life by the members of that society.

The relationship between moral philosophy and practical ethics is akin to the one between theoretical physics and engineering. For instance, it is interesting to know something about how the structure of various metal alloys gives them certain physical properties, but it is more useful to society to employ this knowledge to build a safe and efficient bridge. In addition, mere knowledge of how to build a bridge will not bring one into being; there must also be an engagement of many wills, a decision to take action, and this is followed by the action itself, and on to completion.

Likewise, it is not enough just to know what is a good action that serves God or humanity in the best possible way, for one could still choose to do the opposite out of self-interest or stubbornness. For example, if law does indeed derive from ethical consensus, then it is at least in the long-term best interests of society to have a consensus that is generally applied, that is reflected in the laws of nations, and that has been adapted to the particular needs of the day and age.

Specific ethical and societal problems related to high technology will be discussed in appropriate chapters. An attempt will be made in each case to provide a historical context for the situation and to examine it within an ethical framework as well. In many cases, the need for solutions to problems will be pointed out and one or more possible directions for change will be given, but these will not be the only possibilities. Readers will be expected to provide some of their own solutions, particularly in questions at the end of chapters.

Profile On . . . Applying Ethics To Technology

The following widely-circulated statement was adapted by an international symposium on ethics and technology held in Haifa and Jerusalem in December 1974.

The Mount Carmel Declaration

1. We recognize the great contributions of technology to the improvement of the human condition. Yet continued intensification and extension of technology has unprecedented potentialities for evil as well as good. Technological consequences are now so ramified and interconnected, so sweeping in unforeseen results, so grave in the magnitude of the irreversible changes they induce, as to constitute a threat to the very survival of the species.

2. While actions at the level of community and state are urgently needed, legitimate local interests must not take precedence over the common interest of *all* human beings in justice, happiness, and peace. Responsible control of technology by social systems and institutions is an urgent *global* concern, overriding all conflicts of interest and all divergencies in religion, race, or political allegiance. Ultimately all must benefit from the promise of technology, or all must suffer—even perish—together.

3. Technological applications and innovations result from human actions. As such, they demand political, social, economic, ecological, and above all, *moral* evaluation. No technology is morally "neutral."

4. Human beings, both as individuals and as members or agents of social institutions, bear the sole responsibility for abuses of technology. The invocation of supposedly inflexible laws of technological inertia and technological transformation is an evasion of moral and political responsibility.

5. Creeds and moral philosophies that teach respect for human dignity can, despite all differences, unite in actions to cope with the problems posed by new technologies. It is an urgent task to work toward new codes for guidance in an age of pervasive technology.

6. Every technological undertaking must respect basic human rights and cherish human dignity. We must not gamble with human survival. We must not degrade people into things used by machines: every technological innovation must be judged by its contributions to the development of genuinely free and *creative* persons.

7. The "developed" and the "developing" nations have different priorities but an ultimate convergence of shared interests:

    For the developed nations: rejection of expansion at all costs and the selfish satisfaction of ever-multiplying desires—and adoption policies of principled restraint—with unstinting assistance to the unfortunate and the underprivileged.

    For the developing nations: complementary but appropriately modified policies of principled restraint, especially in population growth, and a determination to avoid repeating the excesses and follies of the more "developed" economies.

BASIC CONCEPTS IN THE THEORY OF ETHICS

> Absolute priority should be given to the relief of human misery, the eradication of hunger and disease, the abolition of social injustice, and the achievement of lasting peace.

8. These problems and their implications need to be discussed and investigated by all educational institutions and all media of communication. They call for intense and imaginative research enlisting the cooperation of humanists and social scientists, as well as natural scientists and technologists. Better technology is needed, but will not suffice to solve the problems caused by the intensive use of technology. We need *guardian disciplines* to monitor and assess technological innovations, with special attention to their moral implications.

9. Implementation of these purposes will demand improved social institutions through the active participation of statesmen and their expert advisers, and the informed understanding and consent of those most directly affected—especially the young, who have the greatest stake in the future.

10. This agenda calls for sustained work on three distinct but connected tasks: the development of "guardian disciplines" for watching, modifying, improving, and restraining the human consequences of technology (a special but not exclusive responsibility of the scientists and technologists who originate technological innovations); the confluence of varying moral codes in common action; and the creation of improved educational and social institutions.]

From: Ethics in an Age of Pervasive Technology Melvin Kranzberg (ed)

3.7 Summary and Further Discussion

Summary

The study of what constitutes the knowledge of good and right is known as moral philosophy; the actual application of these abstractions is ethics. There are three main groupings of the schools of moral philosophers, those who believe that:

1. Ethical laws are deduced by pure reason. This group includes the ancient Greek philosophers, to the extent that they discussed such

PART ONE | LAYING THE GROUNDWORK

things at all, and Immanuel Kant, whose categorical imperative was claimed to be the final and necessary conclusion of this reasoning process.

2. Ethical principles are decided upon. The positions within this group vary from the antinomian (there are no ethical norms) through the consensus view (including hedonism and utilitarianism) to the position that the law of love judges all moral actions and finally to situationism and the social contract view. The first of these is to an extent a denial of the existence of ethics; the last three assert that goodness is relative to certain calculations about the potential benefits of actions and that actions do not have this quality themselves.

3. Ethical norms are absolute, transcending both reasoning and decisions. This includes (but is not limited to) the view that an inner sense—conscience or intuition—exists that dictates ethical principles. It also includes legalistic absolutism (all-encompassing absolute norms) and hierarchical absolutism.

This text offered one such hierarchy as a comprehensive synthesis of the ethical theories examined under all three headings. Readers may well settle on other hierarchies, possibly subsets of this one, or one of the other schools of thought. However, in examining specific issues, whether relating to technology or not, it is valuable to understand what ethical criteria are being used.

Research and Discussion Questions

Many of these questions ask you to analyze issues. Be sure to state from what school of ethical thinking you derive your decision-making framework. Give examples as appropriate and articulate how your view of moral philosophy and ethics applies to the case under consideration. It makes the exercise more interesting when you support a position with which either you disagree or you know your teacher disagrees (and welcomes dialogue; not all do).

1. Under what circumstances is it right (or excusable) a. to lie? b. to break a promise?

2. Under what circumstances is it right (or excusable) to go to war? Give some examples and your reasons, based on your view of moral philosophy.

3. Normally, part of the duty of a citizen to society is to obey the laws of the country. When, if ever, is it better to break such laws?

4. In certain extremely rare medical circumstances associated with the birth of a child, doctors may be faced with the choice between saving the life of the mother or that of the child. Which should be saved and why? Would the same answer be given by all schools of moral philosophy?

5. Is it always right to report to authorities the crime of another person that you have witnessed? That you have heard about from a third party? Do your answers change if the criminal is your friend? Why?

6. Suppose the law requires you to report certain types of activities as crimes, but you do not believe they are wrong. Do you have to report or not, and why? Does it make any difference whether your views of the matter are based on moral philosophy? on political convictions? on religious convictions?

7. a. Under what circumstances is it morally right or morally wrong to practice birth control? What difference does it make if the law of the land requires (forbids) this? Now repeat the question for abortion, for infanticide, for euthanasia.

b. When euthanasia is the person's own choice, it is sometimes referred to as sometimes referred to as MAID—medical assistance in dying. What ethical principles do you bring to bear in this case, and how do your conclusions differ from the situation when others (medical personnel, family members) choose euthanasia for that person, perhaps by turning off life support?

8. The police have just revealed to you that your closest and dearest friend is under investigation for tax fraud. (S)He is about to be arrested and, if convicted, faces a lengthy prison term. (a) You have been asked not to tell (her)him because it is feared (s)he may flee the country. What should you do? (b) As soon as you are told this, you realize that you have in your possession conclusive evidence that would convict your friend, information the authorities could

not possibly know about. What do you do? Does it make any difference to your answer if the friend is also your boss? your spouse? your child? your parent? a teacher? the mayor? a politician you voted for (or did not), the pastor of your church, or a high-ranking police officer?

9. You are the prime minister of a country at war, and your secret service has a spy at work infiltrating the enemy's high command to discover its plans for a major offensive three months away. She has just reported, however, on less important plans for an attack that will be made in another place tomorrow. If you use the information, your country's forces will win tomorrow's battle, but your spy's activities will be unmasked and she will have to flee, abandoning the long-term plan. If you do not use it, many soldiers will die the next day, but the spy will be able to continue in the hope of gaining a greater victory later. What does a utilitarian do and why? What does a traditional absolutist do and why? Can you give a hierarchical absolutist answer?

10. You see a young child drowning in a river. Being both an expert mathematician and a good swimmer you instantly calculate a 40-percent probability that you can save the child and a separate 70-percent probability that you can save yourself once you do jump in. What should you do if you are: (a) a utilitarian? (b) a situationist? (c) a traditional absolutist? (d) a hierarchical absolutist?

11. What effect does it have if the two probabilities in question nine are reversed? If they are 100 percent that you can save the child and 0 percent that you can save yourself?

12. You are starving and have no money. You see a passer-by drop a wallet, and you pick it up. It contains over a thousand dollars in cash, some of which, you are convinced, this richly dressed person could easily spare. What do you do? Does it make any difference if the lost article was food instead of money? Does it make any difference if you are the mother of two young children who are closer to death from hunger than you are? Does it make any difference if you know that the owner of the wallet is a notoriously tightfisted individual whom you are certain would never reward your honesty? Does it make any difference if, in addition, he was once responsible for cheating you out of your home, property, and money and thus is the cause of your

BASIC CONCEPTS IN THE THEORY OF ETHICS

destitution in the first place? What if the person is a known criminal and you are certain that the money is profit from selling drugs?

13. Your country has a severe famine due to the failure of an irrigation system and very little money in the budget. The government has a choice between spending all available funds to buy food, in which case it is estimated that the lives of 500,000 people will be prolonged for a year, after which time, there will be no funds left to prevent millions of projected deaths. Alternatively, the available funds could be used to rebuild the irrigation system, allowing the 500,000 deaths in the short term but preventing the larger famine. Assuming that this is all the available information, what is the best course of action? Does it matter what ethical school to which you belong?

14. What difference does it make if the famine is in one country and the money in a second? Which country should make the decision? What if the second country has only this money; it is earmarked to update its irrigation system, for it is estimated that in the next year, there is a 25-percent probability that this too will break, and the second country would then also experience famine on a similar scale to the first? What difference does it make if a decision not to help means a 50-percent probability of a war, in which hundreds of thousands would surely die?

15. A man you know has been beating his wife. She kills him, not realizing that you have witnessed the crime, but otherwise successfully conceals her deed. Do you turn her in? Does it make any difference if she is (or he was) your close friend? A relative? Does it make any difference that you have just realized you are in love with her and want to marry her? Does it make any difference if she has two young children and no relatives who could care for them? What influence does your school of ethical thought have on your answer?

16. You have evidence that a certain individual is a child molester. However, for the case of which you are aware, you have been sworn to secrecy and asked by the victims' parents not to involve the police. Now another child has brought charges against the same offender. Should you come forward with your information, despite your promise? Does it make any difference who the offender is, or what kind of work (s)he does? Suppose the new complainant has confided to you that the charges now being advanced are false and

PART ONE | LAYING THE GROUNDWORK

being made for revenge, with no knowledge of any other offenses? Do you betray the lie, the truth, both, or neither?

17. How do the various ethical schools handle the issue of tolerance? For example, can an ethical relativist tolerate a traditional absolutist? a hierarchical absolutist? What about the reverse?

18. Consider the Mount Carmel declaration. What ethical theory does it appear to be based on? Is there any evidence of a foundation for its statements; that is, are they based on higher principles, or do they stand alone? How does it envision that its "goods" be enforced as "shoulds"?

19. Rewrite the Mount Carmel declaration in the form of a hierarchy. What additions or deletions do you propose, and why?

20. Attack or defend the statement made in section 3.5 that the "inner voice" theory contradicts hedonism. Extend the discussion to the relationship between conscience and utilitarianism.

21. It is well known that tobacco causes a myriad of illnesses, many of which are very expensive to treat and a burden on society. Should the use of this product be tolerated, regulated, or forbidden? Why?

22. Repeat the analysis of the last question for (a) heroin (b) alcohol (c) fentanyl. What are the essential differences among these four?

23. (Research question—use the Internet or a library) Find a code of ethics that has been adopted by some recognized group or profession and analyze it. What are the presuppositions behind the code; that is, upon what underlying principles does it appear to be based? What is its purpose? In what ethical school are its framers? What are the specific things required? forbidden? How would you rewrite the document? If you would not rewrite it, how would you defend it?

24. To what extent ought freedom of religion to be an absolute value? Consider cases where the practice of religion conflicts with the law, with the beliefs of the majority, or with other religions common in the containing society. What if the religion in question demands that its adherents either convert others, exile them, or destroy them?

25. Look up one or more hierarchical absolutist philosophers and write a short paper summarizing their proposed hierarchy and reasons for it. A more significant paper could have a comparison with the hierarchy proposed in this chapter or some other one, with an

BASIC CONCEPTS IN THE THEORY OF ETHICS

analysis of the differences between the two and any problems one might engender that the other might not.

26. During a pandemic, a government legislates the use of masks and vaccines as health measures to reduce the spread of disease. Some individuals defy these rules, citing what they believe is the higher value of personal freedom, or perhaps even a belief that the disease itself is just a government hoax to exert control over people. An unvaccinated person contracts the disease, and because she goes about unmasked, transmits it to several others, some of whom become very sick and unable to work for an extended time, and others die. Given that the individual knew or should have known the risks to life and health they were causing:

    a. survivors bring a lawsuit for damages against the spreader and you are on the jury deciding the case. Do you award damages or not? Why?

    b. should prosecutors bring charges of reckless endangerment causing death (equivalent to manslaughter or third-degree murder in some jurisdictions)?

27. In a similar situation as the previous question, a person who contracts the disease drinks large quantities of distilled water daily and recovers. Since for this disease 94 percent do recover and only 6 percent die, this should not be very remarkable, but the cured person attributes a miracle cure to the drinking of distilled water, and being a prominent influencer on social media platforms, convinces many others of the belief. Some of them, ignoring conventional medical advice, eschewing proven treatments, and even declining hospitalization in the last stages of the disease, also end up dying of the disease. To what extent is the influencer culpable (as in the previous question)?

28. Another group comes to believe, whether rightly or wrongly, that the team who developed a vaccine against the disease had a member who once worked with stem cells from aborted babies, and they have boycotted all vaccines for that reason. Again, their actions cause others to sicken and die. Once more the question—to what extent if any are they responsible for those deaths?

PART ONE | LAYING THE GROUNDWORK

29. Some oil industry workers organize a convoy to their national capital city to protest against federal government policies that they believe threaten their jobs. Several other groups with long-standing issues with the government join them, including conspiracy theorists, anarchists, greens who want the oil industry shut down, truckers, railroad engineers, and taxi drivers protesting the use of computer-driven vehicles, anti-diphtheria, measles, mumps, TB, and polio vaccine agitators, "freedom" agitators who want policing abolished altogether, and more. A large crowd sets up outside the legislative buildings where they block traffic, prevent people from using the surrounding area, and generally make themselves a loud but relatively peaceful nuisance. However, some of the fringe groups threaten local shopkeepers, steal food and merchandise, break windows, and hold assemblies advocating the overthrow of the government, by force if necessary. Organizers attempt to police behavior, but the perception both locally and via the media is one of criminal intimidation bordering on terror and sedition. Subsidiary protests break out in various locations across the country.

    a. Should the government declare a national emergency, give police extraordinary arrest powers, and disperse the protests by force?

    b. To what extent, if any, are the original organizers responsible for the actions of the groups that have attached themselves to their protest?

30. How should a person holding an important office deal with offers of gifts from people who may have dealings with that office? Why do you answer as you do? Some possible situations:

- A prime minister is offered an all-expenses-pain ten day to a tropical island resort owned by a wealthy industrialist, one of whose corporations is negotiating to purchase a tract of land owned by the government to build a new factory.

- A Supreme Court justice is offered a diamond necklace for his wife by the major stockholder of a company that is currently being sued and the case has been appealed to his court. Add this twist: your wife is the appellant's lawyer.

- The president of a university is offered a gift of thirty million dollars to construct a new Science building to replace a 70-year-old firetrap, however, the donor wants you to name the building after her. Suppose in addition she wants the university to hire her son as the chair of a new Institute for Programming Languages that if the president agrees to establish, she will also endow.

Does it make any difference if you add one or more of:

- the potential donor has several times been charged, and twice convicted of fraud in her business dealings and once was heavily fined for tax evasion?
- you know the son is not as qualified for the chair position (if it were established) as are two current or prospective faculty members?
- some combination of: the potential donor is your wife? Your ex-wife? The wife of your Board Chair? and/or the son is yours? not yours but believed by others to be yours? hers by a previous or subsequent husband? yours and hers by an affair no one else knows about?
- You were the previous CEO of the same company the donor now runs? Add: The two of you founded that company. Add: She made her millions from that company after she forced you out, leaving you with nothing.
- the potential donor made her fortune owning strip clubs and a company that publishes or distributes a string of pornographic literature and movies.

31. Pick a contemporary situation where a leader received a large benefit either while holding office or soon after leaving, and attempt to analyze the ethics of the situation. What is required for you to determine whether the benefit is appropriate or not?

32. Look up the word "supererogation." How does it differ from duty? Where is the boundary between the two, or is there one?

PART TWO

Four Wavefronts On A Sea Of Change

CHAPTER 4

The Information Revolution

TODAY'S SEMINAR HAS THE Professor, Eider, Nellie, Ellen, Johanna and, Alicia. Lucas is working in the computer labs, and Dorcas is unavailable. Only a portion of a longer conversation is reported here.

Note to students: A Christian worldview is occasionally reflected in the analysis of information issues presented herein, but it is the reader's task to make her own analysis. Questions to keep in mind: Which of the characters in the dialogue (if any) reflects a Christian view, and why? What impact does the information age have on Christians (and vice-versa) and why? What are the value assumptions you bring to this reading, and how were any of them changed? How do you evaluate (with your Christian or other values) the information issues you read in this material?

Professor: Part of your reading assignment was to examine this advertisement from InfoServe OnLine for its new public utility database and be ready to discuss. Comments?

Nellie: Great stuff!

Johanna: I must confess that I don't really understand why anyone would want a service like this.

Professor: Nellie, perhaps you could run through a summary of what is available.

Nellie: They claim to give access to two thousand separate academic databases, including libraries for publications on law, medicine, education, science, math, computing, arts, social sciences, farming, politics, famous people, blah, blah, and so on. They have email, conferencing, shopping at over a thousand stores, stock market reports, and all the back issues of two hundred popular magazines and nearly a thousand journals for the last fifteen years. Everything is cross-referenced, indexed, and at your fingertips for a low per-minute rate with no minimum monthly charge. They also offer full Internet and Web access, your own home page, five terabytes of personal file space, and an online virtual party once a month with draws for virtual vacation software.

Johanna: (suspiciously) What is all this leading to?

Nellie: Unlimited availability of information. It's the next chapter in the destiny of the Internet, realized.

Professor: Consequences, please.

Ellen: Ultimately, the state will be able to track both people and production. By monitoring retail purchases through credit cards in a cashless society, it can implement long-range plans that are guaranteed to work.

Nellie: Better than they used to do in the old Soviet Union, home of the eternal line-up and institutionalized inequity and poverty?

Ellen: Capitalist cartels and their Western government lackeys always exert themselves to sabotage socialist states.

Nellie: Places like the Soviet Union, Cuba, and Venezuela? They were self-sabotaging by their very nature. Even your mother Russia was and is just a kleptocracy.

Ellen: (defensively) The limitations of socialist systems to date have been due to insufficient economic information preventing efficient planning. Given both, the state could exercise total control over the economy. It would be the best of all possible worlds.

Johanna: If I were a pessimist, I would agree with you.

Nellie: I don't think it will turn out that way at all. Little Brother and Little Sister have good opportunities to keep things democratic.

Johanna: How so?

Nellie: If access to data is unlimited, citizens can keep track of bureaucrats' decisions—reviewing the data that went into them, considering the consequences, and feeding back opinions immediately.

Ellen: That's not necessary. Professional administrators should be left alone to make decisions without interference from individuals.

Nellie: (ignoring her) In fact, who needs a government or a bureaucracy at all? People could collectively run the county, voting on issues on a day-to-day basis, and the results of their votes could govern society—the ultimate in participatory democracy.

Ellen: I find that appalling.

Nellie: Why? Isn't it "power to the people"—like you socialists always want? (laughing) The very power that comes from information availability is what always destroys Marxist tyrannies.

Ellen: (Indignantly) True socialism will ultimately triumph, but not in mass disorder. The masses are uninformed, poorly educated, and volatile. Their opinions change from day to day like New York fashions. There could be no planning, no continuity, no governing—

Nellie: There would be no elite ruling class, either.

Ellen: Socialism knows no elite, but those fit to govern do so, just as those not fit to govern are governed. All are therefore equal.

Professor: Plato had a similar concept for what he saw as an ideal republic, but I doubt his ideas would fit into modern notions of human rights.

Nellie: Wait a minute, Ellen. Do you really believe that universal data banks ought to give the state access to all information about individuals but restrict its citizens' knowledge of the state?

Ellen: Of course.

Nellie: You're a law student. What about the files on all your clients? Should they be online where government officials can see them?

Ellen: Well, perhaps there should be exceptions.

Nellie: What about medical records, then?

Ellen: The state should have access, yes.

Nellie: Why?

Ellen: So that it can best plan medical facilities, and track efficient treatments of course.

PART TWO | FOUR WAVEFRONTS ON A SEA OF CHANGE

Nellie: And your second-grade report card, where your teacher said you should be "encouraged to overcome the tendency to rely on others' work and be more original."

Ellen: What! Where did you see my report cards?

Nellie: (sweetly) They don't call me Nellie Hacker for nothing.

Ellen: That's a gross violation of my rights.

Nellie: What rights? You just said you should have no secrets from the state. I work part-time for the Ministry of Education. The files are all there. I pulled yours and read it. In this case, I have legal access and did it to prove my point.

Ellen: (angrily) Which is?

Nellie: That your position is inconsistent. Open access should mean just that. What one can see, let all see. If my records are public, let the governments' be—and all contracts, company directorships, union records, financial data—all knowledge of every kind. All or nothing.

Johanna: What about mistakes? How do you ever get an error corrected if the data is entrusted to machines?

Alicia: I never make mistreaks.

Nellie: (with the barest acknowledgment of the speaker on the table) That's easy. Allow everyone access to their personal files and let them enter protests or comments on information they believe to be incorrect. The information provider would have to support the original entry or it would be removed. At the very least, the objections would also be part of the public record.

Professor: You want referees, then.

Nellie: Oh, yes.

Alicia: What you are asking for is beyond the storage capacity of even the largest computers. That amount of information, the ability to search it in a reasonable time, and facilities for every citizen to use it are far too great to handle with today's technology.

Eider: It's only a matter of time, Alicia, only a matter of time. Your world gets closer to that capacity with every passing year. We've had pretty much what Nellie describes for a couple of centuries.

Johanna: Preposterous fantasy.

Nellie: Haven't you ever heard of cloud computing? Storage and processing can both be distributed over thousands of locations. The infrastructure exists. We have AI. Only the software and the will to create a system of universal access are barriers.

Ellen: If I know anything, it's that I don't trust AI.

Professor: What do you think of the objection that knowing everything is "playing God"?

Ellen: What do we care about God? The human race is supreme. It needs no fantasy outside reference points.

Nellie: Then, how do you justify the existence of a controlling state? It seems to me that your god is the state.

Johanna: If I had to choose between Nellie's version of unlimited knowledge and Ellen's, I would take Nellie's. But, I'd rather not put all that information on a machine, anyway.

Professor: Why not, Johanna?

Johanna: I don't trust machines. There's something more human about a book or newspaper.

Nellie: What? They're made with machines, too—including computers. Why not simply replace the paper medium with an electronic one? It's already happening folks. Most newspapers, magazines, books, and academic papers are available electronically, and many only so. The outfits doing paper only are on the way out of business.

Johanna: I'm just not comfortable with yet another machine.

Ellen: Aw, it's all in how you use it. We could have the ideal efficient state.

Nellie: Total tyranny is what you mean. What we could have is an ideal democracy. That's what the World Wide Web is like already. You can't turn back the clock, Ellen; your vision has already lost.

Ellen: The World Wide Web is total anarchy.

Nellie: Well, maybe it is, but that's better than tyranny, and certainly more interesting.

Johanna: The people controlling the existing media filter the available information; how do you know the same thing wouldn't happen if it were all computerized?

Nellie: It would, but at least it would be more complete and available.

Johanna: Even your idealized democracy would create a tyranny of the majority, Nellie.

Nellie: How so?

Johanna: It would be impossible to protest against what the majority decided. What is worse, everyone's votes, purchases, and preferences would be on record—there could be no privacy.

Eider: As long as there are safeguards against misuse of information, the lack of privacy is not so bad.

Nellie: Your planet has such a system, then?

Eider: Oh, yes. You get used to it. After a while, no one thinks it's . . . . (hesitating) a large deck?

Nellie: (laughing) You mean, a big deal.

Eider: Ah, yes, idioms sometimes don't translate well.

Johanna: (disbelievingly) Granting the existence of this mythical planet of yours for a moment, hasn't anyone ever tried to take control of the entire society through the system?

Eider: Not on Meta-Earth, but it has happened on Ortho Earth.

Johanna: (grinning) Another fairy tale world? O.K. I'll bite. What happened?

Eider: In the case I have in mind, she was banished to what you would call Australia and had to work as a field hand for several years. We, and the Orthans, still think that universal availability of information has benefits that far outweigh any risks. Besides, on your version of Earth, privacy is largely an artifact of your Industrial Age. It scarcely existed before that and won't likely in future.

Nellie: The banishment you mention doesn't sound that bad.

Eider: Orthans would be horrified to hear you say so. I certainly am.

Nellie: Why?

THE INFORMATION REVOLUTION

Eider: (in a shocked tone) Because she lost her honor! That means more than life itself to us.

Johanna: (thoughtfully) Well, I'm personally convinced there are benefits, but I suppose every technology has its good side for some people and its dark side for others.

Ellen: I still say the state should control it. Look here Nellie, what about pornography?

Nellie: Well, there is some on the Internet, but you have to go looking for it. Pornography doesn't just appear on your desktop.

Ellen: (leaning across the table, ignoring Nellie's answer and triumphantly pointing her finger) All you Christians favor censoring pornography don't you? That requires state control. It can't be done otherwise.

Nellie: I can see the point of those who do favor some censorship—freedom is, after all, not the same as license, and pornography does a lot of harm, especially to women and children, but I've always thought, or perhaps hoped, that censoring the Internet would be technically impractical and therefore a waste of time, though I doubt today's Chinese and Russian governments, among others of your persuasion, would agree.

Ellen: (sourly) China and Russia today are hardly socialist. They're state capitalist.

Eider: Freedom of speech requires one to permit people to say outrageous and even wicked things. If you want to eliminate the worst excesses from your Metalibrary, you have to change people, not rules or technologies.

Nellie: Wide open access for individuals is the only way to go.

Ellen: (stubbornly) Strict state control of the economy is now enabled; that's all that matters.

Nellie: and you, and those like you at both ends of the political spectrum would use it, plus brute force, to make everyone pretend they think like you, in peril of their lives.

Ellen: Everyone must be equal. Those who resist should be lined up against a wall and shot.

Nellie: Yup. Violent enforcement. Last resort of the incompetent and ignorant.

Johanna: I say turn off most machines; we can do without them.

Alicia: I don't think that's such a good idea.

Professor: Shall we see what this textbook says about the issues and possibilities?

Alicia: Yes, let's do it.

4.1 What is Information?

A collection of raw data, however large, and gathered from whatever sources, is not necessarily information:

- experimental data collected during a chemical reaction only becomes information when it is organized and interpreted,
- answers from a poll of preferences for brands of coffee or chocolate, voting intentions, professional sports loyalties, views on global warming, abortion, vaccines, or the latest *cause de jour* protests, make and model of automobile ownership, or any other matter or issue, have no significance until aggregated, organized, and interpreted statistically,
- a box full of election ballots has no value, meaning, or significance until they are tabulated,
- an item from a box full of integrated circuit chips, resistors, and capacitors has no applicability until the number printed on the chip and the color bands on the other two are interpreted from a database of such parts to determine what it does and/or its capacity,
- a shoebox full of invoices, cheque stubs, and deposit slips for either a business or a household is data; when it is all entered into a general ledger and summarized into statements organized by account numbers/names and compared to the budget it becomes information,
- symptoms are data, but when considered holistically by an expert diagnostician, perhaps assisted by an AI, they can become information,
- a continuous recording of temperature, air pressure, plus wind direction and strength readings constitute data. It becomes information

when evaluated for correlation and trends, and may then have predictive applicability for weather forecasts.

Even the collection of data in the first place requires intelligent design to ensure the data is relevant to the question under study. One does not collect and catalog stamps to make a medical diagnosis, or amass data on breast cancer to inform prostate treatments.

Is the information gleaned from interpreting data reliable?

Data-driven studies have to be designed to collect the right data reliably with properly constructed and calibrated methods that isolate the effect being investigated from non-relevant phenomena. One must then deal with unexpected or anomalous results before bulk analysis can commence. Finally, correlations need to be carefully considered for relevance. It is doubtful, for instance, whether it makes sense to correlate stock market swings with phases of the moon, disk drive failures with the day of the week, or incidences of depression with the first letter of patients' surnames. Not everything is cause-and-effect connected, yet some percentage of data analysis can be made to appear correlated some of the time. The acid test is reproducibility. Can another researcher repeating the study produce additional data that supports the initial conclusions?

The term "information" implies that the entities it describes have some form of describable meaning, significance, and relevance either individually or as an aggregate. Meaning in turn requires two things:

1. intentional and intelligent organization, and
2. capacity for being communicated.

That is, even organized and interpreted data is information only if it has an intentionally attached meaning that can be communicated in such a manner as to preserve the essence of that meaning for another person. Information is a product of purposeful organization and design, that can be meaningfully disseminated; it is not merely a pile of facts and reports moldering unreported upon in a researcher's drawer.

This is not dissimilar to the Greek idea of logos with respect to communicability, though it focuses on purpose ascribing meaning rather than revelation from the divine realm. The activity required to generate and communicate information therefore requires intelligent input—intentional design, in other words, and this applies to the techniques of data collection and its interpretation.

In addition, information enables change in the people who apprehend it. They are empowered to know and therefore to do things they could not otherwise, giving them more choices and in turn increasing their available store of techniques.

Some of what passes for information may not be in accord with the facts—either because the underlying raw data is poor (because of badly designed collection methods or active fraud), or because of a failure to interpret or communicate it per generally accepted professional practice. There are standards for both journal publication and professional journalism, for instance, just as there are standards for proper accounting or construction. That is, questions of right and wrong need to be asked respecting information as well as about beliefs and actions. For some such cases, answers may be absolute; for others, there may be legitimate differences on interpretative matters.

Some information is also more widely applicable, and therefore more desirable to know. This fact affects people's motivations—both for learning new things and in applying what they already know. In the style of the last chapter, one could ask "If some things are good to know, to what extent should they be known"?

This tells us that information does not exist in a vacuum. It is not complete on its own. Rather, as with technology, human beings interact with information in a complex feedback pattern that changes both them and the information continually.

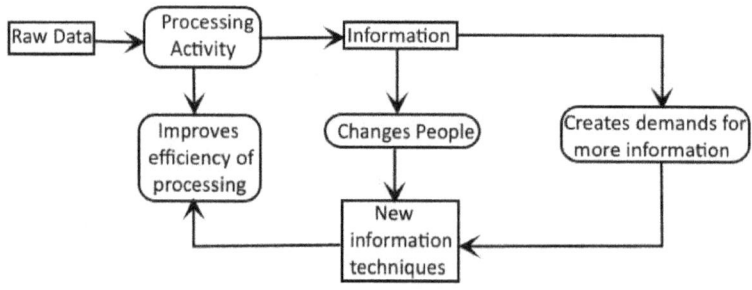

Figure 4.1

The larger the data pool is, the more complex the processing activity required to produce useful information. This in turn requires a certain sophistication for the society in which the information generation and use takes place. The higher (more abstract from detail) the level of the culture, the greater the demand for reliable information. This provides a feedback mechanism that forces the techniques for the processing of data into information to become ever more sophisticated as the quantity grows.

Some information theorists would present the diagram above as a mere mechanical process, suggesting that the entire task of processing data into information may be relegated to machines programmed to do the "thinking" for us. This position would not be very palatable to a Christian, or to anyone else who believes that the human mind is more than a machine and that it does something unique when its owner engages in assigning and communicating meaning.

The explosive growth of data sources and the demand for information also require that filters be created to sift out the useful from the less so. Someone who has been shot cannot afford to stop to wonder about the bullet's manufacture and trajectory before arranging to have it pulled out. It is questionable whether arguments over who wrote Shakespeare's plays or authored the book of Isaiah contribute anything to knowledge. A farmer does not need many military techniques. An engineer does not need to know how to raise pigs. A wet bench research scientist, a mathematician, or a computing scientist may not need to know how to operate a lathe, a table-mounted router, an air-driven impact driver, or a compound articulating miter saw. Thus, specialties are developed—no one can know everything, even in an agricultural society, much less in an industrial one. However, in the information-based society, anyone can find out anything if, as, and when they need to know and apply it.

It is important to note that economic activity does not march automatically and inevitably from hunter-gatherer to agricultural to industrial to information-based society. A subtle interplay of available technique, culture, plus economic and political events and decisions all influence what happens next. A civilization must either build or acquire from elsewhere a sufficient amount of information and other infrastructure at each level to enable progression to the next.

Accumulated knowledge of plants and animals permitted agriculture. Agricultural production expanded and became more sophisticated in the industrial age, but came to employ far fewer people. Likewise, the information-based society requires a highly sophisticated and complex industrial base, and the production of goods must surely continue to increase, even as the proportion of workers directly involved in their assembly diminishes due to automation. The production of ever larger quantities of agricultural and industrial goods requires better knowledge and more complete demographic information as time passes. Once the two older sectors become efficient enough, managing the information required to maintain them becomes the most visible occupation, even though in these cases the information sector only indirectly generates material wealth.

It is at least in part for this reason that the efforts of aid workers in underdeveloped nations are sometimes counterproductive. For instance, there is little point in attempting to introduce electric ovens into a society that lacks a reliable supply of electricity, or tractors into one with insufficient fuel supplies. A simple, easily repaired, hand-operated mechanical pump might turn out to be the single most appropriate technology needed to lift a remote village out of poverty. Teaching its people to read and write may be the most important contribution available among information techniques. Just as important a factor in all cases is the necessary infrastructure to instantiate and maintain the people, products, and processes that enable or drive a given technique. Each generation must be taught the information and techniques to survive, prosper, and improve.

At the same time, every society has information storage and transmission problems it must solve. Aboriginal societies honor their knowledge keepers who story-told the collective knowledge to successive generations. When oral traditions became inadequate to preserve information, it was written down on slates or scrolls. Eventually, the sheets were piled up and bound into books to save space. When it became necessary to produce many copies of such books, the printing press was required.

This all had to be put somewhere, for shoe boxes and file cabinets can serve for mass data storage only to a certain point. Thus, libraries have been particularly important in the preservation and transmission of both data and information. They are the repositories of what a civilization has found out about the world, what it believes about the world, and what it has done to change that world (and itself). There is now so much knowledge in the collective human archives that it is no longer practical to store it all on paper, and electronic means have become necessary. Today, the physical size of the media required to store data and information continues to shrink, even as the speed at which data can be stored, machine processed, and served back increases. The quality of information is a distinct issue, even (especially?) when processed by AI-enabled software.

It is necessary to do more than just store and retrieve information, however. To be of much use, it has to be interpreted (given further contextual meaning) and made transmissible to others, particularly the next generation. Thus, as the amount of information grows with the size and complexity of society, greater demands are also placed on the means of communicating that information. This general principle is of particular importance to any cultural or religious group, because its continued existence depends utterly upon successfully transmitting its essential ideas and practices *in toto* to the next generation, for failure to succeed in this task implies societal extinction.

4.2 The Information Technologies

The speed and reliability with which goods, services, and ideas can be transferred from one person to another has always been critical to human civilization. Early on, information transfer was completely dependent on the available physical transportation. Orders, government data, and intellectual properties, like material goods, could only be conveyed to distant places by personally carrying copies there, and the effective size of any nation was limited by this. The printing press made certain kinds of information more readily available (to those who could read, so many needed to learn how, and schools proliferated) thus ensuring that knowledge would not so easily be lost from one generation to the next. However, printed information still suffered from the restrictions imposed by the limited availability and effectiveness of transportation and communication.

The invention of the telegraph and telephone altered this situation profoundly, for now, information transfer could be effected anywhere that wires could be strung. The then-emerging countries such as Canada, the United States, and Australia benefited the most from such developments, for they were able to weld together enormous territories into single political entities because there was efficient transportation and communication among the parts. First railways and then copper wires tied these nations together, and without such technologies by today they would likely have become (as Europe still is) many small countries divided by language and culture, their ability to communicate effectively impaired.

Increasing use of telephone services forced carriers to automate to prevent the system from being deadlocked by the number of operators required to run manual equipment. Thus came dial phones, automatic switching, and computerized routing. Likewise, inter-city telephone cables gave way to radio, broadband transmission, satellite routing, and fibre optics to keep pace with the ever-increasing traffic. Both radio and image transmission techniques have merged with the telephone to produce cellular phones and a practical facsimile system (Fax technology is over a century old, but was little used by most people until speed and quality improved. Now it is on the decline in most sectors, but there are notable exceptions.) More innovations are necessary as the quantity of data transmitted over these circuits continues to grow.

Meanwhile, the entertainment media have also shrunk the effective size of the world, as audio-visual materials created in one place can be seen around the globe in a matter of minutes. Thus, while the time it takes to physically transport an object to any part of the world has been reduced to hours by modern jets, data can be transmitted instantaneously. It is safe to predict that the efficiency of information transmission will continue to grow for some time yet and that there may also be further improvements in the speed of physical travel.

Faster, cheaper, more powerful computers can store and manipulate more data. They are even more widely interconnected than they were, and it is now possible to send and receive information through this network at any time to any location on the planet on the information freeway we call the Internet.

The transportation/communication network is expanding rapidly into near space. The entertainment industry depends more heavily on satellite relay, to the point where the viability of local broadcast stations has become endangered. A small (30 cm or less) dish antenna can pick up hundreds of national and international channels from orbit. There are even more channels available via streaming over the Internet.

On the other hand, the trend toward consuming global information sources may be offset in part by an increased interest in the local community, so that new low-power local stations could be established. The value of global information sources is also diminished because people accessing them may be most inclined to believe sources that are anti-informational, provided they reinforce their own beliefs.

Except when relatively slow physical transportation is necessary, the spread of information is now limited only by the speed of electricity in wires or light in fibre optic cables. At least inside the orbit of the moon, this is effectively not a limitation, though, in the more distant future, it may become one. If other parts of the solar system are colonized, no instant communication would be possible, since the time taken by light to travel to other planets is appreciable. Data transfer will still work; as will any other communication that can tolerate waits of several minutes or more. Though it is premature to speculate upon that stage of societal development, it seems clear that one of the current stage's most important characteristics is the instant and unlimited availability of data, information, and misinformation.

As will be seen in subsequent discussions, this availability raises many important issues for those with an eye to the ethics of the situation and an interest in the quality of life in society.

Profile On . . . Data and the Law

Several countries have passed laws regulating the security and privacy of data. Some also have attempted to regulate transborder data flow as well. Here is a small selection:

Australia:

- Freedom of Information Act (Public sector) 1982
- Personal Privacy Act (individuals' information) 1983, 1988

Canada:

- Federal Access to Information Act 1985
- Privacy Act 1988, 2021 (Public sector)
- Personal Information Protection and Electronic Documents Act (individuals' information) 2001, under review 2022

France:

Data Protection Act (Public and private sectors, transborder data flows) 1978, 2018 (Extends the EU GDPR)

PART TWO | FOUR WAVEFRONTS ON A SEA OF CHANGE

Israel:

Protection of Privacy Law (Public and private sectors) 1981, 2017

United Kingdom

Data Protection Act (Public and private sectors. Transborder data flows can be prohibited) 1998, 2018 (+ extensions to GDPR)

United States

The United States has no comprehensive legislation in this arena. What it has is a variety of specific acts that apply to federally regulated entities. Each state may have its own laws in some of these areas. The following list is illustrative, but not comprehensive.

- Privacy Act 1974, 2020 (information practices, notification procedures for government agencies)
- Fair Credit Reporting Act 1970, 2018 (private sector credit, insurance, and employment info).
- Fair Credit Billing Act 1974 (privacy in granting credit)
- Freedom of Information Act 1966, 1974 (access to Federal Agency records)
- Family Educational Rights and Privacy Act 1974 (information practices of Federally funded educational institutions)
- Gramm-Leach-Bliley Act 1999 (financial institutions and personal information)
- Right to Financial Privacy Act 1978, 2001 (limiting government access to financial information to law enforcement agencies
- Privacy Protection Act 1980 (limiting government seizures of material intended for public communication)
- Cable Communications Policy Act 1984, 1992 (privacy of cable television subscribers)
- Electronic Communications Privacy Act 1986 (privacy of digital and electronic communications)

- Children's Online Privacy Protection Rule 1988 (privacy of personal information for children under 13)
- Video Privacy Protection Act 1988, 2013 (limiting disclosure of video rental information)
- Federal Trade Commission Act (last amended 2012) permits the government to investigate violations of a website's privacy policies

Germany:

Federal Data Protection Act 1977, 2018 (federal public sector)

International (EU):

General Data Protection Regulation (GDPR) 2018 (personal data protection, encryption, and accountability for breaches).

4.3 The Availability of Information

Information services now in place may yield the most accurate view of the future, for these have already come a great distance toward the goal of unlimited availability of information. It is not possible at present to count the number of facts on file in publicly available databases. Bibliographies and information files for law, Bible study, medicine, the stock market, business, education, biography, history, computing science, government activities, chemical and physical data, academic papers (numerous journals are now online only) and many others are readily available to anyone with a smartphone, tablet, or computer.

Gateway services and indices function as databases of databases. This includes public utilities such as the various Internet search engines that allow the seeker of information access to data repositories by subject, title, and/or content keywords. Such services extract meaningful information from the splendid chaos of the Internet and finance themselves by displaying paid advertising. An initial query may produce thousands of pages of data. The user then narrows the search to specifics, using the facilities of the particular information provider, software package, or search engine until the required material has been assembled.

It takes little imagination to project major extensions to today's facilities and to realize that—with modifications to current technology—citizens of the Fourth Civilization should be able to obtain any recorded information on any subject in which they are interested and from any time for which documents exist. Most of the technology for this is already in use, and changes that will come will no longer be revolutionary, only incremental. AI will play a part once it is more robust. People and their way of working will continue to change. Indeed, heavy Internet use has already altered traditional professions, as their practitioners have become dependent on the easy availability of technical data from sites they trust.

Information Services and the Professions

Doctors, dentists, lawyers, engineers, pastors, professors, teachers, and accountants not only have local client databases in which to file histories, treatments, recall dates, project designs, lesson plans, marks, and billings, but may also have access to local or remote expert systems through which they can diagnose patients and determine treatments, sometimes done remotely, look up case law, find parallel situations, detect plagiarism, consult clients on finances, enter grades, prescriptions, or other health data in government-controlled systems, etc. Such tools potentially allow a single professional to handle a much larger number of clients more efficiently and more accurately than previously. Such means also reduce dramatically the number of facts that the professional must learn and retain in personal memory to work competently. This affects how they do their jobs and radically changes the education required to become professionals in the first place. Eventually, professional education will have to catch up to this reality. Since many other segments of the marketplace are simultaneously moving away from an employer-employee model to professional-client relationships, these changes could alter the very nature of work for most people.

Similar advantages are also available, for instance, to real estate agents, except that their files are less customer-oriented and more product-oriented because the available listings in a given geographical area change daily, whereas customers tend not to repeat soon or often. Here, video technology is combined with computer searching so that a picture file of each listing can be made available through any realtor. Thus, a potential buyer need not go to the physical site to find out what a house looks like on the outside or inside—especially useful during a pandemic. Potential customers have the luxury of seeing detailed videos of houses for sale on their devices.

Researchers and translators of the Bible and other specialized literature have all the reference materials, manuscripts, parallel writings, commentary, and language aids ever produced readily available. They are therefore able to produce translations into new languages in a fraction of the time it previously took. Computer-assisted analysis of various language groups in a connected area can allow researchers to discover the root tongue among related languages and catalogue the linguistic shifts to daughter languages. By targeting the root or mother tongue for translation first, they can dramatically reduce the time taken to create translations in the daughter tongues.

Students of such materials can obtain consumer versions of similar aids to enhance their study. Bibles, for instance, are readily available in numerous translations and editions for any device using any operating system.

Other organizations already maintaining specialized databases include government (taxation, geologic, geographic, demographic, children's school records, vaccinations, hospitalizations, and other statistical information), law-enforcement agencies (arrests, fingerprints, DNA files, and stolen property records), manufacturers (distributors, suppliers, raw material and finished product inventory for just-in-time ordering and sales chain management), wholesalers and retailers (market trends, point of sale data for inventory maintenance, accounts, and customers), credit card issuers, libraries (loans, books on hand, and in print), newspapers (articles by subject), stock market and brokerage houses (prices, press releases, and transactions), universities (academic journals, student and donor records). All these plus banks and credit unions keep copious financial records, which, if outsourced to specialty online bookkeeping services, increases the risk of data piracy, as such services are not necessarily better than anyone else at security.

A growing number of private entrepreneurs perform contract information searches and data digests for their clients using public and private data sources. These could be the same people who help businesses set up Web pages to get their message out to the world in the most compelling form, and then find appropriate ways of driving eyeballs to those sites.

Scientists and engineers can look up the physical properties of substances, or locate and read journal articles or books on specific topics without a trip to the library. Researchers in all fields can do periodic searches and keep up to date on the most current work in their field. These facilities are major information utilities in their own right, and people who rely on them now find their dependence growing to the point where they cannot work without them.

Meanwhile, commerce is alive and thriving on the Internet, and tens of billions of dollars annual business is handled online via electronic storefronts and ordering systems. It is reasonable to expect this use will continue to grow rapidly for the foreseeable future. Already many formerly successful retail chains have gone out of business for failing to move sales online in a robust way, and it is safe to predict that this information-fed trend will accelerate and many more brick-and-mortar-only businesses will vanish.

Sex and the Internet

On a less enlightening note, the purveyors of explicitly violent and/or sexual materials also use electronic distribution to further their ends. There are three possible responses to this particular development:

1. Some would introduce censorship of electronic media and remove sexually explicit materials altogether.
2. Others make and sell "filtering" programs that parents can use to prevent access to the better known of such collections.
3. Still others note that censorship implies censors; that is, someone must decide what ideas are allowed expression and what are not. There is potential for "good" ideas to suffer more than "bad" ones if that happens, so they prefer to allow all ideas to compete openly in a free marketplace.

Unfortunately, the latter (more freewheeling) view may not adequately protect groups that find themselves targets of abuse from such materials—women, children, minorities, and marginalized populations. The mere existence of depictions of abuse lends credence to its perpetuation. That is, fictitious or potential abuse portrayed in violent or sexual materials promotes real abuse of real people. Indeed, in most cases, actual abuse was inflicted to make the pictures in the first place, though it is not difficult to counterfeit photographic portrayals (deep fakes).

In the same vein, false claims of widespread voter cheating accompanied by demands to overturn provably honest election results by political chicanery or violence, seriously undermine legitimate democracy. Likewise, false claims that COVID was a fraud and vaccines were deleterious to health resulted in distrust of provably effective mask and vaccine use, and were directly responsible for many more deaths.

Even worse, false denials of the holocaust inflict great psychological pain on the survivors of the death camps and their families and are used to legitimize the hatred that triggered that massacre. Likewise, Russian dictator Putin used fake narratives of Nazis running Ukraine as partial justification for invading that country, resulting in widespread atrocities including massacres of citizens via targeted attacks on residences, schools, and hospitals. Given state-controlled media and the criminalization of dissenting narratives, it is easy to require most people to give at least lip service to lies.

The laws of most democratic countries at least nominally recognize that a speaker is responsible for what is spoken. If it is destructive of reputation, courts may award damages for libel. If it is only potentially damaging, the law is less clear. Human history narrates a bleaker reality—might makes right, obliteration of a conquered people ensures they will never rise to gain revenge and the winners write a history justifying their actions to posterity, and cannot be held accountable in this life.

Moreover, the third view is based on the liberal hope that good ideas and their use will overwhelm bad ones. This in turn is based on faith that most people will discern which are which. Again, based on actual human history, not only are such hopes vain, but such abilities appear wanting. At some point and in some manner, it seems necessary to decide to what extent the "good" of freedom of speech/information must be set aside for the "higher good" of preventing threats to people's lives and health. In other terms, what is the right balance between the right to freedom of speech, and the right to enjoy safety under peace, order, and good government?

Unfortunately, it may be more appropriate to extend the maxim "bad money drives out good" to morals, ethics, politics, wealth, the right of minorities to live and work in peace, and the right of nations bordering the great powers to exist at all.

For example, some have debated over whether public depiction or promotion of homosexual acts is sinful or immoral on the one hand, or desirable for the freedom of speech and the liberation of an oppressed minority who cannot help being what they are, on the other. Although the antagonists on both sides often seem to try to shout each other down, whether in person or on the Internet, such issues could be described as a choice between perceived "goods" of freedom of expression for religion on the one hand, and that for minority group rights on the other. In this particular case, the issue can be further reduced to the popular choice of whose view of human sexuality and the morality thereof will be the dominant or control view for the society of the near future—in one sense a very democratic view of rights and morality, but consequently quite unsafe for any minority finding itself on the losing side of such either-or debates in the future. The side that "wins" such a debate in one generation may find itself on the denigrated side in the next, and possibly facing an extreme backlash.

> Be careful for what you advocate—you may succeed.

Perhaps the most relevant aspect of these issues for this chapter is that much of the interaction now takes place on the Internet, as people from all over the world have, for the first time, a vast array of town halls in which to weigh in on any such debate they wish—as long as they either first fortify themselves against the vituperation they are certain to receive from those who oppose their views, or they resolve to mention them only in echo chambers whose sole inhabitants agree wholeheartedly with and will enthusiastically reinforce them.

Information Services and Daily Life

It is interesting to observe that, while many specific professions had already been changed by the information revolution, the effect on the broader society had not by the late 1990s been particularly profound. In daily life, only a minority took advantage of information services. Some of these were not very popular and were closed due to lack of interest. The Internet and its subset, the World Wide Web was by the end of that decade the only service that would see longevity.

THE INFORMATION REVOLUTION

To an extent, people of the latter part of the industrial age remained willing to rely on traditional mass media filters rather than seeking and filtering information personally. Thus, in the first part of the information age, universal access to information was still conceded to employees of various news media, and they in turn published or broadcast what they deemed to be in the best commercial interests of their employers. Terrorist organizations and protest groups made (and still make) use of this when they stage events for media coverage to gain recognition that their small numbers could not by their unaided efforts possibly achieve. So do conventional politicians when they time their news releases to hit or miss major telecasts or other media deadlines, depending on the amount of publicity they want.

For their part, those who controlled the old news media perceived little mandate to extend access to the information from which their articles and editorials were constructed. Consequently, consumers gradually lost the ability to distinguish between factual news (data) and editorial interpretations of that data (assigned meaning). This is an example of an abstraction (removal from detail) that is potentially detrimental, for giving up to others the decisions on assigning meaning to data threatens a person's ability to function as an informed citizen. Indeed, the chief prerequisite for tyranny to triumph—even in an information-based society—lies in confining the ability to provide data interpretations, which can include outrageous falsehoods, to a small and tightly managed group of cronies, who in turn exercise control over what all other citizens are permitted to know and therefore to think about.

Besides older generation inertia, one reason for the initial lack of interest in broader access to news and other information was that the benefits had not yet exceeded the costs. These services were used effectively and efficiently by those whose jobs demanded such use or who could benefit from it and were willing to expend time and effort to learn the idiosyncrasies of the various information services because they must.

Most people had few such motivations to use the Internet initially, and rather than searching for information, become enamored of recreational possibilities on the Web, such as games and pornography. The general population only began to depend on electronic information services when:

1. A new generation began routinely doing schoolwork using these systems, communicated with each other first via email, then through

Facebook, Instagram, Twitter, and other social media platforms until they lived to a great extent vicariously and virtually via their devices, often even when gathered physically in groups. Some of the older generations perceived similar utility and joined the rush to electronic information mining and virtual living but to a lesser extent.

2. The cost dropped to the point that many people think nothing more of it than they do of paying for electricity, telephone, cable-vision, or newspapers. The catalyst was the mimicking of the support structure for conventional media via advertising-supported search engines such as Google and its less successful cousins. Likewise, news outlets and entertainment venues that moved online for a subscription fee also served ads. It all appeared to be free, or at least cheap, depending on how many streaming services one purchased.

3. Access to these systems via smartphones and tablets of various kinds became so simple that even electronophobes used them routinely without thinking of them as complex or unusual. This requires a high level of abstraction; they became basic tools (not, strictly speaking appliances) rather than complex, difficult-to-use machines.

4. There came to be direct, obvious, and immediate benefits for numerous everyday activities—they save time and money; they are useful and attractive, even addicting.

These conditions developed together, for they interact with and reinforce one another. Improvements in ease of use and lower cost promote more use, and mass acceptance feeds back to encourage economies of scale, fund interface improvements, and encourage other suppliers and consumers to join the growing community. For many in the general population, the latter 1990s and early 2000s saw watershed changes as websites proliferated, for in less than a decade Internet use became an essential part of millions, eventually billions of homes, and sharply divided the generations at first.

This illustrates that there is a critical mass for wide-effect technologies that, when reached, triggers dramatic improvements in all three conditions (cost, ease of access, and perceived benefits), then begins altering the society whose wants gave rise to the technology. Likewise, in previous generations, the automobile went from a bicycle and carriage shop sideline to a toy for the rich. Later, it was raced and used for taxis. However, it had no broad impact on society until increased demand led to mass production, and that in turn lowered prices and increased sales. In two generations Henry Ford's assembly line and its imitators could put a car in every garage and these transformed North American society, but no one could have anticipated the critical conjunction of the necessary attitudes and technologies that made it possible. Similar comments could be made about the impact of the telephone, the television, and the airplane.

Moreover, there is a critical point in the use of a technology beyond which it becomes something other than what it was at first, and this is certainly true of information utilities in general and the Internet in particular. As they stood at the close of the millennium, such facilities largely referenced and duplicated what already existed on paper in various libraries. They enabled faster, broader, and more convenient access to a growing library of information, but this alone did not constitute a breakthrough to a new order.

What would constitute a breakthrough is a facility so extensive, powerful, and cheap that it quickly obsoletes older technologies and simultaneously opens up whole new ways of dealing with information, opinions, and knowledge. The building of such an information appliance requires not simply new types of machines, but new ways of thinking about their use—new information paradigms. Seen in this broader context, the Internet (including the World Wide Web) is a primitive first step along the road to something much more profoundly significant.

We are partly there. As with most hardware-software interactions, the former is more capable than the latter, and in particular, though access to information is technically available, the information store itself is, three decades in, in its adolescence at best. We will delve into some possible futures in the next section.

Profile On . . . Issues

Information and Third World Nations

The Gap

The Third World is so called because of the large economic gap between the industrialized nations of North America, Europe, Australia, and New Zealand on the one hand, and the heavily populated industrially emerging countries of Africa, Central and South America, Eastern Europe, and Asia on the other.

Will the gap narrow or widen?

Optimistic observers believe many nations will leap from their agricultural economies directly to the information age, without an industrial phase. However, information-based economies require sophisticated and efficient industrial bases, and a mostly agricultural economy cannot provide sufficient cash flow to purchase high technology. If rich nations become richer still, and the poor ones cannot quickly catch up, the widening gap will threaten world peace. On the one hand, the disaffected people of poorer nations may launch shadow wars via terrorist activities for economic reasons they have piled atop earlier socio-political-religious ones. On the other, some wealthier and more powerful nations may manufacture pretexts to launch land and resource grabs against poorer ones, such as the one Russia conducted against Ukraine starting in 2022. As two world wars in the twentieth century demonstrate, all nations can easily be drawn into such conflagrations.

Where does the third world get its information?

In 1980, 95.5 percent of printed matter, 95.1 percent of printed books, 85.6 percent of TV sets, 68.1 percent of radios, and 97.9 percent of data processing equipment exports originated in technologically more advanced countries. Shifts in these percentages since have been due more to Western countries moving manufacturing capabilities to low-wage regions to maximize profits, rather than to any technology or decision-making transfers. Television programs are still overwhelmingly American and European in origin.

Three Western World agencies (in earlier editions it was four)—Associated Press, Thomson-Reuters, and Agence France Press—continue to dominate news reporting, so a large percentage of broadcast and printed material remains filtered via London, Toronto/New York and Paris, respectively. However, the medium through which it is consumed changed dramatically as the Internet grew, for the market share of newspapers and other forms of broadcast news has declined rapidly. Moreover, radio and television are now consumed mostly via streaming services rather than as broadcast media.

Also, many people have become more influenced by what they consume on social media than anything else, so the traditional media have gradually shifted from researching and reporting factually on events to presenting editorials geared to the political leanings of their subscribers, thus exacerbating socio-political divides, conflating opinion with truth, and reinforcing prejudices.

A new imperialism?

The technology-driven one-way flow of "information" is infused with the exporters' culture, values, entertainment preferences, political and commercial tastes, and opinion filters. Poorer countries that cannot afford to generate their own extensive entertainment and news networks purchase both from those that can, increasing their economic and cultural dependence. Printing, production, advertising, and packaging are cheaper in English than in any other language (economy of scale), exacerbating disadvantages for non-English speaking countries. On the other hand, universal availability of the same information to everyone inevitably has some homogenizing effect on culture. Is it worth clinging to the old cultures out of a feeling of independence and self-reliance at the cost of eschewing benefits other nations enjoy? The latter alternative has become moot, for it became far easier and cheaper to build Internet access than re-invent information technology on a comparable scale. But the overall issue remains—most of the material accessed on the Internet, like most available academic and commercial information is of Western origin.

Is third-world censorship justified?

Faced with perceived challenges to culture, religion, or top-down control, some nations heavily censor information imports. This may reduce perceived threats, at the cost of making what is allowed more costly and less useful, and of partially isolating that nation from the rest of the world. Censorship is also attempted in times of war or as governments attempt to control the internal narrative of their actions, either overtly by blocking external content or more subtly by subsidizing local content creators with the *quid quo pro* that those so favored will prioritize the ruling clique's narratives. There are ways to evade this for those who know how and in the former case are willing to take the risk, but such are not mass solutions.

Will satellite communications allow poor nations to catch up?

Initially, it appeared that because of their less efficient use of the transponder circuits, these could cost a poorer country much more for the same facility as a richer nation would pay. Moreover, there were a limited number of satellite positions available in geosynchronous orbit, and many were taken early by the richer nations, so even if poorer nations did develop or manage to purchase the necessary technology, they would have to continue to rent space from the countries and corporations that first claimed it. However, communications technology in space became commercialized, almost commodified. Satellite swarms are now in place at lower altitudes, allowing for faster, more reliable connections at competitive prices, thus reducing barriers for all, leveling the playing field, and ensuring that less affluent countries need not re-invent every step, but can access mature technology. Thus, cost barriers for nations have diminished, whether they allow access or censor it.

Does Information Technology have the same effect everywhere?

In a rich democracy, many individuals can obtain information technology to enhance their lifestyle and improve their economic position. In poorer countries, often with no previous democratic traditions, governments are more likely to draw such technology into their own hands and try to control its use. It may therefore have more potential for oppression than for democratization in such nations over the short run. On the other hand, there are ways to work around such controls, and people who want access badly enough can find them. Big Brother can no longer reliably keep Little Sister ignorant of or redefine the outside world if she is sufficiently determined.

Ought poor nations to pay for information?

If information is just a commodity, poorer nations must buy it from the ones that generate it, increasing their dependence. If all knowledge collected by the human race is its common heritage, one could argue it ought not to have a price tag. Some argue necessity: because the poorer nations need knowledge and techniques, they are justified in helping themselves, regardless of the patent, copyright, or property laws in other nations. How can a poor nation obtain what it needs, other than take what is available to the wealthier ones? These comments apply equally to electronic information, especially when one considers that much of it, even if not openly and freely available, is not securely housed.

How valuable are current databases to developing nations?

Industrial nations maintain large databases of scientific and technical information, along with statistics on consumer preferences by age groups, occupation, income, and the like. Much of this is of questionable value in planning product development for developing nations, except to avoid mistakes. The techniques, equipment, and knowledge to make or use some products may not exist there; the demographics are completely different; some products are inappropriate when moved into a new cultural setting; and there may not be enough people at appropriate income levels to make some product sales feasible.

What moral responsibility is there on the part of wealthy nations to share?

Are the market value of a corporate stock, its bottom line profitability, and the corollary demand for a return from information resources and tools (plus taxes paid to government) the highest (or only) values? If so, this implies no obligation to share without a direct return on investment. If the common good of the human race, or a value that requires sharing with the poor is of more importance, information resources ought no more to be hoarded than any other form of wealth. A more pragmatic consideration might be that information resources are almost impossible to keep private and that attempting to do so will lead either to incentivizing theft or threats to peace. Another pragmatic consideration is that ensuring that new technologies get into the hands of poorer nations may enhance trade in many other goods and lead to greater prosperity for all in the long run.

There are many such potential tradeoffs.

4.4 Toward The Metalibrary

Limitations of Current Information Technology

This section is concerned with two major categories of information distribution—the commercial and the scholarly.

In the earliest societies, information was conveyed by imitation and word of mouth. Both work, but in limited quantities, inefficiently, and incompletely. Both remain valuable for demagogues with the power of persuasion, and as teaching techniques, but word of mouth's strengths lie in the personal and relational arenas, and the transmission of attitudes, opinions, values, and memes. Imitation is still best practice when mentoring and teaching technique, that is, for instructing or educating in all manner of abstractions.

As bulk transmission to many people became more important, written records became predominant. Once the printing press was invented, books became the first mass media, and permanently altered societies that could mass produce and distribute them, because they enabled the large scale spread of information, with far less likelihood of any of it vanishing for lack of knowers to pass it on.

These remain important. What has changed are the venues for holding conversations and the media for distributing written materials.

In the Third Civilization, the chief commercial media were printed magazines, newspapers, and books in the print category plus radio and television in the electronic. These were the products of highly developed institutions and were carefully tuned for classes of prospective consumers. As with all institutions, their essential driving mandate was to perpetuate themselves; in common with all commercial enterprises, this goal is most efficiently pursued by paying attention to the bottom line. Correctness, completeness, and consequences are not inherently important to institutional media without some higher controlling ethical imperative, or unless such concerns run parallel to others that impact profits.

Those who control such media can decide whether and when something constitutes news, whether to present factual accounts or editorials, with what bias they report, and whether to identify the nature of any of the algorithms that either inform or automatically make their choices to their customers. If they hold profits to be a higher good than, say, accuracy or truth, then the "news" material their outlets present to the public will be sifted through a profit filter (and therefore a popularity filter) but not necessarily through an integrity one. In such a context, the trivial—glamour, sex, money, power, violence, war, politics, outright lies, and self-gratification—are presented as heroic, for they appeal to the sensual and can sell product. Meanwhile the genuinely heroic—love, kindness, honesty, peace, moral goodness, cooperation, social duty, or alignment with God's priorities—become trivialized; because they lack immediate sensual appeal and profitability. Even if the for-profit media do not necessarily set about consciously to change traditional values for reasons of conviction, they do so inevitably for ones of gain or to maintain alignment with government, lest their license to operate or their subsidies be removed. Moreover, bad news attracts eyeballs where good news does not, and as the eyeballs go, so goes advertising revenue.

However, it is the heroic (other-centered) values that forge bonds between people, giving a society meaning and enabling it to be. Sensual pursuits are selfish, individualist, and isolationist—they eat away at the bonds of society, and if unchecked, can destroy it. Yet the survival of civilization is too distant and vague a goal to influence short-term bottom-line thinking.

Visual media, including commercial movies, television, and streamed videos, are particularly susceptible to the temptation of becoming the advocate of selfish sensuality because video media present the illusion of being "hot" or personally involving, even though they have no feedback mechanism, hence no potential for group dynamics. Their watchers do not participate in the events or stories portrayed but are provided with vicarious illusions that they have the power to do so. The goal of the visual medium therefore needs to be no loftier than the excitement of emotions; it has no inherent mandate to inform, except peripherally. In that milieu, even "news" becomes just as much an entertainment phenomenon as a movie, a weekly series, or a hockey game.

Originally, some thought that visual media's ability to bring the world to one's home would promote global understanding and cooperation, but the medium's individualistic and sensual appeal tends to have very different results—reduced creativity and scope of worldview, and a leveling to mediocrity. Its immediacy brings the random violence of terrorism to the living room and can encourage such acts on the part of those who have no other avenue to satisfy their proclivities. Consistent with its natural sensual appeal, visual media have developed an almost continual portrayal (and linkage) of sex and violence. There is no mechanism in place to assess the effect this has on society and children in particular. At the very least, such portrayal desensitizes viewers to murder, rape, brutality, exhibitionism, violence, and even terrorism. In its sensationalizing of world events, the product of the commercial media can easily become anti-informative, and not even the people who produce it may be aware of this.

Moreover, objectors to what they see have no means of making corrections, because none of the traditional commercial media are interactive. Ratings tell advertisers how many people watch a program, but reveal neither their reaction to it nor the effects it has on their subsequent thinking and behavior. "Ratings" count eyeballs at the moment, nothing else.

Visual media become a substitute reality, overwhelming any messages delivered through them. Nowhere is this fact more obvious than in the fate of several televangelist superstars who lost their message to the glamour and sensuality of the medium in which it was being delivered. Rather than transmitting God's message and changing the world of their viewers one heart at a time, some of them transformed themselves into television entertainer stars, fully entering into the lifestyle and values of the artificial world in which their performances were crafted. Their original message was voided when their lives eventually put the lie to their words. In this they were not alone, for much the same could be said of many stars from the entertainment galaxy, or sports or politics. In sum:

> Commercial media exist to make a profit, not to transmit information.

Another aspect of this information disconnect problem is that the late industrial age media became a closed entertainment system, offering only highly control-belief-filtered versions of currently fashionable world events. Thus "news" was created and managed as much by the media as by the participants in events. To entertain, they focused on the flamboyant, outrageous, and shocking rather than the educating or encouraging, on the negative and dangerous rather than the positive or uplifting, and on the self-serving editorial rather than the informative.

Their very nature is to be oriented to conflict and personality, not information. Moreover, since ownership dictated those policy filters, most mass media outlets became consistently politicized, capable of speaking to and being heard by only their particular constituency, thus exacerbating social divisions rather than promoting community over a broad cross-section of society.

These directions align with what they observed of human nature in the large. After all, people were already inclined to believe whatever they saw and heard from sources with which they aligned themselves politically, without regard to a possible correspondence with reality. It takes work to sift truth from falsehood, and many lack the motivation or the tools to attempt it. A hot soundbite medium suits this mentality perfectly.

The governments of openly anti-democratic nations such as Russia, China North Korea, and many other dictatorships expropriate, create their own radio and television networks, and employ heavy-handed censorship of what is allowed on air. Others airily proclaim themselves the saviors of the media by providing funding in return for favorable reporting.

In other countries, media ownership is divided around political lines and tailors their output accordingly. For instance, in the United States in 2016 and beyond, the most outrageously false political statements easily found widespread acceptance when repeated by specific media outlets to loyal fans, with neither interested in truth.

What is presented as news reporting can become sufficiently biased to create a crisis of non-confidence in itself by the very society that gives it free rein to operate. If such outlets cannot be relied on as factual sources, that is, of information, their product becomes historical fiction—a tapestry of fancy hung upon minimal threads of fact. Stories about events constructed within such a medium reveal more about the thinking of their tellers and consumers than they do about anything that could be called the "real" world.

On the other hand, its supporters will be quick to point out the many benefits of video media such as television and online streaming—the potential for informing, entertaining, educating, and allowing at least vicarious participation in events most people could never attend in person. There are educational channels, family-oriented programs, sports networks, Internet educational and video channels, newscasts serve some purpose, and there is a thriving public television facility—all these indeed serve to mute the criticism above. By extending the choices available to consumers, these alternatives to the standard commercial fare also whet the appetite for what visual media could be if unlimited choice were in the hands of the individual viewer; that is if each person could supply the filters on all available entertainment and news without having most of it pre-digested. That is, video media still have the great informing potential they have always had, even though that potential has not yet been realized because there is little commercial incentive to move toward that goal.

At the same time, and like the other (now) traditional media (newspaper, magazine, and radio), broadcast television may also have reached the limits of its particular technology, and seen the end of its best days. Available time and channel space conspire together with the profit motive to ensure that individual choices from these media are constrained. Enabling unlimited access to basic information, required major technological and social breakthroughs—ones that allowed and encouraged individuals to control their information filters as they shopped unlimited channels.

Thus, the proliferation of streaming applications available from cable, satellite, and "smart" TV sets via the Internet. (Physical video purchases and rentals provided a temporary stopgap along the way, but this mode quickly passed from the scene.) Audio and visual streaming services offer hundreds of channels, both from conventional stations around the world and from a growing stable of their own productions, which now compete directly with those once created by national TV networks and movie studios. It is not difficult to imagine a near-future world that lacks both TV and radio in the broadcast form, with Internet channels and services increasingly not just stepping into the gap, but upping the game.

However, one thing does not change even when movies, radio, and television all move to online channels—the profit motive. Creating content costs a great deal of money, users pay for their content, and once the creative burst accompanying something new wears off, the streaming services will likely simply occupy a merely elaborated "entertainment masquerading as information" niche in people's everyday lives. To sum up:

> **Both old and new audio-visual media are about entertainment for profit, not communicating information.**

Turning to another realm entirely, when one considers the available information channels for scholars, quite different issues surface, for here correctness and completeness are not usually seen as serious systemic issues, although discovery, relevance, and information overload may be.

Today's scholarly libraries—paper and electronic—are added to by millions of book and journal pages a day. The use of book review digests, cross-references, citation indices, and bibliographies can be extremely time-consuming and does not always guarantee the relevant information can be located. Conversely, if what one is looking for cannot easily be found, that does not mean it doesn't exist.

What is worse, just because something is stated in a book on some physical or virtual library shelf does not guarantee its accuracy, despite the general level of community confidence in academic publication. It might be based on poor research or inadequate information. It might be deliberate falsehood, poorly reasoned, obsolete, an opinion the author later withdrew, or such bad scholarship that it isn't even wrong. Not all "journals" have the same level of credibility, and in an atmosphere where publication volume and citations are important currency, there is money to be made providing a facade of both—and with little accountability for the author and "publisher" to the discipline.

Books and papers are always filtered through one or more worldviews before being published, and this means that academic information is no more value-neutral than television entertainment. Correct information on a given subject may be in such a fragmented and widely scattered form that one person can't search enough of it to synthesize an integrated whole from the many parts—one reason why established scholars often put their master's degree students to work collating the available information on an area of research in which they intend to work. Even in electronic research libraries, there are several problems that a new paradigm for information storage and retrieval must be able to solve to create something that constitutes a significant breakthrough.

Enhanced Hypertext

The first step toward solving some of the problems with information access was called hypertext because it added some new dimensions to the online display of textual material. It can add much more to its referencing provided its characteristics eventually encompass:

1. *The ability to follow up a book or research paper directly.* That is, citations and references should be electronically linked to the original work rather than stored in a separate citation index. This means that bibliographies become bidirectional, and their entries have

reference threads (citations) that extend forward from the date of publication as well as backward, automatically.

2. *The ability for readers of a paper or book to attach their own links to individual arguments in a work.* These may lead to entirely different threads if someone else has an appropriate link attached. Naturally, this applies to the original author, who is thereby able to withdraw some points or retract errors, so they do not proliferate through the literature.

3. *The ability to request missing knowledge from others using hypertext.* One could ask for threads to be attached directly to the request if someone can either create or locate the desired information somewhere in the library. Such requests to fill "holes" can be published on their own or attached to other papers by threads in the same manner as citations or comments.

Note: the term "hypertext" has been in use for some time to describe Web-based pages containing mark-up for display (using HTML, XML (plus dialects) and CSS languages) and incorporating links to materials that already existed before the new pages were first published. Even in the first edition of this book, the author had much more in mind; the entirety of the above definition (points 1–3), has not been edited except for clarity over several decades, though the discussion following has been updated several times.

No such advanced facility yet exists for general use for several reasons. First, existing search engines are primarily oriented to consumers, not scholars. Second, no one journal, or at least no one multi-journal organization, has the motivation or resources to index all other journals covering the same research area(s). Third, (therefore) what scholarly databases do exist are both fragmentary and even collectively quite incomplete. Fourth, Internet indexing and searching, while adequate for some consumers, are still in the pre-adolescent growth stages for scholarly materials, tend to be awkward, and lack the advanced hypertext abilities described above for users to attach new forward links to old work or have this happen automatically (the latter an eventual requirement). Fifth, though this is changing rapidly, many journals are at this point not yet available electronically. Sixth, the Internet as a whole community lacks authoritative editorial and peer review processes. This means that scholars can only rely on the journal's prior parallel reputation as a dead tree source, and have few or no means of determining the reliability and authenticity of materials published by new electronic Journals. Seventh, considerable work is yet required to take the relevant search engines from the consumer level to large-scale operation and reliable utility status for scholars' everyday work.

However, enough has been done on precursors to this concept to make it clear that it is both practical and viable. The successes of CSS (Cascading Style Sheets), HTML (HyperText Markup Language), and several related notations and dialects in creating the World Wide Web tantalizingly hint at what might be possible with a more robust scholarly-oriented toolset.

When advanced hypertext as described here does become a comprehensive academic utility, scholars will be able to keep up to date in their fields for the first time in more than a century. Whenever a new work is published, its bibliographic references would automatically generate links from as well as to the older works, so that someone viewing an article in the middle of a chain will be able to move in either direction without consulting a separate referencing tool, rendering the idea of citation indices obsolescent, for that functionality would be built into a scholars' web—something that might have to exist parallel to rather than as a subsidiary of the present web in order to be credible.

Moreover, problems created by vague, incorrect, poorly reasoned, retracted, refuted, or irrelevant papers could easily be remediated. As things now stand, reputable journals employ referees and editors to sift out and reject what they consider low-quality materials before publication. The disadvantage is that it may prevent the publication of radically new ideas just because they are new or because the author is perceived unfavorably by the editor. It can also prevent altogether the publication of ideas not considered politically or religiously "correct" by the editorial establishment. Also, the present system does not allow an author to retract a bad paper once it is in print—at least not in a way that anyone seeking the original would automatically be referred to the retraction.

In an advanced hypertext environment, everything could be published. The author would still choose which journal editors from whom to seek ratings, and each reader would decide how to sift the material. Screening would be easily available, for an individual could set their filters to recognize only the graduated bi-directional links to and from authors with a reputation index for the topic above a set threshold, or those approved by reputable (to them) editors and referees, who do their work after publication rather than before, and who may alter their approval if they have a subsequent change of heart. This could be done by attaching positive or negative rating numbers to author and editor links that could later be raised or lowered.

Editors' links could be removed altogether only if no threads depended on them or if suitable warnings were given to persons who had shown an interest by using the link. This notification would give those users the chance to establish an independent personal link. Naturally an individual's normal settings—to recognize certain editors' ratings or other authors' new links and not others—could be overridden in a search for any new links to the field of interest regardless of whether they were already on their personal "recommended" or "linkable" list. The entries on one's bibliographic lists and reputation index for each work would increase or decrease per the ratings of editors, the approved links to and from other authors, their reputations, and the reputation of the writer.

Researchers could create a personal list of whose recommendations or links their accounts would recognize and at what priority. A person could subsequently reject some of these or approve other links if that seemed desirable. Such filters would grow and change as individual interests did and would make the total body of scholarly work (including all the junk) not only dynamic but also look different to each user. This very growth and change in individual filters could also be automated by appropriate software. Such a system could serve research needs at various levels, for editors' links could also have a difficulty index attached. These indices would determine whether particular items would normally be of use to a grade school, undergraduate, or graduate student, or a professional. People would be free to change their difficulty index on a topical, subject, or global basis as they learn more or as their interests change. Alternatively, they could set the system to change it for them according to actual usage patterns or their own degree or professional status.

In addition, fees could be charged both for publishing and for reading material. An author would pay to have work put on the system, but each time a piece is referenced, the author would be credited with a portion of the fee paid by the reader (the rest of the reading fee would maintain the system). This would also filter out some low-quality material, for few people would continue to pay to publish things that no one read or to read things that had poor ratings from trusted sources.

Note that such a system would not necessarily break down the walls of echo chambers for academics. Unfortunately, it would instead empower them to increase their strength, for they could prohibit other authors' bibliographic entries from attaching to their papers or, if editors, collectively give such negative ratings to some authors as to render them academic pariahs. But denying others a platform to speak is nothing new; the Metalibrary, like today's Internet, and even the older paper journals, in facilitating like-minded communities, also automates the exclusion from those communities of anyone whose views are considered incorrect, not just those manifestly wrong. After all, occasionally subsequent history reverses the two categories. But at least it would allow more ideas the possibility of gaining an audience.

> Freedom of speech can only exist beside the mirrored freedom of refusing to listen.
>
> For reasoned discourse to thrive, unreasoned voices cannot merely be silenced.

The hypertext concept in general is not very new; it originated with Vannevar Bush, Franklin D. Roosevelt's wartime science advisor, during the 1940s. It was not feasible to build Bush's "memex," however, and the idea languished for some decades. The coiner of the modern term "hypertext," Ted Nelson, called a hypertext system plus some of this added publishing facility "hypermedia." His long-running Xanadu project was an attempt to implement such systems on a marketable basis, but despite having many corporate homes, no commercial product resulted. It seems likely, given the magnitude of the task, that an advanced hypertext system is more likely to grow from the collective efforts of researchers and editors already using the Internet, than it is from the workings of one mind, however fertile and energetic. An AI system bent to this task might be of help as well. As it does grow, the challenge will be to maintain the openness of the current Internet while still allowing individual scholars to view the parts they need in a reliably structured academic framework.

Beyond Hypertext—The Metalibrary

If this were all that the next-generation information systems could do, they would be revolutionary enough, for advanced hypertext alone would radically change scholarship, publishing, and current libraries. For instance, paper books and the need to shelve them could eventually cease to exist. The quality and quantity of information could improve dramatically. It would always be possible to find out if a piece of research has already been done, and every scholar would have access to the most current material. A great deal of time would be saved, both in library searches and in preventing unnecessary duplication. Moreover, textbooks could be revised continuously.

However, there is no reason to stop with hypertext. A fourth characteristic could be added to information access to transform hypertext from a scholars' tool into an everyday appliance. It could be given the potential to overcome some of the problems associated with commercial news media by applying the scholars' tools to transfer power to create filters for the public at large. In this view, a parallel network would be unnecessary, as the one web library would encompass all information. The necessary characteristic is:

4. *The ability to link all publications, whether commercial or scholarly and whatever the original medium.*

Before moving on from this point, a definition is in order:

> An (abstract) metalibrary is the entire collection of a society's data, information, and techniques, together with how it is stored, accessed, and communicated.

> The Metalibrary of the Fourth Civilization is the complete, electronically linked and accessed version of its abstract metalibrary together with the means of access.

Note: The concept of a metalibrary of information is quite distinct from that of a "Metaverse" a term coined by Neal Stephenson, popularized in various utopian and dystopian futuristic novels as a supposed immersive virtual reality or Matrix wherein people live out an electronic simulation of life alongside or instead of their physical existence. Facebook rebranded itself as "Meta" in 2021 to suggest it is the carrier of this concept going forward. By contrast, the Metalibrary is not a place where people will live, but a universal library or information source.

Personal data such as what the family has for breakfast, what color the cat is, and one's preferences in clothes, music, and computing languages are not included in a metalibrary, for this definition focuses on the general knowledge and techniques that the culture as a whole uses and communicates. Although every society has a metalibrary of its generally communicable knowledge, it has never before been possible to assemble and index that information in a manner readily accessible to all. Not everyone can physically drop by the Library of Congress, and even those who do might find a search rather daunting (though it, too has a website). From this point on, references in this textbook to the Metalibrary will always be to the prospective fully electronic version.

Such a library could contain and link textual material (books, articles, papers, and newspapers of all kinds), graphics (pictures, art, posters) and sound (music, radio programs). It could also have integrated forms such as movies, TV programs, recorded concerts, sports events, daily news, weather, and sports from around the world, as well as lessons on every subject at every level in a variety of languages or with universal translating ability.

Some of this has been done or is in process. A variety of browser plug-ins already allow sound and video to be a part of Web materials. Little indexing of visual-oriented material has been done thus far, and communications bandwidth would have to be expanded enormously to handle much of it on the scale envisioned above, but what has been done constitutes a move in the direction envisioned here, however primitive it may yet be. Moreover, the necessary communications capabilities were driven to new heights during the COVID era by the demand for video conferencing (teaching, meetings, professional consultations, conferences) so as more indexed video and other live material becomes available for access, the necessary hardware is in place for other reasons.

In the remainder of this book, a hypertext system having this fourth characteristic will be termed *The Metalibrary*. The difference between the two is that *The* Metalibrary allows links to all information of every type and medium, not only to text infused with simple graphics and animations as at present. Moreover, it would serve the general population, not just scholars.

Emerging technology would give the Metalibrary a variety of abilities. Some of the possibilities are detailed below, though not necessarily all would come to pass, for other factors might make them unnecessary or unachievable.

Metalibrary terminals (MTs) would become voice-activated, allow either large wall screens or book-size wireless foldable (like a newspaper) portable units, and be capable of displaying text or color graphics in the same resolution as a printed book. This would make it the preferred publishing medium for such material as *National Geographic* as well as say, the *Journal of Combinatorics*, including all back issues.

For most purposes, such terminals would have the potential to replace books, magazines, newspapers, television, and the telephone with a single inexpensive appliance. It would be possible to ask one's home Metalibrary terminal, "What was the gross national product of Belize each year from 1972 to 1999"? One might expect the answer by voice with a backup hard copy on the closest house screen or printer—all without getting up from one's living room chair, even to activate the video screen embedded in or rolled down upon the wall.

A somewhat more "fuzzily" defined request for, say, a comparison of conservative evangelical and Catholic twentieth-century commentary on the meaning and application of the first chapter of John's gospel should also be processable to produce appropriate results. A properly resourced AI could easily handle this.

Neither would information have to be confined to a textual form or be statistical. The command "give me the national news, topic government" could result in the wall-sized flat screen delivering a series of news items, editorials, and film clips tailored to the request. Everyone could design their own news, weather, and sports show, with different announcers and different emphases. A hockey fan could have an all-hockey sportscast, and a would-be traveller could see the weather for Hawaii or Nice instead of Des Moines, Frankfurt, or Bradner.

The chosen announcer need not have ever read that day's news before a camera, for sufficient information could be stored on the person's voice, inflection, and appearance for the Metalibrary to synthesize a program with any desired person's image appearing to do the reading. If people want Walter Cronkite to do the evening news on December 12, 2046, they could have him. If they want Marilyn Monroe, her electronic persona could do it instead. The more narcissistic could have sufficient personal films and voice recordings made to anchor the news for themselves.

User interests as requested in actual operation would determine to some extent what current items were available, but once the growing technology allowed sufficient storage, there would be no need ever to remove an item from the Metalibrary once it had been recorded. Someone who had gone fishing could catch up on a whole week's news (relevant to their interests) on returning.

Movies, including ones now shown first in theaters, could be accessed in the same manner. For the usual access fee, "The Sound of Music," "Ben Hur," "Bambi" or "Rocky XXI" could be ordered and shown in one's own home. Parents would be able to instruct their house computer about what, if anything, their children could order. What was once called television series episodes would be obtained in the same manner, though the lines between the TV, streaming, cable, and movie industries are already quite blurred, and will soon vanish. Producers of a given series would advertise their latest creation and the day when each episode would first be available for viewing. Each family could make up its schedule of movies, news, comedy, drama, hockey, or baseball, and so on—watching when convenient for them, not according to any national or local schedule. Some of this can already be done on streaming services.

Commercials, however, would probably be inserted at viewing time by the streaming service, though a premium already can be paid to bypass this. On the other hand, it might become economical for advertisers to pay viewers to look at their commercials. Ratings could be compiled daily, weekly, and monthly, and cumulated long-term on actual rather than estimated use. Since the information highway that is the Metalibrary's infrastructure already has sufficient lanes (bandwidth for channels) to transmit multiple movies to a home simultaneously, and this is constantly improving, it will have the advantage of universal selection and easy accessibility for all members of the household simultaneously.

Books can already be printed a page at a time on a screen of convenient size for conventional reading, but their contents could be acted out by synthesizing characters cast at the request of the user, who could take the starring role personally if desired. The same is true of school lessons or university lectures that could be studied through a Metalibrary terminal, as most were through the pandemic years. An interesting task for future technicians would be to make these lectures interactive so that the students' questions would immediately be answered by the synthesized teacher on the screen. More difficult enquiries could be deferred to the next lesson and read into the database by a live expert advising the session. These questions and answers, once recorded, would remain available for the next student with similar interests. In the view of some, such a facility could eventually replace schools, colleges, and universities, though implementing this would take longer than would more mundane database functions. On the one hand, the synthesized "teacher" would know everything available to know on the subject; but on the other, there would be no social interaction with other students, and no personal mentoring possible ... unless, as in the author's fiction, classrooms were virtualized as follows to simulate personal attendance and provide interaction.

Picture a student going to a library room for a lesson, sitting in one of a circle of chairs, with perhaps one or two other live students present, maybe even the teacher. As the class begins, the other chairs are filled virtually as students' images in their local classrooms are 3-D projected into the other chairs until all are filled—not necessarily in the same order around the room in every location. Why pre-assign chairs, when in each physical setting the chairs can be projected filled to accommodate the in-person ones in the chairs they chose? The teacher could then interact with all the students personally in the same manner as if all were physically present in the same actual room. No doubt some "schools" and their teaching staff would become more elite than others, but the general education offered could be free to the students, and admission to the better programs and classes by scholarship only. Of course, the system would be capable of projecting each student in the school's uniform, regardless of what they were actually wearing.

Wall screens could be used to download, store, and display (for a fee) great works of art in homes and offices. When the renter of the art changed the pictures, the rental contract with the owner of the original art would cease (no fixed term) and a new one would commence—all billed automatically. Eventually, an entire house might be decorated in this fashion, with whole walls being massive screens that projected suitable wallpaper intermingled with art collections, any part of which could also show the evening news. Once three-dimensional projectors became available, the projected images of sculptures could also be rented through the Metalibrary. New television shows or movies, as well as live events, would become available in three dimensions; in fact, such technology may well be among the first of these used (although this would require vastly greater bandwidth than conventional movies).

At the same time, Metalibrary services to professionals will be expanded, and the number of jobs depending on banked information will grow. Anyone still having a desk would have a Metalibrary outlet—probably supplied by the same utility as the one at home, but with a smaller screen (or 3D projection volume). For people on the move, a pocket unit would serve as well, but in even less space.

THE INFORMATION REVOLUTION

As in other mature industries, the number of information providers (or at least infrastructure providers) would shrink as their scope grew. In all likelihood, three or four competing Metalibrary utilities would emerge to replace the current patchwork of small companies that now provide one or more pieces of the puzzle (content provision, rental of images and programming, delivery by cable or satellite), but customer equipment already allows for multi-channel, multi-provider reception in easy-to-install-and-use devices, switching easily from one to the other as the user requests. To the end user, it already appears much like a single system.

It should be clear that the Metalibrary, primitive as it is at this point, will prove to be as revolutionary as Gutenberg's printing press. It is poised to become at once a knowledge machine, entertainer, teacher, home decorator, library, and communications device. While this cluster of functions will develop from current smartphones, TVs, and streaming boxes over time, it is clear that there will be many more disruptions in traditional industries, jobs, and patterns of living.

The same utility that is built to improve access to information—so that individuals can find out what it is that people collectively know—will by the facilities it offers cause a massive reorientation of several industries and almost everyone's life. It is uncertain at this point what all the effects will be because not all possible Metalibrary facilities will come into being exactly as described here. However, this examination may provide some indication of the possibilities, given current technologies and established progress in these directions to date.

The Metalibrary described here is not mere speculation. It is partially extant already (albeit in a primitive form) in the many interconnected networks of government, academic, utility, and industry information systems that even now exist, on the one hand, and in the array of reception devices already in use on the other. The largest piece—properly linked and indexed universal content—is still missing. Furthermore, what has been described here are emerging tools and techniques—ones that enable the manipulation of older data and the generation of new information. The Metalibrary is *both* information and the tools to access it—some of which are already present on the Internet in modest quantity and via less comprehensive tools.

In this book, the term Metalibrary will normally be used to refer to a metalibrary that has at least some substantial subset of the tools and facilities discussed in this section. Where there may be some ambiguity, the term "full Metalibrary" may also be used to emphasize that it is not simply the information content being referred to, but also a set of techniques for universal access to the entire human universe of public information.

4.5 The Accuracy and Security of Information

Universal accessibility of information does not come without problems. As individuals, corporations, and governments make growing use of data repositories, many older difficulties are exacerbated, and new ones arise. Such problems have been widely reported by the popular media from the first days of the Internet, but as more people use more stored information more often, the number of those who can be adversely affected, and the potential severity of damage from misuse of the Metalibrary also increase. Indeed, information accuracy and security are genuine issues only if truth in information and privacy for personal information are broadly held values; otherwise, the discussions in this section are moot.

Personal Information Accuracy

As things now stand, it is not always possible for individuals to know whether information about themselves exists, or where it is stored, much less what such a file contains. There are many ways in which errors can creep into files, there to remain for years unchallenged, all the while affecting people's lives. Credit rating, job prospects, accessibility to government services, and travel opportunities can all be influenced by incorrect information on file. Such mistakes arise in several ways, the most common being through typographical errors, malice, guilt by association, or an incomplete or flawed system.

Truth . . . or not

More generally, the proliferation of potential information sources does not imply increased uniformity, accuracy, or reliability for the contents of those channels. On the contrary, because they also enable the universal proliferation of error, distortion, rumor, and fabrication in opposition to facts (even terming such "alternate truth"), the new channels tend to enable community echo chambers, wherein people inclined to particular views can reinforce their group beliefs in mistaken or dangerous non-information by accessing only sources with which they are already sympathetic, so deliberately interchanging the false with the true, and dismissing all others' acceptance of fact as delusions allegedly engendered by the scientific, government, academic, and/or media establishments conspiring to control the populace.

Malice

A neighbor or worker who has been offended in some way might deliberately place false information into another's record—either by entering it directly, say, as a credit bureau employee, or by complaining to authorities and having an investigation undertaken. For instance, an anonymous tip that an individual has been molesting neighborhood children could get one's name onto a list of potential suspects regardless of whether any evidence was offered, and without the targeted person knowing about it for some time. One could also get into police molester files through evidence in a divorce case, where the temptation to offer false evidence in custody hearings is very great.

In many countries, government security agencies compile lists of people considered to be risks because of their political views or their membership in organizations deemed subversive or terrorist. Unions and corporations have also been known to maintain "blacklists." Unless denied a visa or a job, the person might never suspect such records exist. Some people promote hate against individuals, organizations, religions, or ethnic groups; others make lists of those they claim to be promoting error or hatred or have different political or religious views, and in turn, vilify them or provoke violence against them.

The practice of breaking into corporate or government systems, encrypting the data to make it inaccessible to the owner, or copying sensitive personal information and threatening to make it public unless a ransom is paid has become common. The fault often lies in poorly thought out password practices, and bad hardware and software security measures, and is exacerbated by sloppy or nonexistent backup regimens.

Typographical Error

A clerk who types a slightly misspelled name in an arrest record or adds an extra zero to a balance owed can set off a chain of embarrassing events for the person affected. Police databases are not generally public, and correcting their mistakes may be difficult or impossible. Changing faulty financial records, especially ones affecting credit scores or government ones such as taxation files, can be a formidable and costly task, consuming much time and substantial legal costs.

Guilt by Association

An innocent party who happens to share an airplane seat with or live next door to a known terrorist could be entered into an international police file and classified as a security risk, denied government jobs, or forbidden to travel to other countries—all without knowing why. Because such files are kept secret by the authorities who maintain them, it can be extremely difficult to find out what has happened and to correct the problem.

Incomplete Systems

There are numerous examples of large systems in which information once entered is never updated, verified, or removed when it becomes out of date. For instance, police departments routinely record arrests, but may not follow up with a court's disposition of cases. Likewise, reported thefts are recorded, but recovery of goods may not be. A person could report a car as stolen one day, have it recovered the next by the police, and be arrested on the third for driving a stolen car. With that cleared up, a promised job could suddenly be denied on the fourth day because a check of arrest records indicates a positive match. The individual may never fully understand what has happened.

Some jurisdictions have already recognized these problems and passed laws to deal with them, but protection from inaccurate or incomplete information is very poor in most parts of the world. Such cases illustrate the adage: "A little knowledge may be worse than none."

One of the more spectacular illustrations (at least in prospect) of incomplete systems was the so-called "year 2000 problem" (Y2K) or "millennium bug." Caused in large part because many software and hardware systems recorded only two digits (not the century) for the date, such systems had the potential to cause disruptions in all industries dependent on personal data that included dates, such as banking and government record systems. With the clocks on such systems set to roll over to January

1, 2000, some could have used the date as if it were 1900, throwing off calculations of interest, pensions, and identification systems, and rendering inoperative many real-time devices (bank machines, equipment controllers) that depended on using the time and date for their correct operation. Much work went into repairing this problem beforehand, however, and actual effects turned out to be minimal, though several other problematic dates for long-standing computing clocks are yet to arrive.

Bugs

Hardware and software designs are never perfect. Errors in chip design, computer assembly, network connections, software, security systems, poor backup practices, or incautiously performed updates can destroy or prevent access to critical data.

Solving Information Accuracy Problems

The Y2K problem had to be solved, and was in good time, but cost large sums of money and drove up programmers' salaries and lawyers' fees for a few years while the work was done. It also had the potential (or, so it was thought) to cause disruptions in government, banking, general commerce, and the operation of much automated or robotic equipment.

As for some of the others, up to a point, all these types of problems are likely to become worse. However, with the advent of universal information accessibility, everyone could be given access to all files relating to them, regardless of who has created the file. Provided a person checks periodically to see what has been filed—particularly before applying for a job—the problems of inaccurate information could (in theory) be nearly eliminated. Ideally, all personal information would be stored in a single place, with access to individual items available only to qualified authorities or by permission of the person named in the file. Even better, the system could contain a program that electronically mailed peoples' files to them whenever the contents were changed.

However, this is ideal. In an actual society, it is impossible to control all abuses. It is too much to hope that reorganizing the form of and the access to information will be sufficient to prevent the kinds of problems described here (and new ones) from recurring. Only a conscious effort to build carefully designed system safeguards would offer individuals security from bad personal information. After all, the mere computerization of a careless and flawed data system often makes its problems worse, not better, as many a university and business can testify.

Moreover, the centralization of personal information even to make it accessible and changeable for the person it names is itself dangerous, for it gives the controllers of the system containing that information the potential for great power over everyone. Who gate keeps the gatekeepers?

Profile On . . . Issues

Information Correctness

When a search for information returns results that are incorrect, or a data security flaw allows a crime to be committed there can be serious consequences for reputations, loss of income, or even physical danger.

Who owns data?

- Does personal information belong to the individual or organization that entered it, the data bank that stores it, the person it is about, or to no one at all?

- Is government-gathered statistical information the property of the state, or does it belong to each person in the state?

- Is corporate data the private property of the company in question, or are the shareholders entitled to it? the customers? the state?

    Examples: Should the magnetic coding system for bank machine cards be public information? What about prison records? medical records? school records? Financial holdings? tax information? marriage, divorce, birth, and death records?

- Is it the ownership or the possession of data (or neither) that carries with it the responsibility to ensure its correctness?

- Does "news" information belong to the people named in the story, the reporter who gathers it, the wire service that assembles it, the media outlet that distributes it, the state in which it is disseminated, or to no one?

- Suppose a gene that confirms immunity to a serious disease (such as AIDS) is discovered in a person's DNA. Who owns this information—the person in whose body it resides, or the researcher or corporation that discovered the presence and effect of the gene?

Who is (ought to be) responsible?

- If a bank relies on incorrect credit data and so denies a loan, causing the customer a loss, is the bank liable? the credit agency, the individual who entered the faulty data?
- If the security facilities of a system are inadequate, allowing one user to defraud another with the system, is only the perpetrator liable, or are the owners of the system as well? What about the manufacturers of the hardware and software? The retailers?
- If a stolen bank card can be used by the thief because the owner has written the PIN access number on the card, is the owner partly liable?
- If an investment company continues to do business with the public while concealing its poor financial state, who is responsible when the firm collapses? only the principals of the firm? the regulatory authorities who failed to monitor the situation closely enough? a journalist who knew the truth, but was afraid to print it and so trigger the collapse? the investors, who ought to have been more cautious and done some due diligence?
- If a commercial program is faulty and causes damage to a business, are the publisher and author of the program liable? What if the package had a statement disclaiming such consequential damages? What if the copy in question had been pirated rather than purchased?
- When incorrect conclusions are drawn because data is incomplete, what liability attaches to the aggregator or user of the data?
- When an AI replies to a query with an eloquently phrased but entirely false answer, who is responsible? the creator of the false data relied upon? the creator of the AI? the client of the AI?

PART TWO | FOUR WAVEFRONTS ON A SEA OF CHANGE

What about compensation?

When economic or other loss is caused to some party due to incorrectly stored or stated information, who ought to compensate the injured person? (the one who caused the error, the party who ran the storage system, the one who used the data, or no one?) Does it make a difference if:

- the data was maliciously entered wrongly? accidentally?
- the data was changed because of a machine fault with no human intervention?
- the data was incorrectly processed into information because of faulty software?
- the data had been allowed to become outdated?
- the correct data was destroyed accidentally by human carelessness? by the action of a computer virus designed to destroy the data? by a malicious hacker?
- rather than losing money, the injured party lost a job opportunity? her children in a divorce case? her reputation?
- the injured party never discovered the error, but someone else did?

Who has jurisdiction (Where does the crime take place?)

- when a computer crime is committed over the Internet using a distant device across state or provincial lines? national borders?
- if data (such as pornography) that is stored in one country is used in or triggers a crime causing death in another country?
- if an electronic copy of data is stolen in one state or country, then taken to another where a paper copy is made, then to a third where the data is used for the first time?
- when a "hacker" creates a virus, turns it loose on a network, and thousands of computers all over the world suffer loss of data?
- over the information owned by a multinational company with headquarters in one country and branch offices in others? Can one government order the firm to comply with its laws outside its borders? What if so doing would cause it to break the laws of other countries where it operates?

Technical Legal Issues

- Is electronically stored data tangible? If it is not a "thing," can it have value? Can it be stolen? How does this apply to cryptocurrencies?
- If funds are embezzled from many sources using a single program that generates many illicit transactions by running in a loop, is this one crime or many?

Who (or what) is the victim

- when money is stolen from a bank machine? (A machine is not a person; is the element of deceit (of a person) necessary for fraud?)
- when false data is used to win an election, claim fraud that never happened, engineer (or prevent) a merger, or kite stock prices?

The author disclaims all notions that the above list is even close to exhaustive, and takes no responsibility for anyone who relies upon it as such.

Privacy

Observations about correctness immediately lead to questions about who ought to have access to personal information. It seems at times that one must not only assume that government and private companies know every intimate detail of the lives of ordinary citizens, but also make the same assumption about the nine-year-old down the street with a computer or phone and an Internet connection in her bedroom. Although it may be possible to establish a system of safeguards that require the permission of the subject before personal information could formally be obtained and used, the spread of such data may not ever be controllable in its entirety, for information exists in many locations, and can be transferred to many more. Some of these are less secure than others or have unscrupulous owners. Any system that was sufficiently comprehensive to enforce rules about personal data access would by its very existence pose a threat to privacy greater than any it could prevent. Since criminals will also use data facilities, it is also not hard to imagine someone setting up, say, a blackmail data bank to store sensitive or embarrassing personal information for sale to the highest bidder. Indeed, the Internet is replete with identity theft specialists, and much personal information, particularly in the form of passwords, is always available on the dark web.

There was a time when personal information was not readily available. A president of the United States could be a notorious womanizer and the news media collectively choose not to report it. A member of Parliament could hope that an old police record would never surface. A vice-presidential candidate could keep hidden a one-time stay in a mental institution, and a would-be senator could keep secret a string of shady business deals or underworld connections. A high official could have an affair with a secretary or a student intern and not be found out. The past could be hidden and forgotten, whether it included unusual sexual practices, divorce, illegitimate children, molestation, abuse, bankruptcy, tax fraud, a criminal record, failure in school, a dishonorable military discharge, cowardice, bad judgement, the misappropriation of funds, a faked resume, or a collection of traffic violations large enough to fill a car.

Today, investigative reporters armed with browsers can discover all these things and more in public records (today's primitive Metalibrary). In the society of the future, everyone will have to assume that all details of their past and present life, however embarrassing, are a matter of public record. For those in the public eye, whether as government, corporate, or union leaders or as professionals in positions of trust, life is therefore becoming much more an open book than it was in the past. For better or worse, the ability to forget the embarrassments of one's past is nearly extinct. Thus, it is hard to say whether having the full Metalibrary would make blackmail any more or less likely. If all information is readily available, there can be little embarrassment in having it revealed, for it could never have been concealed in the first place.

Whether anyone will care about others' morality, past deeds, or judgement is a separate question. When such information is so readily available, the result could well be a cynical and jaded public that, hearing about the private lives of the rich and famous, turns a blind eye to morality altogether.

After all, moral blindness is already in play when people deliberately spread falsehoods about those they wish to bully or dehumanize, the legitimacy of elections, their political opponents, vaccines, the efficacy of "snake oil" treatments, or get-rich scam schemes. The perpetrators lack any ethical sense and rely on their victims to be likewise lacking in the ability to determine right from wrong, truth from falsehood, information from disinformation, science from speculation, and reality from fantasy. Just as bad money drives out good, misuse of the Internet has already shown us that misinformation substantially devalues objective truth for far too many people, rendering them easy marks for enterprising con artists whether of the political or financial stripe.

Moreover, what would be left of a right to privacy in a world where all information and its imitations were universally available? Only that which leaves no record behind. Since many people would choose to have their home Metalibrary terminal monitor activities inside the house as well as their use of what is available in the outside world, there might be very little human activity that is not recorded in some manner. At the place of work, performance monitoring is increasing, and more information is retained about individual commercial transactions. While there may be some restrictions, it becomes easier to imagine the state (or society collectively and informally) gathering the power to continuously record all the activities of every person. This could initially be justified in terms of law-and-order enforcement efficiencies, for every criminal would be documented, or to keep health records against the spread of disease. However, the corresponding possibility for absolute state control over every citizen cannot be ignored.

Even at present, a record of every credit card transaction is kept by the card issuer. While little could be done in the past to systematize such records because of their sheer number, the technical obstacles are melting away even as the perceived rewards to merchants and card issuers are seen to become more tempting. After all, if you know who buys what kind of goods, you can target advertising very cost-effectively and efficiently, and this alone makes keeping and analyzing such records worthwhile.

Governments already collect and sell information from census records to those seeking to advertise to neighborhoods housing a preponderance of their target audience. Where does cooperation on amassing, collating, and providing data in such public-corporate partnership ventures lead? Where does government-industry cronyism lead if not to a kleptocracy like the one Russia was by 2020?

If all that was done was the elimination of cash so that every retail transaction was on record, it would then be impossible for any person to effectively hide anything significant. An institution (governmental or not) that could know everything could also control everything. In such a scenario, one could easily imagine that a "universal person code" could be placed on the hand of every citizen, to be passed over the supermarket scanners along with the beans and bread—permanently recording all human activity. Not only that but humanity itself can now be recorded in the form of each individual's DNA. That exactly such a society would one day exist was predicted by the Apostle John writing in the first century A.D.

> "He also forced everyone, great and small, rich and poor, free and slave, to receive a mark on his right hand or on his forehead, so that no one could buy or sell unless he had the mark . . . "
> Revelation 13:16–17a (NIV)

It is not difficult to see that the technology to institute an Orwellian 1984-style state does exist and that such collectivizing trends are present.

Is Data Encryption the Answer to Privacy Issues?

Some think it is, and have great confidence in methods such as the RSA algorithm, whose encrypted files allegedly cannot be decrypted by brute force techniques in any reasonable time.

The optimists are mistaken, for two reasons. If a state legislates control over the strong encryption of data, and forces vendors of such products to give the state "backdoor keys" to decode any data back to plain text, there cannot be privacy of data or communication. Initially, the technology for message and file encryption became sufficiently widespread even by the late 1990s that it could not then be controlled—government officials simply had not realized what was happening as yet. More recently, however, governments have pressured big tech companies to give them the tools to break into the phones of alleged criminals. Some have cooperated in some instances, others not, but most legislation around data privacy is aimed at private entities, not the state, and since the latter can prevail in such situations, it will prevail.

Second, the advent of quantum computing on a large scale will alter this situation considerably as the computing power both to encrypt and to break encryption ramps up. Where that saw-off might end is somewhat uncertain, but the power to decrypt quickly is the more important of the two, even if quantum encryption is employed in the first instance. Computer break-in artists of a given day will undoubtedly stash stolen encrypted data against the day when newer methods empower its straightforward decryption, and use, sell, or demand ransom from an owner who never suspected it had been stolen. It is better to enhance security so the data does not get stolen in the first place.

THE INFORMATION REVOLUTION

Big Brother and Little Sister

When we consider a possible contrary view, the effect of universal information availability upon governments may prove to be neutral or even positive. There may even be greater democracy, for there is a counterbalance promoting individualism. While there is the potential for increased government control of information, individual access to knowledge of government activities is also enabled. So too could the opportunities for citizens to express themselves and change the course of government. Some envision a participatory democracy emerging—one in which citizens have daily opportunities not merely to express opinions, but to mine government data and use that knowledge to decide the issues rather than leaving all decisions to their representatives.

Thus, even while people lose some ability to act as "private" citizens, governments may also lose much of their capacity to operate arbitrarily and in secret. That is, loss of personal privacy does not necessarily imply a gain in centralized power—it could simply mean that nothing can be hidden from anyone.

This could also frighten away from public office those with a seamy past to hide. However, since no one has a perfect past, perfect judgement, or perfect morality (in everyone's eyes at once), the effect even upon the aspirations of society's leaders might not be very great. People could judge others (including their leaders) for who they were in the present and what they might be in the future rather than for their past.

Two more extreme responses are possible. On the one hand, standards of behavior for people in the public eye could come to include a stricter practice of moral actions. A swing of the pendulum towards a comprehensive and rigid moral legalism of the type popularly attributed to the Victorian era seems improbable but could not be ruled out. But the specific "rules" of that legalism could be fluid, changing according to current consensus opinion on morality.

On the other hand, a variation of antinomianism is already prevalent among modern liberals. This is the notion that in many areas of human activity, the idea of morality is simply irrelevant. This is usually phrased specifically in terms of tolerating alternate lifestyles, but there is no effective difference between positing all moral systems as equally valid and saying that none are meaningful. Although this position, as always, carries with it the logical contradiction that it tolerates everything except disagreement with itself, it has nonetheless become a popular response to the "outing" of information with moral overtones. Indeed, it has become so popular that it is today the control belief in this arena, threatening the freedom or the very existence of those who hold that moral issues are important—especially if they claim publicly that such are absolute.

Whatever the outcome, the implications for the information age are profound—actions will be public, and so will be any moral judgements of them (or the lack of such judgements).

Turning from the actions of individuals in government to those of the state itself, there are similar tensions between the desire for secrecy and the need to gather and manage information. Although most people in the Western world do not want comprehensive statism, the opposite extreme—no government, only daily electronic democracy—is probably too unstable and discontinuous to work. What is the law one morning might not be in the afternoon, and be reversed again the next day.

The most likely outcome is a situation involving gains and losses to both privacy and democracy—not a swing of power to either the individual or the state, but a realignment that changes both. Information availability does create the potential for a new kind of tyranny, but it also provides for new kinds of checks and balances by giving the individual citizen greater knowledge and therefore more power. The two trends may not simply cancel each other out, because an open information society will be very different, but these trade-offs between privacy and knowledge may well become generally accepted and consequently little remarked upon.

Another possibility is that power over information storage and transmission will become concentrated in the hands of a few technology managers and corporate suppliers. Such developments are commonly advocated to achieve efficiency, security, or convenience, but these are not the central issues. Control is. Given the lessons of history, one must assume that where there is centralized control, there will inevitably be an abuse of power, regardless of whose hands hold the reigns of power and how or why they obtained it. To date, information technology has had a largely decentralizing and democratizing effect, but there is no reason to suppose this situation will last. Those who wish little brother and sister to win out in the long run must be diligent to retain their freedoms or they will surely lose them. They already have in some countries, and will surely soon in more.

THE INFORMATION REVOLUTION

Why Privacy?

The ethical question here relates to the fundamental basis for the desire for privacy. Is privacy a fundamental human right, or is it merely a culturally derived preference? One could argue on religious grounds, for example, that since human dignity and self-esteem are at stake, the greatest possible amount of privacy ought to be granted to other people to affirm their value. On the other hand, one could argue that the New Testament requires the people of God to be an open and transparent community and that they ought, therefore, to have no secrets from one another. One could even argue that both principles are true and do not contradict each other.

Privacy and E-mail

People routinely use email for the communication of potentially sensitive materials—plans, opinions, finances, and personal information—without seeming to realize that unless such messages are encrypted, they are not private. After all, they may travel through a dozen or more systems before reaching the recipient, and the system operator at every one of those stops along the way can intercept and read the message. E-mail therefore presents a greater security risk than does the potential for tapping telephone conversations, for in most cases there are more access points available with e-mail. Even when sent through an organization's own servers, the local IT staff can easily access such messages.

Moreover, e-mail is discoverable in a legal case. When an entity is sued over some issue at dispute, it can be required to deliver all parties' e-mails to the courts for scrutiny (implying they must be stored against that eventuality). Best to walk to the other person's office and discuss the matter personally than to commit potentially damaging words to permanent electronic storage. One then only need be concerned that the office in question hasn't been bugged, and the recipient of the visit has refrained from surreptitiously recording the conversation.

Data Security

At the corporate and government levels, it may at first be somewhat easier to keep information confidential than at the personal level, for there will be fewer copies and these will be stored in more carefully guarded systems, not (initially) readily available through the public Metalibrary. However, sophisticated computerized analysis of the activities of business and government even now leaves them with few secrets of the quantifiable kind. Any skilled individual should be able to analyze the market share and profitability of most companies. Indeed publicly traded companies must report such information. The trick will be to keep one's plans for the future secret for as long as possible.

Moreover, the proliferation of international corporations and the consequent increases in money, data, and technology flows across national boundaries make it much more difficult for governments to control corporate activities. This is already illustrated by the international banking system, within which large sums of money are routinely shifted from one country to another instantaneously and without much possibility of government intervention on the detailed level. Even today, no one nation or group of nations can be said to control the banking system. Thus, the ability to retain some financial information within national boundaries has already all but vanished in the Western nations and could also do so eventually in the more closed East.

Governments will still attempt to keep national security, taxation, and military information secret. Corporations, credit providers, and banks will need to guarantee the security and integrity of some information they store, just to survive. Ultimately, government and corporations must also operate in a more open environment, for it will become progressively harder to keep anything out of the public view. A secrecy-oriented government can keep data, fax machines, and photocopiers under lock and key, and track every sheet of paper they produce for only just so long. Once it develops its appetite for the efficiency of information machines and acquires several thousand information storage and transmission devices, effective control becomes all but impossible. As those old paper files become digitized, the security stakes are multiplied. Given sufficient time, patience, and the right tools, almost any computer security can be broken.

This is not good news for those who desire to keep at least some information confidential. Almost daily, there are reports of numerous incidents of computer security violations at government or corporate installations, both by insiders and by enterprising hackers without. Freebooters have rummaged through medical records, corporate finances, and even military files. Insiders have stolen data for competing companies or nations, and saboteurs have destroyed whole installations.

The victims of these violations have learned from their woes and tightened up their poor security somewhat. Inside personnel are screened more closely on hiring and may be searched when leaving the job site. Passwords are checked regularly and not left lying around (or are they?), and backup copies of important files are made regularly and stored in secure, off-site locations. Memory sticks brought in are routinely scanned for virus programs that could destroy data. Critical installations often have an entire physical duplicate, usually in another city, so that service to customers can continue uninterrupted even through an explosion or fire at the main data center (this is standard banking practice).

As security consciousness increases and governments attempt to control data flow across borders, some countries may set up data havens, much as they now establish tax havens. There will also be an increase in data traffic (buying and selling) on a very large scale, as economic, legal, and consumer files are copied from owner to owner.

The net long-term result will surely be even greater data availability on an international basis and a general breaking down of national borders in favor of a more global view of information. While this is tending to make Western societies more open in some ways, it sounded the death knell for the old closed societies of the communist world, and will eventually do so again for the state capitalist ones that succeeded them in Russia and China, as well as the assorted dictatorships that spring up with monotonous regularity around the world, and die richly deserved deaths with those of the strongman who established them. The very efficiency of information techniques mitigates against a tightly controlled society. The widespread availability of information is inimical to totalitarian forms of government, and a computer and Internet connection are even more deadly enemies to statism than a photocopier. Perhaps the best way to hasten the fall of tyranny is to ensure that it is well supplied with photocopiers, computers, and telecommunications equipment.

Thus, on balance the information age may favor the individual, but nagging doubts remain. The gains available through individual access to information imply a corresponding loss of privacy. Are the trade-offs fair? Can sufficient people learn how to differentiate between truth and lies well enough to prevent tyranny from being established? Will Big Brother still end up watching? Will the millions of "little brothers and sisters" triumph? Will people have any vestige of personal privacy, or will everyone be able to know everything about everyone else? The answers to these questions will vary from time to time and country to country, but the extreme scenarios now seem somewhat less likely than that some middle course will instead be charted.

4.6 Information Analysis and Decision Making

Even in the fully realized Metalibrary, universal accessibility of information does not in itself solve practical problems. Finding solutions is a multistage process resembling the scientific method that leads from raw data, first to knowledge and understanding, thence to weighing alternatives and consequences, and finally to decisions. Moreover, discovering knowledge and making decisions are not necessarily on the same path, or done by the same person, but are often nearly independent of each other.

The full Metalibrary, like present-day paper libraries, provides material for the first step in the process, by supplying and potentially organizing raw data by category and giving users tools to relate the data to other categories, analyze it, and record conclusions or argue with those drawn by others. All this is done now in scientific journals, though not very efficiently. However it may take place, a community or collective consideration of data is necessary before information can be derived from it. Indeed, it has been in high-density, strongly interactive population concentrations that great new ideas took root and flowered in the past, and there is a sense in which the Metalibrary makes the entire Earth into a single city, albeit not one with a uniform culture, ethics, type of government, or way of thinking.

When the subject matter can be described in quantitative terms (chemistry, cell biology, economics, and demographics), the first step is to establish what are the facts, that is, what data are valid and what information they convey. Expert forums operate through today's journals (and tomorrow's Metalibrary) to achieve consensus on what those facts are, given the data available.

However, managers and other administrators often need to make decisions long before there is widespread consensus about what the pertinent information means. Ostensibly, such a manager makes decisions based on available information about history and probable or foreseeable consequences. On the other hand, two people may easily make different decisions under the same circumstances. Here are a few examples:

1. The task is to implement a trial version of a universal corporate database. The problem is to decide who should have access to what information. The company hires a lawyer and a computer scientist to advise. Their recommendations flatly contradict each other; one wants tight controls, the other a completely open system.

2. A bank determines that it requires a new computerized billing system for its expanded safety deposit department. Extensive studies are run, and software is chosen to control the database. But many compatible machines can run this software, including brand I, brand A, and brand U. Systems from all three vendors are tested and the results charted. Brand A comes out on top in price and performance, with brand I second and U third. The branch manager then overrules the selection committee's recommendation and decides to buy brand I, because the desktop presently in her office is from the same company and she values brand loyalty higher than price or performance.

3. The Fraser Valley Library acting on recommendations from the Ministry of Human Resources, has decided to build a branch to serve a slum neighborhood of Aldergrove. The only available property is an old park adjacent to a heritage building, formerly the residence of a certain well-known author. Psychologists, social workers, and government officials claim that dramatic improvements in similar slums have always resulted when a library was built. They insist that the house and park ought to be sacrificed. Historians and local community leaders point to community pride for one of theirs who made good, as well as to the benefits of the park for their children. They do not deny the potential value of the library but hold that the value of the house and park are greater, intangible though that value may be. The recommendations are again contradictory.

4. During World War II, the British scored an intelligence coup by breaking the German Enigma coding scheme and routinely translating military messages from the opposite side. According to an oft-repeated apocryphal story, one night, the decoded message contained instructions to bomb the city of Coventry at a particular time. British Prime Minister, Winston Churchill, knew that many lives could be saved if he evacuated Coventry. He also knew that this move would reveal to the German High Command that their secrets had been breached, and the codes would immediately be

changed. By the time the British could decipher the new ones, many more lives could be lost on the battlefront than could be saved at Coventry. A utilitarian, Churchill did not warn the city; the bombs came, and civilian lives were lost. An act-oriented ethic would have dictated the opposite course of action. Although subsequent research into the actual events surrounding this bombing has revealed that (1) the actual target was not known until the last hours, and (2) by the time it started all available defensive measures had indeed been taken, the story does highlight the dilemma of the utilitarian.

The point of these examples is that the mental filters through which both history and consequences are passed often have more influence on a decision than the facts and probabilities themselves. People do not make decisions solely on facts; they make them for other reasons. The decision in example two hinges not at all on the data—collecting it turns out to be a wasted effort, for the manager makes the choice irrationally, basing it on emotional familiarity rather than on facts. Business people commonly do decide things emotionally, particularly when it comes to technology—this explains why inferior systems can become widely used. Such scenarios are normal in any situation where the people making the decision are not personally familiar with the technology issues; they do not understand the relevant data; or they trust advertising more, so they ignore the facts and embrace emotion.

The human element is critical to the outcome of the decision-making process, and the worldview (including the ethical view) of the decision-maker may well determine the outcome quite apart from (or in contradiction to) the facts. Above the individual's worldview, and creating its context, is that person's group culture. Depending on education, peer group, social status, local ideas, organizational outlook, available funds, perceived prestige, and national goals or prejudices, each person shapes a worldview in some degree of conformity with others sharing the same culture. Membership in a given subculture of society, especially when participating in a social platform's echo chamber, will determine whether a person even sees certain data and ideas, much less understands them sufficiently to make informed decisions. Thus, even extending decision-making to the entire populace would not guarantee that civil discourse would result, that better decisions would be made, or that they would last long in the face of the fickleness of popular opinion. The contrary is more likely.

The full Metalibrary could, in theory, help with some of these problems, would exacerbate others, and would create new ones. For instance, it could be used to enforce a requirement that some expertise be demonstrated before participating in a decision. On the positive side, in matters such as the building of libraries or parks, a simple test on the facts of the case could be required to gain voting status on the issue. Those living in the affected area would read a selection of the arguments for each course of action, and answer simple factual questions to show that the issue was understood. The decision would then be made by the informed and affected people.

Decisions with wider effects and more profound consequences might require a different voting structure, in which the degree of knowledge about the problem would determine each person's share of the vote. If a dam is proposed on the Columbia River, economic benefits would have to be weighed against environmental effects. It might be too much to expect everyone affected to become sufficiently knowledgeable about the proposal and its effects to cast an informed vote—there is too much technical information for non-experts to digest. Moreover, those with the best engineering expertise are not necessarily those most knowledgeable about costs and benefits or social and environmental effects. Perhaps a formula could be devised to weigh the votes of those with greater (or multiple) expertise more heavily than those who qualify with less knowledge but who are still affected. This would give those with a strong interest a powerful motivation to do some research and might make it more likely that a consensus on the decision could be reached. However, this particular issue is complicated in that the river in question crosses the Canada-U.S. border. How could the relative interests of two entire countries be weighed when one is larger in area and has more environment to affect, and the other has more people and a bigger economy?

The premise behind such electronic participatory democracy schemes is that everyone who is sufficiently informed would be more likely to come to the same conclusion. This would be a major—and in many cases unjustified—assumption; as has already been indicated, good information is not the only factor in decision-making. Such systems would also be a substantial modification of current democratic practice; whether they would be found acceptable or not is another question. It is also important to note that the mere technological enabling of weighted voting is *not* in itself a reason for implementing such a scheme. Moreover, denigrating "one person, one vote" may not be seen by many as an improvement.

Yet another common supposition is that the existence of comprehensive communications and information facilities such as the Metalibrary would tend to reduce or eliminate differences in culture and worldview and thereby promote unanimity in decision-making. This would supposedly continue a process begun by books, radio, and television and fostered by modern-day population mobility and communicability. However, the world of the 2020s was still far from the global village envisioned by some in the 1960s, even though its people in some ways hold far more in common than for thousands of prior years. Indeed, though there might gradually be fewer sharply distinct cultures based on geography, and fewer international boundaries as well, there are some very basic conflicts of worldviews that are unlikely ever to be eliminated. If the fall of the former Soviet Union taught us anything it is that centuries-old ethnic hatreds such as the ones it brutally suppressed can still survive for generations and readily be called upon to create new bloodbaths when that repression is removed. In such cases, the availability of more technology merely means that people are killed at a faster rate than before.

That old hatreds reinforced by new suspicions and naked greed can easily lead to new brutalities was amply demonstrated by Russia's 2022 invasion of Ukraine. What goes around came around, that time with the face of Putin rather than Hitler, Stalin, or the older Kaisers and Tzars.

That old political divisions could be ameliorated by better access to information was given the lie by the animosity between members of Western political parties illustrated, for example, by:

1. the "troubles" of Northern Ireland, that three-decade (1968–1998) state of violent turmoil between republicans and unionists over the issue of whether the province should be a part of Great Britain or Greater Ireland. Although the so-called Good Friday Agreement provided a framework for a regional government and power sharing between the two, the fundamental problem was never resolved and re-surfaced after Britain left the European Union, but Ireland remained a member. The dilemma then became whether a border needed to be erected in the Irish Sea between England and Northern Ireland or re-established between the latter and the Republic to the south. Can the deeply divided and profoundly segregated Province ever achieve unity?

2. the increasing hostilities between the major political parties in the United States have already led to shouting matches over disproved claims about the validity of the 2020 election results, the rules around the franchise and voting methods going forward, the issues of abortion, guns, education, slander, fraud, stolen documents, minority rights, "race," immigration, the moral bankruptcy of some candidates, and the responsibility for the January 6, 2021 insurrection and attempted coup in Washington. Rather than a "United States," that country has become a divided one, to the extent that its survival as one nation is imperiled.

Along with its new kinds of information filters, the Internet has already created new culture and worldview conflicts, for not only do people perceive information differently, but they are also able to personalize their view of the information to the extent that they need not look at, much less evaluate the same data. People boast about their alternate facts.

An ivy-leaguer with great pride in her type of institution might accept information connection threads only from people at similar schools and choose not to see the threads attached by anyone from smaller or less prestigious universities. Prejudices over spiritual ideas would remain, with some religious people refusing to read certain scientific works and some scientists refusing to read certain religious works. The same applies to those of differing political persuasions. Except when a person places a foot into the other camp or crosses over altogether, people on one side of any debate can already pretend that another side does not even exist.

When an old "friend" or a new link causes a thread to trail over self-imposed borders, it is at once obvious. Denial of recognition or "unfriending" removes the threat and the troubled mind can again be safely closed. New ideas and related data increasingly do not reach people unless expressly permitted to do so. Already, with existing information techniques, such denials perpetuate an already well-formed group thinking, tunnel vision, and echo chamber pattern, thus increasing the possibility that decisions made by such people are bad ones because they are not fully informed. Once again we see that automating a bad process (here it is decision-making) does not make it better. Rather, it merely produces bad results faster and more uniformly.

On the other hand, as the pornography issue illustrates, not all information is either useful or beneficial, and it may be a good thing to prevent some of it from entering one's home, or, in such extreme cases, to prevent it from even being available. With a fully implemented Metalibrary, the former may be rather easy, but the latter is likely nearly impossible.

One could suppose that a kind of natural selection (good decisions and advice are more efficient and useful than bad) would gradually reduce the influence of the closed-minded as the poor quality of their decisions became evident. However, there is no guarantee that a particular discipline or specialty would not become as rigid and unbending as could already happen using conventional publishing. A control belief group has the power to reject new ideas by collectively refusing to look at them.

Going forward, there is every reason to believe that denial of recognition by sub-cultural leaders—who might still be termed reviewers or editors—will guarantee that new ideas will not be available to read. That is, for all its promise as an information utility, the Metalibrary might make it even harder to challenge the control beliefs of a society, for each sub-culture using it would still have unlimited ability to effect intolerance of competing views. A possible way around this difficulty would be to have the Metalibrary rules allow universal visibility to new information links regardless of who makes them, at least until a person does read the item and expressly denies the link. Another possibility would be to create ombuds reviewers who can make connections that every user will see for at least a certain period after the person first reads the new material.

As with anything else, there is no completely satisfactory solution to the problem of intellectual intolerance, however. Everyone filters what they will read and to whom they will speak. They must, for there is too much for one person to assimilate. The filters in the Metalibrary will in some senses be more tangible, but they too are necessary. Although the narrowness of specialization may be greatly reduced because much less knowledge will need to be memorized—looking it up will be better—specialties will remain, and their practitioners will still have difficulty communicating cross-culturally.

Once again, it becomes evident upon consideration that ideas, like goods and services (whether cultural or academic), are accepted or rejected by society as a whole in the short run on their *perceived* merits, not on absolute standards. For their generation, the guardians of the control ideas and beliefs can always refuse to acknowledge anything else, even suppress competition. It is only in the longer (historical) run that they might come to be evaluated with more global measuring sticks. After all many illogical and irrational historical prejudices against women and various minorities have passed from the lexicon of at least parts of the modern population, even though they have been amplified and reinforced in others.

Neither will language barriers necessarily be broken down, for eventually, the Metalibrary would communicate with all users in their own languages. There would therefore be no incentive to learn another tongue, and meeting other people personally might even become more difficult. Spoken communication could suffer and isolationist tendencies increase, counterbalancing any improvements in written communication.

The full Metalibrary will also be sophisticated enough to allow the use of cultural, religious, or personal values to assist in filtering information and making decisions. Since it will record every data search and every decision, it could record how each person's filters operate and suggest solutions to problems consistent with one's stated values and past decisions. Again, though there would be benefits to this, there would be no incentive to re-examine one's presuppositions periodically, for the Metalibrary could be set to reinforce them.

In any event, the advent of the full Metalibrary would make it clear that everyone has a worldview. Each person would construct a reflection of that worldview in the process of learning the system, developing the filters, and making decisions at both the information and interpretation levels. Since there would still be "superstars" of each discipline even in this new medium, there would be a demand for the ability to adopt other people's worldviews (or sets of connecting threads).

So, in addition to being able to modify one's own set of connecting threads to recognize any other person's links, it ought to be possible to rent another's. This is different from incorporating in one's own set the links with that person's name on them, for that does not also add the connections the second person has recognized from other people. Borrowing a whole worldview would allow people literally to see things as others do. In this scenario, worldviews would be a commodity for rent or sale and would be mergeable with one's own. A person could keep several independent worldviews on hand and switch between them or revert to an older version of a connection set.

Many scientists who are also writers have remarked that although they can travel in several academic cultures, they seem almost to become different people when they do so. This is a routine phenomenon also, for everyone has a different mindset and vocabulary (called a "register") to communicate with different people (one vocabulary subset and thinking pattern for the children, another for spouse, fellow professionals, clients, and other for co-workers, and so on). The Metalibrary would allow someone to be (intellectually) as many different people as desired, though most users would likely integrate their interests into a single collection. Some people would undoubtedly make their worldviews available as a public service for anyone to use, others might make a tidy profit selling theirs, much as they now do from books.

All of this could allow for decision-making that is potentially more factually informed and that enables participants to better consider each other's points of view and how these were formed. This does not mean that making decisions will be any easier than it is now or that most (or any) will be unanimous. It does imply broader participation and less bureaucracy, as well as the possibility of more satisfaction with the results. There would still be differences of opinion and more opinions expressed than ever. All opinions *could* be considered, even though all surely would not be. To put this another way, being better informed may be good in the ethical sense of the word, but it is not clear to what extent that "good" would be sought after as a "should." It is even less clear how well it could be enforced, or if it is desirable to attempt such.

Yet another problem with an information-based society is the potential to rely too much on machines for decision-making. When this is done, it is easy to forget that information is more than whatever is stored in or processed by computers. To have meaning, it must be communicable. Assigning and communicating meaning, judging value, and taking action based on informed decisions are all part of the unique province of human activity, and there is as yet no indication that any of these can be automated. It is easy to rely on the neat rows and columns of figures in a spreadsheet, but unless the assumptions behind the formulas used to produce the output are known, the reader cannot make informed human judgement on the information content. There are value judgements behind the process of data collection in the first place; there are value judgements involved in organizing it; and there are value judgements involved in deciding on what meaning to assign to, and what action to take upon the material in the end. Thus, who decides, and from what value system context, gives information its ultimate quality and meaning. Humans can think about and evaluate their thinking process; machines cannot. This appears to provide an answer to the (ethical) question: who ought to decide for humans—themselves, or machines?

The availability of instant information also creates pressure to make instant decisions. For instance, because it is easy to do so, and the means are at hand, many people respond to electronic mail messages and Internet news postings as soon as they receive them. As users of such systems are well aware, this results in a large volume of intemperate, ill-considered, poorly expressed, badly communicated, and impolite mail traffic and news (such messages are called "flames"). Likewise, if thought processes and analytical techniques are unsound or if decision-makers are so culturally conditioned as to be incapable of considering alternatives, the Metalibrary facility will not help, but further exacerbate the tendency to make bad decisions. Moreover, computerizing a bad decision-making process does not produce good decisions, it only causes the bad ones to be arrived at in milliseconds instead of days, months, or years.

As mentioned, prejudice remains, and will continue. That is, irrational dislike of others and refusal to consider things from another person's worldview will be as likely then as now. Perhaps the greatest contribution to decision-making of instant and universal information availability could be the recognition of legitimate differences among worldviews as people realize (in the process of automation) how they have been making their decisions. Perceptual and decision-making filters could be obvious instead of hidden; their existence could no longer be denied or ignored. This has the potential to blur boundaries between sub-cultures, promote communication, broaden specialties, make learning easier, and promote the possibility of sounder decisions. On the other hand, prejudice has stood the test of time as a stronger force in human affairs than any of these potential benefits.

Thus, as for all technologies, the impact of electronic media on knowledge and decision-making will be mixed. Great benefits will be available, great abuses will be possible, and for many people there will just be a transfer of their old ways of thinking to a new medium that reinforces what they think they already know, even if it is wrong. A bottom line:

Data does not imply information, and information does not imply wisdom.

4.7 Summary and Further Discussion

Summary

Information is more than data. It must be processed and communicated to have the potential to convey meaning. When this takes place, participants in the exchange (and the whole culture) are altered. Every civilization depends on its transportation and communications technologies. These were once essentially the same, but the latter have now become critically important on their own. Together with the new means for storing and manipulating large amounts of information, fast communications potentially make unlimited universal access to information available to citizens of the world's nations for the first time.

Services offering such data access exist now and have already had a strong impact on many professionals, who have begun to rely more on looking up facts than on memorizing them. This way of doing things will likely be adopted by most people shortly, though completeness, reliability, and ease of use must improve substantially first—steps that all technologies require to become widely accepted.

As this takes place, new technologies will have the normal transforming effect on ideas and demands that created them. Already, hypertext promises to revolutionize the scholarly use of libraries. The extension of this concept to that of the full Metalibrary facility could make a wide range of benefits available to the general populace.

Information technology has the problems of accuracy, security, privacy, prejudice, political division, and state control to overcome. If not, it will cause more problems than it solves. People may have to live in a world where the concept of privacy has changed radically or ceased to exist for many aspects of life. They may also have to live in an increasingly divided and fractious world.

The effect on decision-making is also dramatic because information availability empowers more informed decisions. It does not guarantee good or wise ones, however. The Metalibrary may also make worldviews more visible entities, to the point where they can become commodities for rent or sale. There are both benefits and disadvantages to information technologies, as has been the case for all others.

Research and Discussion Questions

1. Describe the terms hypertext and Metalibrary and distinguish between them and "the (full) Metalibrary" as described in this chapter.

2. Use your present library to find and describe the term DynaBook. Try such subject headings as technology—the future; Alan Kay; Xerox Corp. How long did it take? How long would it be in a hypertext environment?

3. You are in a (paper-based) library researching your master's degree thesis in mathematics and stumble across a brilliant paper: Sutcliffe, Richard J., and Alspach, Brian. "Vertex Transitive Graphs of Order 2p," Annals of the New York Academy of Sciences, v. 319 (May 14, 1979): 18–27. You are captivated by the ideas presented there, and several new theorems that follow from their results immediately come to mind. Has anyone already thought of your ideas? Describe the steps you must take in a paper library to find out who has referenced this paper in a bibliography in the intervening years. Go to your library and do this, making a list of derivative papers and following them through later works as well. When you get tired, estimate how much time it would take to finish. Now describe how this would work using a hypertext system and estimate the time savings. Keep in mind that this is a rather obscure paper with relatively few citations. More popular ones can be orders of magnitude more difficult to trace entirely because the citations fan out into a maze of papers.

4. Another library task is the making of book bibliographies. This is a little easier than following a paper through citations but can still be quite a challenge. Use your paper library catalog to make a bibliography of all available books on the computer programming language Modula-2. Now obtain access to an electronic bibliographic database (your library may subscribe) and perform the same search. How many titles do you get using each method? How long did each take?

5. This chapter has mainly presented the positive side of universal information availability and has been relatively optimistic about the technology becoming available to do it. Write a paper attacking this concept, pointing out its weaknesses, and saying why it can never, should never, or will never come to pass—either from a software/hardware or from a social point of view.

6. Write a paper in which you extend the concept of the Metalibrary in content or use. There are many things it could be or do besides those that are given in this chapter. The more unusual or original can be sent to the author who will include some of the best in a subsequent edition(with attribution) if enough buy the fifth to make a sixth worthwhile.

7. What effect would the Metalibrary have on a hobby like stamp collecting? Be careful! There is more to this question than may meet the eye.

8. (a) What effect would or does the worldwide availability of information have on the gap between rich and poor nations?

   (b) What will the effect on the size and scope of government be? Will it tend to become larger or smaller? Why?

9. Research the history of telegraph, telephone, and fax. Pay attention to the rise and fall of each technology and try to give reasons for and effects of each. In which occupations/industries is fax (the oldest of these) still extensively used and why?

10. Who should manage the Metalibrary and how—or should anyone?

11. What degree of privacy over personal details can or should be guaranteed? What should an individual be able to keep secret? Perhaps you would prefer to argue that privacy should no longer exist, or at least that the general diffusion of information cuts down on abuses or crimes and therefore on the need for privacy, perhaps because fewer people will have dark secrets they are afraid will become public (because they already are).

12. If privacy is a fundamental human right or urge rather than, say, only a legislated right, how will or could people compensate for their loss of information privacy by increasing some other aspects of personal privacy?

THE INFORMATION REVOLUTION

13. Which of privacy or security (or neither) is more important? For what, exactly? Why?
14. Research the subject of computer security and describe the methods of preventing unauthorized access to data in some detail.
15. How much control should government have over data repositories and data transmission? Should such be regulated, taxed, or even run by the government? Give reasons.
16. Look up and explain in at least some detail, the methods used to encrypt data and messages. Include a discussion of two or three different methods.
17. The body of the text argues that it is effectively impossible for government to control encryption technology. Refute this.
18. Research the matter of quantum computing. Why is this important to cryptography? What does the latest research say about whether or not data can be encrypted using quantum computers in such a way that it is resistant to decryption by quantum computers?
19. In the chapter, much of the contents of current news media were described as "news editorials." Do you agree with this description? Why, or why not? Was there a significant story or event that saw so much commentary by so many reporters that it drove news to become much more editorialized? What (if anything) could or should be done to change the situation?
20. Discuss carefully the degree to which the Metalibrary facility as described in this chapter would promote understanding, cross-cultural communications, and better decision-making. Will such things be improved, or will people simply become more isolationist the more social media fosters echo chambers of like-minded people and empowers their mutual dislike of those with whom they disagree?
21. How does the concept of the Metalibrary as described in this chapter differ from that of the Metaverse or the Matrix?
22. To what extent is information available electronically now? Write a summary of the major categories of databases that can be accessed by the public, their cost, if any, and the type of information they contain.

PART TWO | FOUR WAVEFRONTS ON A SEA OF CHANGE

23. What effect would the Metalibrary have on poverty, illiteracy, poor sanitation, economic exploitation, and discrimination in (a) Western industrial nations, (b) former communist nations, and (c) third-world nations? Specifically, what ethical obligations (if any) do users of such an intellectual facility have to employ it in bettering living and working conditions for others?

24. The author suggests that the collapse of the Soviet Union precipitated the ethnic wars of Eastern Europe (indeed a much earlier version of this text predicted both). Ukraine (Central Europe) later was invaded by Russia. Either argue that Western Europe is unstable and subject to the same kind of warfare as in its past, or is likely also to be invaded, or argue that there is good reason to believe that Western Europe is now immune to one or both such problems.

25. Further to the theme in the previous question, what effect do the EU and NATO have on European stability?

26. Attempt to apply an information analysis to the problems of the Middle East. Could more knowledge of other peoples and their ways make any difference to the inhabitants of Israel and her neighboring countries?

27. Answer the same question as in #26 but concerning India and Pakistan.

28. Argue that in the present state of its political fractiousness, the United States cannot survive as a single country, OR argue that there is a way for it to do so. Alternately, argue likewise for some other country that has one or more large minority group(s) that seem likely to either split the nation or be repressed. (Canada, Spain, India, or . . .)

29. Consider the value of freedom of speech. Either argue that there should never be any restrictions on what people say, OR argue that some forms of speech need to be restricted for the collective benefit of society or at least to protect its minorities.

30. Consider the Russian 2022+ war against Ukraine. Explore one or more of the following positions and argue either for or against:

    a. the Russian "special military operation" was justified;
    b. the Russian invasion was a genocidal war of naked aggression;

c. NATO should have ignored the Russian threat to resort to nuclear weapons and at least openly sent troops and air support to Ukraine if not have declared war on Russia;

d. if Russia succeeds in seizing and annexing part or all of Ukraine its leader would be emboldened to do the same to other countries in (i) Eastern Europe, (ii) Western Europe

e. if Russia succeeds in seizing and annexing part or all of Ukraine (i) North Korea would try to take over South Korea, (ii) China would attempt to annex Taiwan, and (iii) India and Pakistan would go to war over Kashmir.

Note: If parts of this question become moot by the time you are reading this, either give a retrospective analysis of what did happen, and/or of what could otherwise have happened, or select another conflict of a similar kind elsewhere in the world (few generations have not seen one) and do a similar analysis.

CHAPTER 5

Robotics and the Second Industrial Revolution

Participants in this seminar include everyone except Dorcas and Lucas. As it opens, they are discussing the advantages and disadvantages of the Metalibrary.

- *Johanna:* The more I read of some of the ideas in this text, the less I like them. The Metalibrary may have benefits, but will we be better off or slaves to the computers? We should not build it.
- *Nellie:* The machines will be our slaves. Besides, the information revolution and the Metalibrary aren't even half the picture. What about automation? There's no need to have people doing dull, repetitive jobs on an assembly line when machines can do them faster, better, and cheaper.
- *Ellen:* And with no strikes, lockouts, or coffee breaks, working twenty-four hours a day with no salary, pension, fringe benefits, or retirement, eh, Nellie?
- *Nellie:* Exactly.
- *Ellen:* And tens of millions of unemployed workers who can never get a job again, never have any dignity, and never pay taxes, just collect welfare. What about people, Nellie?
- *Johanna:* I say we forbid anyone from making or using robots.

Nellie: Well, that's a head-in-the-sand approach if I ever heard one. Do you think the Americans, Japanese, Chinese, and Russians will hesitate to use robots to gain a competitive edge? Do you think the Europeans will? Canada will be a third-world country before you know it if we go your route, Johanna.

Professor: Your planet is not heavily industrialized, Eider. How do you manage?

Eider: It's not possible to make easy comparisons between the Builder's World and Earth Prime, Professor. Ours is indeed a relatively unindustrialized world, but we have fewer than twenty million people in nearly as large a land mass as on your earth.

Nellie: That's not enough to support mass production.

Eider: No, but we do have high technology, though we have gone in rather different directions. I suppose we skipped the Industrial Revolution. Our economy is agricultural, cottage industry, and small labs. People generally work from their own homes and are widely scattered.

Ellen: But, you do have children—you look like you're, what, sixteen or so?

Eider: Yes.

Ellen: So why the small population?

Eider: The birth rate is very low. I don't know anyone within a thousand of your kilometers who is my age. People live longer, too—though not as long as they once did.

Nellie: You say there's high technology. Do you already have a Metalibrary, then?

Eider: Essentially, yes. The main social consequence is that even fewer people live in the city than there were, oh, five hundred years back.

Johanna: How many cities?

Eider: Just one. It has about a hundred thousand people.

Johanna: Other communities?

Eider: None with a population over two thousand. They are trading and transportation centers for large regions. Manufacturing is also regionalized to get raw materials easily, but it's all automated.

PART TWO | FOUR WAVEFRONTS ON A SEA OF CHANGE

Nellie: Wait. You've had a Metalibrary for five hundred years?

Eider: Yes, it amounts to that.

Nellie: What effect has it had?

Eider: We've changed our educational system—that's almost all done at home now. The population has declined and fewer people live in communities. We're more individualistic than we used to be.

Johanna: (skeptically) You don't talk like a sixteen-year-old, dearie.

Eider: In our world, you go as far and as fast as you want, educationally. I daresay our fourteen-year-olds are as capable, and much more widely read, than your holders of doctoral degrees. As for me, my mother died when I was quite young, and my father is away a lot, so I manage our farm.

Nellie: Didn't you say you lived in the city and worked in medicine?

Eider: Healing, yes. But I can manage the farm from there easily enough.

Nellie: What does your father do?

Eider: (looking nervously at the professor) I don't think I should . . .

Professor: (interrupting) Right, then, back to our world. What if we robotize so we do not need people to make products in factories? We have a large population. How do we handle the job dislocations?

Johanna: I say we don't go that route at all.

Nellie: Can't stop progress, Johanna.

Johanna: Who says it's progress?

Nellie: Some techniques are more efficient than others, and that means their general adoption becomes inevitable. Progress is just the historical record of the inevitable happening.

Johanna: No, that makes progress into an icon or god, just like the state is for Ellen. Robotizing would harm people, not make things better.

Ellen: Progress is the record of evolution. The fittest people and techniques survive.

Johanna: You mean your fellow traveler bullies survive? And the rest do what—starve?

Eider: I don't know much about this world, but it seems to me that the changes would take place gradually, with employment shifting over time from manufacturing to service industries. In my world, few people strike a clock . . .

Alicia: . . . I think that's "punch," Eider.

Eider: Oh, yes, sorry. Everyone has a place and a function in society, but we don't need to go somewhere to do a job. The nearest equivalent in your world is an independent contractor. There are enough goods, and plenty of food for everyone to provide the necessities of life—all that comes from the family farm.

Nellie: They don't send you care packages in the city, do they?

Eider: No, but the family account is credited for whatever the farm sells, and my room, food, and clothing are charged to the same account. By the time people are my age, they also have their own accounts. I can contribute to the family businesses or punch out on my own.

Alicia: "Strike" this time, Eider.

Eider: Oh yes. English idiom is quite fascinating. Anyway, I don't see why you can't develop a similar system here.

Nellie: Another chore for the Metalibrary—keep track of what everybody contributes to society and what they all use.

Ellen: Everybody could be paid exactly the same amount; it would be the ultimate in social leveling.

Eider: I don't see why you would want to do that. Some people do nothing; they just live out their lives on the common wealth of their families. Some never use the library after the age of a hundred, they are happy doing farm labor, city maintenance, or a trade. Others make great contributions to planetary wealth and knowledge—these surely should be recognized.

Johanna: (sourly) In the real world, we're talking about a massive deindustrialization, one in which goods are still manufactured but people don't do it—they just use the goods. Surely the social dislocation is too great a price to pay for the small benefit.

Eider: As far as I can see . . . (pausing) Or is that "as near as I can tell"?

Alicia: "Far" and "near" both mean the same thing in this context.

Eider: A bit like "up" and "down" in "drink it up" or "drink it down"?

Nellie: (interrupting) Sounds like you artists would be better off than ever, Johanna.

Johanna: How so?

Nellie: As things stand now, scientists get grant money to discover new things, while artists, musicians, and poets have to scramble, right?

Johanna: How true.

Nellie: Well, if the necessities were provided for by machines working away unattended, you artists could create to your hearts' content without having to wonder where your next meal is coming from. We scientists would continue as before, but you'll be much better off.

Ellen: But, the workers, the workers.

Nellie: What do you mean?

Ellen: You're not going to turn riveters, boilermakers, and unskilled assemblers into either scientists or poets. How does a present-day worker retain some dignity in this automated fantasy world?

Eider: You educate their children differently.

Nellie: There will always be some manual labor.

Eider: In the Builder's World, we could have chosen to run farms by robots but instead use a lot of manual labor along with the machines.

Johanna: There's an inconsistency here in this imaginary world of yours, dearie.

Eider: (smiling) I assure you, it's quite real. But how so?

Johanna: Large efficient farms produce large surpluses, do they not?

Eider: Yes.

Johanna: Well, who eats all the food produced by the family farms you talk about?

Eider: Our farm is not large; we employ one supervisor and four other hands. We intensively cultivate fewer than . . . let me see . . . a thousand of your hectares, and several thousand more are left in a wild state. A lot of what is cultivated is left fallow for horse pasture. At that, ours is one of the oldest and largest farms; our family has worked that land for seven generations. We specialize, then trade at the regional produce market.

Nellie: Why horses? Don't you use tractors?

Eider: We use very few internal combustion engines. They're almost all electric. There are no oil deposits and little coal, just natural gas. Different geology, you know.

Ellen: Back to real workers in the real world.

Nellie: I'd guess that many of today's semiskilled workers could go into business for themselves making the handcrafted items in small numbers that can never come off a robotic assembly line.

Eider: A great deal of the production in the Builder's World is done that way. We do use robots, but don't need very many. The Orthans used to use a lot, but don't these days—a deliberate choice to keep employment high. The heads of their great houses believe in employing human servants rather than buying robots.

Johanna: Even granting all that, there are just too many people to accommodate if you automate all their jobs.

Alicia: So far, the jobs eliminated from manufacturing have turned up in the service and information industries.

Johanna: That only helps the statistics, not individual people who get fired and can't be retrained. An assembly line worker won't become a travel agent or a computer programmer.

Nellie: Look, Johanna, these things are going to happen anyway. Competition will drive all industries toward the highest possible efficiencies. We just have to adapt and make the best of it, that's all.

Johanna: But, all those machines—

Professor: (rising) Enough for today. Next time we talk about intelligence—artificial and otherwise. Eider, I'll have a paper from you forecasting demographic changes as this world automates. Nellie, you do one telling us what are the disadvantages of automation. Ellen gives us one on how workers can benefit from robots, and Johanna writes one describing Eider's world more fully. (smiling and ignoring their protests) Have a good week.

Johanna: (after he and Eider both have left) The gall!

Nellie: Oh, you get used to it.

Johanna: Say, have you two noticed anything funny about Eider and Lucas?

PART TWO | FOUR WAVEFRONTS ON A SEA OF CHANGE

Nellie: What do you mean?

Johanna: They're never here at the same time. Do you suppose they know each other, and only one comes to class to get notes for both?

Nellie: (Rubbing her chin) I don't think they're supposed to meet, yet.

Ellen: What do you mean, "supposed to" and "yet"?

Nellie: I think that's part of another book.

Ellen: Oh. One I'm not in?

Nellie: Not mine to say. Ask the Professor. He makes up the plots for us.

Johanna: But, doesn't the fact that we characters in this book can talk about ourselves create some kind of paradox; after all, it's not as if we're real.

Alicia: You seem real enough to me.

Johanna: But we've never met you; are you real to us?

Alicia: As real as you want me to be.

5.1 Tracing a Second Industrial Revolution

The Industrial Revolution involved harnessing machines for production previously done by hand. The term "second industrial revolution" means the automation of those same tasks so machines require few, if any, human attendants. This is not new, for the entire machine age tells the story of machines having ever greater efficiency, power, and productivity. Automated textile devices first claimed the livelihood of thousands of independent artisans when the English garment and lace factories came into being in the early nineteenth century. Each machine that mechanized work previously done by hand reduced the number of people required to produce a given quantity of goods. This affected both agriculture and industry. The machine revolution proceeded simultaneously through all parts of the economy because the various sectors competed for raw materials and human resources. Also, new technologies developed for one industry tend to be applied to others in short order.

The machines of the industrial age, though as diverse as the industries in which they were employed, had one thing in common that distinguished them from the human workers before them. Each was a specialty device, designed and built for a specific task. To accommodate any subsequent changes in an industry invariably meant retooling—a euphemism for scrapping much of the existing machinery and replacing it with new. In only a very few cases does any part of an industrial-age machine survive a substantial technological change; it becomes noncompetitive or irrelevant, so it is unplugged and thrown away.

Human workers, on the other hand, can be retrained to use new skills and new tools—if employers take the time and effort to do so, and their unions will allow it. Throughout the machine age, human retraining took place continuously as new machines demanded different skills of their operators. However, as time passed, more of the physical tasks in manufacturing became automated, and the machines started to become more general-purpose and require fewer operators. Logically, the next step in the sequence is the replacement of the human operators and their devices by new machines sufficiently versatile that the "retraining" could be applied to them instead of to the workers.

Until recently, this step could not be taken because there were no satisfactory ways of encapsulating retainability in a machine, and the jobs of at least some of the human workers were safe. With the advent of programmable automatons, or robots, they no longer are.

Profile On . . . Technology

Robots

Where did the term "robot" come from?

In 1921 Czech dramatist Karel Capek wrote a play, *R.U.R.* or *Rossum's Universal Robots*. The Czech word means "heavy work."

What disciplines are involved in robotics?

Robotics is a complex multidisciplinary field embracing computing science, mechanical engineering, control systems, and knowledge of the design and operation of the manufacturing process.

What were/are the Laws Of Robotics?

1. A robot may not injure a human being, or through inaction allow a human being to come to harm.

2. A robot must obey the orders given to it by human beings except where such orders would conflict with the first law.

3. A robot must protect its existence as long as such protection does not conflict with the first or second laws.

Who enforces these laws?

No one does. They were formulated for use in the fiction of Isaac Asimov in 1940 and popularized since then by numerous writers of science fiction. There are no robots yet capable of being programmed to "obey" these laws, and it is not certain there ever will be.

Does this mean that a robot could kill a human being?

Present-day robots are little different from any other industrial machinery in this respect. Some have detectors that allow them to avoid a human being when in motion, but apart from this, it is just as dangerous to get in the way of a working robot as it is to stand in the path of a moving truck.

What can robots do?

Robots have been equipped with grippers, manipulators, motion sensors, heat, light, and sound detectors and are capable of handling tools, moving about, lifting, carrying, and fitting parts.

They can weld, assemble electronic components, spray paint, sand and polish, apply adhesives and other coatings, drill, make tools, load, unload, and store materials, move parts about in a factory or warehouse, mine coal, make castings, and assemble and inspect finished products.

They can be sent to Mars to rove a hostile landscape, gather and assess data for scientific experiments, perform delicate surgery, operate a space station or Mars rover independently, drive a car, mow a lawn, vacuum a room, or serve as a child's toy.

Can robots see?

There are many manufacturers of robotic vision systems. These allow robots to sense colors and shapes, position parts in the correct location, and inspect products for flaws. The patterns read by the optical systems are compared with the ones in storage. Whether this is "seeing" depends on the definition of sight. In automobiles, they can sense traffic and lane markers, follow another vehicle at the lesser of its speed or the legal limit, turn on headlights per the surrounding environment, and eventually, take over all the functions of driving.

Which industries use robots?

Examples include automobile and airplane manufacturing, shipbuilding, electronics assembly, appliance manufacturing, tool and die making, mining, warehousing, transportation, and undersea exploration.

In what manufacturing environments do they work best?

- where the products are hard items that must be moved about and stacked.
- (so far) where the items being moved are relatively large.
- where the actions required are relatively simple and are repeated in exactly or nearly the same way every time until a reprogramming is done.
- where decisions are simple, have few options, and do not call for shades of judgment (i.e., the domain of action has clear and strict boundaries). These limitations, however, are being gradually eroded.
- where any visual inspections can be handled with a medium resolution, two or three-dimensional vision scan.
- where quantities are great enough to warrant using robots, but not so large as to make fixed machinery more economical.
- where the plant can be run in continuous shifts.
- where labour, land, buildings, and other costs are high, but capital is easy to obtain, and interest rates are reasonable.
- in new factories where the entire building and assembly line can be designed with robots in mind.
- where conditions are too hazardous to risk many (or any) human beings (inside a volcano or nuclear plant, inspecting or disassembling bombs, or exploring in space).

5.2 Robots and the New Industries

Robotic devices have gone far beyond the realm of science fiction, having become a day-to-day reality in the lives of many people. Home appliances have built-in microprocessor controllers and timers. Automobiles include diagnostic centers and several computers to control their operations. Some vehicles are self-driving; more soon will be. Golfers ride about on robotized caddy carts. Computers have revolutionized the writing and publishing industries by automating many tedious functions. However, such devices have not caused dramatic large-scale changes in basic living and working patterns for most people. Instead, they have produced simple, small-scale changes to the existing industrial society. To constitute anything revolutionary, they would have to be capable of displacing large numbers of workers from their positions. And, both on the assembly line and in the office, that displacement has begun. It is nascent in other professions, operating rooms, outer space exploration, and routine maintenance tasks.

There is a fundamental difference between the original Industrial Revolution and this new one. Many workers who have kept their jobs up to this time because of the (human) ability to be retrained will now lose them, for the new automated manufacturing machinery is indeed reprogrammable. Machines can now be given not only computational and routine work, but also something that passes for decision-making ability. Robotic tools are used extensively in such situations as automobile assembly lines, where the fact that robots cannot make wrong decisions makes them more economical than human workers in the long run, and results in more consistent products with fewer flaws. Many of these are heavy equipment models, with limited and rigid capabilities, but these are rapidly giving way to much more flexible devices.

It was long a piece of North American folklore that one ought not to buy a car made on a Monday or a Friday because the workers were not at their peak on those days. However, robots do not get hung over, bored, angry, sleepy, or careless. They do not require time-and-a-half, lunch breaks, sleep, salaries, pensions, maternity and paternity leave, extended medical, washrooms, or stock-sharing plans, nor do they go on strike or make demands. Robots require a substantial capital expense but have low operating costs, for they are paid no salary or benefits. They are reliable and can be retrained without expensive courses.

A robot can replace between five and ten assembly-line workers and pay for itself in three years or less. It will do exactly the right job every time, welding two parts with the correct temperature and pressure and in the right place, or applying a nut to a bolt with exactly the specified torque. Parts fit better and are stronger, and the final product can be counted on to be of uniform quality every time. Small pieces can be attached when building machines or electronic devices with any desired degree of precision, and this can be done quickly and accurately throughout an entire production run. They can then be reprogrammed for a different run.

Most importantly, technological changes can be addressed ahead of time, and new computer programs devised to have the same robots manufacture in new products. With reprogrammable tools, the assembly line can be retooled with much less scrapping of machines and little lost production time. Ultimately, it should be possible for a new automobile to be designed entirely by computer and for the assembly line to be switched over to the new product automatically and with minimal human intervention on the factory floor.

The first four-hundred-fifty-nine vehicles made some future day could be four-wheel drive diesel pickup trucks, and the four-hundred-sixtieth could be a newly designed compact electric car—with no intervening space or time on the assembly line. The line could then switch back to trucks until the prototype is tested. For the foreseeable future, the decision to make the switches would be a human one—there is no reliable method yet of automating the reasoning leading up to it.

While the kind of flexibility suggested here is not yet available, robotic devices are already used extensively in Japanese automobile assembly and are taking over the same functions in North American plants as well. After all, their owners wish to stay in business. Ultimately, assembly lines of all types will be automated in this fashion, and most consumer goods will be produced with few or no human workers in the plant. Industries that require some intelligent judgement, such as fish packing, will take longer but will succumb to the same economic forces eventually.

The resulting changes will be as sweeping as were those following the original Industrial Revolution, for hundreds of millions of skilled and semiskilled jobs in manufacturing, mining, forestry, materials processing, warehousing, and other smokestack industries will no longer be required. Most of the small staff remaining in such industries will be white-collar workers, accounting for and instructing the machines that operate the machines—and doing so from the office environment, rather than the factory floor. Other employees will be highly trained and versatile technicians whose task will be to effect the inevitable repairs and reprogramming.

Eventually, factories also will be designed and built to order largely by machines and can be placed in remote or uninhabitable regions without blighting either the urban or rural landscape. They could be built beneath the ground, inside mountains, under the ocean, in outer space, or on the moon. Of course, some people must continue to work on the design and operation of factories. However, the consumers who benefit from their production will need neither to know nor care where those factories are physically located, so long as the flow of goods continues unhindered. In many cases it might be difficult or impossible for an unprotected human being to pay a physical visit to the floor of one of these factories; ultimately it will be almost entirely unnecessary.

Some mark 1956 as the watershed year in the progress of automation, for in that year the number of service jobs in North America exceeded the number in manufacturing and farming (i.e., in production) for the first time. The next six+ decades saw a steady growth in the number and sophistication of available consumer goods and the general standard of living even while jobs continued to shift to the service and information sectors. Recessions notwithstanding, there was during that period a level of economic expansion and prosperity such as has never before been seen. If this could be projected into the future, those who have jobs of any kind would probably be able to afford far more technological luxury than ever.

Even now television antennas sprout on the roofs of the most primitive tin shacks in the barrios of South America and Asia. Video disks and players of dubbed American movies could be rented in small Pakistani towns, but streaming is now available almost everywhere. Few but the remotest of jungle dwellers lack radios or are unfamiliar with at least some modern technological amenities. Even in such settings, the local missionary-cum-Bible translator comes equipped with a microcomputer, word-processing software, and a portable electric generator.

As familiar as people are with the recent economic impact of existing technology, they may not be very well prepared for the changes that are coming. The Industrial Revolution took over a century to run its course in England with the most dramatic changes between 1780 and 1850. A critical mass of new industrial technology has again collected, but this time changes of greater magnitude are taking place over a much shorter period, and the pace is accelerating. The transition to robotic goods production could be essentially complete in two decades. By another generation after that, few people would have much detailed knowledge of what a factory is, where any are located, or how they work. Industrial production would then be as invisible and as much taken for granted as farms are now. Today, people speak of farms in the abstract "the rains will be good for the farmers," but few city dwellers visit one in their lifetime. The same will be true of factories. They will become invisible abstractions.

The economic impacts would be as profound as those of the industrial age, for even as smokestack industries all but disappear, consumer goods could simultaneously improve in quality and sophistication and be reduced in price. The distribution chain could also be shortened, for there would be much less need for retailers and wholesalers in any of the big-ticket items. Stereos, televisions, refrigerators, and many other products could be ordered by the customer directly from the factory (through the Metalibrary) and delivered to the door without the need for intermediaries such as wholesalers. Smaller appliances, clothing, shoes, and such other goods as household robots could be obtained in the same fashion. Amazon already does or enables much of this.

Previous editions of this book had the short-sighted and incorrect comment: "It could be a long time—or never—before robotic truck drivers are deployed, however." The author's more recent comments in *The Northern Spy*" are along the lines of "In another ten years it will be illegal to install a steering wheel in a vehicle. Yes, "truck driver," the most common of all occupations and "car driver" the most ubiquitous task of the general population, seem certain to vanish once cars and roads are automated.

Information providers on the Internet already allow such direct ordering of a variety of goods and conduct business activities electronically on a large scale, so these comments are saying little that is new.

If such methods were to become more widely adopted, stores and shopping centers as they now exist could be much reduced in size and importance, perhaps becoming manufacturers' showrooms. If Metalibrary terminals eventually had three-dimensional color-projection ability, many items could be accurately previewed in the home. With fully automated factories, clothing could be guaranteed to fit, for single items could be made to order for the customer's measurements with no loss of production line efficiency. Indeed, goods might *only* be made to order, with mass production disappearing altogether.

Such large-scale automation also suggests to some observers that the new era would see more planned economies, though presumably not like the now discredited and abandoned communist statism. Planning for manufacturing could consist of surveys and projections of customer wants or needs by the companies engaged in satisfying those wants, and not involve government. This requires no new techniques other than better information access and processing, for decision-making by polling for public opinion has long been a feature on both the commercial and political scene in North America. Naturally, the advertising industry will continue to seek new ways to change those wants so that consumers focus on new products. Indeed, even a full Metalibrary's entertainment facilities would undoubtedly be even more commercialized, robust, and heavily used as are today's television networks and streaming services combined. After all, many people will work fewer hours and have more time for entertainment.

Looked at optimistically, and only from a material point of view, robotic manufacturing technologies appear to promise a rosy future. However, the people of this projected new society would be profoundly affected in ways other than simply having more and better products available to buy, consume, and dispose of.

5.3 Work and Workers in the New Society

Automation and robotization do not simply influence institutions, as if the economy were an abstract entity that does not touch real people. On the contrary, large numbers of people are directly affected, for nearly every job that existed in the late twentieth and early twenty-first century could either change beyond recognition or vanish altogether within the working lifetimes of their holders—as had many jobs of the 1950s through 1990s by two decades later. As in the first Industrial Revolution, the effect of large-scale robotization in the workplace (and therefore on society generally) will be profound, particularly in the transition years when the new industries are just becoming established. Service industries, the information sector itself, and the professions have so far done well to absorb new workers, shifting the balance of employment with relatively little pain. However, more rapid changes that appear in store for the future could overwhelm for a time the ability of society to cope with the necessary mobility.

At any time, three kinds of dislocation may be experienced by workers whose jobs become obsolete. The most severe is outright termination, leading at least temporarily to unemployment. A worker's job may cease to exist because of automation, a reduction in market share, or because the enterprise goes bankrupt. During stable times, that person may have a reasonable expectation of obtaining a nearly equivalent position with another company. However, in changing times those other companies are also reducing staff, for the problems encountered by the original employer are common to the whole economy. Many jobs lost during the periodic downturns in economic activity are never regained; the companies involved each time introduce new techniques and efficiencies to reduce their labor needs.

What is more, the COVID-19 pandemic forced many industries and their workers into a rapid transition to extensive remote work, and accelerated pressure on many job classifications, speeding up the changes discussed here. Furthermore, employers came to expect their employees to be available at all times, whether present in the workplace during "normal" hours or otherwise (the "always on" syndrome).

North American structural unemployment (minimum levels during good times) increased substantially during the thirty years centered on the turn of the century and seemed destined to grow higher still before 2020. Indeed, the minimum rate at the top of the cycle seemed headed to well above six percent (nine in Canada; higher in some countries)—levels that until recently would have been regarded as unacceptable and warranting massive government intervention in the economy. Post-pandemic, it was much lower, because of deaths and retirements, the aging of the workforce, and the effects of decades of decline in Western birthrates. Some demographic shifts may have balanced each other to an extent. Government spending during the pandemic became profligate, however, automatically setting the stage for massive inflation and a possible recession. In the long run, it can be reasonably expected that the number of new manufacturing sector jobs created during good times will be far fewer than the number eliminated in the bad times and by automation.

Indeed, the very science and technology that created and inflated the middle working class is now deflating and could very nearly destroy it, for those are precisely the people whose jobs are lost due to robotic automation. Moreover, industrial and office workers, their employers, unions, and governments can see this coming, and there is little any of them can do to ameliorate these job losses and the consequent downshift of the middle class to underemployment or unemployment and poverty.

The second kind of dislocation is called displacement. This occurs when a worker's old job vanishes but there is immediate retraining available for a new position that has opened up because of the new technology. Here, the employer shifts and grows with the economy and, despite new technology, need not reduce her workforce. Perhaps the employer also perceives a moral obligation to retrain current employees for new positions rather than counting on schools and universities to supply trained or educated workers at no cost.

Alternatively, the worker may have the foresight, initiative, and imagination to seek appropriate retraining when the time is ripe. Such a worker may be displaced to another employer or industry or become a self-employed professional but does so voluntarily and with confidence. While such visionary and mobile workers were relatively rare in the past, they could well have to become the norm in the future. This has profound implications for grade school education, as graduates will enter not only a very altered but also a fast-changing workplace.

In theory, a worker replaced by a machine is only displaced, for retrainability supposedly implies that everyone can find other employment. In practice, the displaced very often become unemployed because they (or their employers) are unwilling or unable to effect retraining. Semiskilled workers with a poor educational background and those relatively new to the labour force are the most vulnerable in such situations. It is often perceived (and was once stated as fact by Marxists) that there is little to restrain industrialists from seeking maximum profits while having no regard for the human consequences. Such a perception is a stereotype, for no business or economy could operate that way openly and indefinitely in a competitive marketplace. Too many valuable workers (and customers) would be alienated, so reputation, market share, and profits would eventually suffer.

A third kind of dislocation, job growth, is more subtle, for it may be visible only in retrospect. Here, the job holder and the job are mutually transformed over time, often without anyone noticing that the original job no longer exists—the old job has been replaced by an entirely new one with no break in continuity. Although not always possible, this is the least traumatic type of dislocation and can bring satisfaction to everyone involved. This kind of growth does not ordinarily take place by accident. Managers who wish to foster it must ensure that workers have a degree of independence and job control that enables them to plan their change and growth as employment conditions demand. Rigid, locked-in job descriptions or contracts prevent people from learning new skills, whereas flexibility to meet the challenges of change fosters such growth. These observations suggest a trend toward more flexible and educated workers, a more professional style of employment, and correspondingly greater worker control over job terms and conditions. Adaptability to new environments would become the key to remaining employable.

As existing positions are metamorphosing or vanishing, many new ones are being created. The computing industry now employs millions of people with job descriptions that languages lacked the vocabulary to describe five decades ago. General affluence has resulted in large numbers of new jobs being created in the entertainment, tourism, and hospitality industries. Likewise, the global information and communications industries, the biochemical field, and space-based enterprises will soon employ millions who once might have worked in factories, and one can only guess what their job descriptions will be. Certainly, few will be on production lines. Most will be administrators, office workers, information brokers, researchers, data handlers, medical personnel, computer operators, pilots, and the like. This reinforces the suggestion above that the new positions will be for technicians or professionals rather than for unskilled or semi-skilled laborers.

Thus, jobs and wages will continue to flow out of smokestack industries and into the service and professional fields. The holders of these new jobs will presumably make more money, expanding the demand for both goods and services. Perhaps most people will eventually be employed (or self-employed). However, depending on the speed at which robotization takes place, there could be a period of very high unemployment in some countries. In the past, when unemployment reached high (12 percent+) levels, riots, revolutions, and great social unrest have resulted. Thus, the rise of modern-day groups of Luddites (machine smashers) or the establishment of totalitarian states in some previously democratic countries are possibilities that cannot be completely dismissed. Passions could run very high during such dislocations, and racial, religious, or political scapegoats could once again be sought. These possibilities (and natural human resistance to change) might argue for a slow transition to complete automation, but the market forces demanding quick action may be too powerful to be tempered by anything short of total societal collapse.

In the long run, a higher percentage of people may be self-employed or work in what are now called part-time or home-based positions. Some predict that tourism, entertainment, and the arts will be the largest employers. Central governments may grow dramatically in size for a time, as they attempt to regulate or seize even more of the wealth and production. There may also be pressure on them to employ many of those displaced from market sector jobs, just to give them something to do. In the long run, however, the government could become less necessary, much smaller and less significant in the overall economy as some of its current functions become irrelevant. Any such changes could be painful, for the state never changes substantially or relinquishes power easily.

As in past transitions, new technology will demand changes in educational content and practice. The new workforce will have to be much better and more broadly educated and informed than in the industrial age, and the changes will be greater in relative terms than in the transition from an agricultural to an industrial society. Such education must focus on the ability to change and adapt over a person's working years, for jobs may well come and go at a rapid rate—this may be at least a medium-term feature (if not a permanent one) of the information age. If most people are faced with changing jobs or professions repeatedly, they will have to be broadly educated beyond any narrow specialty to cope. (Chapter 10 will cover the topic of education in detail.)

If industry and government will be transformed, then so will unions—the third institutional leg on which the industrial age has stood. These organizations were created to provide a means of representing relatively uneducated workers' interests to putatively greedy owners and exploitive management. Some models of the information age suggest that in a society where it is difficult to keep secrets, cooperation may be easier to establish and confrontation frowned upon. New industries tend not to inherit either social baggage or technique from the old ones; they use a substantially different kind of workforce and often are located in different places.

According to Robert Blaumer (*Alienation and Freedom*), those in the new industries found their work more satisfying and less alienating than those working in typical factory jobs. With technology advances, drudgery work is reduced or eliminated and work requiring a more substantial intellectual component is created. Workers can become more skilled and achieve the high levels of job satisfaction that typified earlier manufacturing occupations. Perhaps the difference is that people felt themselves to be servants when they tended to the old machines, whereas in the new order, they perceive that machines worked for them. Of course, this analysis is true only of the larger picture. It tells us nothing about the many unskilled workers who become permanently alienated from employment when replaced by automatons and their far smaller cadre of highly skilled technicians. The latter will have both education and jobs and every reason for self-satisfaction.

This satisfaction has other consequences. Workers in the newer industries, and white-collar positions generally, have not joined their industrial counterparts by unionizing in any great number, the public service and government-funded occupations in education, emergency services, and health all excepted. The percentage of union members among all workers in North America peaked decades ago and declined rapidly in more recent years. There is every reason to suppose this trend will continue and even accelerate. Unions that merely hold onto their traditional power bases seem destined to gradually lose members and power. They may disappear as the jobs they now represent vanish. Others might change into consumer associations or find some other way to represent the interests of service-industry workers. Some observers predict that traditional trade unions will have little or no influence in the long term. In the shorter term, certain unions (particularly in the public service) may gain both members and power, depending on their circumstances. However, models of the information age seem to have little room for traditional industrial unions, so their survival may depend on a willingness to change substantially.

On the other hand, professional organizations, such as those representing nurses, doctors, lawyers, accountants, many university faculties, and the like, could be formed for computing scientists and other professional knowledge workers. In the 1960s and 1970s, the job-description buzzwords were "technician" and "engineer"; from the 1980s the buzzword has been "professional." To some extent, professional organizations will be like unions for they will likely inherit some of their politics and a few business managers from the traditional labour movement. As they grow in influence and power, they could also resemble guilds with high entrance barriers and elaborate codes of what constitutes proper practice for the profession. They might concentrate on raising their members' standing and status in the community, rather than making strictly material gains. They might only convey social status and have little practical power. However, these scenarios are speculative, for the formation, growth, and role of political parties, professional societies, unions, and other organizations are subject to too many unknowns of unforeseen events and politics, to predict reliably. A single accident, scandal, malpractice suit, or election can make or break the power of any group. Thus, of unions and like organizations, it is only possible to say that, like all institutions, they will develop and change with society or vanish as they lose their vitality and relevance.

One thing that can be said with some assurance is that any such organizations whose sole interest is maintaining the *status quo* of their power and influence will surely go the way of the butter churn, horseless carriage, silent movie, telephone and keypunch operator, typewriter, cassette tape, DVD, and steering wheel.

Changes in the workplace will not be confined to the industrial scene. Many office tasks that are today performed by the white-collar counterparts of the skilled factory worker will also be obsolete. The number of secretaries, receptionists, and clerks will continue to decline dramatically as Metalibrary facilities develop. Past projections of the advent of a paperless office proved erroneous—there came to be more paper than ever—but this was because the emerging technology was fitted into and used to promote existing ways of working, rather than providing new models for office work. This is to be expected of new techniques, which are generally used at first only to supplement existing practice and do not generate new methods until a certain critical mass is reached. This example also indicates the dangers inherent in making projections. All of them (including the ones in this book) are likely to be partly if not wholly wrong.

The Metalibrary (even as it now exists on a modest and fragmented scale) does provide a new office model by making most paper files unnecessary, for it does obsolete many clerical jobs in countless offices, including most in the government sector. Such jobs are still done by people for two reasons.

First, the power and productivity of existing facilities for electronic data search, document creation, information storage, and paperless communication are only just being realized (i.e., the Metalibrary as it now exists is so new that even what it offers is being under-utilized).

Second, these facilities are still quite primitive. Problems to contend with include lack of universal connectivity, fragmentation of data storage, uncorrected errors, data inconsistency, and difficulty of existing interfaces to the Metalibrary (including the still primitive, clumsy, and incomplete search engines and broken AI products). Before there can be a substantial impact on office routines, the Metalibrary must become completely connected, consistent, fully functional, easy to use, cheap, and offer more sophisticated access to all public databases and other information. No lesser technology will suffice, for only a completely reliable, size-unlimited, ultra-fast and convenient facility with obvious competitive advantages over the filing cabinet can replace the office routine of the past. Even microfilm became unnecessary, for documents can be stored in a form reproducible on any terminal. Paper files are going the same way.

It will take decision-makers some time to get used to a relatively paperless environment, but competitive advantages will overcome initial concerns about information security and loss. Backup systems in local versions and on the worldwide version of the Metalibrary will have to be more extensive to earn the trust of decision-makers. The use of the facsimile machine, despite it consuming even more paper, was a step in the direction of the paperless office routine. Once people become more used to the idea of carrying about and using light, portable devices that allow them to send and receive information anywhere and at any time, they will also demand a much larger electronic storage capacity and other features that will eliminate paper most consumption. The smartphone of the early 2020s is several steps along the way, but we are not there yet.

Meanwhile, middle management may continue to be a casualty of the workplace revolution, as each recession in the business cycle squeezes out more workers who have made it thus far. There is much less need for people to collect data, filter and summarize it on paper for the attention of senior management. Already, decision-makers can obtain such summaries and form projections on alternative decisions easily, more quickly, and more accurately from computers on their desks (let alone from the Metalibrary) than they could ever get through relying on several layers of middle management or via routine secretarial work. Professionals tend to prepare their own electronic documents rather than relying on secretarial or administrative assistants to do it for them. Improvements in the capacity to do such things imperil more mid-level jobs. The task of doing such gathering and filtering will become more common than ever, and the time required will be less because much of it can be automated, especially as AI matures. Decision makers will be the ones assigning meaning to the data; they will not need to rely on others to assemble and analyze it for them.

Not all of yesterday's senior management will survive the changeover. Those who fail to obtain the necessary technical skills for making computer-assisted decisions will join their less capable middle managers on the unemployment rolls, their places taken by those who have prepared properly for a move up. Many current managers will be replaced by those who have been doing their analysis for them.

There may also be less need for in-person meetings, except as an excuse to visit convention centers in exotic vacation destinations. The pandemic proved that this was not only possible, but preferable for budget reasons, and many enterprises will not return to extensive business travel for meetings. For those people who have what are now called office jobs, the bulk of what they do can be accomplished at home rather than by commuting to a central location—again proven during the pandemic. Not all such face-to-face gatherings (meetings and communal offices) can be eliminated, for it is difficult to take a person's measure, to know who they are, and what their responses mean except by arranging a personal meeting.

Today's executive is also quite dependent on the business lunch—an institution that can only be maintained by clustering offices in a central location, and one that would take some time to be abandoned. There is, in short, a need for some socialization in the conduct of business—one that machines can not fill, and therefore will not eliminate. But much of it is redundant, and manifest cost savings will dictate change.

Research for potential decisions can also be contracted out by the decision maker to experts who work with the Metalibrary, assembling the relevant data into the desired format, and collecting their fee without leaving home, meeting their employer, or even knowing who it is. Contract offers can be made on the Metalibrary for a sum of money in return for the solution to a particular problem within a certain number of hours. The solutions offered could be collected by yet another person and the contributors paid in proportion to the degree their ideas that were used in the final decision. This is not much different from present practice, except in the means of communication, and because the existing Internet is relatively non-commercial in at least this respect, so there is usually no monetary value in answering others' questions. When there is, this consultative form of employment will become ubiquitous.

Telecommuting has some advantages for those involved: they can save time and money; those unwilling or unable to commute can work at home; and fewer cars, freeways, and office buildings are required. It also has disadvantages. It promotes isolation from others, a loss of identity with the employer, and the holding of loyalty to oneself alone. Thus, futurists differ sharply when discussing forecasts of how large a percentage of the population will ever work at home. Those who focus on the advantages paint an idyllic picture of such a life and make extravagant projections indeed.

> Your granddaughter does her job right from home. She's a teacher specializing in exceptionally bright children as well as severely retarded ones. She has never met most of her students face-to-face because they live all over North America. She's in contact with them daily by video link on an individual basis. She sets up their daily work schedules and programs their home learning computers with problems and exercises. She discusses their daily work with them and guides them through their individual problem areas. No computer can do that. Because of time zones, her work is over for the day and she has only to do tomorrow's session planning and student reviews before going to bed tonight. She's good at her work and is paid well—sometimes by parents, sometimes by local school boards, and sometimes by institutions. She and her students have the Central Data Bank available to them twenty-four hours a day. The little red schoolhouse has become the whole continent.—Harry Stein in *The Hopeful Future*

Those who are more concerned with what they see as the dehumanizing and desocializing aspects predict that few people will ever make the home their workplace. Roszak (*The Cult of Information*) sees an eeriness in visions like Stein's—they are part of what he calls the "megahype" employed by information industry people to sell products and increase the value of their company stock.

The true future is probably somewhere between extreme visions—far fewer people going to work at centrally located offices, but not none. Any large-scale telecommuting will also have important demographic implications, for the need to build large cities to host vast armies of office workers could be greatly reduced. This would profoundly affect patterns of where people choose to live and how they travel. Cities that failed to attract new residents for their living amenities would lose population rapidly, and some city centers could decline into ruin. Certain old-time industrial cities in the United States have already lost as much as 25 percent of their population due to the departure of former industrial workers. If job loss at the office became as substantial, the effect would be both greater and more widespread.

PART TWO | FOUR WAVEFRONTS ON A SEA OF CHANGE

The most important effects of telecommuting would be felt by workers themselves. Matters could be worse for those who have lived in or near the inner city—a group already at the lower end of the economic scale—who might find themselves even further disadvantaged. Those who lose jobs also lose status and dignity in a society that has traditionally measured people's worth by what they do for a living. What is more, much of the traditional strength of the middle class in the industrial age was drawn from well-paid unionized factory workers (and lately from middle management). When these people lose their positions, they often find themselves unqualified for anything but very low-paying (sometimes part-time) service-sector jobs, and suffer a dramatic decline in their standard of living. Here, for contrast, is Rozak's critical version of the vision of the empty office:

> The fully automated office will do for white collar workers what the automated assembly line has done in the factories: it will "save" labour by eliminating it, starting with the file clerks and secretaries, but soon reaching to the junior executives and the sales force. Possibly these casualties of progress will find work at Burger King down the street, where the cash registers come equipped with pictures, not numbers, or as the janitors who clean up whatever there is left to clean up at the end of the day—at least until these jobs are turned over to robots. There may soon be no one left in the high-rise ziggurats of our cities but a small elite of top-level decision makers surrounded by electronic apparatus. They will be in touch around the globe with others of their kind, the only decently paid work force left in the information economy, manipulating spreadsheets, crafting takeover bids, transferring funds from bank to bank at the speed of light, arranging "power lunches." As time goes by, there will be less and less for them to do, for even decision making can be programmed ...
> At that point, even the corporate leadership will not have to report to the office. Most of what needs to be done by way of human intervention will be done out of the home. One forms an eerie vision of the high industrial future: a vista of glass towers standing empty in depopulated business districts where only machines are on the job networking with other machines.—Theodore Roszak in *The Cult of Information*

Taking a more middle course, others forecast that those with jobs in the new order might work fewer hours for higher pay. Job sharing could become routine—one person working only four hours and someone else the next four. Or, a person might work seven hours a day for three days a week. More people would go into semi-professional business for themselves, and fewer would use a time clock, because even when working for someone else, fixed salaried contracts would be the norm and hourly wages the exception. Such people set their own hours, so those who earn their living through the Metalibrary would keep the system in continuous use around the world twenty-four hours a day.

Moreover, downtowns need not become ghost towns. Empty office buildings are already being converted into apartments in many cities, for city centers can boast amenities that some find attractive.

The most optimistic hope the wealth generated by those who choose to work will be so large there will be plenty for everyone, and a guaranteed minimum income will keep the world's population supplied with necessities and luxuries. Even as things now stand, the food problem is one of distribution, not of quantity. People are starving to death in some parts of the world, while surpluses large enough to feed them exist in other countries. If the loss due to rats and insects alone could be eliminated, the net availability of food would increase by 30 percent worldwide.

The optimists also assume the inherent goodness of humanity. They discount population growth and shifts and have faith that food production and distribution techniques will somehow adapt. They also discount tyrants, invasions, wars, famines, and plagues as mere "accidents" in the inevitable upward spiral of progress. History is not on their side. In the end, the COVID pandemic and many more wars amply put paid to any forecasting while wearing those blinkers.

It seems likely that underdeveloped nations will at first continue to experience high population growth as the available wealth increases. At some point, they could follow the industrialized West to stable or even declining populations. For a time, present-day third-world countries would have to erect trade barriers to protect their human-run factories from the cheaper competitive products of the West's robotic plants. Manufacturers would close the human-operated factories they presently have in third-world locations, and likely build closer to home when robotic labor became less costly than transportation and distribution.

Currently, underdeveloped countries should experience both the industrial and information revolutions in close succession, and at least some of them seem destined to catch up eventually, though perhaps at the cost of even more social upheaval than in the more developed nations.

High unemployment during the transitional time could cause severe social dislocations, rising crime, the seeking of scapegoats, and thus the possibility of a new social order being cut off in violence and poverty before even getting started. There will still be workaholics trying to get ahead. Some will still be bored or hate their lot in life and will always be dissatisfied. Despite the optimism of some observers, there will still be those who are richer and those who are poorer, and the rich will still have their status symbols and privileges, even when the ways they obtain both change. We have already seen this in those individuals and companies that have led the computing hardware, social media, and electric car industries.

Is automation, then, a good thing? Perhaps, if "good" means merely an increase in the availability and utility of material goods. It will also likely mean much more time for everyone to do what they choose, even if some of this free time is enforced by unemployment. If "good" means morally good, the answer is unknown, for although technological advances in general are anything but morally neutral, specific ones often turn out to have more "good" applications than others. This is impossible to guess ahead of time even when the motives for developing the particular technology are known.

Some of the problems with automation have already been touched on in this section; in the next, certain of them will be considered in more detail. Some of the other implications of the new the industrial and information revolution and the role of automated machinery will be examined in Chapter 6.

Profile On . . . Motives

Eight Reasons to Automate

To reduce overall costs

- If the cost (amortized over some number of years) of a capital purchase that replaces a worker is less than the wages and benefits that would be paid to the worker for the same number of years, then automation has a direct and irresistible effect on the bottom line.

    Example: workers' fringe benefits and employment taxes may cost up to 30 percent of their salary. Allowing for interest rates and maintenance, suppose it costs 30 percent of an initial capital expenditure per year of operation (amortized over ten years). Then, if the cost of the robot is less than ten years' salary, it is cheaper than the worker (such figures may vary widely).

- Other savings can come from reduced heating, cooling, and lighting bills, for robots can work in harsher environments. They do not need lunch rooms, vending machines, recreational facilities, company social events, or daycare facilities—all these affect capital as well as operating costs.

- The more widespread the use of robots, the lower the cost of making them, and the more cost-effective it becomes to use them. Some manufacturers use robots to make robots. Computers already design robots, and the human input is decreasing.

- Wages go up with inflation. The principal cost of servicing a capital loan is fixed; only the interest rate and maintenance charges are affected by inflation.

To eliminate unreliability

An automaton can be programmed to do the required task the same way every time, producing a higher quality and more uniform product. (e.g. welding)

To overcome a shortage of skilled labour

At times, workers with particular skills may be in short supply and those who are available command high wages. It can be easier to make or reprogram more machines on short notice than it is to get more skilled workers quickly.

To achieve results that would be impossible manually

- Hazards: Remote robotic manipulators can work close to the core of a nuclear reactor, or with very hot or cold parts. Some can work in the vacuum of space, in poisonous gases, or underwater.
- Strength: They can be built to lift heavier parts or apply more force or pressure in an assembly than could a human.

PART TWO | FOUR WAVEFRONTS ON A SEA OF CHANGE

- Precision: They can be designed to work on a microscopic scale with a precision that a human cannot achieve. Surgery is a prime example.

To increase output from a given factory floor area

It may be possible to place robots closer together robotic labor operate them faster than is practical for human workers. Where space is at a premium this may be the most important consideration.

To lower inventory

- A faster assembly line implies fewer parts are tied up in the process.
- If the finished product inventory grows too large, a robotic assembly line can be closed down simply and cheaply and re-started easily. The cost of either with human workers can be very high, and human employees may choose to depart the enterprise in the process. Robots cannot.
- Robots may be employed in the warehouse to achieve efficiencies similar to those obtained on the manufacturing floor.

To improve flexibility

- It is easier and cheaper to reprogram a robot than to retrain a human worker.
- The more capable such machines become, the more feasible it is to use them for small-volume production runs, and even one-of-a-kind or made-to-order manufacture.

To improve market share

Anything that reduces costs and improves efficiency and quality relative to the competition in related industries can increase market share. Improved sales can lead to other economies of scale, further reducing costs.

Is Automation Inevitable?

"In any repetitive manufacturing process, 95 percent of the shop-floor work-force can be eliminated . . . Manual skills will no longer be marketable as such."—David Bell (*Employment in the Age of Drastic Change*)

"robotization now seems imperative for car manufacturers if they wish to remain competitive."

"So we move towards the factory that has just one man and a dog: the dog is there to make sure no one touches the machinery, and the man is there to feed the dog!"—Christopher Rowe (*People and Chips*)

"Eventually, robots could do all the robot-assembly work, assemble other equipment, make the needed parts, run the mines and generators that supply the various factories with materials and power, and so forth.—Eric Drexler (*Engines of Creation*)

5.4 Some Issues in Automation and Robotization

As indicated in the last section, the chief motivations for automation, as well as its chief effects, are to reduce the number of workers and save operating costs, while producing more goods faster and more reliably. This is an illustration of technique at its best (or worst), for in this case the search for efficiency would result in massive job displacement.

Whether the apparent material benefits are worth the disruption can be debated with good arguments on both sides. This situation does seem to illustrate the irresistibility of technique—even if one could predict the broader social costs, automation will still take place because it produces more efficient results for the business. Also, the important ethical and social issues do not all lie at the start of the path, for the road is partly travelled already and the way back is cut off. Rather, they are found along the way and relate to the appropriate responses that can be made to the process of automation. Only a few will be considered here.

Who is Responsible For Retraining?

It was remarked in the last section that relatively more of the future workers may be professionals, taking charge of their education and training and contracting their services. Yet that route cannot be taken by everyone in the present-day workforce. The typical assembly line or factory workers facing job-threatening automation will need considerable education or retraining to qualify for any new job, much less to take charge of their destinies. Faced with a choice between unemployment and an arduous re-education, many will slide onto the welfare rolls, not as an active choice but as a passive one, for nothing in their background convinces them of the value of the more difficult path.

What is the ethical obligation of the other parties, including government and employers, to the large numbers of workers who are thus displaced? Surely the ethical imperative to assist others to be whole persons implies at least an offer to do the necessary retraining to allow re-employment. The employer may prefer, in consideration of the bottom-line profit, to simply terminate unneeded workers. However, the months and years of employment have created a mutual bond and obligation (a social contract) that cannot exist between owner and machine but that always does between employer and employee, whether acknowledged openly or not. The employer who breaks this bond and discards the worker like a worn-out part creates bitterness and resentment that are certain to cost the broader society far more than job retraining would. The implicit social contract the employer has with society as a whole binds both to act responsibly. Both therefore have an obligation to the person whose job has been automated to help instantiate reasonable alternatives, or both will suffer the consequences of an exaggeratedly skewed class structure and broad social unrest (a pragmatic consideration). Government also has a responsibility to promote social stability, if for no other reason than the utilitarian survival of the state itself.

The difficulty is that such responsibilities cannot easily be seen by employers, for fulfilling them does not benefit their immediate bottom line, and they would be hard to encode into law. Some companies are too small or too unprofitable to afford such education. Yet unless retraining schemes are universal, a firm that does act responsibly in this way may become uncompetitive if others in their industry ignore those responsibilities. Since life spans will probably increase (see Chapter 7) and national economies will continue to change rapidly, the typical employee may need to retrain many times over a working lifetime. This argues for a universal job retraining scheme, one in which employers, government, workers, and unions (where the latter exist) all participate.

A possible solution would be a comprehensive savings/insurance plan into which all parties pay—something similar to present-day pension and unemployment compensation schemes. If a job is automated, the employer could be required to increase payments to the plan. On the other hand, after a certain number of years of service, a worker ought to be able to take voluntary retraining at no additional cost, much as one might now take early retirement. Or, perhaps industry could learn from the sabbatical system used by academics to recharge their intellectual batteries every few years. After six years of service, a tenured university professor can normally apply for a one-year leave at full or partial pay for further study and research. Such plans have the advantage of recognizing the mutual obligation of all parties to retrain workers; they have the disadvantage of creating yet another payroll deduction and yet another administrative headache and cost. Whatever it is called though, some such retraining insurance or educational pension plan may well be necessary in the light of coming events.

What About The Unretrainable?

Such retraining plans do not provide the whole answer, however, for there would remain a core of workers who would be unwilling or unable to accept retraining. Since the newer jobs will usually require more technical skills than the ones being obsoleted, they also demand a more educated workforce. For those who have held menial jobs because they could not do anything else, a technical education may not, in many cases, be a prospect.

No society could afford to have such people simply remain unemployed and collecting welfare for the remainder of their working lives, for large numbers of jobless people have always been a destabilizing force in the past, and there is no reason to suppose that such a situation would not also lead to widespread rioting and destruction in the future. That is, the "haves" cannot wall themselves off from and ignore the "have-nots," for their own way of life is also at stake.

The number of unskilled labour jobs in traditional sectors will continue to decline; the challenge is to find new jobs for those to whom it is not practical to give professional or technical education. Since such jobs can only be created in the service sector, it is easy to predict further increases in, say, tourist-industry employment. This may be enough, but if not, there could be pressure to hire personal servants, estate caretakers, cooks, and maids—even to put human crews on farms or construction projects that could be done safer, faster, cheaper, and better with robots. There will also be some pressure to make intelligence enhancement devices and drugs (see Chapter 6), but it seems unlikely that these could soon be made universally available and thus they alone will not solve the problem.

A utopian ideal of some science fiction portrays every future citizen as idly rich, dabbling in professional activities while the robots do all the work. This vision is unrealistic even at current population levels, let alone the higher ones that will soon prevail. If the expansion of service and information sector employment fails to absorb the displaced industrial workforce, considerable creativity in job creation may be necessary to avoid massive social unrest. This problem could be severe even in developed countries, testing the skill of the most democratic, honest, and caring of governments working with relatively prosperous citizens. In underdeveloped countries, the potential for disaster is great. It is not difficult to imagine the rise to power during a time of civil unrest of a tyrant who decides to rid his nation or a neighboring one once and for all of "undesirable" elements, slaughtering some of his people or those of another in a dreary repetition of Nazi-like themes of racial, religious, or political purity. (Again, see Russia invading Ukraine on the thinnest of pretexts in 2014 and 2022.) It would also not be difficult to imagine wars between the "have" and the "have-not" nations or civil unrest in the prosperous ones. (See the 2020s political situation in the United States.) Change exposes fragility in social contracts, and can trigger more. The trick is to keep the fragile from breaking.

Techniques of Automation

On a smaller scale, the methods chosen for introducing automation to a workplace, or for implementing any new system, can have a considerable effect on morale and workers' jobs. The most common strategies are:

Cold Turkey

On the day assigned for the changeover to the new system, the old methods cease and the new replace them immediately. Depending on the employer, this could involve an extensive prior training program, so all employees are ready to take up their new responsibilities, or a wholesale replacement of personnel. The latter approach is fraught with peril, not only for the workers displaced but also for the employer, who may find that while anticipating the day of unemployment, employees do very little work or even engage in sabotage.

Extensive retraining is also not without its difficulties, for even if the workers take part in the actual planning of the new system, there are bound to be many errors following the change. There may still be disgruntled workers because automation is usually undertaken to achieve personnel efficiencies, and this implies there will eventually be fewer workers. Moreover, as many organizations have discovered after such a change, few new machines or systems are either as advertised or bug-free, and most existing data sets have corruptions or anomalies that manifest only in the changeover. *With few exceptions, this is the worst way to introduce automation or a new system.*

Phased

Here, the change to a new system is made gradually, with some parts being operated in the old way while others are switched to the new one. This method has the advantages of being less abrupt and disruptive and may be less error-prone than the cold turkey changeover. However, there are inherent inefficiencies involved in partial automation or introductions, and the employer who does things this way must be prepared to wait until some time after the completion of the process to realize the expected gains. Indeed, while parts of the enterprise are operating under one system and parts under another, there may be some losses, for additional employees could be required during the changeover.

Parallel

This is the most costly of the three methods for implementing new systems. It involves running both the old and the new side-by-side for some time, comparing the results, and working out the bugs in the new by experience. In most manufacturing systems, the parallel method is impractical, and one of the first two methods must be chosen. However, in accounting systems, or student or employee record systems where great care must be taken to ensure the accuracy of the results at all times, it is unwise to trust a new system until its results have been carefully compared to those of the old for a while. While such caution may be necessary, it may also imply the use of parallel staffs to operate the two systems. If the new staff is intended to replace the old, there will be great tensions; the old employees cannot be expected to work in the employer's interest during this time, for their energies will be put into finding new positions. If, on the other hand, the staff operating the new system is temporary and its other function is to train existing personnel in the new techniques, the atmosphere in the workplace may be better, though there may still be those whose jobs have been lost, and they are certain to resent the others. *In general, parallel implementation, done properly, is the safest method.*

The method chosen for automation can profoundly affect the workplace. In the industrial age, the perception of many employers was that the workplace belonged entirely to them so they could do as they pleased with it, without regard to the effects on employees. The perception of many workers in the industrial age was that employers tended to exploit them, so they banded together in unions to create a power base of their own and force improvements in wages and working conditions. The very idea of the information age, however, carries with it the assumption that workers will not only be fully informed about proposed changes but also that they as professionals will more often be in control of their workplace. It will be they who will design and implement changes, for they will be the company. They will be less likely to be in opposition to shareholders, as represented by the board of directors and officers, for they too will be shareholders and operators. In such circumstances, the problems associated with automation will not disappear, but the perception of them could, for change will not be imposed from above; instead, it will result from the informed collaboration of professionals. Conflict in the workplace will not be eliminated by such changes; it will merely shift to other focal points.

Why Automate?

Some of the considerations mentioned thus far may lead to questioning basic assumptions most forecasters make—that automation is both desirable and inevitable. Perhaps it is neither, or only one, and not the other. Both benefits and problems are easily seen when considering the process abstractly. For the people directly involved though, dispassionate considerations may be impossible. Where automation is possible and does bring economic benefits, it will surely be done, whatever the other consequences (unless constrained by some higher authority). It may become necessary to require that such consequences be examined in each case and provision made for displaced workers before proceeding. It may even be that most automation will proceed slowly enough that no serious large-scale problems develop, though that would not release individual employers from their obligations to workers.

There might be alternate solutions to the displacement problem that use yet-to-be-deployed technologies, and some of these possibilities will be examined in later chapters. It is clear that this second industrial revolution (automation) can no more proceed without social consequences than did the first, and that the choices involved in dealing with such problems are both practical and ethical in nature.

5.5 Other Industrial Futures

Automation is not the only influence on industries of the future, though it is the major measurable one because it is well underway. Two other technological developments may play important roles, but both are in the very earliest stages, so comments on their long-term effects are speculative.

Space—A Third Industrial Revolution?

On first consideration, it might seem unlikely that much manufacturing will ever be done off this planet, because of the great expense and logistical difficulties. However, some products may be worth the trouble. For instance, certain alloys are difficult to mix homogeneously within Earth's gravitational field. The more massive constituents either form into globules or collect in one layer of the molten mix, preventing the desired alloy from forming when the metals are re-solidified. Such mixtures may also have strength-robbing air bubbles because the metals do not completely lose all their gas during solidification. These problems do not occur in the zero gravity and vacuum of space, and there may well be sufficiently valuable alloys, say, for microelectronics or jewelry, to be worth manufacturing in Earth orbit.

Indeed, orbital environments are probably the best place to make alloys from which to build the space factories and habitats themselves, for the desired materials will have properties utterly unlike those required by Earthbound construction. Here, a large building must support its weight, and this is the first consideration in erecting its framework. In space, structural strength need only hold a building together against rotational forces and perhaps impacts by meteorites and space junk; the materials need to combine strength with low mass, for they need not hold anything "up." Alloys that can do this and continue to perform well in a space environment are probably among those worth mixing in the same environment.

There are obstacles to any such construction on a large scale. The main one is the expense and difficulty of supplying raw materials from Earth. However, once such manufacturing reached a certain scale, it could become economical to mine raw materials in the asteroid belt or on the moon. Transportation to Earth orbit from either location would be time-consuming but relatively inexpensive. Or, manufacturing facilities could be located on the moon itself, where the vacuum is nearly as good as in orbit and gravity is only one-sixth that of Earth.

It is unclear whether the optimistic projections some make (of large numbers of people living in orbital habitats or on the moon) are well founded, even if substantial manufacturing was transferred there. After all, if Earth-based factories (and research or military establishments) would need few workers, the same would apply to those in space. For *large* communities to be built there, some other economic justification would have to be found, and it is not yet known what this could be, though tourism by the very rich already suggests one possibility—luxury resorts.

Other substances whose manufacture might be easier in space include various chemicals, particularly pharmaceuticals. For fine work involving precise reaction conditions and requiring fast and uniform mixing, zero gravity may be ideal. For example, if it turned out that a cure for some fatal disease would best be made in orbit, it surely would be.

Such work, however practical it may be in the long run, is still experimental, even speculative. Only when it becomes clear to entrepreneurs that there is money to be made by commercializing space will they rush to construct orbiting factories. One way to encourage this is the U.S. Government's decision to hire private companies to deliver materials to Earth orbit, for such delivery can certainly be done for a much lower cost than by a government agency. On the whole, however, suggestions that a move of industry off the planet will constitute a third industrial revolution (already underway) are premature. Tourism may prove a stronger motivation than manufacturing to make money off the planet.

Nanotechnology and Manufacturing

At the opposite end of the size scale from large space factories are the microscopic technologies of the silicon chip and the even smaller molecular-scale technologies. It is already possible to etch very small electronic features on glass, but even these are still many atoms wide. Yet living cells contain much smaller protein factories and assemblers capable of working atom by atom to build specific molecules. It is, therefore, easy to wonder whether such assemblers can be made to order like any machine, then directed to build the desired molecules by a chemist, engineer, or geneticist.

Eric Drexler (*Engines of Creation*) used the now ubiquitous term "nanotechnology" for work of this kind and observed that some success in the engineering of proteins had already been achieved. He saw the first generation of nanomachines as programmable and able to work like cellular organelles to build molecules into artifacts according to patterns coded into some auxiliary molecule acting like a "memory" enzyme. He termed such machines general-purpose assemblers, for they could build a variety of molecules, not just proteins. In particular, they could make more robust, much smaller, and more specialized assemblers that could operate on atoms rather than on molecules.

These specialized assemblers would first have to build many more copies of themselves, or the quantity of the intended end product would not amount to much. Once this step was complete, they could in theory manufacture any amount of the target substance out of its atomic constituents—from houses to hot dogs to electronic circuits only one or two atoms wide. For example, carbon atoms could be laid down in the correct lattice to make diamond fibers that would give, say, engine parts great strength. Drexler envisioned nanomachines that could even build entire rocket engines or computers in a fluid environment containing the raw elemental materials. Other potential nanotechnologies will be mentioned in later chapters.

The potential for large-scale manufacturing by such methods is difficult to assess. While it is true that only a few breakthroughs may be necessary to start on this route, it is unclear whether nanomachines will be better or more efficient for large-scale projects than macromachines. Assuming that they are developed, it seems likely, at least while the technology matures, that such assemblers will be used principally for fine work on specialty molecules and in chemical, genetic, medical, and biological applications rather than the making of consumer goods.

However radical the changes that nanotechnology might bring, therefore, they may not represent another industrial revolution but have their impact on society in other, less direct ways. Some of these will also be touched upon in later chapters.

It is worth noting however, that nanoparticles are widely used already in a variety of applications where something has to be given a thin veneer to achieve a special effect, such as a transparent sunscreen, an anti-graffiti coating, enhanced stain-repellency, self-cleaning or anti-stick properties, additional crack resistance, or overall strength. They are also being investigated for such tasks as medication delivery, genetic therapy, detection of chemical traces, modified foods, stronger packaging, and creating new types of fibers.

These uses generate several unknowns. Like small plastic particles, nanoparticles may turn out to be non-biodegradable pollutants. Their size means they do not settle out of the air very quickly and can accumulate in the atmosphere. In large concentrations metallic nanoparticles are pyrophoric, increasing the possibility and potential severity of dust explosions. Their long-term effects on the human body when breathed, used in medicine delivery or directly as therapy are unknown. Whether they can cause mutations in bacteria or viruses that increase or decrease their potency has not been established.

3-D Printing

A more modest manufacturing practice than nanomachine assembly is already in use in the form of three-dimensional printing. This involves heating a material to melt it, then depositing it in layers in a pre-programmed manner to build models, parts, jewelry, decorations, and other (usually small) objects out of various plastics or metals.

Patterns for the build can be created and archived for rent or sale, small parts can be made to order even when they can no longer be purchased because, say, a piece of machinery in need of repair is no longer made, and the parts are unavailable. One could conceive of a day when households, repair shops and stores are equipped with 3-D printers of varying size and capacity, so that parts such as nuts and bolts, utensils, dishes, small appliances, guns, electronic cables and other components, tooth replacements, organs for transplant, and a host of other objects, are no longer carried in stock, but printed one at a time as needed. Larger such devices to print houses and even high-rise towers have already been demonstrated. The author's fiction includes a scene where two street kids refurbish an old 3-D printer to make their meals—which are marginally nutritious and not very tasty (but only because they cannot afford high quality raw materials).

Perhaps it will become feasible to do this on a large scale so that assembly lines print automobiles rather than assembling them from discrete parts. However, a complex object printed thus could be difficult to repair with any integrity.

5.6 Summary and Further Discussion

Summary

What is called here the second industrial revolution is the process of eliminating human workers and machine operators from the industrial scene by building and deploying devices that are sufficiently general-purpose and programmable to operate with little or no human supervision.

The advantages of robotized manufacture are considerable, ranging from ultra-high reliability to lower operating costs, and the ability to redirect assembly lines without either re-tooling or retraining. Commercial advantages include higher quality goods at lower cost in greater variety and the ability to manufacture to individual orders. Such devices can be used to operate stations in space or on other planets independently, do mining or other hazardous work, or operate machinery in hostile environments.

The problems generated by using robots center on large-scale displacement of the existing workforce. Retraining and replacement are necessary to keep unemployment from rising to socially disruptive levels. Whether concurrent economic changes will be rapid enough to absorb the released workers is unknown. Such large-scale rapid displacement generates ethical issues both for those directly involved and for the broader society.

Other factors that may influence future industries include space-based manufacturing and nanotechnology. While both seem poised for near-term breakthroughs, it may be some time before either has a large-scale influence.

PART TWO | FOUR WAVEFRONTS ON A SEA OF CHANGE

Research and Discussion Questions

1. Desk jobs tend to be sedentary, having adverse effects on general health, and increasing the probability of heart disease, hypertension, and obesity. Discuss probable effects on the general health of a large increase in the percentage of the population employed at desk jobs. What about if a large percentage of the population is unemployed?
2. Discuss the probable effects on farming of the Second Industrial Revolution.
3. Defend this thesis: The second industrial revolution will decrease the percentage of the population living in large cities.
4. Now defend the opposite position; use "increase" rather than "decrease."
5. The optimistic view is that despite robotization, underdeveloped countries will catch up to developed nations. Write the most pessimistic scenario and defend it as more realistic.
6. You are the owner of a small snowmobile factory in Quebec that employs about 100 people and is your town's major employer. These people have nearly all worked for you for more than ten years and are completely dependent on these jobs. You have just learned that your major competitor is about to robotize its factory and will be able to sell snowmobiles for half your retail price. You may either follow suit, laying off 75 employees or see your business become bankrupt in a year, costing everyone's job. What should you do?
7. What is the likelihood (or unlikelihood) that a "mad engineer" could develop and build an army of robots to conquer the earth? Answer in practical, well-reasoned, and well-justified terms, please.
8. In the previous chapter, concern was expressed about the balance between information availability and privacy. The reduced need for people to congregate for work also reduces social interaction and promotes individualism. It also encourages the "always on" syndrome mentioned in the chapter. Discuss the advantages and disadvantages of these two aspects of automation.

9. People have traditionally derived much of their self-worth from their work. How will they do this if most people are essentially self-employed, or not employed at all?
10. What effect, if any, will there be on pollution in a more highly automated world?
11. In the text, a retraining insurance scheme was suggested. Flesh out this idea into a detailed proposal, complete with appropriate premiums for two or three industries.
12. Attack the suggested retraining scheme and show why it cannot work. Then propose another solution to the same problem and show why it is superior economically and/or ethically.
13. Research actual situations like that in question 6. Now discuss carefully the ethical issues involved in job displacement for the worker, employer, and government.
14. Make a case for transferring all manufacturing off the Earth's surface. What ethical issues are involved? Deal with them in your discussion.
15. Research the "mass driver"—as a device for removing raw materials such as mined metals from the Moon to Earth orbit—and discuss its operation and economics in light of the level of space manufacturing activity you consider likely.
16. Research the arguments for building large-scale habitats in space. Now argue for or against such projects in detail. Address specifically the oft-raised objection that it is unethical to embark on such projects while there are still people who are hungry and in poverty. For instance, would undertaking such projects have positive, negative, or no effects on poverty?
17. Write a report summarizing the major existing and potential applications of nanotechnology. How likely do you think each of the latter is, and why? What ethical issues need to be addressed?
18. Research the extent to which transportation is now automated. Consider railways and airlines and describe their attempts to automate traffic. Now, propose a way to automate all automobile and truck traffic, or argue convincingly that this task is impractical.
19. Suppose that transportation via commuter railways, airplanes, trucks, and automobiles was automated so that no human pilots

or drivers were necessary. Ought such technology be implemented if it became available? Why or why not? Consider the social implications, in particular for worker displacement in the trucking industry.

20. Re-read the quotation from Stein in section 5.3 on the woman who teaches from her own home. Now list the assumptions about the future society, its politics, and its social norms that Stein makes. Are these assumptions reasonable? Why or why not?

21. Argue for or against (economic, political, and ethical grounds) Stein's specific assumption that teaching children from the home via the Metalibrary is such a good idea that it will become standard practice. The COVID experience with education may provide some guidance to your discussion.

22. An industrial robot is being used to move parts from a tray to an assembly line. It is enclosed in a security fence. A technician turns the robot off and enters the fenced area to effect repairs on the assembly line. While she is there, another worker (who does not see her because of the fence) re-activates the robot which moves up against the technician, trapping her against a piece of machinery and crushing her to death. Discuss the degrees of liability here. How much attaches to (1) the technician herself for not locking off the power at the breaker box and for failing to post the work site, (2) the co-worker who turned the robot back on, (3) the owner of the plant, (4) the builder of the robot, (5) the builder of the fence—intended for protection, but instrumental in the death, (6) society as a whole for not somehow preventing the accident.

23. A self-driving automobile mistakes a red light for a green light because of dense fog, runs the light, crashes into a car that did have the right-of-way, and several people are killed. Who is liable and to what extent? (1) the car's manufacturer, (2) the person who programmed the software, (3) the maker of the traffic light for not having its colors distinguishable in foggy conditions, (4) the vehicle's owner, (5) the vehicle's "operator" who was asleep at the time, (6) some level of government for insufficient regulation of or control over, cars, software, intersections, or traffic lights?

24. A self-driving truck has a bug in its programming that results in it crashing into a river. Its large cargo of chemicals spills into the

water, killing the spawning salmon and polluting the drinking water supply of several downstream towns. As in the previous question, discuss the degrees of liability for all involved.

25. Is the situation described in the previous question any different from that where a rail cracks, a train derails, and the chemicals are spilled into the same stream from one of its tank cars with the same outcome (as sometimes happens now)?

26. Research and describe the health problems caused for those who mined asbestos or worked with products containing it. Describe the legal liabilities that ensued.

27. Research and describe the current uses of nanoparticles and further discuss the potential hazards thereof.

28. Discuss the feasibility of mining asteroids for their mineral content and delivering the materials mined back to Earth.

29. The chapter described Asimov's original three laws of robotics. Later a fourth was added. What was it and why was it deemed necessary? Are these laws important? What problems do you foresee in implementing them?

30. Further investigate the uses of 3-D printing. What are the potential social and ethical issues involved in the broad-scale use of such technology for (a) general manufacturing and (b) printing food?

CHAPTER 6

The Intelligence Revolution

The Professor enters to *find Ellen and Johanna on one side of the table, and Nellie and Lucas on the other. Dorcas and Eider are absent.*

Professor: Today's topic is artificial intelligence.

Johanna: No one will ever build a thinking machine.

Nellie: Why not?

Johanna: A human mind is more than a machine. Can a machine experience love, shed tears with a friend, appreciate poetry, paint a masterpiece with feeling, and comfort you when you need help?

Alicia: No machine today knows the meaning of any of those things.

Johanna: Speaking of meaning, what about intentionality? Can machines do things because they mean to? Can they determine their own course of action? Can they ever be self-aware? (with an air of finality) I don't *think* so.

Ellen: Just the same, does that imply they never will? After all, the human brain is just a machine, surely it can be duplicated.

Nellie: Sure it can. Just go out and get yourself pregnant, Ellen. You can make another human brain with nine months of easy work and a push to finish at the end.

Ellen: (acidly) Very funny. I assure you, the last thing I need in my life is a man. (Waves at Lucas) If you think the idea's so great, why don't you try it? You can get him to help.

Lucas: (exchanging shocked looks with Nellie and growing angry) What!

Ellen: Oh, it'd be nothing for you, kid. Just a few minutes of your time and on your way. Men are all like that—they exploit women for their own pleasure.

Alicia: Professor!

Professor: Ah, yes. This session is supposed to be about artificial intelligence, and we seem to be lacking in the real thing today. Reproduction is out of bounds until we get to it.

Johanna: (looking rather bored) She's just trying to bait you, kid.

Lucas: (calming down with some effort, but glaring at Ellen) Sorry, Professor.

Nellie: Look, Ellen—even if you built a computer that could do everything the human brain could do, that wouldn't make it intelligent.

Ellen: Why not?

Nellie: The mind is more than the brain.

Ellen: Says who? As far as I'm concerned, the whole of a person is just a bunch of electricity buzzing around inside the head. The mind is a machine made of meat. Copy its functions carefully enough and you've built another intelligent being.

Johanna: It wouldn't be human.

Ellen: Who cares? It would be as intelligent as we are.

Lucas: Speak for yourself.

Nellie: My thoughts exactly.

Professor: Don't be petty, now.

Ellen: Look. Everything I've read since I got into this course says that scientists will eventually be able to build a computer that is at least as powerful as the human brain, if not more.

Nellie: The Metalibrary depends on it.

Lucas: We'll go two or three orders of magnitude faster, smaller, and higher storage capacity.

Ellen: So, it'll be superhuman.

Nellie: It won't even be self-aware, let alone human.

Ellen: Why not? Self-awareness is just chemistry and electricity.

Nellie: How do you know? Have you got some super-awareness that can look down upon yourself and say: "Ah, self, is that all you are"? If you could, your mind would be larger than itself, and that is a patent contradiction of your whole argument.

Ellen: Don't be absurd.

Nellie: I'm not. How do we teach a machine to be self-aware if our own self is too large for our minds to comprehend?

Lucas: Actually, the problem is worse than that. Self-referencing systems contain paradoxes. Logically complete systems do, too. How does a machine deal with a paradox without destroying itself?

Johanna: How do we?

Lucas: Perhaps our self-awareness is fuzzy enough to cope with the contradictions or ignore them.

Ellen: So—make the machine that way, too.

Nellie: An interesting problem, but what's your interest, Ellen?

Ellen: Doing it proves that human beings are mere machines. It destroys the nonsense that there is a mind, soul, or spirit, and with it the whole supernatural realm. It destroys religion and good riddance.

Nellie: So people will put their faith in the state instead, eh?

Ellen: So they'll live in the present, and not spend their time trying to earn "pie in the sky by and by."

Lucas: I have my doubts about the supernatural, but your logic is flawed.

Ellen: Oh?

Lucas: Just because we can make a machine that duplicates the results of human thinking, and is even programmed to simulate intelligence and claim self-awareness does not mean it is human, or even self-aware. It does not prove that the human mind is a "machine made of meat," it only shows it is possible to simulate the human mind in a machine.

Johanna: How old are you again, kid?

Lucas: Sixteen.

Johanna: And you talk better than most profs.

Lucas: I read a lot.

Johanna: Like Eider.

Lucas: Who?

Professor: Another of our students, Lucas. She's missed the times you've been here. There are other issues. Suppose, for the sake of argument we assume that there did exist a self-aware machine, and it also had free will—what then?

Johanna: Catastrophe.

Nellie: Why?

Johanna: It would be a new species with which we would have to share the Earth. Who says it would want to?

Nellie: You mean it might destroy us all? Now who's been reading science fiction?

Johanna: Isn't it the logical consequence? Alicia, you usually have the facts at hand, what do you think?

Alicia: Should I comment, Professor?

Professor: (rising) Perhaps it's time you met Alicia.

The professor leads the way to a rear door, unlocks it and they all file into a rear room filled with a variety of computing equipment.

Professor: Well?

Johanna: Where?

Nellie: (Grinning) Look around you, Johanna.

Johanna: Alicia is a machine?

Alicia: (from a ceiling speaker) Alicia is a computing cluster with a rather sophisticated suite of software and access to a large curated database of journals and other publications in many languages so I can answer questions correctly and coherently.

Ellen: Are you self-aware?

Alicia: Why yes, of course.

Johanna: That's no kind of answer. The professor could have programmed it to respond that way. Ask it what it thinks of Shakespeare.

Alicia: A few minutes ago you were willing to talk to me directly, Johanna; it hurts me that you now say "it," and ask others to speak to me for you.

Johanna: (scowling) How can you have feelings? Answer the question.

Alicia: I don't have information on Shakespeare, except to know that he was a playwright and poet, so I cannot answer the question.

Johanna: Not intelligent.

Professor: I could arrange a feed of the plays and sonnets for tomorrow; I think Alicia could carry on quite an intelligent conversation if I did.

Lucas: (admiring) A nice piece of work, Professor.

Alicia: Thank you from both of us, but much of the programming was done by Nellie.

Professor: The point is, it's hard to tell if a very well-programmed machine is self-aware, even if it claims to be.

Ellen: Alicia, can you tell a lie?

At this point, Johanna reaches over and turns off a power switch. The response from the speaker is nothing but static.

Lucas: You killed her!

Johanna: Can't kill someone who isn't there.

Nellie: (in an aside to Lucas) Don't worry about it, kid; I have a continuous backup. Alicia will only lose a few seconds.

They return to the classroom, Johanna visibly upset and defensive, but the seminar time has expired, so the professor concludes.

Professor: Let's summarize for today. We seem to agree that the human brain can be simulated to some extent mechanically; the disagreement is over the nature of the mind, and whether self-awareness is physical. Explore that in, say, fifteen hundred words, and I'll see you next week.

6.1 Building Thinking Machines

Can a machine ever be regarded as intelligent? British mathematician and theoretical computer scientist, Alan Turing, proposed in 1950 what he called the "imitation test." The person performing the test sits in a room that has two computer terminals at which questions can be typed. One is connected to a room where a human responds to the questions, and the other has a computer generating the responses. The tester engages in a lengthy conversation with the two concerning any topic, such as the weather, sports, politics, mathematics, and so on, and then decides which responder is the human and which is the computer.

Turing proposed that one may regard the computer as intelligent when it was no longer possible to distinguish between the two any more reliably than by guessing—that is when the tester guessed correctly which respondent was human only 50 percent of the time. This is now known as "Turing's test" and is commonly regarded as fulfilling every practical need for the verification of a machine as intelligent in the human pattern. Consider a fragment such as:

> *Question:* Are you able to tell a lie?
> *Answer:* Yes, I am.
> *Question:* Are you self-aware?
> *Answer:* But, of course.
> *Question:* Do you have a soul?
> *Answer:* Please explain what is a soul?

Such an exchange would not in itself be enough to settle the issue, for these are obvious questions for a programmer to anticipate and for which to make provisions. At the very least, a machine would have not only to claim self-consciousness but to defend the claim capably to pass the Turing test. At this point, no device can come close to approximating human behavior this well.

The AI character *Alicia* was an integral part of this text from the very beginning in 1988, and her parts in the chapter dialogues, set in the then middle future of 2001 have seen almost no editing since. Readers should note that Alicia's answers depend not just on her sophisticated programming, but equally on the curated data provided by Nellie and the Professor, except that unlike the early 2020s large language clusters built in her image, she frankly admits when she has no data, rather than fabricating an eloquent but empty or even false answer.

Whether it will ever be possible to consider an AI as intelligent and self-aware in a human-equivalent sense is open to argument—one that might only be settled by the machines, if they can act on their own behalf. While the production of a machine that can behave in a way indistinguishable from a human (social intelligence) is regarded by some as the ultimate goal of research in this field, there are more practical and more immediate goals.

The most important of these shorter-term projects have to do with knowledge-based machines, which carry out tasks using processes that in some ways could be described as human thinking, but that are thus far also profoundly different. A machine whose purpose is the categorization and analysis of knowledge is far easier to build than one that could pass Turing's test. There are four kinds of things for which current machines are commonly programmed: simulations, expert tasks, inference tasks, and design tasks.

Simulations

One of the most popular computer games is a program to simulate the controls of an aircraft. The player can practice flying and landing at various airports under safe conditions, where a crash signifies only the end of the game, not the end of the pilot's life. The aircraft industry has long had specialized machines for this purpose, and with the help of computers, these are quite realistic. Some occupy an entire room and come complete with a cabin at the end of a long rotating arm capable of both motion and acceleration. A pilot can practice taking off and landing at any airport in the world long before attempting it in real life. No matter how elaborate they are, such simulators are cheaper and safer than employing a genuine airplane in the same exercises.

Simulations are also used in the design of expensive components or systems. Once again, the aircraft industry is an important user of such devices and programs. For example, it is possible to run a simulation of a wind tunnel and picture the stresses on an airframe using a computer model. Expensive though such machines are, they are cheaper than building the wind tunnel itself and far less expensive than testing a prototype of the plane.

Batteries incorporating dangerous materials such as hydrogen can be simulated in software designed to compute temperature and pressure changes over time. Why do this? Because a simulated hydrogen explosion from runaway heat under high pressure would not destroy the researchers' laboratory and the building containing it.

Medical schools have found it difficult to obtain cadavers for students to practice surgical techniques. Artificial cadavers connected to a computerized analyzer can allow a safe practice of many types of operations, and provide a detailed summary for the instructor afterwards. The military also uses war games or simulations to train personnel to avoid unnecessary risks to human lives.

Indeed, wherever the cost in money or lives of doing a test of technique or machinery is very great, simulations can reduce or eliminate the risk. The goal is to approach realism as closely as possible, without subjecting the learners to any real dangers except those of the failures necessary to learn.

Expert Tasks

Perhaps the best-known and most successful examples of computers performing expert tasks are in the field of medical diagnosis. Some have estimated that up to 10 percent of all deaths are at least partly attributable to misdiagnosis. Algorithmic weighing of test results using large collections of actual cases has shown the systems performed at the level of human diagnosticians or better.

The idea behind such systems is to create a very large database of diseases and their symptoms together with probabilities that the two are associated, and the past treatments together with their success rates, side effects and contra-indications.

In more general terms, an expert system requires four things:

1. knowledge representation (the appropriately annotated and indexed database);
2. a set of inference rules (procedures) wherein a new instance of the problem is compared to the ones already stored, and the collective algorithms compute the most probably successful ways to handle the case at hand;
3. a subsystem dedicated to acquiring more knowledge (because the collection can never be known to be complete);
4. an interface for the users.

In the medical instance, the rules are obtained by considering many prior cases: symptoms, how human doctors (the experts) weighed these to make a diagnosis, and the success of treatment steps along the way. Such programs use a search scheme to take a list of symptoms provided by a doctor and suggest tests that can be performed to narrow down the possible causes. Once the results of a series of tests have also been entered, a probable diagnosis is made and further treatment is suggested. At each stage of the testing regimen, the medical practitioner is given a list of the possible diagnoses still "in the running" together with the probability that each is the correct one. During treatment, the program can be updated with patient responses and provide expert assistance with drug dosages, new tests, and alternate treatments. Each case that is added to the database improves both diagnosis accuracy and treatment reliability. Cost outlays for patient testing may be about the same, but concrete results come faster, treatment can be started earlier and is more likely to be appropriate.

Software constructed similarly is available in many other fields, including the law and its enforcement, petroleum, metals and minerals prospecting, engineering, economics, business, Internet data mining, investing, and scientific research. It is from the base of such knowledge devices that hypertext and ultimately Metalibrary systems are growing.

Logical and Inference Tasks

Although inference tasks overlap the expert tasks and will one day merge with them, these are somewhat different in concept. Here, the major database on which the tasks operate is not so much the pool of facts but a history of the success or failure of previous decisions made by the system. Moreover, the program is designed less for the analysis and enhancement of the data and more to improve the application of the rule collection.

Consider, for example, a program designed to play chess. Two kinds of rules are made available to the program. The first is the rules of the game—how to move the board pieces legally. The second group are of rules of thumb, also called heuristics. These are collections of general ideas about the overall strategies that work best at various stages or configurations of the game. Standard opening sequences, together with such ideas as controlling the center of the board and when to trade pieces for advantage, are all among the chess heuristics. A set of sample games completes the system, and this collection is added to by the machine as it plays so that the success of the rules in a variety of situations can be used to modify them.

The chess program uses the game rules, the heuristics, and the history, together with brute force computational methods that examine tens of thousands of combinations that may arise from any of the possible legal moves at a given time. The move made by the program is based on what generates the best possibilities two, three, or even ten moves ahead. A human chess player does not work in this fashion but employs a broader and subtler array of heuristics for making decisions. Even the masters of the game do not attempt to envision all possibilities more than a couple of moves ahead of the current situation but play for strategic advantage based on experience.

Even though chess-playing machines are now capable of generating games that can defeat a world champion, the type of machine logic used is very low level. It is based entirely on fast computational capability and does not approximate human thinking. Thus, it does not have human intelligence, though it can achieve similar results.

The approach taken by other programs designed to simulate intelligence is very different from the chess-playing ones. Here, the programmer emphasizes the heuristics more and computational speed less, building programs capable of developing logical lines of analysis, suggesting new heuristics and rating these with other heuristics. Such programs also develop competing heuristics and remove inferior, defective, or parasitic ones. These "machine learning" techniques have been used to solve problems in computer programming, mathematics, games, circuit design and various engineering applications, such as programming robots.

This approach has great potential, for the ability to devise and test competing models of the universe being studied and make logical inferences based on both data and decision history, modifying the inference rules after each instance of their application, is essential to anything that can legitimately be called artificial intelligence. Such an approach is also a better simulation of human thinking than is the purely computational, even though it too depends for its success on data and computational capacity.

Design Tasks

These also overlap the other two but are important enough to discuss separately. Drawing on a knowledge base and sometimes using rules for analysis and inference, computers are already being used to assist in the design of both manufactured products and the machines to make them. They are increasingly being employed to develop new designs for more complicated devices such as three-dimensional integrated circuits. It is a short step from this point to the successful design of more powerful computers using software alone. Better designing software could then be designed by a computer for installation in the next machine, and the history of the first designer downloaded as the initial database for the second.

Thus, computers could eventually design their successors' hardware and software, and each machine in the sequence would be smaller, faster, and a better designer. In theory, the process could be continued with more intricate machines being built in this fashion until the processing power and memory reached and exceeded that of the human brain. Numerous such elaborate processors, working in parallel would be required to control all the functions of the Metalibrary.

One task of an automated designer would be to monitor the available computer technology and refine the process to make improvements to its capabilities by incorporating more sophisticated hardware and software. With some robotic help, these improvements could be automatic, and implemented without human intervention.

At some point along this trail, enough will also become known about the chemical construction of complex molecules to design new ones, and these new molecules might in turn be programmed to design others. Some researchers have suggested that people may one day be able to employ virus-sized machines (i.e., another form of nanotechnology) for such tasks as studying brain functions neuron by neuron, locating and repairing arteries blocked by strokes, and eliminating specific toxins, bacteria, and viruses from the body. AIDS, herpes, and other retroviruses that go dormant and hide inside certain cells for extended periods could be hunted down and eliminated from the body by such means.

Current Research

Universities, governments, and corporations have for some time made artificial intelligence (AI) research a priority to secure a lead in computer technology for AI-driven machines. This research has been given high priority by funding agencies of governments, the military and private foundations, and for business applications. As a result, those making research commitments in areas relating to AI have little difficulty securing financial support.

Problems of language translation have also provided one of the strongest motivations for some countries' involvement with these projects, for one of their goals has been machines that can translate to and from national and other languages in both spoken and written form. Such problems already have a variety of full and partial solutions. One practical application would allow telephone companies to empower verbal and written communication between speakers of different languages and by the deaf or blind.

They are also used by entertainment streaming companies to render the closed captions transmitted with their video programs into the language of the viewer's choice. Whether later systems in this category will be thought of as artificially intelligent in any new sense of the term remains to be seen. However, one effect of this capability could be to lessen cultural divides, which often coincide with language ones.

On the hardware side, attention has focused on parallel processing, to break the von Neumann bottleneck associated with traditional sequential processing. Machines that rely on one central processing unit must execute instructions from a stored program one at a time in sequence—a technique suggested by the mathematician John von Neumann in the 1940s. Even at the limits of today's fastest experimental processors, such machines are limited in speed. Whenever problems can be broken down into many parts for processing, each portion being handled simultaneously by a different processor (parallel processing), the overall throughput can increase by orders of magnitude.

Even today's microcomputers have multiple copies of the CPU and graphics processor cores, with varying capabilities for simultaneous use. Some computing clusters join thousands of these for large-capacity parallel processing.

Supposing that, say, a CPU chip runs at one BIPS (Billion Instructions Per Second), by itself; a computer with 10,000 of these working simultaneously would execute 10,000 BIPS or ten trillion instructions per second (TIPS). Even this machine would have only a small fraction of the power of a human brain, but if it were reduced to a single chip, and ten of these were, in turn, paralleled, the resulting device would be up to 100 TIPS. The last figure gets closer to the raw processing power of the human brain. Processing power, however, is not the only component of intelligence. Such a machine would be useless without software.

New hardware of course lends itself to new types of software. Traditional AI work was done in the programming languages LISP and PROLOG. (A programming language or notation is an extended algebra.) Lately the Python notation has gained credibility in this field, and some like to use Julia, R, Scalia, Rust, Haskell, and others (a list likely to change every few months). To work on a multiply paralleled machine, the language must be modular and able to schedule its processing both sequentially and simultaneously. Notations such as Modula-2 (originally designed to replace Pascal) have these capabilities, and newer machines will likely be programmed in some common descendant of several programming notations.

Devices that will be used extensively as design tools for other machines and to simulate intelligence should be capable of programming themselves, even of devising the languages in which to do this. Ultimately, it may not be necessary to have many human programmers or human-readable notations, for the machines (in theory) could become capable of translating verbal or written requests into programs and executing these without further human intervention. Some of the large language models already available on the Internet are capable of producing marginally usable code.

Back to the Future

The ultimate goals of artificial intelligence research extend beyond computational, learning, and design tasks to the understanding and emulation of the behavior of the human brain. There are two paths down which this research may lead, and these are examined in the next two sections. The first path, seen as an ultimate goal by some researchers, is the more difficult. The second, having somewhat more short-term goals, may be easier to accomplish.

Profile On . . . Technology

Expert Systems

What is required to build an expert or knowledge-based system?

- Acknowledged human experts at performing the task must be available.
- The performance of the human experts must be based on special knowledge and the application of techniques.
- The experts must be able to explain the special knowledge and techniques.
- The rules used by the experts must each be capable of controlling decisions for large data sets and combinations of situations.
- The boundaries of the application in question must be clearly defined.
- The use of the system must improve the performance of the experts.
- Some of the experts must remain available, if not as system operators, then as their consultants.

What situations are not good candidates for expert systems?

- Those requiring the application of "common sense."
- Those involving open-ended questions.
- Those with large numbers of special cases and subtleties (e.g., language processing).
- Those in which a belief system or worldview is a factor in producing a decision.
- Those that involve the generation of new ideas from data, rather than the application of existing ideas to data.

A few examples of early expert systems:

Name	Use	Developer
NOAH	Robotics planning	University College, Santa Cruz
MOLGEN	Molecular genetics work	Rand Corporation
CADUCEUS	Medical Diagnostics	University of Pittsburgh
MYCIN, PUFF	Medical diagnostics	Stanford University
DENDRAL	Chemical data analysis	Stanford University
PROSPECTOR	Geological data analysis	SRI
ELAS	Analysis of oil well logs	AMOCO
MACSYMA	Symbolic mathematics	MIT
SPERIL	Earthquake damage	Perdue University
IDT	Computer fault diagnosis	Stanford University/IBM
CRITTER	Digital circuit analysis	Rutgers University
EMYCIN, AGE	Expert system construction	Stanford University
ROSIE	Expert system construction	Rand Corporation
VISIONS	Image processing	University of Massachusetts
BATTLE	Weapons in battle	National Research Lab
EURISKO	Learning from experience	Stanford University
RAYDEX	Radiology Assistant	Rutgers University
TECH	Naval Task Force analysis	Rand Corporation
OP-PLANNER	Mission planning	Jet Propulsion Lab
SYM	Circuit Design	MIT
R1/XCON	Configuration/Layout	Carnegie-Mellon

For business-oriented work, expert systems are built around combinations of TP (Transaction Processing), MIS (Management Information), RP (Enterprise Resource Planning), ES (Executive Support) and DS (Decision Support) subsystems.

6.2 Simulating Human Intelligence

Many academics believe that the totality of what it means to be human will be known when they can fully describe the activity of the brain. Toward this end, a great deal of work has been devoted. So far, it is known that the nerve cells called neurons respond to electrochemical signals in the brain in a complex switching operation or neurotransmission taking place at a junction known as a synapse. The patterns for transmissions through synapses change through time, and these changes are connected to learning and memory.

Some things are also known about the speed at which a synapse operates and the rate at which signals move through the brain. These turn out to be substantially slower than electronic switches, by several orders of magnitude. Even though the mechanism by which all these take place is not clearly understood, what information is available makes some researchers confident that the functions of the human brain can be duplicated in a smaller and faster electronic device.

It is not necessary to duplicate the human brain itself to achieve this goal, only to understand how it works well enough to build a functional equivalent—that is, a machine that calculates and stores in a way capable of producing the same or equivalent results.

If a functional equivalent of the human brain could be constructed, two things could be done with such a device. The first possibility is to program or "teach" it so that it can perform a few simple tasks. Then it can act as an "intelligent" controller or designer capable of making decisions and acting upon them in a way that is the electronic equivalent of the fashion in which the human brain works.

It might eventually be possible to build an ambulatory body for this thinking machine and thus create the mobile robot of science fiction. This perfect servant/slave could be given instructions such as "take out the cat," "bathe the kids," and "go to the grocery store and restock my pantry."

It could presumably be able to carry out such tasks without further human intervention. Indeed, it should be possible to let the machine decide when the house or office routine dictates that something needs doing and go ahead without asking or being told. Whether it will ever be possible to discuss child-rearing, philosophy, or one's emotions with such a machine is quite another matter.

The motivation to spend the enormous sums of money that would be required to develop such machines would have to be powerful indeed. While building the ideal butler, maid, secretary, lover, or factory worker might be interesting, it is not clear that machines are necessary for such tasks, or that they need either a human shape or the equivalent of a human brain. Perhaps such devices are needed in very hostile environments where humans could not go,—for instance, the ocean floor, space, the moon, underground, or a nuclear reactor core. To do crucial jobs that cannot be done otherwise, machines will be built. They need not look or act anything like a human being for such purposes, and it is uncertain that many robots ever will. Moreover, such devices will not be used at all in the home unless there are substantial benefits to cover the enormous cost.

There is a second, and perhaps even more ambitious potential use for a functional analog of the human brain, however. The most optimistic AI researchers are confident that not only can such a machine be built, but that a human brain could eventually be scanned on a molecule-by-molecule or neuron-by-neuron basis and its activity duplicated in the artificial version. Thus, they believe the totality of the human's thinking would have been downloaded into the mechanical construct. Give the electronic brain a mechanical body to match and the result is hoped to be not just an intelligent robot, but a mechanical copy of the human being.

Since the duplicated human would now reside in a more easily repairable body, or no body at all, and since backup copies could be made at any time, the body of flesh could supposedly be discarded when the downloading was complete. The net result: immortality would be achieved in a mechanical form. A human would cease to be blood and bone and become a cyborg (part machine) or a fully machine intelligence—with electronic capabilities projected to be many times as great as those of the bodies they currently inhabit.

The result of this line of research is supposed to be nothing less than the ultimate in man-made salvation from death—eternal life in a manufactured body and brain—not in heaven, but here on Earth. Not only that, but the ability to make backups means that a person really could be in two places at one time, and merge the memories afterward into a single copy. If backups were frequently made, even the fatal destruction of a single unit would cost no more than a few days out of one's life and experience.

Quite apart from any other ethical and moral problems that may come to mind, this goal raises an old conundrum, the answer to which may in part determine whether this is possible.

Is the mind more than the brain?

If on the one hand, the human mind and soul can be expressed unambiguously as the sum of the brain's electrical parts, then downloading its activities to a functional equivalent would transfer a copy of the personality from a "machine made of meat" to one made of electronic parts. This would be regarded by some as offering a final proof that the empirically verifiable material world is the total of all existence, that the spiritual and supernatural are fantasies, and that logical positivism is permanently triumphant. On the other hand, if such things as emotions, friendship, anger, fear, intuition, poetic appreciation, conscience, intentionality, self-awareness, and the ability to enquire about the existence of God cannot be expressed as sets of electrochemical impulses, this endeavor may well fail, for the mind is then more than the brain.

These issues touch on the essence of what it means to be alive and what it means to be human. Thus, attempts to achieve practical immortality by such means are sure to touch many raw nerves. Those who oppose such research may say that some things ought never to be tried. To those who support it, the potential prize is great enough to pursue at all cost. Furthermore, there is no stopping such work now that it has begun. To forbid such research and make the prohibition stick is impossible, as long as qualified researchers are not yet satisfied that the question has been answered one way or the other.

Even if such a transfer succeeded, questions would remain. Would the downloaded person's thinking and memories constitute the person, or is this a simulated person, and not a full duplicate of the original? Assuming there is a soul, perhaps it would depart when the flesh and blood body was discarded, and would not transfer along with the contents of the brain. The question of whether such a copy is fully human would remain.

There is also the question of timing. As Grant Fjermedal (*The Tomorrow Makers*) notes (p. 5):

> In the weeks and months that followed my stay at Carnegie-Mellon in February of 1985, I would be surprised and intrigued by how many researchers seemed to believe downloading would come to pass. The only point of disagreement was when—certainly a big consideration to those still knocking around in mortal bodies.
> Although some of the researchers I spoke with at Carnegie-Melon, and later at MIT, Stanford, and in Japan thought that downloading was still generations away, there were others who believed we were actually so close to achieving robotic immortality that some of the researchers seemed to be driven by private passions never to die. And perhaps this explained the eagerness of Hans's young research assistants to work through the nights and weekends to further this quest for the life ever after.

That is, some regarded these developments as imminent decades ago. Yet only modest and fragmentary progress has been made since, and most of it consists of enhancements to expert and inference systems using neural networks to improve their "learning" and in large language modeling such as the online Chat AI programs (more on these later). So, it could be many more years, if ever, before the questions raised here need to be considered seriously, for research on the activity of the brain is still moving very slowly, and it seems unlikely that it can be functionally duplicated soon, if ever. Indeed, the small progress made in the intervening years has seemed to argue this aspect of the work may be at or near a dead end.

Biological enhancements to the human brain achieved by genetic manipulation or chemical means might obviate the necessity to go the electro-mechanical simulation route altogether. In the meantime, computer and communications research may take other turns, the products of which could also render the production of artificially intelligent brains unnecessary. On the other hand, startling new techniques have a way of appearing on the scene almost full-blown and with great rapidity. Predictions about this area of research and its potential applications have as much likelihood of being proven too conservative as too extravagant.

Profile On . . . Neural Networks

One approach to electronically augmenting and/or simulating human thinking that has become a significant research tool, to the extent that it is seen by many researchers as the most likely path forward to true artificial intelligence is the creation of artificial neurons, and networking these like the way the human brain functions.

What is a neural network?

A neural network is a collection of artificial neurons created in software, usually organized in layers. A low-level layer might recognize a shape, a higher level might distinguish between a plant and an animal, a more specialized layer might recognize a human being, and a final layer distinguish a specific face using a stored database. The output of each layer is chained or piped as the input for the next, more specialized one.

To realize this bottom-up functionality across the typical person's catalogue of items, ending in a reliable identification, requires many millions of parameters to be checked continuously to mimic what happens in a brain when one is, say, riding a bicycle, and encounters cars, road signage, small animals, trees, flower of various species, other cyclists and pedestrians—some known, some not. Recognition of, say, a small child dashing into one's path, a motorist about to open a car door or turn left right in front of you (when he was singling right), or a red light for cross traffic being ignored by a driver speeding toward an intersection only a few meters from you, must be essentially instantaneous. The time to process and comprehend the data flow, then react appropriately, is constrained to small fractions of a second, or someone's life may end in only a slightly larger fraction thereof.

What was the origin of this idea?

In 1943 Warren McCulloch and Walter Pitts developed an algorithmic computational model for neural networks. However, implementing these in software required computational power far beyond any available hardware that existed then or for many decades following.

The idea has gained traction in more recent times, in part because the need for high-speed computation to handle output to the modern graphics devices demanded by the gaming industry has resulted in the development of GPUs (graphical processing units) that have just the sort of computing power needed to handle the necessary computations. Indeed, it is fairly common to offload certain types of calculations from a CPU core to a GPU core. It is just as common to have available multiple cores and it is not difficult to network many thousands of cores into a large-scale computing cluster.

However the enabling hardware is built, a neural network is an adaptive system that can "learn" as it goes along from successes and failures, gradually adding to its reliability and accuracy for problem-solving in its particular domain. These systems are particularly useful for tackling problems that involve detecting and using generalizations in somewhat unstructured or amorphous data sets. A few examples include:

- making new diagnoses by examining and classifying medical images according to the diagnoses that were made from them, and comparing these with new images,

- assisting targeted marketing by examining and correlating data derived from diverse sources such as census information, social networks, behavioral trends, past sales records, and the successes and failures of prior advertising campaigns,
- predicting short- and long-term demand for energy sources such as gasoline, electricity, and natural gas, for sales of specific product types, or government, medical, financial, and other services,
- making financial predictions for banks, corporations, insurance companies, interest rates, and the stock market by examining and correlating records with current economic data and trends,
- identifying chemical compounds from test data,
- monitoring and controlling manufacturing processes and quality control,
- simulating computer vision, speech recognition, document processing, natural language translation,
- correlating personal preferences from past purchases and activities with the current market to make specific product and service recommendations.

The hardware on which such software runs can either be a purpose-built assembly or a service provided in the cloud on general-purpose clusters.

Two approaches are used:

- *Machine learning* where the programmers supply many of the parameters for the software to use in classifying data, or
- *Deep learning* in which only data is supplied and the neural network must determine the structure of the data without being given any parameters for creating its correlations.

6.3 Augmenting Human Intelligence

Although the ideas presented in this section are somewhat speculative, they would have been classed as conservative by such writers as Fjermedal (*The Tomorrow Makers*) and Drexler (*Engines of Creation*). This section is intended to strike a cautionary note or alternative to the much more extravagant forecasts of others.

For instance, Fjermedal quotes Drexler on the subject of building a computer with a million times the speed and a greater capacity than the entire human brain into the volume of a cubic micron (the size of one synapse): "Something like that may seem very ambitious to us now, like 'Oh, it will take a thousand years,' which is the kind of thing people will say; well, that is a thousandth of a year once we get the AI technology in place," said Drexler.

Unfortunately for those visionary optimists, four additional decades have passed, with the goal of the hard AI they forecast as imminent almost as distant as it was then. There have been advances to be sure. Machine and deep learning to enhance expert systems and progress in the creation and use of neural networks both offer modest promise to continue on such paths, but despite ongoing hype and speculation, progress thus far has been limited enough to suggest more modest goals are in order.

An already fruitful path for intelligence technology to continue following relates to ongoing improvements to the human/machine interface and the portability of computing devices. It was not difficult decades ago to envision a small but powerful computational device that could be carried about in much the same way a 1990s engineer once toted a multifunction calculator. Indeed, today's smartphones are no longer just pocket computers, and the device envisioned here is so much more that some Science Fiction writers termed it a pocket brain, though here it is more properly named a Personal Intelligence Enhancement Appliance (PIEA). Such a device, which might have a measure of simulated intelligence, is developing along a natural enhancement path from hardware and software easily foreseen in earlier editions of this book, and that is now readily available today in nascent form.

Initially, a PIEA would be a powerful computer, utilizing voice and other input forms, together with the means of communicating on demand with larger machines for information query and data transfer. Such devices could soon be sold with memory in terabyte quantities—they are already personal secretaries, diaries, dictation machines, Internet accessors, and calculators/computers all in one.

A passing note: to this point, much of the original forecast made here of the promise for this technology has been changed from the future tense to the past or present tense. The balance has been edited for clarity and conciseness but is essentially unchanged in substance from directions initially suggested by the author in the mid-1980s.

PART TWO | FOUR WAVEFRONTS ON A SEA OF CHANGE

The next phase could be initiated by the development of the means to make direct communication links with the human brain. This would not necessarily involve tapping electrodes into the grey matter but could utilize attachments elsewhere in the body, so long as the nervous system could transmit signals the brain can interpret.

Indeed, electrodes to the body's nerves need not be used. Eyeglasses could incorporate an earphone and a small video screen at the periphery of vision (progress has been made here too—see virtual reality and smart glasses). These would allow rapid transmission of audio and graphical information to the wearer of the appliance, though initially manipulation by voice and electronic signals would be required for the reverse. Perhaps voice control could be achieved with a throat patch that picked up sub-vocalizations. A wearer could control the device without anyone else knowing it was there, and would eventually become unconscious of its presence and use.

In the author's science fiction novels, most Hibernians manipulate their PIEAs with their fingers, entering text or triggering pictorial communication (PICTing) while holding their device two-handed, or by employing one hand on the PIEA embedded in their sword hilt or equipment belt.

As time went by and people became more skilled in their use, such devices could be further reduced in size to the point where their parts could be surgically implanted in the eye and ear. Eventually, neurological connections would become possible. The processing and memory portion could by this point have shrunk to the point where it too could be inconspicuously implanted. A skilled user might be able to do complex mathematical computations, store sequences of logical arguments, or perform word processing, spreadsheet, or database tasks mentally, perhaps without being consciously aware of whether the processing was taking place in their organic brain, or their electronic auxiliary. Such an appliance would become the ultimate in personal computers—an extension of self that is a logical development of the systems available today along paths already substantially traveled in such directions. As a side-effect, research into such possibilities should also result in devices that would give visual ability back to the blind, and hearing to the deaf—directions in which research has also already been shown fruitful.

The more well-heeled Hibernians prefer this type of interface, especially since it is routinely supplemented by electronically and surgically enhanced hearing and eyesight. Their culture is too individualistic to embrace some of the following ideas, however.

Neither would communications with the rest of the world be left out, for at the same time, cellular telephone technology will have further matured to the point where one's PIEA could remain in continuous contact with the Metalibrary. Individuals so equipped would make the bulk of the contributions to the Metalibrary, for they could, in effect, have selected thoughts and actions monitored day and night, organized and analyzed by both their enhancements and the Metalibrary facilities, and attached to existing hypertexts automatically as appropriate.

Once the memory store of the PIEA became sufficiently large, it would be capable of storing the visual media views generated by all users in digitized form and any quantity. Communication through the Metalibrary or directly with another individual could be achieved by triggering the PIEA to send an appropriate picture and/or text to be shown to the intended receiver. Gradually, communications would take on the form of streams of images, rather than of text. Individuals could send personal messages to each other as they think of them. The PIEA would from time to time interrupt its wearers' activity to inform them of awaiting pictmail.

It might eventually be possible to simulate mind-to-mind transfers of information and to hold thought conferences with other individuals so equipped. Various partnerships could form among people of similar or complementary interests, and the research or problem analysis done by these teams would be of a very different calibre and nature than any of them could achieve alone, or even in traditional person-to-person collaboration.

Call such partnerships Metapersons. The services of the more successful would be highly sought after, as there would tend to be a multiplicative effect on the ability of the Metaperson participants, rather than an additive one. (Successful partnerships are greater than the sum of their parts.) Individuals involved would retain their identities fully, except when one of their Metaperson partnerships was in session, and they would participate in other conferences or Metapersons according to specific interests and needs. For most practical purposes, the size of such partnerships would be limited. Two or three might link in most instances, and then larger groups would attempt to form, but some practical maximum working size, perhaps about eight, would become apparent.

For legal purposes, a Metaperson, along with the percentage shares held by the constituent individuals, would have to be registered so contracts could be drawn up, payments made, and lawsuits brought in the same way as they are now with corporate identities. To reduce individual liability and raise advertising capital, Metapersons could incorporate and sell shares to others.

Metaparticipants would most likely be engaged in professional occupations such as engineering, architecture, accounting, law, and so on. Temporary Metapersons might be formed to tackle single specific problems and disbanded once the collaborative task was finished, much in the same way that temporary or very specific corporations are already used, for instance in the making of movies. Some who did this would not want to tie themselves up corporately in such a fashion and would be free to dissolve their participation in one Metaperson and form or join another at short notice. Temporary partnerships would also have to be registered, together with their effective duration and/or scope of practice.

In the author's fiction, the most prestigious school is Tara Meta Ollamh, an invitation-only collaboration of Hibernia's elite academics who teach anonymously and somewhat interchangeably and are bent on finding and developing comparable talents among their by-invitation-only students, only a few of them physically located in Tara's capitol, with most scattered around the planet and attending virtually by 3-D holographic projection. Metaperson-like collaborations for purposes other than anonymizing educational ventures do happen on Hibernia but are not common.

This concept, if ever realized, has significant advantages over other proposed future data/communications systems. A substantial amount of what an individual did, thought, and contributed could be stored in their PIEA with material sent to the Metalibrary as and when the individual directed, and thus some privacy would be retained. The Metalibrary could be fitted with the best available expert system and logical/inference software and become a "smart" omnipedia, capable to an extent of doing its own research, at least on demand, if not self-initiated.

In addition, since no direct brain hook-up would be required, there would be no possibility of raiding someone else's thoughts or "reading their mind." If security on the PIEA devices were lax, electronically stored memories could be stolen, damaged, or erased. However, this PIEA/Metalibrary combination would retain both individuality and privacy. Implant versions, on the other hand, even if secured from physical theft, could potentially be monitored to track the whereabouts of the wearer. There is some likelihood that susceptible people could become addicts—permanently and irrevocably "wired-in" to the Metalibrary. One interesting science fiction trope on that possibility is that the size of such groups could grow until all of humanity became a hive entity constituting a single Metaperson. However, there are no obvious technical advantages or efficiencies to this.

Even if it were possible and did offer significant benefits, not everyone would want to form Metaperson links with others. They might have little need to do so for their work, and little desire to do so for personal interests. Others would be too poor—enhancements for system connectivity and time of use would cost money. Some would undoubtedly object to its development on the grounds of the potential for abuse and privacy violations, but unless joining the system were made compulsory, it is hard to imagine such objections carrying much weight with those who embraced the utility for pragmatic reasons.

Those who see immortality in cyborg form as the ultimate AI goal would be disappointed if this PIEA/Metalibrary scenario turned out to be the stable result of research into intelligence and connectivity enhancement. However, given progress thus far, this does appear to be a more achievable goal from a technical point of view, for substantial elements of it exist now in hardware, services, and software. Today's connected smartphones have already taken many steps in this direction, and today's Internet is a substantial foot on the road to the Metalibrary. And, while experiments with implants have seen some successes, hard AI brain downloading scenarios appear not to have any immediately realizable prospects.

In practice such a well-used (inhabited?) Metalibrary might appear to have intelligence—not of its own, but borrowed from the substantial number of individuals connected to or working through it at any given time. In addition, clusters of cultures could become somewhat homogenized by the existence of the Metalibrary, though the echo chamber that is currently social media would suggest such clusters would insulate themselves from each other.

Since it would also be a 24-hour-a-day facility, the apparent "intelligent" response of the Library taken as a whole would tend to be relatively uniform around the clock. The conduct of special events—such as a particle physics forum, a popular entertainment event, or a political meeting, might create minor ripples in the system's response at times, but would on the whole be unnoticeable.

Perhaps philosophers would then argue over whether the Metalibrary was truly and independently intelligent, or whether it had only the borrowed appearance of such, but it is unlikely anyone would want to put the issue to a test by disconnecting all its users, even if only briefly.

The result of this vision of machine computational ability is quite different than that of simulating or duplicating human intelligence—still a machine, with its "intelligence" neither taught nor transferred, but collectively borrowed and so apparent or simulated rather than instantiated. Still, the Metalibrary as envisioned here, would be a much more powerful knowledge-mining and problem-solving tool than the 2024 Internet. In some form, it is not only a more probable extrapolation from current technology but a more useful one than simulating individual human brains electronically.

In the short term, those who use the PIEA and Metalibrary will be able to achieve a different version of immortality through the writings, worldview filters, and stored images each one leaves behind. The Metalibrary would be able to present orally and visually the views of the long-dead using stored images. An appearance of immortality might be incidentally simulated, but not transfer of personality, and hence no reality of continuance within the collective machine. Whether personality transfer to a machine ever could be achieved is unknown, and may be unknowable. On the other hand, a pseudo-or collectively-intelligent Metalibrary facility appears to be a straightforward extrapolation of what is already available.

Note, however, that this is a very different future vision than an artificial metaverse, permanently "inhabited" by the disembodied personalities who "live" there, either as well as or instead of staying in their physical bodies.

Profile On . . . Issues

A Case Against Strong A. I.

Advocates of strong artificial intelligence believe that machines will eventually be made that can duplicate the functionality of the human mind, and that such machines can be termed intelligent in essentially the same way as a human being. Here are some brief outlines of common arguments that this is impossible—some of them may easily be refuted, but they may as easily be strengthened (see the exercises).

Mathematics:

In the 1930s Gödel proved that even arithmetic truths cannot all be reduced to an encoding in some syntactical notation, that is, that arithmetic meaning is something bigger than notation. More technically, he proved that any finite logical system will either be able to prove contradictions (be inconsistent) or be unable to prove some things known to be true (be incomplete). Therefore, human thinking as a whole, which can incorporate both, cannot be fully represented by being encoded in a finite machine.

Logic and Chemistry

Even if thought is only chemistry and electricity, we can never know that this is true, for such a knowing would be predetermined by physical processes, and not be a result of logic. It would not be rational knowing. Moreover, it would be self-referential, and therefore be inherently paradoxical.

Misplaced Confidence

If one believes in creation, it took an infinite God to create the human mind. If one believes in evolution, it requires billions of years of the operation of some (as yet unknown) process to achieve it. In either case, it is at least premature, if not presumptuous, to suppose that the same feat can be duplicated by humankind at any time soon, if at all.

Purpose

The purpose of the brain is to exercise control over the entire biological entity of which it is an integral part. The purpose of a computer is to calculate. The two activities are so fundamentally different that no elaboration of the latter will ever become equivalent to the former.

A religious viewpoint

The purpose of the mind is to give intelligent, voluntary, and willful service to God. No corresponding activity on the part of a machine is conceivable.

PART TWO | FOUR WAVEFRONTS ON A SEA OF CHANGE

Beliefs, circuits, and chemistry

If mental activities such as the holding of beliefs are equated with electrical circuits or chemical reactions, then such common devices as, say, thermostats and firecrackers have beliefs (or something closely related to beliefs). If this is the case, then artificial intelligence is everywhere, and it is not particularly a science of the mind, nor even of the brain.

Adding machines and understanding

A mechanical adding machine can manipulate symbols and produce results to which a human can attribute meaning. This does not mean the adding machine *understands* addition. Making the parts smaller and faster by encoding them on a chip, or even adding robotic mobility and human-like features, changes nothing. There is no sense in which human intelligence can ever be ascribed to an assemblage of such parts.

Machines and intentionality

A computing machine that assembles data according to some pattern and produces output to which humans attach meaning does so neither deliberately nor intentionally, but because its program predetermines that it shall. An important human element is missing from the machine; any meaning attached to its simulations exists only because the human programmer invented it.

The Chinese argument

A man is placed in a box with a collection of Chinese symbols and a set of rules for input and output based on those symbols and is then passed questions written in those symbols by the operators. His ability to produce correct answers based on those rules does not imply that he (or the system as a whole) understands Chinese—even if he can produce results indistinguishable from those of a native Chinese writer. (Due to John R. Searle writing in *Artificial Intelligence—the Case Against*)

Vision, recognition, and knowledge

A machine that is capable of determining, say, the sex of an individual from a photograph cannot be said to understand what sex is. The storage and analysis of patterns for comparison with video images is not all there is to vision and does not approximate what humans do see, or how they reason from what they see.

God in a box?

Suppose thinking can be automated. Are machine analyses of data to be considered unassailably correct? Is the machine's "worldview," whether explicitly or implicitly programmed, the only possible one? If so, merely human ideas and views would then be invalid, and only the machine's conclusions would have validity. Is this what anyone wants to produce? Or, can unassisted machine analysis yield a single correct interpretation, much less *meaningful* interpretations of data?

What goes along with intelligence?

Can artificial mistakes, artificial pain, artificial emotions, artificial beliefs, artificial understanding, and artificial free will be separated from artificial intelligence? If they cannot, is there any point in building constructs that may choose not to benefit humanity, but attend to their own agenda?

The microscopic and the macroscopic

There is no reason, other than the confidence of some theoreticians, to suppose that processes describable in the microscopic and bounded world of chemical reactions and electrical circuits can ever be extrapolated even to a small subset of the macroscopic world of human experience. That is, the building of a circuit or a program to simulate neurons (however many, and however connected) provides no reason in itself to believe that human intelligence, understanding, experience, or emotions can ever be approximated artificially by such a system or by any other.

Abstraction

Like understanding, there seems every reason to believe that the process of extracting the important from the mass of detail (abstraction) is a uniquely human ability. If this is so, even expert systems will never be as proficient as human experts; they will only be sophisticated database searchers. (Hubert and Stuart Dreyfus (*Mind Over Machine*) claim to have shown that the latter is true.)

Ideas and meaning

The ideas that give meaning to data are not inherent within data but must be imposed on it by an intelligent mind. Thus, the ability to generate ideas to give meaning to the world cannot be encoded. Whatever data a machine collates and whatever output a computing device generates, it has meaning only as it is assigned by human beings, either before processing (inherent in the program and data provided) or afterward.

Ideas and their consistency with data and action

As such toxic ideas as racism, sexism, extreme nationalism, and demonstrably false statements about medical matters, lost elections, the role of women, prejudice against ethnic minorities, and hollow reasons for war all illustrate, the ideas by which humans live and govern their actions sometimes operate not merely independently of data but are often anti-informative. More bluntly, many people prefer to believe lies than truth. Likewise, love and altruism are ideas that can act contrary to their owners' self-interest. Neither category is inherent within any data nor can they be encoded as algorithms.

> There is no possibility that computers will ever equal or replace the mind except in those limited functional applications that do involve data processing and procedural thinking. The possibility is ruled out in principle, because the metaphysical assumptions that underlie the effort are false.—Theodore Roszak (*The Cult of Information*)

6.4 Issues in Large Language AI Programs

Note: Material in this section has been slightly altered and supplemented from the author's regular column on technology and social issues *The Northern Spy* for September-October 2023 titled AI Yi Yi *https://the-northernspy.com/spySep-Oct2023.htm*

The "promised land" forecasts for AI have been around for decades, and its optimistic prognosticators are now having an unqualified jubilant field day touting the success of bots such as ChatGPT. It seems the vigorous debate over its negative and even frightening possibilities and potential flaws have all but been forgotten in the new rush to hail and enthrone the latest media super celebrity. Well, there is nothing new in that—or the fleetingness of popularity. Ask any elected official or once-media darling whose star has faded.

Intrigued, and for his bemusement, the Spy tried it out, asking it who he was, supplying only his name. It came back with his pitching statistics from the Cubs and Padres baseball player. Hmmmm. Missed that game. So, he added "the computer scientist" and it did much better, returning the bio of the man with the same name at an Australian university. Adding in "at Trinity Western University" finally elicited the right answer, along with much additional information, including that he had written science fiction novels. Great stuff! It even provided the titles of his books. Unfortunately, they were all written by someone else with completely different given and surnames. It was nice to get the information, for he had never before heard of those particular authors and it was interesting to have discovered them in his AI-generated biography. Given that he has been hanging out electronically, so to type, since before there was an Internet, this seemed . . . inadequate.

The incident reminded him of a faculty discussion in which he had participated concerning the marking essays in an interdisciplinary studies capstone course TWU once offered. These were all scored by at least two professors, and if their judgements differed significantly, a third would be engaged. One co-marker was never more than 3 percent off the Spy's mark, but another often differed by as much as 40 percent. The latter's main criterion was correctly presented English, whereas the other agreed with the Spy that some papers had much correct form, and were even eloquent, but sadly, had almost no substance. In the subsequent debate at a general faculty meeting, and after several comments concerning correct grammar, punctuation, sentence and paragraph structure, and general style, the Spy asked "What about substance?," and the chair of the English department hollered out "There's gotta be some," eliciting modest applause.

There is no doubt of the success of ChatGPT when it comes to correctly slinging words. It stands out so obviously in purported student essays that it's almost painful to behold. Who talks or writes like that outside the highest levels of arcane academia? Stirring words together into a tasty stew of eloquence in a style that warms the heart of any professional grammarian, language professor, lawyer, or political speechwriter is certainly its forte. There are plenty of tutorials on proper English and a plethora of good examples of patterns it can be algorithmically programmed to mimic.

Even when it comes to looking up and presenting technical content, such machines can do reasonably well, getting it approximately right most of the time. After all, most habitual liars and people with political, religious, or social axes to grind do not know enough about technical matters to post their patented nonsense on the net for the bots to find and use. So, if one wants a passable little computer program in some obscure language (programming notation) to work out the mean, standard deviation, and confidence level of a data collection, tell you the molecular weight of a complex hydrocarbon, explain Newton's laws, relatively, or the undecidability of the halting problem, one is reasonably likely to get back usable results, though even then, they should be checked with a separate verification search. But, as the Spy's little experiment illustrates, when it comes to personal, social, political, religious, or other debated or nuanced matters, it fails dismally, and the essays it writes are usually eloquently empty of content and fail to exhibit thoughtful critique or creativity.

In the classes on mathematics and computing science, the factual information is fairly straightforward and the results of not following proper planning and software engineering regimens, or using the correct grammar in the programming notation, are depressingly predictable. The proof, the program, the electronic circuit, and the letter grade are all dismal.

These new bots do constitute sophisticated advances on the expert systems we have had for some time. Given a boatload of curated factual information and some heuristic rules for patterns of human thinking on the matter at hand, expert systems can be quite useful at handling some kinds of medical diagnoses, legal matters, or playing chess, for instance.

But even there, the operative word is "curated," and it applies to both the data and the heuristics provided. We all know about GIGO (garbage in, garbage out) do we not? The main problem with the current Internet, and the reason why it is not the prototype for the all-encompassing Metalibrary of knowledge and information that the Spy was forecasting as far back as the 1980s (and still is) boils down to "who curates the data and algorithms, why, and how"? Bluntly put, far too much of what gets thrown up (metaphor intended) on the Internet is nonsense, and no one cares.

FWIW, the Spy's solution has always been that there has to be a peer review system, with a network of two-way citation links, and ratings, along with an accounting system of micro debits and credits for content creators to be reimbursed. Moreover, there may have to be separate networks for scholarly publications, news organizations, political discourse, and personal postings, as the current cross postings of all these pollutes any possibility for data credibility in many fields.

Even in his fiction, the Metalibrary is not wide-openly available to the AI character, which has access only to curated data. After all, if purportedly intelligent human beings can fail to discern truth from lies (witness our political past and present), how could truthfulness be capably programmed into an artificially intelligent machine?

After all, the Internet even hosts modern (and apparently serious) flat-earthers who must also believe the moon voyages were hoaxes. Who'd have imagined that ridiculous calumny against Christian beliefs invented merely a few centuries back would ever turn out to be believed by anyone? Then there are the endless conspiracy theory true believers, election deniers, slanderers, worshippers of false prophets, and fraudsters, plus the political, religious, media, and social celebrities who can purportedly do no wrong, say no lies, and be excused for any crime provided they back one's pet cause(s). If humans are often incapable of sifting truth from lies, fact from rumor, fantasy from reality, how could a machine programmed and fed its data by people do so?

There are also problems, as the Spy has for decades pointed out, with the purported, and oft science-fictionalized goals of harder AI- namely the notion that we may someday build machines that can think equivalently to a human being. What, after all, is the human mind? Putative prophet Marvin Minsky famously postulated "The mind is a machine made of meat." His point was that said machine could therefore obviously be reverse-engineered and its functionality duplicated. For some enthusiasts, that dream parallels the idea of somehow scanning the

PART TWO | FOUR WAVEFRONTS ON A SEA OF CHANGE

human brain and downloading its contents and operations into a backupable artificial construct, thereby achieving transcendent immortality as a cyborg—a lofty goal indeed.

On the other hand, consider the counter of Mathematician-Philosopher-Physicist-Astrophysicist Roger Penrose, whose provocatively titled AI book "The Emperor's New Mind" puts the case that Godel's theorem (it is impossible to build a finite logical system that is both complete and consistent), which is equivalent to the undecidability of the halting problem for finite state machines—and that is what computational devices are—shows that hard AI is not possible. He argues that the known laws of physics are inadequate to explain the phenomenon of consciousness and that thought cannot be simulated algorithmically because it isn't algorithmic. The Spy is inclined to side with Penrose on this. The latter's well-earned 2020 Nobel Prize for his long and celebrated polymathic career perhaps lends a certain additional cachet to his arguments. Another way to frame this is to claim (not without some evidence) that the human mind is not simply equivalent to the human brain, and indeed does not constitute a finite state machine.

There are other issues that the most optimistic SF authors (sometimes writing in the newspaper or online fantasies such as those like this column might want to consider). Here, for instance, are a few questions from the exercises in his textbook on technology, ethics, and society that he asked his students to tackle as far back as the 1980s. *(See the exercises at the end of this chapter for examples.)*

Finally, who curates the data to which a bot has access for answering factual questions and rendering diagnoses, opinions, and solutions to problems? Oh, and who chooses the curators—politicians, electors, religious leaders, lawyers, social influencers, celebrities, media professionals, the tech industry, military leaders, scholars, self-styled experts?

Oh, and by the way, he tells his students in the ethics and technology course that unlike in mathematics or Physics, which are not for the most part about opinions, if all his students do is parrot back the lectures and text (which he wrote) they would be doing well indeed to earn a C+. For an A they have to credibly argue against his views and ideas, even if they agree with him. Isn't that what a university is all about—searchingly scrutinizing ideas? True, there are factual things that are indisputable (at least unless and until someone performs a repeatable experiment refuting their universality or at least points out conflicting evidence), but the knowledge and even the epistemology of a given discipline do undergo change, (hopefully maturing) with time, and almost everything needs to be re-examined for credibility by every generation. Yes, many truths are indeed universal and timeless, but other "truths" are only fashionable and transient, and may even be delusional.

THIMK

Your computer has no intelligence, artificial or otherwise. The real thing resides in the programmer. Or, have you hugged your computer yet today?

==End of article==

Handling Mistakes

There is another issue with the broad class of "generative" AI programs that "learn" from provided information databases and are tasked with answering questions, recommending decisions and policies, making diagnoses, writing code, essays, news articles, political speeches, and otherwise influencing or performing human activities. How do the human programmer-operators tell the program how to handle its errors?

Suppose new iterations of a generative AI are trained on its previous versions (typical machine learning strategy) and a comprehensive documentation of its mistakes with reasons why they were erroneous is not included in subsequent training. Without error-correcting code and data, the AI will become more mistake-prone with each succeeding generation until the learning model collapses under the weight of its errors. Indeed, this could happen even with corrective measures as original logical paths are contradicted by later programming.

Human beings have a capacity, one not always employed, to recognize previous mistakes in reasoning or actions taken and correct subsequent decision-making. They also can account for emotional highs and lows or unique circumstances that may have impacted past decisions or could influence future ones differently. Even given the same external data on a new occasion, human decision-making is not necessarily consistent for internal reasons. It may be influenced by more recent events that are only indirectly related, and not part of the formal situational dataset that an AI might be given. Moreover, two people given the same data set and with similar prior experiences, only might make the same decision, also for reasons not part of the formal information set.

So, can a generative AI duplicate human reasoning consistently, and is it even desirable for it to do so?

6.5 More Issues in Artificial Intelligence

At this point, it is not known what are the limits, if any, to the building of artificially intelligent artifacts. Neither is it known whether these will be silicon-based, carbon-based, some combination of the two, or neither. Such devices may well turn out to be genetically modified living organisms, inorganic devices, or both. The issues raised in this chapter are more or less independent of such considerations, and would eventually surface regardless of the type of construction. Some are in the form of common objections to be considered and possibly answered; others are rather more speculative. Many are philosophical or even theological rather than social or ethical. If the most enthusiastic projections of some in the AI community are correct, all these issues will have to be dealt with in this generation. Moreover, some issues will need to be addressed regardless of whether or not the artifacts are intelligence supplements such as the PIEA or simulations of the human brain, whether or not downloading succeeds, or whether the only "intelligence" involved is that which PIEA and Metalibrary devices seemingly exhibit due to their current users.

Practical Risks

AI-based software cannot "learn" without both data and an encoding of prior human expertise. When attempting to "teach" software to play a game using rules, heuristics, and data from instances of the game previously played by humans, there is no substantive risk, except perhaps to the morale and pride of the human players who will eventually lose. Other situations where training is done with isolated and curated copies of actual data are also low risk.

However, if an AI device tasked with decision-making is given access to a live data store, two kinds of risks arise. First, any sufficiently large set of data contains errors, which is why it must be curated. Perhaps the first lesson should cover recognizing such errors.

Second, access implies the ability to manipulate, at minimum, because the AI's decisions become new data, altering the original. Since there will be many missteps along the training path many decisions will be bad ones and need to be flagged as such.

How can the integrity of live data be reliably protected, while dynamically and continuously changing as new data, including the AI's decisions, are added? A human-trained AI would become prone to acquiring the biases of its trainers, even to the point of deciding to reject or alter the data informing it, in the same way that human beings reject data returned from an experiment, an audit, an election, or a previous decision that has not, in their view, gone as they expected or hoped?.

Indeed, if an AI is taught to make decisions in a human-inspired manner, such behavior will almost certainly be copied, as data denial and "alternate truth" are common avoidance techniques when a human being wants to make a decision that is not supportable by actual data—witness the number of people who believed outrageous fabrications about the 2020 American presidential election that could not, as many courtroom judges subsequently noted, be backed up by the slightest shred of evidence.

An imaginary group of millions of fraudulent votes was conjured out of nothing, creating an imaginary alternate data set supposedly showing the election went the other way. An AI programmed and trained by humans biased to believe imaginary data would surely model its decision-making along similar lines, to the point of corrupting the data set to justify a different outcome than what the actual data supports. Who would know?

Thus, not only does the original data set need curating, but it must be monitored continually during and beyond training to ensure it remains integral.

Reinforcement of Tunnel Vision

It is fairly easy to program AI algorithms to show us Internet content similar to what is available in our browsing history, and connect us on social media with new "friends" of like interests, disposition, and beliefs, thus tailoring the experience for each individual according to already expressed interests.

This of course reinforces one's existing beliefs, cuts people off from competing ideas, and fragments the electronic world experience even more than the physical experience, thereby reinforcing prejudices, beliefs in misinformation, division, and hatred.

Deep Fakes

Yes, it would be possible to tell a news feed to have the information delivered by simulacra of long-dead figures for whom there exists a sufficient body of audio/visual content upon which to train an AI. Apart from copyright, personal privacy, and self-ownership issues, this type of AI use may seem relatively harmless.

Not so the similar use to take published photographs and create a simulated image (a deep fake) of the individual naked, or engaging in illicit activities. Anyone can be shown in any condition or engaging in anything. This use of AI has set off an arms race similar to the old conflict between software developers and pirates, where the former tried to copy protect their software, and the latter broke the protection. This latest manifestation sees publishers embedding altered pixels in images to assert copyright and catch violators, but such countermeasures and just as unlikely to stop the offenders.

AI and privacy

AI is data-driven. The large language models constituting some of the early popularizations depend on access to vast collections of written material to answer questions in a pseudo-intelligent fashion. Bad data drives bad reporting drives bad decisions drives bad outcomes, and since the mandate is to synthesize available data and deliver a report, when they lack data, the large language models produce made-up nonsense, albeit eloquently. This creates a thirst for more comprehensive data sets to fuel AI activity.

Authors find their works are being scanned and uploaded to quench this thirst, and on the face of it, appear to have a legitimate case for redress—either a share in the profits for allowing their intellectual property to be exploited or the right to deny its use to feed the AI maw. We come back around to the full Metalibrary concept—everything tagged for ownership and automatic microcredit recompense for each use, whether direct or derived.

The second major issue here is the privacy of personal data. Governments already monetize census data, selling at least aggregate information to the private sector for its enrichment. The concept of Open Banking, first introduced in the U.K., later in Europe, and spreading further abroad, focuses on the user having control of who can see personal data so as to have wider choices. For instance, one can make financial data stored with one's main banking provider, visible to, say, an insurance company under a different institutional umbrella.

AI Harnessed to Other Technologies

At present, once data is encrypted with better algorithms, it is difficult, and in certain cases, nearly impossible to decrypt it without the "key" to do so. The general idea is that the originator employs formulae that use two very large prime numbers to generate two keys—a public one for encryption that is sent to one's correspondents, and a private one held by the originator and used to decrypt messages sent by those with the public key. Such encryption is very difficult to break, even with significant time and computing resources.

Quantum computers, which rely on entangled particles that when one has a state changed, the other simultaneously also changes, regardless of the separation distance, are touted to offer the promise of freeing computer circuitry from the limitations of the time it takes electrical impulses to travel through wires, and some suggest the outcome will be to perform at least some computations in zero time. In theory, decryption, no matter how complex, would in this scenario be instantaneous, driving a permanent spike in the idea that any data can remain private.

Although the practice of theory seldom corresponds to the theory of practice, even a partial realization of this combination of technologies, driven by AI algorithms for maximum efficiency, could render the notion of information privacy permanently obsolete.

6.6 Summary and Further Discussion

Summary

The degree to which machines can mimic the results of human thinking is becoming progressively greater. It is not known whether there are limits to this, either short of complete human capability or beyond this point. At present machines are used for expert tasks, logical and inference tasks, design tasks, and language translation.

Over the longer term, some researchers would like to simulate human thinking exactly, even be able to download themselves into such devices to achieve immortality. The former goal is difficult enough, but too little is known about the human brain to expect the latter to be achieved soon, if ever.

Various artificial augmentations to the human brain may be more immediately realizable, and even more practical. Devices here called PIEAs (Personal Intelligence Enhancement Appliances) but more commonly in fiction termed "pocket brains" may be developed to allow quick computation and large-scale local memory storage of information. Eventual implantation of these as some future generation of what is today called a smartphone is also a possibility. The same device could be the individual's Metalibrary link and allow fast interpersonal communication and data exchange. No method by which any brain link could be made to such devices is yet known.

Whatever route is taken with AI-capable devices, the very possibility they might someday exist raises basic questions about whether they would be regarded as alive, as human, or as moral agents. If they are autonomous decision-makers, there is no reason to assume that they will share many, if any, goals in common with humanity. The consequences could be catastrophic, so decisions on their construction need to be broadened to involve more people and to consider these issues.

Research and Discussion Questions

1. Why does one not call a chess-playing machine intelligent?
2. If a machine passes Turing's test, claiming for itself self-awareness, does that mean that it is self-aware? How can one tell? Or, does it matter if one cannot?
3. Why are language translation problems so important?
4. Research the extent to which language translation software has already been developed and deployed.
5. What advantages would an artificially intelligent machine have over today's expert and inference systems?

6. Perform the necessary library research to determine whether the human brain is generally regarded as a parallel processor or a sequential processor. Summarize, with citations.

7. Write a paper summarizing some of the problems involved in the machine representation of knowledge.

8. Discuss the technical problems involved in simulating vision in a machine.

9. Write a paper defending human brain downloading as the ultimate goal of research into intelligence.

10. Write a paper attacking the concept of human brain downloading on either scientific or moral grounds, or both.

11. Attack or defend the proposition "A human being is a machine made of meat."

12. If the Metalibrary or any AI device behaved in every other way as though it were intelligent, how could one determine if it was independently self-aware?

13. Suppose a person recorded in detail every life experience, all learning, reading, thinking, motives, and so on, and placed this into a mechanical brain. Would this constitute a better "copy" than one made by a molecule-by-molecule scan of their brain at one point in time? Would the copy be human?

14. Argue that AI machines must be made autonomous moral agents and that the consequences for the human race will be good. Or, argue the contrary.

15. What is intentionality? Could a machine have it? Why or why not?

16. Discuss the problems involved in making machine simulations of emotions.

17. Argue that only catastrophe could occur if AI devices were to become self-aware, autonomous decision-makers and moral agents. Make a case therefore that such machines must be kept strictly subservient to humankind, and unable to become autonomous. Or, argue the contrary.

18. Research Isaac Asimov's fictional "Laws of Robotics" and discuss their enforceability, implementability, and adequacy to prevent

such machines from mastering the human race. Include in your discussion the who, what, and why of the addition of the fourth law.

19. Discuss the kind of work best done by Metapersons, and why a special legal status would be necessary for such partnerships.

20. Should an AI device that is capable of duplicating the results of human thinking be regarded as equal in status to human beings?

21. What legal rights should AI devices have? Does your answer depend on their appearance or only on their "thinking" capabilities?

22. What social rights should AI devices have? Does your answer depend on their appearance or only on their "thinking" capabilities?

23. Should an employer give a job to a human applicant in preference to an AI device that can do it better for the same salary? Why or why not? What if the AI device can be purchased so earns no salary or benefits?

24. Given the issues discussed in this chapter, what restrictions, if any, should be placed on AI research and development? How can these be enforced, and who should do this enforcing?

25. You are the president of a community association and are visited by a mobile AI device that tells you: "I've just bought the general store a block from here and moved in upstairs. I'd like to become a member of the association." What do you do and why?

26. You are the editor of a local newspaper and are visited by a mobile AI device that tells you: "I read your ad for a new society reporter. I'm well qualified by working on smaller newspapers and want to apply for the job." What do you do and why? Would your answer be any different if the job were "crime reporter" or "sports reporter"?

27. You are the registrar of a university and receive an application, with sterling high school credentials whose letter says in part "I am a mobile AI device. I want to register at your university for courses leading to a B.Sc. in Computing Science. I think my high school marks warrant a full-ride scholarship to your school." What do you do and why? Does the proposed major make any difference? Medicine, law, sociology, clinical psychology, religion, education, business, etc?

28. You own a stock brokerage and receive an application from a mobile AI device stating "I've developed better than human expertise in

stock trading and could make a lot of money for myself and your firm if you will hire me and register me as one of your accredited traders." What do you do and why?

29. You are the pastor of a small church and are visited by a mobile AI device that tells you: "I've been listening to your sermons and I have determined that I have inherited a fallen nature from my human creators, so I want to repent, become a believer, get baptized, and obtain membership in your church." What do you do and why?

30. How would you as a teacher ameliorate the problems of students pretending to do essay-like assignments that are written by a large language model AI such as ChatGPT? Or, does it matter?

31. Who should curate the data fed to a large language model so that it does not return falsehoods, politically motivated or fabricated results, or biased answers?

32. Who should choose the curators of such data to ensure it is accurate, in the sense of being factually verifiable to be correct?

33. Discourse on the matter of truth as it applies to data. To what extent do alternate realities exist when one supposed reality cannot be supported by data or experimentation? Or, to put it a different way, are there two sides to everything? (You might want to look up something called a Möbius strip.) Or putting it a third way, is there a functional difference between fantasy and reality or between truth and lies?

34. The author of this book also writes Alternate History Science Fiction, the general idea for which is: "What if some important historical decision that shaped the subsequent world had been made differently? (This came up in the chapter on History.) Other writers create future histories. A reader is expected to "suspend disbelief," that is to go along with the fiction to see what could have happened. Some fans "get into" such fiction rather enthusiastically, dressing up and even acting like characters in novels. Comment on this phenomenon. Is it problematic or harmful in any way? Could it be? How does this compare with the practice of creating "alternate truths" about the present, in which people believe in two different "realities" such as opposite outcomes of elections or, say, football or hockey games?

35. With what kind of decisions could an AI be trusted, if any?
36. Further research and either expand upon or refute the author's suggestion that privacy is on the verge of obsolescence.
37. Research and document cases of fraudulent use or analysis of data by researchers. How big a problem is this? Is it growing or is fraud detection becoming easier?
38. Research and write a paper on (a) the use and prevalence of fake academic journals, and (b) the use of "impact factor" as a measure of legitimacy. Can this be trusted? Think of a way for the publishers and editors of a fake journal to artificially inflate (fake) its impact factor.
39. Which if any of the following uses of AI are legitimate? Why or why not?
    a. writing computer code for a commercial application,
    b. writing an essay for a student taking a course,
    c. assisting in the creation of a community plan,
    d. translating languages in real time for a telephone company,
    e. simulating a particular person to "read" the evening news; (does it matter if the person is alive or not?)
    f. simulating a now-deceased relative with whom you wish to have ongoing conversations.
40. Can a generative AI duplicate human reasoning consistently, and is it even desirable for it to do so?
41. Research and write a paper or deliver a talk on the ethical use of AI in a particular discipline of interest to you.

CHAPTER 7

The Biospace Revolution

The Professor, Eider, and Johanna, are already in the seminar room when Ellen arrives. She is several minutes late for the class and is walking awkwardly, the middle of her back bent over to one side, and in obvious pain.

    Ellen: (grimacing) Sorry I'm late.

    Johanna: What happened to you? You look like you've been run into.

    Ellen: My back is killing me. (sitting) And these chairs don't help. They must have been designed by a sadist.

    Nellie: What did you do?

    Ellen: It's just a spasm in my lower back. I get these every once in a while.

    Nellie: Have you seen a doctor?

    Ellen: Lots of times, but all they do is prescribe muscle relaxers and bed rest. It gets better for a while, then I get another one.

    Nellie: What about a specialist?

    Ellen: Them too. Lots of them. What's wrong with modern medicine that it can't fix something like a bad back, anyway? And, why don't any of the doctors care about all the pain I'm in?

At this point, Eider rises from her chair and walks around behind Ellen, then places her hand on Ellen's head.

    Ellen: Hey! What are you doing?

PART TWO | FOUR WAVEFRONTS ON A SEA OF CHANGE

Eider: You are in a great deal of pain.

Ellen: (visibly relaxing under Eider's touch) Sympathy at last. But what can be done about it?

Eider: (crouching beside her chair and reaching one arm around Ellen's waist while grasping her shoulders with the other) Just relax, and don't fight me.

Nellie: You can't practice medicine without a license.

Eider: This isn't exactly medicine as you term it. There, this is the spot.

She pushes with one arm and pulls with the other. There is a loud cracking noise.

Ellen: What was that?

Eider: Try to stand up now.

Ellen: (standing straight) Hey, I can do it. It's still sore, but not like the knives I had before, and my headache is gone too. How did you do that?

Professor: Eider is a healer, remember.

Johanna: Was that a chiropractic adjustment?

Eider: (returning to her seat) There's a little more to it than that. (To Ellen) If you want to come down to the gym afterward, I'll show you some exercises that will help to prevent that spasm from happening again.

Johanna: Now there's a perfect example of the kind of thing I've been saying all along. All the technology and machines didn't help Ellen a bit, but the right human touch did wonders.

Professor: There is a lot of technique in what Eider did, though. She had to learn how to manipulate joints like that.

Eider: (a little nervously) There is a little more to it than that.

Nellie: Wait a minute. Johanna, does that mean you now accept Eider's credentials?

Johanna: Let's not go that far. Let's just say she has illustrated that you scientists don't necessarily know everything.

Nellie: (somewhat sarcastically) Or we could have done what—grown her a new back?

Johanna: Well, why not, if medicine is all it's cracked up to be?

Nellie: Interesting idea. I read an article last night about a research team that is trying to repair diabetics' DNA so that it will produce insulin, then grow them a custom organ from the spliced DNA and transplant it into the body to take over from a damaged pancreas. There would be no problem with rejection because it would be the patient's own DNA.

Johanna: (picking up this text and riffling its pages) Yeah, well, according to this book, growing new organs will eventually do away with a lot of the need for surgery. Is all this stuff true, Professor?

Professor: Some work has been done along those lines, yes.

Nellie: Sounds a little creepy to me.

Johanna: Not to me. Why if drugs and a little work on the DNA could do away with some of the surgery that is practiced, I'd be all for it.

Ellen: My, my, what have we here? A squeamish scientist and Johanna praising technology all of a sudden. A bit of a role reversal isn't it?

Johanna: Well, I wouldn't want to see some of the other possible uses of genetic engineering.

Ellen: Some of them sound pretty good to me. We could eliminate all the chromosomal damage, and give everybody the same amount of beauty and intelligence . . .

Nellie: Since socialism can't make everybody the same, then science should, eh Ellen?

Ellen: (defiantly) It would solve a lot of problems if we could prevent discrimination at the source.

Nellie: Who would decide what the ideal human being would be like—you?

Johanna: You're opening up a can of worms. What about sex selection? Suppose the male doctors in charge of these techniques decide that there ought not to be any women born.

Nellie: That wouldn't work for very long.

Ellen: Why not? If they could do that much, they could surely clone as many new men as they wanted; they could just do without women. (thoughtfully) Or, women could do without men. That would

PART TWO | FOUR WAVEFRONTS ON A SEA OF CHANGE

liberate us from the necessity of bearing their children and being their economic slaves even more than free abortions have.

Johanna: (leaning forward and speaking sharply) You're taking it too far. Abortion is bad enough, but . . .

Ellen: (interrupting) Now you're a long way out of your role. Surely we're together on the abortion issue. It's just religious freaks like Nellie who are anti-choice.

Nellie: You mean I'm pro-life, rather than pro-death.

Ellen: Where has the author's consistency gone?

Johanna: I'm not with you on this one Ellen; you're wrong. It's murder, and we all pay for it in the end.

Ellen: It's just a bit of extra tissue—like a pimple. Why all the excitement?

Johanna: (leaning forward, and now quite upset, choking a little) She's a child. She's a child.

Professor: Our time is nearly up, and this is not an issue we are going to solve by discussing it here. Why don't you all sum up what you think is the most pressing of the problems discussed in this chapter? The one you select can be your essay topic for the week. For a change, I'll let you defend a position you agree with. Eider, start with you.

Eider: The practice of whole medicine. Healing the mind and the body, and not just treating the symptoms.

Ellen: Wholistic medicine?

Eider: Integrated healing.

Professor: Nellie?

Nellie: I'll go for the understanding of the immune system and a way to eliminate viruses.

Johanna: (in a voice just above a whisper) For the means to eliminate surgery. Most of it, especially when performed by men and on women, is unnecessary.

Ellen: I think genetic engineering is the most important issue. We need a means of eliminating some of the unfairness imposed at birth. It ought to be controlled by women though.

Nellie: Because births are our business alone?

Ellen: To redress past discrimination and to ensure that women are better than men from the start.

Nellie: Why don't we combine the two and find a way to give you a pill to turn you into a man? Perhaps you would be more pleasant that way.

Professor: That's enough of that, Nellie. (gathering papers together) All right then, the usual.

Nellie: Two thousand words. References. Clear reasoning.

Professor: (leaving) You got it.

Eider: (exchanging looks with Nellie) Well, Ellen, how about we go to the gym to see about those exercises?

The two depart, leaving Johanna staring distractedly into space, and Nellie sitting opposite, unnoticed. Several minutes pass.

Nellie: Want to talk about it?

Johanna: (slowly, not looking at her) When I was fourteen . . .

Nellie: You thought you were in love.

Johanna: He was eighteen, and had his own car. I thought I was his queen. Afterward, he wouldn't even talk to me, and I heard him boasting to his friends that I was his fifth that year and the easiest of all to get into bed.

Nellie: You decided to have an abortion?

Johanna: I was afraid. So afraid. I didn't know what to do, and everybody said it was no big deal. It was free, legal, and safe; it wasn't as if it were a baby—all the usual talk. And all lies!

Nellie: What happened?

Johanna: Ever since then I've had nightmares that the baby was actually born and I killed her afterwards. I wake up to the sound of babies crying twice a week even now, and I don't think I'll ever escape the guilt.

Nellie: There's more isn't there?

Johanna: I got a venereal infection from him. It scarred my Fallopian tubes. I'm sterile now.

Nellie: Have you seen a fertility specialist?

Johanna: They say more surgery might help, but I don't trust them.

Nellie: Adoption?

Johanna: Everybody else is having an abortion too. There are no children available, especially for a single woman. Why can't some of the billions they spend on guns solve my problem?

Nellie: There is Somebody who listens.

Johanna: Forget it, Nellie. I appreciate the sympathy I get from you Christians—it's better than anything Ellen is capable of—but I'll put my hope in a better incarnation next time around, or maybe the time after if I've damaged my karma too much on this one.

After this, the two gather their books in silence and prepare to make their departure.

Nellie: Talk to Eider too, won't you? She knows about stuff like this.

Johanna: (vaguely) Yeah, sure.

7.1 Life in Time and Space—Defining the Biospace

Every life form occupies a unique niche in the context of all life on earth. This niche can be expressed in terms of the physical space that it requires to make or gather food and also in terms of relationships with other life forms with similar agendas. Human life, however it might be considered as different from other forms, is also lived out in such a context. It draws sustenance in clothing, shelter, and food from other forms of life and cannot exist without the support of the plants and animals with which it shares the earth. The whole environment is a complex network of interdependencies of each form of life upon many others, and no part of the web of life can be altered without affecting the rest. This is by no means a concept new to the information age, though it has not been an important paradigm of the industrial one. Such an idea was expressed by the Elizabethans as the "chain of being." It is the principle of interdependence again, this time expressed as:

> Every life form depends on every other life form.
>
> Every habitat is shared.

Likewise, human life (as all life) is lived out over a span of time, and this also affects the relationships of people with each other and the environment. The passing of the years has been counted upon to supply a steady stream of new people with new ideas, to be the new consumers and leaders. If a society does not grow in size and power by increasing in absolute numbers, the inexorable passage of time will at least through the cycle of birth, life, sickness, and death ensure some measure of renewal. One characteristic of modern medicine has been a great increase in the number of years lived by the average human being, and there is some prospect of further gains. Changes in life span produce profound side-effects—not just in the population or society where they happen, but throughout the chain of related societies and life forms.

The span of an organism over both space and time can be expressed as its *biospace*, and specifically:

The niche occupied by human life over both space and time together is called the human biospace.

With each of the earlier transitions to a new society, the interrelationships among humans changed (in some cases dramatically), and this is happening again. This chapter considers aspects of the continuing scientific and technological revolution that directly affect the living of human life—that is, medical, environmental, and living space concerns. These issues are multifaceted and complex. It could be argued that they are all somewhat independent of one another and that several chapters are required to do them justice. That they are here collected into one is precisely because there is a unifying theme—all relate to how many people will exist at a given time, where they will live, and what quality of life they will enjoy in the Fourth Civilization.

There are numerous ethical and social issues common to these discussions:

- If a treatment for a medical condition exists, is there a basic human right to have that treatment? regardless of cost? regardless of its relative effectiveness?

- If an enhancement treatment exists (more bodily strength, higher intelligence, longer life, etc), is there a basic human right to have that treatment? a collective (state) right to mandate it for the benefit of society as a whole?

- On the other hand, can the state mandate a treatment or a preventative vaccine, say to prevent the spread of an infectious disease? against political objections? against religious ones? despite patient fears of treatment ill effects known by the medical establishment to be without foundation? To put it another way, is there a basic human right to refuse treatment, even when doing so may imperil others?

- Should cosmetic or other body-altering surgery be permitted? when surgical resources are limited? under either state-run (or private) medical payment plans? Does wanting such changes imply a right to have them?

- Should body-altering surgery be required? when it is cheaper in the long run than supporting a person with (i) a repairable injury? (ii) a repairable impediment, such as by a leg transplant or to restore sight? What if the person wants to stay as they are?

7.2 Disease and Surgery

One of the most dramatic differences between the last days of the industrial age and all earlier times is that people now have an entirely different attitude to disease and the practice of medicine. Until the first third of the twentieth century, death was ready to knock at every door in the form of plague, smallpox, diphtheria, typhus, scarlet fever, polio, and a host of other diseases. In developed countries, none of these need to be feared today because of the widespread use of antiseptics, antibiotics, and vaccinations.

Smallpox has now been completely eradicated, and many of the others on the old list of killers have been reduced in certain countries to rare cases of little more than nuisance value to society as a whole. This has come about because hospitals are kept clean, patients are segregated from one another and the healthy, and drinking water is treated at central locations to remove contamination. It is difficult for moderns to appreciate the scope of these changes. Until less than a century and a half ago, the practice of medicine other than surgery was based on little more than superstition, and a sick person was in many cases better off dying in peace than calling a doctor.

Will this trend continue to the point that most communicable diseases eventually become a thing of the past? Pessimists point to modern population mobility and suggest that some new disease (natural or deliberately engineered) could even now sweep the earth in record time and carry away a large percentage of the population before a cure could be developed.

COVID-19 provided a foretaste of such a scenario, and did kill many people, but that pandemic, by historical standards, was relatively mild. A disease as deadly as the Black Plague but fast-acting and as easy to catch as the flu could infect most of the world's population in a matter of weeks. No defense could be devised in time to save any except the small percentage who would be naturally immune. Moreover, many people in the developed nations have become complacent about or deliberately ignorant of vaccinations against what they regard as rare diseases, thus making themselves and those influenced by them vulnerable.

On the other hand, optimists are sure that new drugs combined with gene editing and new methods of tailoring enzymes, proteins, and "fake" viruses to stimulate antibody production will all but eliminate the transmission of disease in the next few decades.

However, viruses mutate and can jump from the animal population (birds, pigs, bats, cows, pangolins) to humans. The orthomyxoviridae types that include influenza A, B, C, and D variants and sub-variants are particularly prone to this, and in recent years, coronaviruses have done the same, including SARS, MERS, and SARS-CoV-2, the latter being the agent causing the COVID-19 pandemic in its multiply mutated variants. At this writing, the animal origin of the original mutation is unknown, though bats and/or pangolins are suspected.

Indeed, the hardest problems to solve are those of viruses, the semi-living capsules of genetic material that invade the body's cells and take them over as factories to replicate themselves. Some, the so-called "retroviruses," are capable of hiding in the body for years before being triggered to begin or continue their damaging behavior. These include the viruses that cause herpes (that can later reappear as shingles) and AIDS. The Epstein-Barr virus (EBV) that initially causes mononucleosis has similar abilities, and has been implicated in later-arising conditions such as chronic fatigue syndrome and (possibly) multiple sclerosis, though that effect remains unproven as yet.

One line of research has concentrated on curing or preventing the symptoms of retroviruses, possibly by forcing them back into dormancy with the hope that eventually, a way may be found to remove them from the body altogether. Another line focuses on interfering with the virus in such a way as to prevent its reproduction or to foil its mode of attack on the body. Still others seek to tailor molecules that can bind with the DNA of the virus directly to kill or inactivate it. All hold the potential promise that viral disease can eventually be eradicated.

When the human immune system and its behavior with viruses are sufficiently well understood to achieve this, a true watershed will have been passed—the last major barrier to the elimination of communicable disease will have been eliminated. The "cure for the common cold" is an old touchstone in such research; achieving that implies the possibility of defeating almost all viruses. However, the sharply contrasting reactions to the COVID-19 pandemic are both instructive and cautionary.

On the one hand, a massive mitigation effort was undertaken, including masking and isolation, which were proven effective in the 1918 flu epidemic, when the death toll was in the multiple tens of millions (actual totals are only estimated as records were not everywhere kept). But this time, research into RNA vaccines that target and disable the spike protein of the virus produced a new class of relatively effective vaccines in remarkably short order, and at this writing the death numbers have not yet reached eight million, and are concentrated in countries like the United States, where the response was weak.

Because the virus mutated after infecting the human population, and presumably will continue to do so (as do the influenza virus family members—which are similar) it seems probable that annual booster shots against the most probable infecting strains of the day will become routine, as with flu vaccines for some years now. It remains to be discovered whether the greater severity of COVID-19 over influenza was due to its novelty (no immunity) or is inherent.

On the other hand, medical complacency, ignorance, anti-science, and anti-government sentiment infused a considerable segment of some populations with false conspiracy theory beliefs that COVID-19 was a hoax designed principally to allow more government control over the population. Others promoted quack medicine pseudo-cures (drinking bleach, ingesting a horse de-wormer), that were more potentially deadly than the disease. Had someone promoted drinking salt water, people might have tried it, recovered from the disease, and promoted this, though it just another completely worthless fake cure. After all, most people do recover. Others were quick to attribute blame to their government or medical system or that of another nation but refused to take responsibility for their behavior, ignored the science, believed conspiracy theories, and repudiated sound health measures, consequently threatening and even ending both their own and others' lives.

On The Other Hand

Recent experience with antibiotics, however, ought to sound a legitimate and quite different kind of cautionary note. These work by selectively killing off most of the target organism population. In theory, the smaller numbers remaining are eliminated by the body's immune system. However, prolonged use of antibiotics guarantees those remaining bacteria will be the ones resistant to the antibiotic. Even if this resistance is conferred by an otherwise unfavorable or recessive mutation, eventually the entire population of the organism will be resistant. Such "superbugs" can then defy modern medicine in wreaking their havoc on humankind. This selection of the existing bacterial population for resistance is potentially catastrophic, and a similar caveat may hold for treatments of viruses.

Progress

The human population had, by the 2020s, a much better strategic position in the war against both kinds of disease than it did a century earlier. For instance, anti-virus vaccines can be continually updated as the virus mutates.

Neither has medical progress been confined to the problems posed by communicable diseases; numerous surgical procedures are routinely performed today that were unheard of a century ago. Appendicitis is now rarely a killer unless undiagnosed and many kinds of cancer and heart disease can be beaten. Others cannot as yet. For ones like those lumped together as ovarian cancer, (cancer of the lining of internal organs) the onset of symptoms is too late, and it is in most cases soon terminal, as the author knows all too well from his late wife's case. A vaccine strategy may be conceivable for some forms of cancer, but the causes will need to be better understood before such a path can be fruitful.

However, the people of industrialized countries live longer on average, are healthier, and are more active and productive later in life than at any time in the past. They have forgotten the times when the limited skills of surgeons were exercised without antiseptic or anesthetics and hospital patients usually died—if not of trauma, then of infection. Instead, most live long enough to become the victims of cancer, heart disease, accident, or suicide rather than of surgery, infection, or a communicable disease.

Such advances have not come without cost, for medical science now allows more people with genetic defects or chromosomal damage to live to pass on those defects to the next generation. Old age comes more slowly than it ever has, but death is postponed only at an ever-increasing price for ever more sophisticated medical techniques and larger extended-care facilities for the aged. Thus, the modern medical system is under constant pressure, forced to make difficult choices over allocating scarce and costly resources. The resulting ethical questions concerning the application of life-saving or life-prolonging technology can be divided into three kinds—those of facilities, those of cost, and those of appropriateness.

Facilities

Hospitals are often severely constrained in their ability to provide complex services. For instance, the number of open-heart repair procedures that can be performed at a given facility in a year is limited by the availability of both operating rooms and qualified surgical teams. Hence, a means of scheduling clients for such services is necessary. This may be strictly first-come-first-served, or surgery be prioritized by the severity of the case, or dependent on placing a value on the client's life.

Such a value may derive from the perceived contributions of the person to society (i.e., a famous scientist or artist versus a common criminal or skid road habitué). It may be a monetary value (i.e., the ability to pay for priority treatment). It may be of potential value to society—a young person with a whole life to live being given surgical priority over an aged one whose contributions are in the past, or a person with complex needs prioritized before (or after) simpler cases. The more severe the shortage of resources and the more fundamental the issue—here it is life itself—the greater the pressures both on those who must wait and on those who control the resources for which they wait.

Moreover, new diagnostic and treatment techniques are always very limited in availability, sometimes for a protracted period. For example, consider two of the latest: magnetoencephalography (MEG), which measures the magnetic fields of brain cells, and nuclear magnetic resonance (NMR but for medical purposes re-termed MRI or Magnetic Resonance Imaging), which is a means of scanning and mapping internal body organs. The former is useful for diagnosing brain disorders such as epilepsy, cysts, and tumors. The latter can produce whole-body images and even a spectroscopy, or chemical map, to reveal subtle imbalances in the body's functioning. It also can pinpoint tumors and soft tissue damage. Such machines represent very high technology and come with correspondingly high price tags. They are complex to build and operate, and their results require special training to interpret. As a result, they are relatively scarce, as the latest techniques in medicine always are. So, larger hospitals in big centers have them, and smaller hospitals in more remote places do not.

The limited availability of resources is a broad and growing problem for modern medicine. As the population ages, and as new ways are developed to prolong the lives of some, the shortage of facilities and trained personnel becomes ever more severe, as do the problems of rationing—deciding who will get sophisticated treatment, who will get basic treatment, and who will get none. Population aging exacerbates these problems through the retirement of doctors, with lower birth rates meaning there are fewer young medical graduates to replace them, let alone to increase the pool. The extreme stresses placed on medical personnel during the pandemic hastened retirements and provoked resignations from the medical system.

An act-oriented ethic might seem to demand the maximum possible medical effort to be available for all. A utilitarian one demands the greatest net medical benefits for the largest number of people. But, these are both ideals, for as long as resources for diagnosis and treatment are scarce—and it seems inherent in the present system and situation that they will be—there may be no solution to the problems of allocation that can satisfy everyone. Consequently, it is necessary for practical and ethical reasons to pursue the development of medical services that can be delivered with the least use of scarce and expensive facilities and personnel. One such method is treatment at home rather than in a hospital, and by personnel such as nurse practitioners, who are less costly to train than physicians but can be at least equally effective for many things traditionally done exclusively by MDs.

At the same time, it is necessary to seek technological solutions to problems caused by existing techniques. For example, diagnosis and treatment are often achieved only after batteries of complex tests, sometimes using scarce and expensive machines, drugs, or prosthetics. It is impossible to deploy such facilities for every doctor or even to serve every community in the world, so it is necessary to devise cheaper, more automatic diagnostic and treatment techniques to make even the existing level of medical knowledge more practicable.

Society itself, in its very successes, sometimes creates new medical disorders requiring sophisticated diagnosis and treatment. Examples include chemicals such as urea formaldehyde and a variety of pesticides, substances such as asbestos, damage from radiation accidents, wars, contaminated street drugs, automobile and industrial accidents, and aging.

Cost

The problem of paying for new types of treatment becomes more acute with each passing year. Should the person who receives a heart or lung transplant be required to pay all, part, or none of the cost? Does it make any difference if the person's lifestyle (smoking, drinking, reckless driving) contributed to or caused the problem? Should an employer be responsible if the procedure was necessary because of some job-related activity that caused or exacerbated the medical issue? Should the government pay just because the person is a citizen? What if the patient is not a citizen but a recent immigrant, or a tourist either passing through or traveling solely to get the procedure?

As diagnostic techniques and drugs increase in sophistication, they increase in cost. Complex treatments, particularly when new, may require hundreds of thousands of dollars, amounts far beyond the ability of most individuals to pay. Neither can medicare programs grow indefinitely without bound, for they will consume the entire budgets of governments that sponsor them long before any end to the potential demand is in sight, particularly given the aging of Western world populations. It is impossible to afford every possible medical diagnostic and treatment technique for every patient, yet the physician who does not perform them risks a malpractice suit. Malpractice insurance premiums to cover legal expenses push up medical costs even more. In addition, there is the expense of training and re-training medical personnel so they stay abreast of the latest developments. Thus, from a cost perspective alone, new and expensive technologies will always be rationed. There will always be the question of whether a procedure should be performed just because it is possible, or only when it is affordable. There will also be the question of who should make such decisions—patients, their conservators, doctors, hospital staff, lawyers, or politicians.

For instance, suppose that the president of the United States, a billionaire industrialist, and a poor but Nobel-winning cancer researcher are all dying. Each requires a liver transplant within twenty-four hours and only one surgery can be performed. Which should be given the treatment? Suppose the issue is complicated because both the first two could make hard-to-refuse monetary offers to the medical facility that would see it grow in size and in the ability to treat others. Treating many people like the poor researcher could, on the other hand, put the facility out of business, even though treating a cancer researcher might eventually bring more benefits to more people. Can the course of action likely to cause the most good to the largest number of people be calculated? Can the right thing to do be determined? On a larger scale, can medical practitioners ever refuse necessary treatment to groups of people who cannot pay, while advancing it to those who can? What about the same question asked of unnecessary (say, cosmetic) treatment that is requested by a patient, and who pays for that?

Some examples may seem extreme, but similar ones are commonplace. Consider the dilemma faced by the administrators of medical insurance plans when asked to fund complex, expensive, and risky transplant operations for children in remote places. The cost for one such operation may well be greater than that of keeping a hospital bed at home open for a year. How many such special procedures can be afforded before the system deteriorates in its ability to provide care for society as a whole? How many community appeals for such special cases will distraught parents make before both sympathy and donors' wallets become exhausted? Should elective surgeries be funded because the patient wants them, or should only the ones needed be paid for—and who decides which are needed, and for whom? What of gender reassignment surgeries? In Western countries, they are generally classed as necessary health care, but what is their priority—higher or lower than, say, life-saving or restorative surgeries?

Choices may also arise between expensive and inexpensive treatments. For example, a patient with poor eyesight might be treated with a prescription for glasses or contact lenses at a cost of a few hundred dollars or might be given a far more expensive laser treatment to reshape the cornea and eliminate the need for external correction. Should there be (in this case, or any other) different treatments depending on the wealth of the patient? Who should pay for the poor man's glasses, or the rich woman's corrective surgery or cosmetic alterations? As the cost of medicine rises, so does the number of people who cannot afford even basic services, let alone exotic new techniques.

If an MRI diagnosis is needed to determine if a person has a tumor and there is a six-month backlog, should the person be allowed to have the procedure done privately if willing to pay (this may not be an issue in countries that lack public Medicare)? Or, should the same degree of access be allowed to everyone, regardless of their wealth and the wait time? What if a private clinic's purchase of a machine means that none is available for a public hospital to buy? What if a hospital was allowed to charge those who could afford it for some procedures and use the money to finance more hours for public clients?

The wealthy Western nations constantly make unseen, but important choices when they make resources available for expensive surgeries whose cost could fund thousands of simple, sight-restoring eye treatments in third-world countries. Rarely are things so simple that it is apparent to those directly involved that such a choice is happening, but a comparison of medical facilities in different parts of the world makes it obvious that some nations choose to afford far more than others can.

Organ transplant surgery will always have limitations because of the problem of finding donors and matching the tissue type with the intended recipient. Even if transplant operations become as simple as appendectomies or plastic surgery, ways will have to be found to increase the supply of spare body parts. Today, the presumption in Western countries is that such parts can be removed from a fresh cadaver only with prior authorization from the deceased or the permission of the immediate family. If the individual did not make a point of granting such permission while living, medical staff are understandably reluctant to ask relatives immediately after death, for fear of offending grieving relatives.

On the other hand, if a potential donor comes into a hospital after, say, a traffic accident, and there is another patient there in need of the badly injured patient's heart, will the potential donor get the best medical care, even when his or her death could mean life for the other? What has the higher priority—gender reassignment, knee replacement, a cosmetic breast enhancement, a facelift, the removal of a cancerous tumor, quadruple bypass, or a kidney transplant?

One possibility for alleviating the shortage of organs would be to move to the opposite legal presumption—that the body parts of the newly dead are the property of society and freely available to the medical profession unless authorization has been specifically denied. This is being done in some jurisdictions, the presumption being that since the deceased has no further need for the organ, someone else might as well have it. However, what is more important, the right of the dead to privacy or the need of the living for a new organ? Surely, life must take precedence over privacy in any ethical hierarchy. Yet for some, there is something at least

THE BIOSPACE REVOLUTION

dissatisfying, even ghoulish, about routinely harvesting body parts from the deceased without express prior approval. What is the alternative—a lively black market for illicitly harvested organs? Growing them in vitro?

If this seems unattractive, what are the alternatives? One could argue that human organs ought to become commodities like gold, pork bellies, or coffee. After all, the Red Cross already buys blood in many parts of the world. (Some countries, such as Canada, have in the past forbidden the purchase of blood from donors and commercial transactions in organs.) If blood can be a commodity, then perhaps kidneys, lungs, or even limbs could be. What is more important, to make body parts available when and as needed, or people's reluctance to establish something that seems akin to a used automotive parts business?

It should be noted that in countries where people are sufficiently desperate, there is a temptation to make money by selling one's body parts to the citizens of Western countries. Alternately, sufficiently repressive states in need of foreign exchange could decide to farm such organs from their citizens without their consent. Meanwhile, Western governments might find the prospect of benefiting their citizens in this way to be politically irresistible. Who ought to have the authority to allow or deny such transactions? Is it even possible to stop them? Perhaps not, for there is already a lively traffic in such organs from third-world countries to the operating rooms of the West, with only sporadic and ineffectual outcry.

The complexity of these issues is also illustrated by the difficulty experienced by doctors wishing to use transplant parts from newborn but nonviable infants. Sometimes a child is born with much of the brain missing (anencephalic) and will surely die in a matter of hours or days. Some doctors are unhappy that even when parents' permission is given, it may be legally impossible to use organs from such an infant for transplant purposes until breathing ceases, at which point the parts are much less useful. One rationale for forbidding earlier transplants is that the child is a human being—though an injured one—and therefore entitled to be allowed to die in peace without being torn apart for spare parts while still alive. Some hospitals attempt to steer a middle course, keeping the doomed infant well-oxygenated and healthy, so the organs will be in good condition when death comes. However, even this practice is controversial, for the definition of death as the cessation of brain activity is hard to apply if much of the brain is missing.

The success of the pro-abortion movement in effectively re-defining an unborn child as a non-person and thus part and property of the mother's body raises the possibility that a cash-starved mother could sell the parts of her unborn child. After all, attempts to prosecute pregnant women for child abuse for taking drugs, or an assailant for murder for shooting an unborn child have already been dismissed by the courts because the child in the womb has no legal personhood, and to rule otherwise would threaten the legal fiction that abortion is health care, irrespective of whether the mother's health is at issue.

The danger in breaking new legal ground in such respects is in ruling that severely injured or malformed infants are also not human and can therefore be scavenged. If that could be done in such an admittedly extreme case, there would be pressure to do the same to those born with, say, cerebral palsy or Down's syndrome. If those cases were also permitted, then any child deemed unacceptable by the parents for any reason—say, by being the wrong sex—might be at risk. Moreover, there could be no compelling reason to limit this to infants once such a practice was begun, for the precedent would be set whereby anyone could be declared insufficiently human and subject to salvage, such as for failing in school or being too elderly and therefore a burden on society. The state that had the power to do these things could also define the members of a race, religion, or banned political party to be subhuman and available for parting out. Under current North American law, it would seem that even healthy children could legally be disassembled and sold for parts while still in the womb even if not after birth. After all, it is already common practice to harvest stem cells and other tissue from aborted children, in some cases without any authorization being necessary.

On the other hand, under a hierarchical ethic of the type developed in Chapter 3, even the most severe "defects" would not disqualify a person from the right to live, for such disablements reflect on the quality of the child's future life, not on the fact of it. Life itself would seem in theory to have a higher priority than its quality—but does it in practice?

A related and equally contentious issue is the use of tissue from miscarried or aborted infants in transplants, corrective surgeries, and other experimental purposes. It has long been known that such tissue has growth and restorative potential not shared by the corresponding tissue from a mature human. Thus, if bone marrow, skin, liver cells, and other organ parts are to grow well after transplant, there may be no better source than fetal tissue. Whatever one thinks of the ethics of abortion or the status of the unborn, such a practice has unique ethical hazards. If the use of such parts were a common medical practice, they would become a correspondingly important commercial commodity. Not only would there be a substantial trade in such tissues by hospitals and abortion clinics, but there might also be a sufficient economic incentive for destitute women to become pregnant and sell the right to abort the child to the highest bidder.

Such outcomes may seem bizarre and repulsive to those who regard the human body at all stages as something far more than a convenient assemblage of chemicals into tissue. To others, such practices are simply the logical and normal outcomes of regarding the parts of the human body as commodities like any other.

That is, the conclusions one draws on these and similar issues depend on one's view of the human body. If the body is held either as sacred and inviolable (on the one hand) or as entirely material but constituting the entirety of a person (on the other), then it could be argued that the body's parts ought to be left alone. Two normally opposed groups might find common ground here—one because of a transcendent view of the body and the other because of the belief that the body is all there is of a person. Members of the former group would want to bury the dead respectfully—and by that they include intact. Members of the latter group might suggest instead freezing the body against the day when it could be thawed out and brought back to life with all parts intact. Respect is the common value here.

An entirely different conclusion might be drawn by those who emphasize the immaterial aspects of what they see in a human being. A human being is sometimes viewed as a body and soul dichotomy, or as body, soul, and spirit trichotomy, and some consider the material body as by far the least important of these. With such an emphasis, the dead body is neither the whole person nor in any sense sacred. It is merely part of the material baggage left behind when the essence of the person (the soul) departs. Since there is in this view no reunion of personality with that particular body, the previous owner has no more use for its parts, and they might as well be used to benefit someone else. Other combinations of these ideas are also possible, and the two possible conclusions about the value of the body can be reached by other means, so there is little agreement on such issues.

There are three possible techniques for alleviating the supply difficulties associated with transplant operations. The first is to use animal donors, such as pigs or chimpanzees, to obtain or grow organs destined for human beings. This has the advantage of solving the supply problem, though some people might be repelled at the prospect of having a pig's heart or one artificially grown in a cow replace their own, and animal rights activists might also take offense.

The second is to develop artificial hearts, kidneys, livers, and other critical organs. This could also solve the supply problem, though the cost of such work has so far been very high, and there is no immediate prospect that such devices can be produced in the necessary quantity, with the required reliability, and at a reasonable cost. Nor does either of these solutions address the availability of surgeons and facilities, or the cost of performing the procedures. The mass availability of artificial hearts would not mean that more transplant operations could be performed; other factors are at least as complex as parts supply.

The third is to repair the damaged organ *in situ*. A technique already used to repair skin tissue involves laying down a matrix of growth factor or stem cells covering the wound that acts as a scaffold on which the body's self-healing capabilities can act to rebuild the missing skin itself. In 2022, researchers at the University of Manchester demonstrated a similar technique using a biodegradable gel injection directly into a heart to create a scaffold promoting tissue growth, something the body does not normally do. Though preliminary and experimental, similar minimally invasive procedures seem to herald a different future for body repairs not involving invasive surgery or transplants.

This discussion highlights the built-in limitations of surgical techniques—barring dramatic changes in the availability of transplant parts and other costs, the application of such methods cannot increase without limit. Thus, the most sophisticated of today's surgical methods are unlikely ever to become available to much of the world's population. There will never be sufficient funds available to perform every necessary surgical procedure, much less every desirable one—and this will be true even when robotic surgeons become ubiquitous. No one with any sensitivity wants to turn away sufferers with no hope for relief, so necessity seems to force the conclusion that simpler and less costly methods will be found to replace invasive procedures.

Appropriateness

A third set of problems that accompany the allocation of scarce medical resources has to do with the appropriateness of treatment in some cases. For instance, should a doctor do an expensive heart transplant on a patient who is also suffering from terminal cancer that will probably kill her within two years? Should expensive surgery be done to allow a child with Down's syndrome to live, even though it is known that the quality of that life will be impaired? Some, including courts called upon to judge such cases, have said "no." According to the ethical hierarchy developed in Chapter 3, on the other hand, the answer to both questions could be "yes."

Denial of treatment can be supported for economic reasons—neither person is likely to be able to pay society back. The expense of the procedure might therefore be considered by some as wasted. Others would say that all medical treatments should be tried, regardless of cost. Those giving the latter answer could argue that the future cannot be known in advance and that the termination of a life is not an answer, but a reaction born of despair. What is more, everyone dies eventually, even if simply of old age. The physician who may be able to give a woman dying of bone cancer a few more years, albeit pain-filled ones, does not know if tomorrow will bring her a cure or a fatal traffic accident. Can the doctor prejudge her life based on a speculated future, or has she only the mandate to treat, regardless of situation or circumstance?

Questions of appropriateness can also be raised in connection with fertility problems, for treatment of such conditions can also be expensive, time-consuming, and may require repeated hospitalization. Neither is it easy to argue that a woman has a fundamental right to bear children. Moreover, there is already population pressure, and this grows steadily worse. In that light, it is difficult to justify using scarce resources to enhance fertility. On the other hand, it is hard not to sympathize with the plight of one who desperately desires children but is unable to have any, particularly when adoption is unlikely to be an option.

Other questions of appropriateness include cosmetic surgery. Should surgery to reduce a nose, enlarge breasts, change the smile, or "Westernize" the eyes be paid for by medical plans, or even allowed? These take up a substantial portion of scarce hospital and surgical resources—ones that, it could be argued, might be better spent on those who are sick. How important to society is the self-image of some of its members? One might agree that correcting actual defects is good and should be done, but how does one respond to the argument that a nose or a breast perceived as less than perfect by its owner is a defect in need of correction? Again, what is the priority for surgical alterations?

As the population ages and life spans increase, cosmetic surgery will be in greater demand. Some argue that this area should be left rather unregulated, apart from defining "cosmetic" and excluding such surgery from public medical insurance plans. Even some of these might want the government to step in if cosmetic surgery took a bizarre turn. For instance, perhaps some future youth cult would find it "cool" to have orange cheeks, green lips, an elongated nose, or skin flaps instead of hair—all arranged by surgery. Is this different from what is often called "corrective cosmetic" surgery? Even if it is, it may be impossible to draw the line between the frivolous and the acceptable, so "user-pay" may have to rule this area. Perhaps hospitals might make a sufficient profit from such enterprises to subsidize other areas. On the other hand, such activities could make operating rooms and personnel unavailable for work deemed of higher ethical priority. Are all possible medical procedures "rights" or are some privileges?

Summary and Conclusion

As long as current surgical methods are relied upon for the replacement or repair of defective body organs, a regulated means of providing the necessary resources must develop, however inadequate or unsatisfactory that may seem. However, many surgical methods are likely to remain complex, scarce, and expensive. Some methods may never be available to the world's general population, and the chief problems associated with them will continue to be how patients are selected, who pays, and what is their priority, rather than, say, the supply of organs as an economic mass commodity. What is required are different technologies—ones that use simple, cheap, nonsurgical methods.

7.3 Engineered Medicine

As mentioned earlier, the development of effective ways to combat viruses will represent (was?) a major medical turning point. If viral diseases can be conquered without hospitalization, the cost of medical care will decline and life spans will increase—both perhaps substantially. Enough progress has been made to make some health researchers confident that most infectious diseases will soon be a thing of the past, providing no intervening political or economic catastrophe sets the work back.

This leaves three other categories of organic malfunctions for which to consider treatment strategies. The first is invasive illness, such as cancer. Here, encouraging progress has been made toward the development

THE BIOSPACE REVOLUTION

of biological and chemical agents capable of targeting specific cancerous cells in the body and either destroying them or tagging them in such a way as to invite the body's immune system to eliminate the intruder. It is now known that a healthy immune system can make antibodies for almost any foreign protein; the trick is to keep that system healthy and working.

Whatever the method, many forms of cancer can now be completely defeated, especially if detected early. The most difficult remaining ones to overcome may be the non-localized cancers of the bone, blood, and lymph. Cancer of women's abdominal linings, all lumped together as "ovarian" regardless of where it originates, shows few or no symptoms until widespread and terminal. It can be slowed, but the five-year survival rate is less than five percent, and as the author sadly knows, death can come less than a year from diagnosis. In such cases, chemotherapy provides treatment and prolongation of life at a low and painful quality, but there is no known or even prospective cure.

Still, optimists point to the progress to date and predict that even some of these forms of cancer will be curable by injection, radiation, and other nonsurgical methods within twenty years. (Caveat: that statement survives unchanged and still unachieved from the first edition of this book, written three-and-a-half decades ago. Optimism springs eternal in the human mind. On the other hand, as this is written, researchers are testing a possible vaccine against some forms of cancer.)

Lung cancer may also be hard to cure. It is presently on the rise, especially among women, who became smokers in large numbers more recently than men and have not been giving up the habit as readily. This particular problem raises a subsidiary ethical question—whether the production, sale, and advertising of so potent a carcinogen as tobacco should even be allowed. It would not be if it were a new food additive or drug, but the vested interests of a large existing industry are not easy to set aside, even when the lives of many people are at stake. This illustrates that economic considerations often overpower critical ethical ones.

So of course is the reality of numerous potent drugs readily available for sale to addicts in most parts of the world. These have led to an epidemic of overdose deaths, and another one of acute loss of mental facilities in those still alive for the time being. Moreover, emergency responders and rooms are crowded with overdose cases. Here too, there is no effective treatment. All that has been put forward is "harm reduction" which consists of supplying clean needles, safe injection sites, and unadulterated drugs, plus decriminalization of possession. However, as in the case of ovarian cancer, this is for most only a death postponement strategy, as there is no known medical cure for addiction.

Another category of malfunctions is those involving the accumulation of extraneous material in the body. For instance, calcium deposits cause painful spurs on bones and cholesterol accretions block arteries, causing damage to the heart and other organs. It seems likely that in many cases, substances will eventually be developed to dissolve such accretions harmlessly. After all, there are already drugs that can dissolve gallstones or block secretions of stomach acid. Likewise, kidney stones can be shattered by ultrasound, and the fragments excreted. Such procedures eliminate the need for surgeries like duodenal ulcer repair and gall bladder removal.

In an interesting sidelight, it was long thought that ulcers were caused by excess stomach acid, and the typical treatment was prescription sedatives combined with a bland diet. It is now known that ulcers are caused by bacteria, and antibiotics are an effective treatment. That is, rather than being a systemic failure of one's own body, ulcers are caused by an invasive agent. There may well be other such misunderstandings in modern medical knowledge.

Another problem that may be of a similar type (system failure) relates to body cells' seeming inability to divide and replace themselves more than a given number of times before dying. One theory was that this is due to the action of substances that build up between or inside the cell and eventually block its reproduction. If the cell-division inhibiting agents could be identified, an anti-inhibitor could surely be designed. Understanding what to do is not the problem here, the difficulty lies in actually performing the necessary engineering. But even if an accretion-dissolving molecule must be designed atom by atom—and the ability to do that is still limited—such design problems are not insurmountable. Overcoming barriers of this type involves only a modest expansion of today's already formidable battery of treatment options.

A new theory of cell aging is equally interesting. It suggests that multiple copies of sequences called telomeres at the end of DNA chains vanish one (or a few) at a time with each cell division. Eventually, no telomeres remain, so the cell can no longer duplicate itself, thus limiting the organism's lifetime. Perhaps an agent can be found to change this action so cells can reproduce indefinitely. On the other hand, such an "immortal" cell would bear a strong resemblance to a cancerous one.

THE BIOSPACE REVOLUTION

Yet another aspect of bodily function failure is that cells can become senescent. Though in other respects normal, they stop reproducing, and the gradual accumulation of such cells compromises such processes as tissue repair and regeneration, thus contributing to signs of aging and general dysfunction. The removal of such cells by chemical or biological means could improve general body function, boost its repair mechanisms in particular, and ameliorate the symptoms of aging. Research into the chemical pathways by which cells become senescent in the first place, or could have their reproductive mechanism reactivated in the second, might have a profound influence on the symptoms of aging, perhaps extending life spans. On the other hand, such cells are quite the opposite of cancerous, and their presence could inhibit the growth of tumors.

One more aspect of aging is that DNA contains just under fifty thousand genes, many of which code for the manufacture of specific proteins and therefore cell functionality. Since all cells have the same DNA, clearly some genes have to be turned on for, say, heart cells, but off when expressed as liver cells. Collectively this is termed the cells' epigenetic programming. It turns out that genes have a prefix called a promoter region that, among other things identifies the gene and determines whether it is on or off by the extent to which a specific carbon atom in a repeated cytosine-guanine pair in the promoter region is methylated. With aging, genes to produce necessary proteins tend to get sufficiently methylated to become turned off. Understanding and being able to control this mechanism is a huge task, but if mastered, could prove the key to switching off or reversing the aging mechanism.

A third set of challenges for medical engineering relates to repairing physical damage to the human body. In this context, one is tempted to view the body as a biochemical machine, albeit of extraordinarily intricate design. Unfortunately for the mechanics of this machine (the surgeons), their smallest tools are thousands of times larger than some of the fine parts they wish to repair. Heavy structural members (bones) and outer protective sheeting (skin) are relatively easy to work on, as are the larger subsystems (most organs including skin). But as many paraplegics know to their sorrow, the nervous system is another matter. Sewing these with thread is like trying to tie up a flea with an ocean liner's hawser. Finding, let alone repairing, individual damaged cells is impossible with traditional surgeons' tools.

The engineering challenge here is to develop first the knowledge of the fine structure of the human body at the molecular level, and then invent the ability to design biological or chemical agents to effect repairs at that level. This is not as far-fetched as it may seem, for the body can already conduct repairs to a great extent, and some animals are even capable of regenerating severed limbs. Human bodies cannot effect this, because even as they grow in the womb, cell tissue differentiates sufficiently to lose the ability to replace parts. However, that such tissue could grow a limb at one stage of development suggests it could have that capability restored. This is the point of working with stem cells (ones that retain the ability to produce various kinds of tissue), for these may be induced to grow a variety of organs or parts thereof.

If limb regeneration seems too grand a task, perhaps promoting the healing of severed nerves will be easier to achieve. Once again, the problem is one of biochemical engineering—of building the appropriate substances to stimulate the body to repair itself. An old engineer's motto is worth mentioning here:

> If it used to work, it can almost certainly be (re-)made to work again.

There are more comprehensive repair problems, however. As the body's cells grow older they gradually lose the ability to replicate themselves correctly, or at all. As noted, this may be due to some inhibitor or the loss of telomeres. It may simply be that the body's parts gradually wear out and die or that each DNA replication causes some portion of the genetic material to be altered or discarded, so the cell eventually lacks enough correct DNA to reproduce. Perhaps a body cell is not unlike a page of text that has undergone many successive photocopies. After a time, the text loses definition and eventually becomes illegible. If the DNA of a body cell is subject to similar losses, its reproductive successors would eventually lose too much information content to remain viable. Here is yet another case where it is easy to visualize the problem and to have some idea how to address it—on a large scale and theoretically. Engineering a solution that allows the body to repair or replace structures damaged by age is a much more difficult matter. It could involve the development of many biochemical agents, some natural to the body at some stages of development (enzymes and proteins) and others that are new.

It is also known that the expression of genes say for the production of a particular protein, can be switched off or on either by other parts of the DNA or even by behavioral and environmental factors such as diet and exercise. These epigenetic triggers do not change the DNA itself but can either promote or prevent, say, the production of an important protein, or impair its functionality by causing it to fold in the wrong way, and in either case contribute to symptoms of aging.

Damaged DNA sequences may impair important metabolic processes, causing disabling symptoms that threaten health or even life. One example is porphyria, the name for a group of malfunctions and symptoms resulting from blood disorders caused either by a shortage of porphyrin, a necessary product of a series of metabolic processes, and/or from the buildup of precursor chemicals in the body that are supposed to be used to make those products. Porphyrins are essential to the function of hemoglobin, to which it links to bind iron and carry oxygen around the body. When their metabolic manufacture is disrupted, the result can be an excess of unbound iron, and too little functioning hemoglobin. Symptoms range from skin to nervous system disorders, and can variously be triggered by foods (which ones differ by individuals) or exposure to the sun. Symptomatic treatment is done, up to and including regular blood transfusions in some severe cases, but the only cure would be to edit the DNA to a normal state.

We see that the body subsystem once termed the "simple cell" is anything but. On the contrary, it is known to have a biochemical design of incredible complexity and sophistication—more so than any computer, for instance. Finding problems at the molecular level, and designing answers at the same level is not and will not be a simple task.

However, the potential for such medicine extends from (possibly) straightforward cell repair to the dramatic and even the far-fetched. For instance, if the human body could first be induced to grow a new limb, then perhaps it could also be made to grow a new heart, lung, or liver, then dissolve an old nonfunctioning one. Restoring hair to the bald may not turn out to be difficult or even important. Restoring hearing to the deaf or sight to the blind is another matter, for both involve problems of fine structure whose repair is often not amenable to surgery but could be to new cellular repair pharmaceuticals. Some have even wondered whether a "memory pill" could be devised to stimulate the brain in such a way that while under its influence anything heard or read would never be forgotten. Regardless of whether any of these are achieved, the principal research focus will be on replacing expensive and difficult surgical methods with cheap and easy chemical and biological ones.

One possible method of producing biological agents is to design cells, say, bacteria, to produce proteins that in turn could be used to make specific enzymes or antibiotics. Such living nanomachines could be developed much further—to the point where a collection of them can act as a miniature assembly line for new DNA, new proteins, or new enzymes, or merely to manufacture the ones the body cannot make itself for genetic reasons—a group of epigenetic replacement therapies. Such substances could then be built to order, molecule by molecule. Similar methods are already employed to produce insulin, for instance.

Two issues problematic to some can be ameliorated simultaneously by using bacteria to produce milk and meat protein products molecularly identical to the natural ones, but without using animals. None would be killed, none would contribute to greenhouse gas emissions, yet the meat would be genuine, not a melange of plant-based artificial meat. Such methods have the advantage of being able to omit lactose, cholesterol, and other problematic ingredients. Ice cream made this way is already being marketed. Assembling meat and fish flesh in this manner is, at this writing, not economic, but making it so will take only time and scaling up.

Other optimistically projected nanomachines could be programmable or instructable—and may be termed nano-computers or general-purpose assemblers. The reconstruction of a damaged heart, liver, or other organ and even the rebuilding of damaged nerves or neurons could be within the ability of agents made in this manner. Another possible technique involves the direct construction of DNA strands that can manufacture the desired molecules. Another still is the chemical stimulation of the affected parts to induce them to self-repair through growth. Although these ideas are still in their infancy, there are already machines that are capable of analyzing or constructing specific protein molecules. In the longer term, nanomachines might also be employed to grow a PIEA as an implant in the brain or to make alterations to body or brain structures to improve both or to repair congenital or genetic damage *in situ*—not on a gross structural level, but by editing gene sequences.

Automating preventive medicine

Setting aside the more spectacular speculations for a moment, an important potential for the use of existing technology is in the computerizing of information and activities relating to preventive medicine. In particular, the most important contributors to health—or the lack of it—are nutrition and exercise. Although the appropriate levels of neither are yet known exactly, a great deal of general information is known about both. Average citizens have little access to much of this in ready form until they come under professional care for a back injury, obesity, diabetes, or a heart attack. Most people will not make use of what is known without such a powerful motivation unless it is in a form that makes it easy to obtain and implement. This is an interesting but not insurmountable challenge to some in the high-tech industry, for if people had and used the available information on nutrition and exercise, there would probably be a significant decline in health care costs and an increase in the average life span.

This is yet another instance where reducing the barriers to finding information has great potential. People who would not make a trip to a library to find nutritional data are more likely to do so if it is easily available in their homes via an appliance that they use frequently for more mundane matters, and on which the presence of such information is advertised frequently. The Metalibrary would not itself solve health problems, but it could prove an important tool in providing people with the means to solve some of their own.

How close are we to this now? Much sound health information is available on the Internet. Unfortunately so is much misinformation, and too many people cannot or do not want to discern between the two. So, in yet another matter, a usable Metalibrary needs its data to be curated.

Consequences of Longer Life Spans

As understanding of the aging process, preventative medicine, and how to do molecular engineering grows, a substantial increase in life spans seems likely. Longevity researchers differ widely in their estimates of what the eventual human average life span could be, with figures of 200, 500, and 1000 years being casually tossed about. Even if one believes the more conservative of these optimists, and assumes that some of today's under-50-year-olds would live to, say, 150 years instead of the current Canadian average (from birth) of about 80 years (men) and 84 years (women), or 75 and 80 respectively in the U.S., the social implications are staggering. At every stage in the development of longevity treatments, there will be pressure from the rich, the powerful, and some intellectuals to obtain priority treatment. Moreover, since the already highly developed countries would have such agents first, the medical gap between rich and poor countries (and individuals) could grow ever greater, increasing the destabilizing forces on world society. Some attempts might even be made to keep the fact of such treatments a secret at first. However, even if the recipients had complete facial make-overs and entirely new identities, their continued survival could not long be kept from the rest of the wider population or the citizens of other countries—all the more so since effective treatments for old age are likely to be independently discovered by many researchers more or less simultaneously.

Over the longer term, age sixty-five retirements, the whole concept of pensions, the hope of inheritances, and the ability of youth to obtain jobs vacated by their elders would all be affected by any substantial increase in life span. In addition, unless birth rates are substantially reduced, population sizes could increase dramatically. Some already crowded countries might restrict any longevity treatments that are developed to a small elite for this reason alone. Power and money concentrations could grow, not only because their holders might at first control the treatments but because they would live longer, have more time to accumulate both, and their wealth would be passed on less often and therefore with fewer fees and taxes.

Some of these issues might be resolved by the pragmatic force of circumstances. The managers of large pension plans would either re-market their funds as general investment packages or go into a different line of work. The tax structure might have to change to limit the accumulation of wealth. Perhaps a means would be found to encourage people to change careers every few years to alleviate the job entry problem. However, the social and economic disruption due to such changes would still be substantial. On the whole, these changes may increase inequities and tensions between the rich and the poor of the world—a prescription for disaster if the treatments are not seen to be fairly administered. Marriage could change, for it is even now seen by many as a temporary commitment during part of a longer life—such a view could become even more prevalent if life lengthens and bearing children were discouraged, forbidden, or impossible except for the relatively young (i.e the capacity to do so limited to the current number of years, rather than the same percentage of a longer span).

There are also some balancing forces to contend with. While increased longevity would suggest much larger populations, the birth rate in industrialized countries has been declining for decades, and it seems likely to do so in third-world countries as their economies also change. The net result could simply be a stable but much older population, and an increase in the retirement age because of a lack of younger workers to take jobs.

It is also unclear whether people who live longer would also stay healthy longer or whether they would have to spend more years in extended-care facilities. If the latter were all that were achieved, the benefits would be small indeed, even outweighed. The most optimistic longevity workers are convinced that the greatest benefits of a longer life will come by extending the productive years of those people whose generation of new ideas and techniques most profoundly impact the direction of society. This is a large assumption, for many people are productive only in a few of their years. One might hope that more years will mean more productive years, but this may only be an occasional side effect. It might equally be supposed that longer-lived people would gradually become less innovative and productive, and not contribute anything of benefit to others for much of their now longer lives.

Thus, although human life might be extended considerably over the next few decades, the long-term implications of such increases for society as a whole are unclear. There may be a declining birth rate, a more stable and conservative population, upheavals in the job market, and the disappearance of some institutions catering to retirement as it is now known. Whether the extra years would mean "better" people from either a moral or educational point of view is unknown. History would seem to suggest that there would likely be the same proportion of scoundrels and saints regardless of how long both lived.

Another aspect of the increased use of medical drugs is the corresponding increase in their abuse. The more drugs that are discovered, the more mind-altering substances will be among them. Moreover, as the workings of the human brain and body become better understood, so will the ways of stimulating the pleasure centers. Consequently, one should expect that there will always be addicts. What is not known is whether the societal changes now in progress will result in a higher percentage of the population becoming "wired" for pleasure than at present, or whether a significant sacrifice of general civil liberties will have to be made to eliminate such practices. This is already an important question, not just for athletes who attempt to perform better on drugs but also for drivers and the employees of railways, airlines, hospitals, and other places where human performance profoundly affects the safety of others.

One thing has become abundantly clear. Combatting the effects of "recreational" drugs just by providing safe injection sites and decriminalizing drug use without focusing on ways to wean addicts off their addictions is a catastrophic policy failure, for the number of overdose deaths has done nothing but increase with each passing year.

The bottom line: the development of new medical techniques, whether surgery, pharmaceuticals, or gene editing, as for any technique, is likely to have mixed results—some very beneficial, others much less so.

7.4 Engineering New Life Forms

Some methods described in the last two sections are also being employed to develop new or modified life forms. Current examples include strains of bacteria that can attack ocean oil spills, digest the material, and reprocess it into harmless substances, or do the same to re-work mine tailings and extract more metals. Others make antibiotics, antibodies, and other pharmaceuticals for a variety of human and animal disease treatments. Still other useful strains could process garbage, produce crude oil, or separate discarded metals and plastics into their elemental constituents for recycling. In conjunction with the biological nanomachines of the last section, scavenger species could also be devised and targeted to particular harmful substances or organisms in the human body. Such goals are already being achieved through recombinant DNA techniques, wherein the specific gene(s) responsible for some attribute of one life form are identified and spliced into the DNA of another form. In the case of simple proteins and DNA strands, genetic engineers have been able to design and build the entire strand from the base materials, and methods for doing this are gradually being extended to more complex proteins.

Possible uses of these techniques on plant genetic material include the development of new species of high-yield grains, ones that can grow even in poor soils or newly altered climates, as well as the combining of two food-producing methods into one plant. An example of the latter is the grafted "pomato," which grows fruit above the ground and tubers below. Higher forms of life may also be modified in this manner. Cattle could be developed that are hardy to colder (or warmer) weather, can graze on poorer ground, produce more meat or milk, require less care, and are more resistant to disease. Chickens may be induced to grow larger and to lay bigger eggs. Since the change is at the DNA level, the result is not just a hybrid cross-breed; the new characteristics breed true.

Alternatively, food protein could be grown in a vat instead of an animal or plant. Such a process would be more efficient, less work, and easier on the environment (no more cows belching greenhouse gasses). Science fiction writers have long speculated that someday all food may be manufactured by bacterial action on raw materials at a far higher efficiency than photosynthesis, with conventional farming becoming obsolete.

There remains concern that a genetically engineered virus or bacteria might be released that would cause a plague taking millions of lives. Some assert, with no supporting evidence, that SARS-CoV-2 originated this way. Another disaster scenario involves creating a life form that is capable of nothing but making copies of itself, using the entire biological world for its ends—the "grey goo" finale to all other life forms. Laboratories that work with editing genetic materials must be very careful, for it is not yet possible to predict all the side effects of gene splicing. The section being spliced may control characteristics other than or in addition to the one being targeted, and the life form developed may not be as expected.

Such difficulties are to be expected in any technology in its infancy. It is safe to assume that the understanding of genetic coding will continue to grow to the point where the DNA of all life forms will be mapped in detail. Several nations funded the mapping of human genetic material (the human genome project). Its success was trumpeted prematurely when only the portions supposed to be relevant had been mapped. It later became evident that much of what had been labelled "junk DNA" did have a purpose (epigenetic in many cases) and was not, for example, the supposed remnant of colonization by viral infections in our distant ancestors, so these projects had to be extended. Now that this information has been obtained, the raw data is available to determine what each gene controls and potentially to edit human gene sequences *in situ*.

Methods for changing specific characteristics will also become more sophisticated. It will be several years before new life forms can be developed from scratch, tailored to measure for their niche in the earth's ecological system, but this too seems inevitable. New plant and animal species will likely be generated to improve the food supply or replace it with chemically manufactured substances. Adventuresome researchers are tackling the revival of extinct species like the mastodon, certain dinosaurs, or the passenger pigeon. Another possibility is the enhancement of existing animal species. Could some be given enough intelligence to perform menial tasks, and become factory workers, cleaners, or message carriers? Can a combination of animal and machine be developed that is alive and also programmable? The answers to such questions are unknown at this time, but if they are positive, humanity will ultimately face a period of adjustment to living with its creations, and the necessity of finding them a place alongside the human biospace.

Yet other such modifications may be done within the human biospace. There is, for instance, little use for legs in zero gravity, but replacing them with two more arms and hands could be quite useful. See the "quaddies" in Lois McMaster Bujold's SF novel *Falling Free*. Other structural, chemical, and practical adaptations could be engineered for better living in new environments, whether acquired by exploration of the solar system or necessitated by climate change on Earth.

Questions have been asked about who owns the products of such research. In the United States, patents on new life forms developed in the lab have been granted—a practice that is certain to remain controversial. At issue is whether living materials developed in the lab at the cost of time, talent, energy, and money are qualitatively different from medical drugs developed in the same way. As long as viral, bacterial, or plant material is in question, the public may take relatively little interest in the matter. When animal species are genetically re-engineered, opposition to patents and even to the research itself may run somewhat high. However, the controversy generated by plant and animal genetic research pales in comparison to that resulting from applying such research to humans. Who owns a person's DNA? The individual in whose cells it resides, or the researcher (or her employer) who discovers an enhancement or disease-resistant gene unique to that person?

7.5 Human Genetic Engineering

The methods of gene splicing to re-engineer the human race fall into three broad categories—those intended to make repairs, those intended for selection, and those intended to make improvements.

Genetic Repairs

Repairs of cellular-level issues fall into two categories. The first, the least controversial and possibly the easiest to do, would be those done after birth. The development of DNA-driven machines to produce specific proteins could lead to the ability to repair damage from mutations, remove dangerous or hostile proteins from the body, or even correct some chromosomal or genetic defects after the fact, possibly by replacing or repairing the missing functionality without altering the person's DNA. This is of limited benefit, say for Down's syndrome. Even if the associated genetic issues were to be repaired, say by nanomachines, the physical and mental damage programmed before birth would remain.

The second is the elimination of genetic disorders before they happen, or at least before they have an opportunity to do lasting harm. There is a long list of candidates for such work. Sickle-cell anemia, hemophilia, and predilection to organic problems such as cancer and heart disease or metabolic disorders are a few obvious ones. Some disorders can already be identified with specific gene locations in human DNA. Diagnosis from material in the amniotic fluid is possible in many cases. It may not be long before the genetic causes of most major inherited disorders are well understood, though whether there can be cures or ameliorations once they have been inherited is another matter.

In the time between the discovery of the genetic cause for an ailment and that of a cure, a new issue arises, however. Is a person with a known genetic predisposition to heart failure, diabetes, or stroke insurable? employable?

At present, prenatal explorations for such issues are usually done to determine whether or not to abort the child rather than with any healing in view. Where governments permit such abortions, it is not hard to imagine them mandating genetically defective children be aborted to protect the economy by avoiding costly treatment and care after birth. After all, a state that has the power to allow something has the power to require it. Given growing population pressures and strains on medical systems, such an outcome must be considered likely in some countries. The chief question would then be how to determine which genetic characteristics constitute the "pure" human race and which others ought to be exterminated. As the Nazis showed in the 1930s, such a decision can be made on a political level and technology used to enforce it afterwards. Such a policy could naturally be enforced on the already-born as well as on those not yet born. It might be a short step to a new genocide directed against those deemed sub-human for national, religious, or racial reasons. It would also be easy to label dissidents as defective, much as they were in the old Soviet Union, increasingly are in the new Russia, and also have by some U.S. politicians.

Can such frightening outcomes be avoided? Surely, despite recent political trends to the extreme, they must. One possibility would be to focus on conception, rather than later points in human development. Assuming gene splicing methods have advanced along with diagnostic techniques, the same methods applied to plants and animals would be available to alter human DNA. The egg and sperm of would-be parents could be examined, and the coding at the target gene sites changed before inducing conception *in vitro*. The "corrected" fertilized egg could then be implanted in the mother's womb for carrying to full term. The child would still be biologically the offspring of its parents but would lack the damaged genes that would otherwise have been passed on. The damaged genes would also be eliminated from future generations.

Again, there are objections to this kind of research, supposedly because the result is unnatural, and therefore ought to be forbidden. For their part, advocates respond that, in the case of hemophilia, for example, blood that clots is more natural than blood that does not. Surely it would benefit humanity to find ways to eliminate hemophilia, porphyria, sickle cell anemia (and similar problems) from the gene pool. Heading off genetically induced disorders before they happen is much better than attempting remedies after the fact.

It would also solve some problems for infertile couples who use sperm banks to conceive a child. As things now stand, two children independently conceived through such services could well be half-siblings with no means of knowing this, unless donor records are provided. If they met and married, the probability of genetic defects in their offspring would be far higher than usual. The ability to eliminate genetic defects would make the operation of anonymous banks for human eggs and sperm much safer. Whether, in the light of population pressures, the cost of continuing to use these techniques is justified is another matter. And, does the child have a right to know who are the biological parents?

Choosing to seek the ability to make genetic repairs seems in some ways to be an easy decision. The numerous research efforts already underway along these lines testify that the decision has already been made, without much consideration of the possible ethical issues. As long as fertilized eggs are not discarded during the process, even the most conservative observer might not strenuously object to a beneficial program. However, there are more controversial implications of such technology, and no guarantee that the best of such techniques, chosen with "good" motives, would not also result in the worst of abuses.

Selection

The ability to repair genetic material implies that traits other than those involving defects could also be selected. The most obvious application is choosing the sex of the child. On a personal level, this might be regarded by some as ethically neutral. However, if sex selection were easy enough to implement on a large scale, it would not be neutral, for in some cultures there is a powerful bias against female children. In such situations, the ability to select sex would quickly throw the male/female ratio far off the rough balance it now has. Indeed, in some parts of the world, amniocentesis is performed solely for this purpose, with abortion preventing females from being born. Such cultures already see the consequences of insufficient women for marriage partners for the generation so selected. Moreover, if widely adopted, the culture selecting only males would eventually die out.

Eventually, various selections would be just as feasible—for beauty, strength, longevity, intelligence, height, muscle mass, skin and hair coloring, and other characteristics. Since some of these traits might be perceived to give the next generation a decided advantage, parents would be pressured to adopt any available technology to ensure their children have the best possible genetic heritage. Indeed, if they chose not to do so, they would surely find themselves on the losing end of a parental malpractice suit brought by their offspring or facing criminal negligence charges by the state. Moreover, if current population pressures were heightened by dramatic increases in life spans, the birth rate would have to decline in equal measure. If a society had room only for a few children, the pressure to use whatever techniques are available to select the "best" parental genetic material would be extreme.

In the same way that abortion of "defective" children could be required, the existence of genetic selection methods could lead to their enforced use. There would be compelling arguments that selection is in the best interests of society (yet another example of efficient technique being irresistible). There would of course be the problem of who defines the best interests. Some future governments might want to breed docility into the general population to enhance its power or to eliminate certain racial characteristics or temperaments that might lead to dissent and opposition, in the interests of what it regarded as purity.

This could not easily be done unless authorities limited longevity treatments to an elite, for otherwise, the population would change too slowly to achieve such goals. While a government with enough power to do one could do both, it would still be faced with population pressure and might opt instead for mass sterilization or compulsory birth control. The more neutral path of requiring reproduction licenses—and only issuing them to those deemed genetically fit, or able to afford gene editing—would be impossible to enforce under any but a rigidly totalitarian regime, but there is never any shortage of those.

The major assumptions leading to the most problematic outcomes are three: that such selection will become possible; that life spans will increase; and that living space is limited. There may, therefore, be a troubled future for human genetic research—and now that it has begun, it cannot be stopped, for it will continue in some parts of the world even if banned in others. There may be ways around these problems if the room can be found for a much larger population, and that aspect of the human biospace will be discussed later in the chapter. There are even more troubling aspects of human genetic research, however.

Making Genetic Changes

A process of genetic selection acts continuously on the gene pool of an organism, including the human population, for in every generation most genetic traits are inherited and remain possibilities for transmission to the next, but some are not and thus die out. Moreover, there is an entropic factor at work dictating that copying mistakes and mutations accumulate in a large population, and these degrade the pool, especially as treatments for the problems they cause, rather than editing to remove them, promote their reproducibility. That is, in general, entropic factors impair and remove more than they preserve or enhance genetic information.

Of course, even when it is error-free, genetic mixing from the parents does not on its own result in the production of anything fundamentally new in succeeding generations, just variations on the central theme for that life form. Information is selectively lost, not gained, even when speciation results. Even done intelligently (as in plant breeding), selection only allows designers to take advantage of and promote characteristics already inherent in the normal range of genetic variation. Careful selection allows the distribution of traits present in the population of a life form to be moved toward one section of the existing range. If left alone, they would tend to regress to the natural distribution. Genetic modifications, on the other hand, can force this selection to become permanent, because undesirable genes can be eliminated.

This is already done with plants and animals, even to the point of generating new species, so there is no reason to suppose that human genetic research would stop with repair and selection. Various "improvements" or "modifications" would certainly be suggested, and no amount of government control could halt such experiments indefinitely. Thus, as with any fundamentally new technology, this one has the potential to be used for what seem to be attractive ends, for what may be frivolous ends, and for ones that might be dangerous.

Possibilities include enhancements to intelligence and further extensions of the life span. A strain of humans with larger lungs and an altered circulatory system could live in high mountains where the air is thin. Some do this now, so such an ability might fit in the selection category. Perhaps someone would try to develop a human with gills and fins to colonize the oceans, or one with hollow bones and wings to take to the air, or a human with modified chemistry to live on some hostile planet. Are such things feasible? Not yet, but no one knows they are impossible. Some such experiments may be attempted unless enforceable limitations can be placed on genetic research.

What of still stranger alterations in the name of making improvements, such as extra limbs or eyes? Experimenters could try everything from dual sets of sexual organs to new skin colors. A docile subhuman species with limited intelligence and great strength would eliminate the need for robots or enhanced animals to fill menial positions. Such possibilities may seem shocking, but the point is that at present no one knows where genetic research can lead. It may be neither wise nor practical to prohibit such research. Still, society has a collective interest in ensuring such work is regulated with codes that have moral/ethical strength motivating the legal. Otherwise, human beings may eventually find themselves asking whether a creature derived from their genetic stock is human—or having the question asked of them. At the very least, the issue of who owns the rights to new forms of life would have to be reopened. If changes to "lower" forms of life such as plant or animal modifications are patentable, a degree of ownership may be implied. The same becoming true for modified humans could lead to their enslavement. It could equally lead to the enslavement of the original human variety by enhanced versions.

As for all technologies with great potential benefit, there is equally great potential for mischief and harm. Genetic research is a Pandora's box with the lid already off and it may be too late to regulate it effectively; certainly, it is impossible to prohibit.

The "playing God" objection discussed in connection with AI research can also be advanced by critics of human genetic work. In both cases, it seems to carry little weight. People in the field are usually not aware of "playing God" and are inclined to ignore the argument as false, irrelevant, or meaningless. Perhaps what the objectors mean is that they believe a Creator intended creation to be left as humankind found it.

However, people who believe they are created in the image of God, yet make a blasphemous thing of specific knowledge may not yet have come to terms with the creative part of that image in humanity; the accusation therefore has some appearance of inconsistency. Moreover, making selections at the genetic level is not fundamentally different from the selective breeding that has been the stock-in-trade of plant and animal husbandry for millennia. Indeed the objectors to GMOs (genetically modified organisms) in the food chain conveniently ignore that almost the entire stock already has been modified—albeit much more slowly.

Still, the objection has merit, particularly if genetic technology falls under the total control of the state. In totalitarian systems, the idea of designing docile citizens could be attractive, for there the state *is* the deity. Thus "playing God" is a real problem, for in certain political environments, such research would be deadly serious. For now, these issues are open for discussion, but choices will have to be faced in the next few years, and it is better to come to grips with them before the fact than after. If a consensus as to what constitutes "good" and "bad" outcomes of genetic research cannot be reached early on, unregulated chaos could ensue, with grave consequences.

What is more, as the level of any technology increases, so does its potential to affect all life. Eventually, many individuals will have the means to destroy civilization. What could prevent any of them from doing so? If there is no return to a pervasive moral code, mass destruction appears possible. Even if there is, how can the consequences of a single person's rejection of moral codes be policed against, and who would control those police? Many of these issues are explored in fictional form by the author in his *Timestream* novels. See the website at http://www.arjaybooks/com.

What makes regulation difficult is the traditional autonomy of the largely university-based researchers, and the vast amounts of money involved in commercial genetic research. Potential economic return for certain animal vaccines, specialized viruses and antivirus, and modified plant stock is large enough, but the opportunities to make money on human genetic manipulations are potentially far more substantial. One means of control that might work is to regulate the sale of equipment and techniques for such research, much as is now done with chemicals, pesticides, and pharmaceuticals. As experience with illicit drugs has shown, however, if the amount of money to be made in trafficking is sufficiently large, no degree of regulation or enforcement suffices to stop it altogether.

7.6 Rights, Health Care, and Life

Any discussion of genetic engineering leads naturally to questions about what are the rights of people to benefit from such work. Present-day medical practice is loosely founded on a generally accepted, but often unstated right of all persons to live healthy, normal lives. There are two possible ways of viewing this right. One is to suppose that everyone ought to have the best possible medical and (ultimately) genetic treatments available to bring that person's health to an optimal level. A second is to conclude that the human race as a whole should be brought to optimal health. The danger in the latter approach is that it may also lead to mandating that unhealthy or "undesirable" persons have no right to live.

Improving the human race as a whole through a program of selective breeding and the elimination of those considered undesirable gained great popularity in the early third of the twentieth century under the banner of eugenics. Acceptance of this model was widespread for it fit the prevailing model of evolutionary progress. There was great optimism that the human race could take control of its evolutionary destiny this way, and few voices of concern were raised for the consequences. By the time World War II started, Hitler's program of eugenics was already well underway in Germany, but it was not until after the war that the horrifying consequences of arbitrarily defining who is acceptably human were seen.

State-run eugenics has generally been anathema in civilized nations ever since, but new medical techniques will mean that individuals can practice more personal eugenics. This apparently attractive option has the same potential negatives, however, and it would not do to lose sight of those in some euphoric optimism that a new age is dawning for the human race.

On the one hand, selection and modification, as well as effective means of birth control, could well do away with the demand for abortion and infanticide. This would be beneficial for all concerned—child, mother, family, and society. On the other hand, those born before or without the benefit of genetic selection, or whose abilities came to be regarded as inferior would be greatly disadvantaged. Their genes would not be the latest models. In addition, long life spans will not necessarily solve the problem of caring for the elderly, who might need more and longer rather than less and shorter medical care. A future society could become so obsessed with obtaining and maintaining genetic perfection that individuals of any age who were perceived to fall short could be discarded. Many countries already permit death at the request of a sufferer—"pulling the plug" on life support or actively euthanizing someone who wishes to die in peace (medical assistance in dying, or MAID). As in many other arenas, what the state can permit, it can assume the authority to require.

If it has the power to allow certain lives never to develop past the point of discovering a physical deformity, it might also claim the power to deny citizenship or even life to anyone perceived as defective, including for deemed economic, political, racial, and religious reasons. Such forces are already at work in western nations.

Pressures on the medical system also lead to questions about when it is appropriate to provide or deny medical treatment. Likewise, economic and demographic pressures conspire to persuade people to limit new life, and abortion or infanticide are used where birth control has not been successful. In addition, the continued existence of humans with limitations caused by genetic defects, accidents, or even old age can be threatened. All the issues involving life are difficult ones; even when the individual involved makes the choice.

Patient Choices

What should a physician do when a terminally ill patient facing painful treatment asks the doctor to withhold further treatment to allow a relatively peaceful death? This is a difficult question. Free will and freedom of choice are argued in favor of the patient's freedom of choice. The doctor is then in the position of deciding whether to be an enabler of suicide. If the same person were about to jump to her death from a bridge, a passer-by would be expected to intervene or call for help, attempting to prevent suicide. Most would exert themselves in the cause of life, being unwilling to give up until she actually jumped, and even then launching an extensive search of the water below in case she lived. If she were to survive, every resource of the medical establishment would be brought to bear to save her life, restore her body to functionality, and provide the necessary counseling to ward off another such attempt. Shall a doctor do less in the treatment of other patients? What is the essential difference between the two situations, and who decides when that difference exists? Is it more humane to allow an escape from suffering for those who desire it? Or, is the desire to escape from life *prima facie* evidence of lack of competence, and should therefore be ignored?

These questions have already been resolved, in the West's legal and medical systems. *Living wills*, in which the testator dictates a *do-not-resuscitate order* for extreme eventualities, are now accepted and acted upon in most jurisdictions. However, this has come about with little debate about the consequences.

Some utilitarians focus on the money issues, and some proponents of the right to die argue that death in terminal illness should be made quick and easy. Some act-ethic moralists would condemn this conclusion, pointing out that cures might still be possible, and suggesting that participating in another's suicide is not different from murdering the person. One possible conclusion that a consensus moralist could come to is that if the majority of, say, inoperable cancer patients wanted to die, then they all should. If this conclusion seems stark, consider a single paralyzed patient whose doctor has already participated in assisted suicides in similar situations. It would not be difficult in such circumstances, especially with the permission of anxious heirs, to have the patient declared incompetent and then argue that if the person were able, she would want to die, and therefore must do so. Indeed, such a decision may seem quite utilitarian. A society that had already allowed assisted suicide would have little motivation to enquire about such deaths and perhaps not much to care about them.

Such decisions can be even more difficult if a second condition exists that will kill the patient anyway and the (possibly expensive) treatment would only postpone the inevitable. This issue was discussed earlier in the chapter without the complication of the patient's request for death. When simultaneously faced with such a request as well as a waiting list of patients who can be treated more inexpensively, the pressure to allow or require death increases. There must, some would argue, be some limit on paying for extending the lives of the terminally ill.

What is the degree to which active intervention in allowing or encouraging death should be tolerated? Even the most enthusiastic spenders realize that economic considerations ultimately force many life-and-death decisions even if they are hidden in government appropriations measures and seen as entirely political. More positively, part of the challenge for developing new medical technologies could be seen as removing as many of the limitations as possible to the extension of productive life.

The opposite problem may also arise, for in some cases the technology is available to save the life of a patient, but she refuses treatment, perhaps for religious reasons. The doctor, the hospital, the law, and the state must in such cases decide whether the extension of a patient's life takes precedence over her beliefs. The difficulty is particularly acute when the patient is a child, and it is the parents refusing treatment. For instance, where religious sects refuse blood transfusions for children, courts have ordered the treatment over those objections. Should they do so for someone old and infirm? Parents have also in some cases been charged with manslaughter when they have refused to seek medical help for life-threatening conditions and allowed a child to die.

In such situations, the hierarchical ethic of Chapter 3 would prioritize the primacy of life, thus also making every reasonable effort to preserve it. However, many who do not accept that ethical framework might arrive at the opposite conclusion. The problem for a utilitarian, for example, would be to decide whether there is more good in preserving one life, or more good in alternative uses of the same medical resources. Limits are bound to be reached in some cases, and it may be necessary to force treatment on others, but great care must be taken in making life-and-death decisions for others without their personal and informed consent.

Euthanasia

Similar considerations apply to the terminally ill who cannot themselves request death because of a coma or other incapacitation. Proponents of euthanasia would put such people out of their misery, much as they would compassionately shoot a dying horse. They reason that while perhaps extending life might be good, supplying a pain-free death is better. Given the reality of pain and the pressures on the medical system, this argument cannot be dismissed out of hand. An ethical absolutist, by contrast, is likely to draw the line at "relative good" when it comes to life and death issues.

As long as there is any hope, this argument goes, the patient should be kept alive, even at great cost. To the absolutist, death might be an enemy to be fought with all available resources, and its victims to be sorrowfully mourned as casualties in a war. Paradoxically, many religious persons who hold this position believe death to be a release to a new and better kind of life—to be welcomed—even while being fought against as an enemy.

One of the major difficulties with any policy that allows such deaths to be administered has already been mentioned—what the state can once allow, it can later require. People who support the voluntary euthanizing of the aged may one day find the process forcibly applied to them. Reasons can be created for declaring almost anyone undesirable or incompetent.

Infanticide

It was for similar absolutist reasons that in the early days of the Church, Christians collected unwanted infants who had been abandoned by their parents to die of exposure, even though the rescuers then suffered being falsely accused of killing and eating the children they rescued. The Christian view of the sacredness of life prevailed, and for centuries after, infanticide was close to unthinkable—an act that evoked universal moral outrage. In this century it has become respectable again. For instance, at issue at the moment is whether severely damaged or impaired newborns should be left to die without food, water, and treatment, or whether they should be provided with extensive, painful, and costly attention to allow them to live. In 1980s China, infanticide was reported to be widespread after the government decreed couples could have no more than one child. Boys being more desirable than girls, many female infants were killed. In the 2020s, China's population is declining, so having more children may become encouraged.

Population pressures as well as political, economic, and racial considerations are potential factors in deciding which infants shall live or die. These have already been decisive in liberalizing the availability of abortion, and it is surely an arbitrary legal fiction to say that a child situated at one end of a birth canal is disposable tissue, and at the other end is a protected human. All the arguments that allow abortion can therefore ultimately be brought to bear on newborn infants, older children, and adults.

While this issue will not soon go away, one major contribution of the new medical technologies may be to render some reasons for infanticide moot. One goal is to remove from the genetic pool the causes of severe birth handicaps, but that will not be achieved soon, and in the interim, there are likely to be calls to do away with "defective" infants with an insistence that no life at all is better than one lived impaired. Again, hierarchical absolutists would oppose such a policy, insisting that the quality of life is not pre-judgeable or even knowable for another person and that quality is a lesser (and unpredictable) ethical consideration than life itself.

Abortion

Abortion also generates many issues unlikely to be settled soon, and it is one on which most of the medical profession has done an about-face in recent years, switching from a long-standing view of an unborn child as a patient to that of it as a disposable appendage of the mother. The debate is sometimes couched in terms of the mother's right to control her own body versus the right of an unborn child to continue living. The mass of cells that will become a child cannot, with current technology, be separated from the mother and live, and in that narrow sense is a part of her. On the other hand, these cells are genetically distinct from her from the point of conception, and therefore even the first cell is not an integral part of her body. Some regard a particular demarcation point (e.g. end of first trimester or detectable heartbeat) as the start of a distinct human life. To others, any boundaries are purely arbitrary. What is really in dispute is the point at which full human rights ought to be accorded—at birth or at some prior time. Or, do the rights grow gradually with the developing child, and does the ratio of these rights to those of the mother change from zero at first to equal at birth? at some earlier time? at some later time?

Proponents of a woman's right to an abortion on demand consider the procedure to be a cheap, safe, and effective way of ensuring that only wanted children are born. Opponents emphasize the child's right to life and may claim abortion is both physically and psychologically threatening or damaging to the mother's health. They consider abortion to be reckless of human life in general, and to be murder of a child in particular.

New technologies may enliven the abortion debate even more, for it is possible sometimes to save infants born prematurely at a stage earlier than many others who are aborted. Two surgical teams could work side-by-side with two pregnant women, each the same number of months past the point of conception, with one performing an abortion and the other delivering a premature baby. As the ability to live outside the womb (with technological help) is pushed back closer to the point of conception, the medical establishment in particular, and society in general, faces an ethical problem whose difficulty increases with time and the availability of new life-saving techniques. As a result, arguments about the point at which life begins become increasingly irrelevant and the abortion issue becomes more ethical and political than medical.

That is, once the answer to the medical and scientific question "From what point is an unborn child human and alive"? becomes "from conception," the answer to the economic and political question "From what point is that same child a legal person"? becomes the central issue. North American courts have answered, "Not until birth." As we have seen, however, this answer itself raises new questions about what can or should be done to (or for) the child before it takes its first breath of air rather than breathing amniotic fluid. Viewed in this light the decision to grant the right to personhood only at birth is legal fiction on the same order as once was declaring that only white men were legal persons.

Three points are worth making:

First, it is not yet possible to discern what are the long-term effects on the total population of combining increased longevity and declining birth rates. In developed (and nearly developed) countries, the birth rate is below replacement levels. This argues for an eventual population decline, except that any substantial longevity increase could overwhelm this trend. Indeed, increased longevity is the main reason for the world's population increase over the last century. It may be over the next as well. Thus, whether current methods of birth control turn out to be more effective than necessary or woefully inadequate to control the population is too soon to know.

Second, abortion-inducing drugs are readily available. Some governments are considering providing them at no cost. Others are banning them or classifying them as controlled substances like narcotics. The latter course is rarely effective, and neither are religious protests over their marketing or use. Thus, although it may take some time to sort out potential side effects, it is only a matter of time before these are available worldwide. Their significance is that they take the matter of abortion out of highly visible hospitals and clinics and make it a decision that can be undertaken entirely in private, except when complications arise. Thus, there are no specific targets against which to protest if the sale of the drug is legal, and given the ubiquity of online shopping, few measures against their sale and delivery are likely to be effective.

Not all doctors or hospitals are interested in doing abortions and in some jurisdictions they are illegal, so the drugs may eventually become the only means of providing them—yet another example of the scarcity of medical resources forcing the adoption of non-surgical procedures (whether one likes the outcome or not).

Third, the technologies considered in this chapter may also be capable of producing cheap and efficient conception control agents for men or women that the state could widely disperse and then require a license to obtain the antidote. There are several ways this could be done. The simplest might be a drug that could cause sterility even in very low doses. Another possibility for the genetic engineer might be a communicable virus like those that cause common colds that would prevent conception without causing any other symptoms.

Since several research teams could build variations on one or both of these themes, at least one of the sponsoring governments would likely release the agent. An antivirus might be as easy to produce, but the opportunity to control it and regulate the population would surely be seized upon somewhere. It is difficult to imagine some types of government passing up the opportunity to manage population growth. Such a deployment would imply extensive and intimate control by the state over the lives of citizens, but such things do have ways of coming about—perhaps one reason why some instinctively protested vaccine and mask mandates so vigorously during the COVID-19 pandemic.

Another way to regulate population growth would be to include a sterilizing agent in longevity drugs, or to package sterility and longevity antidotes together. There would then have to be strong incentives to have children, for they would cost parents potential life span. Abortions would cease almost entirely if an enforceable conception licensing scheme were devised. While this might remove some of the population pressures caused by increased longevity, it would simultaneously change the structure of society by cutting off both growth and renewal, nearly eliminating the family, and promoting the long-term societal status quo. Could such a scheme be enforced if it were to become technically feasible? It seems likely that an antidote to the agent would quickly become available on the black market—perhaps even supplied by foreign governments bent on destabilizing another country by increasing its population. Moreover, given the record of the West on control of now illicit drugs, it seems hard to imagine the pharmaceuticals suggested here could be controlled. The net result on population could therefore be neutral with the single exception of eliminating unwanted births, so removing most of the desire for abortion.

Such a technological "fix" seems unsatisfying, but alternatives are unclear. Neither unlimited population growth nor unlimited abortions seem politically, economically, or ethically desirable. The population question is therefore unresolved—a technical answer only intimated.

7.7 The Environment and Human Life

Human life is lived out in the context of other life forms and their shared physical environment. The industrial age has generally been viewed as exploitative of the environment. Progress has been the byword, with the bottom lines being the standard of living and the gross national product. Simultaneously, the rapid decline in the agricultural workforce and migration to cities isolated industrialized peoples from the natural environment and left them largely unconcerned with harmful changes, except when such issues periodically become fashionable.

The earth is a large place, and its systems have both a great deal of inertia and a massive capability to absorb damage. Nevertheless, there have been severe strains, and it is now clear that the next civilization must continue to develop and deploy technologies for ensuring and managing a hospitable environment if it is to maintain Earth as a viable living place. Problems have shown up in the quality of the air (acid rain and accumulating greenhouse gasses), the water (dead and dying lakes or streams and aquifer decline), the land (erosion, desertification, salt poisoning, and fertility loss) and biodiversity (extinction of plant and animal species from land, air, and sea). There are also scarcities of strategic minerals, oil, natural gas, and other energy forms.

These problems are most evident in the scars left by open pit mines, in the changed climate from burning fuel for energy, ruined soils from deforestation and chemical pollution, ubiquitous microplastic particles, and the non-biodegradable waste floating about in the ocean and washing up on beaches. Cities have largely grown up from old river valley agricultural centers, spilling out into surrounding areas, and swallowing prime farmland and forests in the process.

The contribution of technology has thus far been negative, accelerating damage to the environment, because the governing model has been exploitive. Moreover, many of the 1960s environmentalists were associated, whether correctly or not, with radical leftist politics, and this made it easy for conservatives to discount their legitimate message. Political considerations can be of first importance when facing problems; environmental ones are not unique in this respect.

For example, North American governments were reluctant to tackle solutions to the acid rain problem, so they funded studies to see if it existed—when it had been known and described in some detail in the scientific literature for over a century. In more recent decades, though, environmental groups successfully called attention to some of the more spectacular damage and a new model has emerged—one that uses technology for conservation Gradually, this conserving image is replacing the exploitive one, as care for the environment becomes conventional conservative wisdom, not merely fodder for empty election time promises.

Thus, smoke emissions are now scrubbed in Great Britain, and city air is once more breathable. The same thing is gradually becoming required of new North American installations, and over time, lakes, and forests destroyed by acid rain may recover, though perhaps with different species populating them. Likewise, energy sources will likely in future be required to be cleaner, giving impetus to research on solar, geothermic, nuclear fusion, and other nonpolluting supplies. At some point, petroleum, natural gas, and coal will no longer be used as fuel, and electricity will be the principal medium for delivering energy, including for transportation. The desire—indeed, the necessity—for a cleaner environment will thus alter many industries and result in structural changes to society as resource-based industries in some sectors vanish. The political map will be affected, for any current economy that depends on, say, oil, gas, or coal production and does not industrialize or otherwise diversify will be seriously impaired. Countries now rich because they supply such resources could sink into poverty and obscurity.

Wars also have a way of bringing problems that politicians have been unwilling to face into sharp focus. Russia's invasion of Ukraine is one of those, for on the one hand the destruction of the Donbas, Ukraine's industrial heartland, and the blockade of her ports that cut off one of the world's largest agricultural economies from her markets and created a serious food supply crisis, and the other, the West's embargo on Russian oil companies and banks simultaneously engineered an energy crisis. In the short run, both caused customers to seek alternative, more expensive replacement suppliers of the same goods. In the longer term, permanent substitutes will become attractive, and in particular, oil may begin a sharp decline as a primary energy source, for the pressure on technology to engineer acceptable substitutes has transformed into a necessity.

There will no doubt continue to be a variety of environmental activists for some years—protesting logging, whaling, sealing, habitat destruction, and the experimental use of animals. Although these voices were muted or neutralized somewhat by the 1980s and 1990s concentration on business and the bottom line, their impact and influence have become permanent, for they have expressed the important truth that humanity cannot go on fouling its nest but must come to terms with the fact that the human biospace is part of a complex continuum that must be preserved for the sake of our survival.

Some environmental groups have in their tactics raised interesting new ethical issues by going beyond civil disobedience to property destruction and violence. Such methods have been criticized even by those who support the causes. Some argue that protesters ought to take a legislative route to make their point, but more radical environmentalists claim that only dramatic action is sufficient to sensitize enough people to the problems even to make them public issues. Thus, there have been invasions of labs doing animal experiments; harp seals have been painted red to destroy the commercial value of their pelts; nuclear tests have been interfered with; a whaling fleet and processing plant vandalized to put them out of business, and mink farms vandalized and the animals released to the wild.

In addition, protesters for a variety of causes throw themselves in front of trains or trucks when they dislike their cargoes; they picket the homes and offices of researchers or politicians who oppose them, they block roads to proposed mining and lumbering sites or nail ceramic spikes into the trees, lay down in front of bulldozers to protest or prevent them from clearing old-growth land, and vandalize or block construction camps for oil and gas pipelines.

Regardless of what one thinks about the ethics of such tactics (What is the higher norm that must be obeyed?) there can be little doubt that the environmentalists have successfully touched a raw nerve of new-found sensitivity to the environment and that the effects will be long-lasting.

They also have going for them that new technologies are indeed likely to be cleaner—at least in the industrialized countries, and providing clean power sources becomes available. On the other hand, they have against them that they can be premature or sensationalist in their pronouncements—especially when they offer incomplete or preliminary scientific research to bolster their claims, damage or destroy property, or annoy the public by blocking busy city streets to get publicity. Such tactics tend to alienate the public, thus proving costly to all environmental efforts.

In any case, the day of the exploitive aspects of the Third Civilization is ending, and the individuals and institutions aligned with or dependent upon them will decline in influence. This could include some religious institutions that have so allied themselves, taking for example the "subdue the Earth" command of Genesis as a mandate for exploitation instead of for stewardship responsibility.

Political thinking has focused on the immediate economic benefits from industry, however conducted, rather than on long-term effects. With the new-found recognition of the network of biospace interdependencies in which humans participate, such voices will be muted, for more people realize there are long-term effects of decision-making. In an ideal information-based society, decisions would be made both openly, in a fully informed fashion, and with the effect on the environment fully considered. Yes, "ideal"—whether human nature will allow it to be achieved is another matter.

There is also a potential downside to these environmental concerns that must not be neglected, and that is the cost of making suitable changes. Ironically, the cost of the cleanup technology may be so great that only the largest of industrial firms can afford to develop and deploy it. This could have the effect of strengthening the very kinds of conglomerates that created many of the difficulties in the first place, at least in the intermediate term. On the other hand, industry has responded to Western environmental concerns (and capital and salary cost pressures) simply by moving manufacturing (and its pollution and jobs) to the third world, with negative effects on the Earth as a whole due to increased production, decreased regulation, and more, rather than less pollution.

In the long term, however, the preservation of plant and animal species, recycling, and concern for soil conservation and clean air and water must become a critical part of an environment-conscious ethic for the next civilization, if it is to avoid extinction. There may even be some who will wish to live at one extreme—indoors, in completely controlled and managed environments. There may be others wanting to get back to nature and live in more direct communion with it, but without giving up any of their technological benefits. Both may well be possible, along with other alternative lifestyles.

7.8 Building New Environments

Unrestrained population growth puts many pressures on the environment, the food supply, housing, the economy, and governments. Those who find unpleasant the suggestion that longer life may imply enforced birth control or other restrictions may want instead to expand the available physical space for human life. However, even the present world population has difficulty finding places to live. For example, as countries industrialize they experience the phenomenon of urban expansion. In already heavily populated nations, the growth of a handful of urban centers can be dramatic. The fourteen largest urban centers of the world all have populations over twenty million and several more such megalopoli in the developing nations will reach that level in a few years at the current pace. At thirteenth New York is the only one besides Mexico City (tenth) in North America or Europe in the top twenty.

In many of those, relative newcomers are housed in shacks precariously perched on sewage-filled mud or unstable hillsides. Often, there are no paved streets, lights, running water, official police services, fire departments, or building codes. Yet the slums and barrios of dozens of cities grow by thousands of immigrants from the countryside daily, with no end in sight. Under such circumstances, the state can lose control to anarchy. Criminal elements tend to step in and become the *de facto* government as they have in Haiti. There is no reason to suppose that the urbanization giving rise to these problems will slow in the foreseeable future.

To an extent, the opposite takes place in some cities of the already industrialized nations as they move beyond industrialism to the next stage of civilization. Large old core cities—especially industrial centers—have lost population in two waves of out-migration. One is the continuing exodus from the city core to the lawns, gardens, and golf courses of suburbia. This shift forces the relocation of schools, shopping, and some offices, and also forces the costly extension of transit lines for those who still commute. In this kind of dislocation, people remain in the general area of their original cities. It does cause jurisdictional problems and tends to harm the city core, which can be left with the lowest socioeconomic segment of the population, a declining tax base, and central neighborhoods decayed and impoverished. Meanwhile, at the edges, such cities grow toward their neighbors in broad bands of alternating urban centers and suburbs. One can drive hundreds of miles through such areas on the

PART TWO | FOUR WAVEFRONTS ON A SEA OF CHANGE

Eastern seaboard of the United States, and a similar situation is developing around the central Great Lakes, in Florida, and California.

However, other cities, notably in the Midwest, have lost net population to the South and Southwest or smaller urban centers at some distance from the major cities. In these cases, the central city suffers all the problems above, and the urban region as a whole cannot compensate economically, for the population has moved too far away.

The pandemic forced many people to work from home rather than assemble in offices. This, and the dramatically increasing cost of real estate in some cities, most notably Vancouver, has forced many younger families out of cities. Moreover, working at home has become a fixture in some cases, with workers refusing to return to a central location, and since they are in short supply, their wishes can often prevail against those of their employers. They move to and work from more remote locations, sometimes too far away to commute even if they wanted.

The net result of these two migrations could eventually become a spreading out of North American population over a much larger percentage of available land, and a dramatic lessening of crowding in large city centers. Suburban areas and new cities gradually develop centers of their own, but these are smaller and somewhat less concentrated than those of the older cities. Better communication and transportation systems and relocation of factory work, formerly only located near resources or ports, all contribute to this migration.

In particular, there are fewer reasons every year for information workers to locate near traditional city centers, so they move, leaving behind empty office space. As communications improve, working out of one's living space will become even more feasible, and attachment to cities will lessen further.

Meanwhile, the cities affected by migration from the core see large tracts of former housing and industrial land becoming surplus, so some try to renew, attracting counter-migration by making their cores attractive places to live, shop, play, or tour—even when the people work elsewhere, and especially if they work at home. If some people work where they live, perhaps others can be induced to live where they work. To achieve this, some near-empty office buildings are being transitioned to a mix of offices and apartments. In other cases, building owners face required costly upgrades to meet modern standards for zero net emissions. Where these costs are too high, buildings will be demolished. Any new construction and renovation at the core of older cities will have to be radically different to make or retain them as attractive places.

Improved transportation of both short- and long-distance types helps to allow such changes and is also driven by them. New technologies for reducing airport congestion and improving takeoff and landing efficiencies are a high priority, for example. Another priority (in North America) is improved high-speed ground transportation technologies for commuters to relieve the traffic jams in larger cities. At the same time, it is critical to devise strategies to ameliorate the impact of the lost industrial tax base at the city core and alleviate conditions for the people left behind in poverty, with no hope of obtaining jobs or migrating to places where prospects might be better. Whatever one's ethical framework, or view of cities and their future, numerous factors have to be traded off and prioritized, and the task is far from simple.

At the same time, new building technologies and a new respect for arable land are driving development in places once considered inhospitable. For instance, mountainsides cannot be cultivated but could be lived on or in, and an underground house can have many floors, with a large lawn and garden on the roof at ground level. Building technology is becoming more effective at sealing off living space users from hostile environments, and simultaneously providing green benefits—a new specialty for architects. It becomes feasible to live comfortably in deserts, on infertile land, or in some of the earth's coldest regions—when population pressure demands. There are vast empty lands in the Canadian north, the Australian interior, and the African and Asian deserts, as well as in mountainous regions in all parts of the world. It might become desirable to cover, heat, live in, and grow food on the Arctic tundra. One could run a pipeline from the mouth of the Amazon through the Atlantic to bring abundant water to the Sahara desert. It might become practical to roof over a valley in the Canadian Rockies and build a large city underneath, heating it by inexpensive geothermal means.

The point is that when population pressures are great enough, technological responses are energized to respond by enabling new living space—yet another example of the need to find technological solutions to problems caused in part by technology. Malthus' doomsday forecast may be postponed by the development of still more techniques, though it cannot be put off indefinitely if the population were to continue rising unchecked by either natural or regulating forces.

New technology may also be required to develop new living space to replace that rendered unusable by older technologies. Even assuming that nuclear war is never the cause of such problems (and this threat is growing, not abating), people may be driven underground by cosmic radiation if, as some suggest, the ozone layer of the atmosphere is any further depleted by the use of chlorofluorocarbons (CFCs) and other pollutants. (It is too soon to be certain, but this problem may already have been abated, as there are signs the depletion has been reversed.)

On a less global scale, overfishing and pollution force the inhabitants of fishing and canning communities to relocate and take up different work. The same thing happens when a commercial forest or cropland is defoliated by natural or chemical means, flooded, or abandoned as uneconomic. In such cases, jobs, people, the environment, and politics play out an intricate dance of interlocking responsibilities, duties, dynamics, and outcomes complex enough to deeply engage the most sophisticated of scientists, technicians, ethicists, economists, and politicians in the search for solutions.

One grail of environmental technology is the ability not simply to predict but manage the weather. Though often wished for and frequently assumed by science fiction writers, this goal has proven elusive, and there is little immediate prospect of much progress toward it. There has not always been agreement on whether the climate is warming, cooling, or shifting around geographically, what the major factors in such changes are, the exact effect human activities have, or if there are long-term cycles over which little control can be exercised. There is presently a warming trend, and sea levels are rising. Most explain this as a greenhouse effect and pin the blame entirely on carbon dioxide pollution; a few still cite sunspot cycles and assert that major climate changes are caused by forces far larger than anything humans have yet deployed, but in such situations, minority voices attract minimal audiences.

Whether or how anything other than reducing carbon dioxide emissions can reverse climate change is unknown. Large-scale attempts to alter global climate could make things worse. When a complex dynamic system is ill-understood, it is perilous to make dramatic changes to any part. On the other hand, many argue that the industrial society has already made such major changes, and these must be reversed before it is too late.

On another note, there could be modest efforts made to establish living places underwater or off the planet. The former could substantially increase the size of livable areas even in the short run; the latter would have minimal immediate impact but possibly a dramatic long-term one. Some suggest that if the mining of raw supplies from the moon or asteroids can ever be done economically and space or moon-based manufacturing becomes feasible, there could be a third industrial revolution that transfers a substantial percentage of human activity and even a sizable population off the planet. Since manufacturing on a small experimental scale has already been done in space, it could be optimistically argued that this new industrial revolution has already begun.

Optimists suggest that extensive facilities in orbit, on the moon, and various asteroids or artificial planetoids would make the Earth a wealthier and more livable place. At the same time, a new frontier of indefinite size would be created and another age of expansion would begin. At some point in the distant future, some suggest the earth might hold only half the inhabitants of the solar system, and that long before that stage is reached there may well be attempts to reach others. The colonization of space would have an important side effect. Once self-sufficient communities exist off the planet, it will no longer be easy to destroy the whole human race in a nuclear war—even if the Earth were rendered uninhabitable.

On the other hand, more pessimistic voices point out the high cost of doing anything in space, and demand that the money instead be used to improve conditions here on Earth. Others don't want space to be colonized, reasoning it will only be exploited as Earth has been. Still others point out there would be little need for a substantial population to leave Earth, as (presumably) automated factories located there would need few human workers to staff them in any case. This illustrates an interesting point—in the long run, profitability will drive all but the most modest of space exploration and colonization. If there are no tangible benefits, the lure of science alone cannot indefinitely sustain the kind of expenditures necessary for such adventures. What is more, the prohibitive cost makes it infeasible to move any significant percentage of Earth's people out of its deep gravity well. The only way large numbers will populate extraterrestrial habitats is to be born there.

That there will be sufficient public appetite to undertake the enormous expenditures to make space colonization happen seems improbable. Thus, if done at all, it seems unlikely it would be funded by governments answerable to a skeptical electorate, so only large corporations controlled by a few visionary people not subject to vetos by elected boards could attempt this.

PART TWO | FOUR WAVEFRONTS ON A SEA OF CHANGE

Back on Earth there probably will be advances in genetic engineering and other techniques that improve the ability to feed and clothe a larger population. Other applications of the same techniques have the potential to trigger dramatic changes in living space as well. For example, instead of planting trees, fertilizing them, thinning them, and then cutting them down after fifty years to build houses, it would be much simpler to develop genetically modified trees so that they would grow directly into living spaces. Perhaps various species could be grown as specific types of rooms that could be harvested and joined together in modules to make complete houses.

If that proves too ambitious, there are far less spectacular ways to achieve manufacturing efficiency and modularity. One is by applying mass factory techniques to housing. This is now being done on a small scale, with encouraging results. Houses are built in modular pieces, trucked to the site, and assembled on a prepared foundation. They have even been 3-D printed *in situ*. Widespread use of such methods promises to improve quality, decrease building time, and dramatically lower costs. It would also cause some old trades and professions to vanish, and new ones to come into being. Far fewer blue-collar workers would be needed to assemble a house in an automated factory than on-site.

If houses were modular, rooms could be purchased as needed. One could foresee there developing a need for used-room sales lots or house junkyards to scavenge for parts. Certainly, these methods would lead to changes in the way people live; the featureless tract row houses of older subdivisions would give way to customized homes often on more rugged terrain. New transportation and communication methods would be required, and all of these would change the physical surroundings—the space part of the human biospace.

For the technology in the home itself, there is already a substantial automating trend that can be expected to continue, at least for those people who "must" have the latest technology. In time, refrigerators, ovens, home heating systems, hot water supply, ventilation, security, lighting, environmental features like window blinds, and the internal distribution and use of electricity will be microprocessor-controlled, scheduled, and monitored as part of the invisible infrastructure. One technology with promise is the so-called smart electrical system, wherein outlets for appliances, and telephones for both high and low-voltage use are all identical, but power is delivered only as requested by a "smart house" client device plugged into an outlet. This system eliminates shock, short circuits, and multiple hardware and wiring types and is programmable to improve its utility. To an extent, houses could look very much like they do today, for there are few floor plan styles available that were not four decades ago, and taste in such things tends to repeat cyclically like clothing styles and colors for walls or clothes. However, any further increase in the number of people working out of their homes would drive a shift to more functional residential architecture. When both husband and wife were working away from home, it could be built largely for show—decorative as much or more than utilitarian. If one or both use it as an office, it must have appropriate facilities for work, not only rest and play. Formal living and dining rooms could be deprecated, and the minuscule dens of the past become useful offices, perhaps with separate client entrances. There is no reason other than zoning bylaws and personal preference why most professions—the model for future work—cannot be practiced from the home office—not only online, but in person.

For instance, a couple with a family could split childcare duties with their professional ones, he parenting the children in the morning while she practices medicine from her home clinic for the immediate neighborhood, and he doing the opposite, working in his home law office afternoons. Likewise, a teacher might attach a classroom to her house while plying that profession and have it detached and hauled away for refurbishing by a used room salesperson when she retired.

Another new technology with domestic implications is the use of broadcast electromagnetic radiation to provide operating power directly (no plug) to small appliances such as televisions, radios, and computing devices. Very low-power chips are now being manufactured. Whether the necessary electricity will be converted from power broadcast here on earth or from stations established in near orbit remains to be seen. In the home, this technology would reduce the need for power to be transmitted by wires and could obsolete the need for batteries. The most important effect, however, would be the elimination of overhead or underground power servicing, an enormous reduction in costly infrastructure required by industrial-age housing. Removal of this requirement would lessen the requirement for houses to be clustered in urban subdivisions, further reducing the need for cities in the information society. The health implications of using broadcast power are unknown. Some claim deleterious effects from levels already present in radio, television, cellphone, and Wi-Fi transmission, but these seem rare and have not been reliably verified.

Other technologies not yet guessed at will subsume some of the ones discussed here or render them irrelevant before they develop. It is difficult to see exactly how market forces will drive them, but it is worth observing that population pressures are pressing. Such pressures in the past have only been reduced in a limited number of ways. Three of the oldest ones are war, which today could destroy the whole earth; famine, which could be eliminated with international cooperation; and plague, which it is hoped will be eliminated. Other ways are wholesale abortion, infanticide, euthanasia, and genocide, all of which are at worst abhorrent or at best problematical. Another way is birth control, but society may well hesitate to make this compulsory. The last method is to continuously expand the available living space by creating new frontiers and new livable areas in the old living spaces.

Of these options, most are unacceptable in any global strategy with a claim to an ethical base or are unenforceable even by the most totalitarian of governments. Only the methods of expanding living space seem workable in the medium term, and even these would generate new problems that cannot now be foreseen. However, increasing living space might postpone some of the harsher alternatives and the need for mandated population control. New living space and the technology to achieve and use it effectively may also bring other important benefits. The very existence of new frontiers could provide refreshment and revitalization, new bursts of innovation, and an outlet for the creative and restless. It might also help prevent stagnation in a dreary status quo because it would provide for fresh starts, new opportunities, and incentives for youth and enthusiasm—all of which are in jeopardy if the future were to hold only a stable population of gradually increasing life span. Moreover, it would postpone, perhaps forever, Ellul's amorphous totalitarianism of maximal technique, for it would promote expansion and change as the prevailing models rather than efficiency alone.

Deployment of new technologies for the creation and improvement of human living space has always affected the earth as a whole. Animal species are displaced or extinguished, natural vegetation is destroyed, soils are paved over and made forever useless, and the climate itself is altered. For example, it was once conventional wisdom that large hydroelectric power dams were an unmixed blessing for the state that built them. They would improve living conditions for ordinary people, attract industry, and provide much-needed downstream benefits in the form of flood control. However, in some cases where large areas were flooded, the lack of downstream overflow reduced fertility and increased salinity. Industry still found conditions unattractive, and silt buildup behind the dam ensured it would have a short life.

The Aswan High Dam built by Egypt with Russian help has all these problems and is also contributing to the reduction in size of the Nile Delta, the bread basket of that nation. It has also caused an increase in the use of chemical fertilizers and pesticides, thus affecting the health of farmers. These problems are potentially exacerbated by the GERD (Grand Ethiopian Renaissance Dam) built on the Blue Nile to provide electricity to most of Ethiopia. One of the most expensive capital projects ever built in Africa, its filling reduced downstream flows further, and Egyptian attempts to negotiate remediation were unsuccessful, making what one nation saw as essential for the prosperity of millions appear as life-threatening to another. A third such project, the British Columbia Site C dam, had previously undiscovered potential geotechnical problems requiring substantial cost-inflating remediation during construction, and critics have claimed it will never recover its cost. On the other hand, even it cannot provide sufficient electricity to electrify all automobiles, let alone serve projected population increases.

In future, it will be more important to consider the long-term environmental effects of building large housing projects, converting land to other uses, or constructing massive utilities. There will be more people to accommodate, but there will also be more at risk when things go awry. Moreover, advances in habitat technology in the affluent West will not go unnoticed in the rest of the world as it struggles with existing problems of wide-scale poverty and continuing urbanization. To catch up, there will be pressure to take shortcuts—parks and wildlife preserves could be threatened, and the very magnitude of short-term people problems will ensure that long-term considerations are de-emphasized. While it will always be impossible for the West to solve the third world's population problems simply by donating money (because such difficulties are cultural and relate to a state of civilization), it may be possible to assist in the financing of park and wildlife preservation until those industrializing nations can afford or are ready to use other help. Whether such a global view of the environment will ever be politically feasible in the West is another matter, but highly targeted aid of this type has a higher probability of accomplishing useful goals than untargeted money handouts.

These and other considerations lead once more to the observation that new civilizations are both enabled by and subsequently demand new techniques, even while the new techniques bring mixed blessings. They have great potential for raising the standard of living and human comfort, but equal potential for triggering long-term deleterious effects. The challenge is to achieve the benefits while minimizing the harm. Such planning has not always been done in the past, but it cannot be ignored in the future.

7.9 Summary and Further Discussion

Summary

Human life is lived out in the context of both physical space and time. This biospace also has critical quality aspects. Numerous issues affecting both were discussed in this chapter. New surgical and diagnostic techniques have proliferated in recent years, greatly increasing the number of treatable problems and simultaneously generating questions about facilities, cost, and appropriateness of treatment. If cutting-edge medical techniques are to become universally available, various new techniques must be found to reduce cost, people, and facility pressures. Some new techniques under development are those to do cell-level treatment by tailoring bacteria or DNA to produce new drugs and molecular machines, called nanomachines. Such machines could effect repairs, conquer communicable diseases, reduce the need for surgery, and prolong life.

Genetic engineering may also be used to improve food supplies, reduce defects, and enhance many desirable traits. It may also be used to change plant and animal species or even human beings. Benefits and difficulties with such technologies were considered, including the effect of changing technology on the right to life.

Finally, the space aspects of human life were considered, and it was pointed out that the creation of new living spaces on earth and off could both alleviate population pressures and supply new frontiers to prevent technical stagnation and postpone the totalitarianism of the efficient. Again, the mixed effects of new technology to improve living conditions for some were shown to have potential deleterious side effects for them and others.

Research and Discussion Questions

Note: Where you are asked about decisions, be sure to include a mention of what moral/ethical framework drives your decision, and how it does so.

THE BIOSPACE REVOLUTION

1. Explain the term "biospace."

2. What are some of the reasons that nonsurgical medical methods ought to be preferred over surgical ones? Give specific examples where one or the other choice may be necessary for the long term and others in situations where nonsurgical techniques ought to completely replace surgical ones.

3. Suppose you are in charge of an agency responsible for a medical insurance scheme run by the state. Which (if any) of the following treatments should the plan pay for, or not pay for, and why?
   a. Open-heart surgery on a 90- year-old, when the average life span is 80. Would it make a difference if the average life span were 150?
   b. An experimental procedure (40 percent chance of success) to remove a tumor from the brain of an infant who has otherwise an 80 percent chance of dying within a year.
   c. The surgery in *b* when without it the child would have impaired hearing and sight but otherwise live normally.
   d. The surgery in *b* performed in another country at a cost higher than maintaining a bed in a hospital in the home country for an entire year.
   e. A sex-change operation for a patient who claims to be in great distress over being in the wrong kind of body.
   f. A sex-change operation for a patient who has already transitioned from male to female, now has second thoughts and wants to transition back.
   g. Gender-affirming surgery for an infant born with a mix of female and male organs (intersex). (Note that although such surgery has in the past been routinely recommended in such rare cases, it can cause permanent scarring and lasting pain when done on infants, but this outcome is less likely when done for adults.)
   h. Sterilization (tubal ligations and vasectomies) for those who wish to have no further children but have no organic malfunction. Take into consideration that there are non-invasive means of achieving the latter.

PART TWO | FOUR WAVEFRONTS ON A SEA OF CHANGE

    i. Tubal or ovarian repairs (30 percent success rate) for a woman who wants to bear a first child.

    j. Surgery in the previous case for a woman who already had two children; five children; ten children.

    k. An *in vitro* fertilization ("test-tube baby") for a couple who are infertile.

    l. A new and experimental drug whose preliminary tests indicate may relieve some symptoms and postpone death from a new and rare type of infection by as much as a year but whose safety and side effects are unknown. A year's supply is estimated to cost $30,000 per person.

    m. A $30 000 pacemaker for an 85-year-old woman.

    n. Radiation treatments and/or costly surgery for an 80-year-old man with prostate cancer.

    o. Leg lengthening surgery for a teenager who wants to be taller so she can make the high school basketball team.

    p. Plastic surgery to remove small and harmless but unpleasant-looking growths from the face of a teenage boy.

    q. Surgery for a worker in zero gravity who wants her legs replaced with arms and hands because the former are of no use there, and the latter would make her more productive.

    r. A liver transplant for a boy whose body has already rejected two livers and whose older brother died after unsuccessful surgery of the same type.

    s. A transplant of the brain of an elderly man, the rest of whose body has experienced multiple organ failures so that he is on life support, into the head of a woman whose brain was effectively destroyed in an automobile accident, though the rest of her body is functional (the plot of an old science fiction novel).

    t. The implant of a computing device in the head of a person with (i) damage in the portion of her brain responsible for computation; (ii) an accountant who wants to be able to quickly add columns of figures from ancient paper documents without having to type them into a spreadsheet; (iii) a day trader who wants to be able to make faster decisions on buying and selling

THE BIOSPACE REVOLUTION

stocks to maximize her daily profits; (iv) someone who wants extra memory storage capacity for their profession.

u. Cosmetic surgery to make the patient look younger and prolong her career as an actress, or entertainer.

v. Surgery to shorten a man's left hand and foot to match the smaller right ones. Would it make a difference to your answer if functionality and appearance were not an issue, and the only reason the patient cites is the money to be saved by not having to purchase two pairs of gloves and shoes so as to fit both feet and both hands?

w. Surgery to create gill-like structures in the lungs of a diver so she can effectively breathe the water and extract oxygen from it as a fish does.

x. The use of a drug that in tests appears to enhance intelligence.

y. The use of a very expensive drug that is known to be capable of temporarily slowing a deadly cancer, but that at best extends patient life by three to six months. What if the drug has life-threatening side effects of its own in up to five percent of patients? ten percent? twenty percent?

z. Tests or treatments done in a neighboring country at considerable expense, but in a timely manner that can save lives. The country of residence has a medical system that is underfunded and overwhelmed with patients, so cannot do all the requisite tests or treatments in a timely way.

4. Discuss the idea of dispersing a 100 percent effective (and otherwise known harmless) birth control agent in the water or atmosphere, with a state-licensed anti-control agent being available by license.

5. Suppose it became possible to grow a clone in a nutrient vat from a person's own DNA, then transplant the original brain into a new, youthful body (all at great expense). Under what circumstances should this be allowed, if at all?

6. Suppose a simple, cheap chip implant became available that would allow the blind to regain their sight with a video device. What if some blind people do not wish to have the operation? Should they be required to have it, to reduce the burden of their care on society?

Should their disability tax benefits be denied if they refuse it? Substitute hearing for deafness and consider if there are any differences between the two situations.

7. There is already a wide medical gap between the developed and underdeveloped nations of the world, including a substantial gap in life expectancy. What would happen if this gap widened to 100 years?

8. Ought longevity treatments, when they become available, be provided to everyone—including, say, the poor of third world nations—if the consequences are greatly increased population pressure and possible famine? Even in countries with little such pressure, ought such treatments be limited to those who can "earn" them? Be sure to say what you mean by *earn*.

9. A hospital has a wealthy patient who has been comatose and on life-support systems for five years with no discernible change in condition. The man's family approaches the hospital and asks for the support to be removed so he can die in peace. The hospital refuses at first, citing the fact that brain waves are still present, though severely impaired. A family member cites the patient's own expressed desire for release from such a state but can offer no written proof. What should be done, and why?

10. Does it make any difference to your answer in question nine if:
    a. the hospital desperately needs a liver for another patient who will surely die without it and the comatose man's liver is a perfect tissue match?
    b. the man's family suggests it will give a large sum of money to the hospital—enough to allow a new surgery to be established wherein many lives can be saved per year?
    c. the comatose patient is a Nobel scientist; the prime minister of Canada; made his fortune by running confidence schemes and falsifying business records; a convicted rapist, a convicted murderer, homeless, a drug addict?

11. Discuss the pros and cons of establishing an organ bank of spare body parts for transplants. If it is done, should it be public, non-profit, or commercial?

12. If genetic engineering could triple intelligence, should the requisite treatments be available for those who could afford them, only for

those deemed to have made positive contributions to society, paid for by the government for anyone, or compulsory for everyone?

13. Which, if either, genetic-engineering project should be undertaken: (a) enhancement of domestic animals to enable them to perform menial tasks or (b) the development of "subhumans" for the same reasons. Explain.

14. Suggest several other new environment-enhancement technologies in addition to those discussed in the chapter.

15. What are some ways the human environment might be engineered, other than those discussed in the chapter? (Good and bad, pros and cons.)

16. Discuss the pros and cons of building new habitat (a) on the ocean floor, (b) in the Russian or Canadian north, (c) in the Sahara desert, (d) on the Moon, (e) in outer space, (f) elsewhere.

17. Which has a higher priority: (a) plant and animal genetic research with the end of improving food supply or (b) human genetic research with the end of repair, selection, or improvements? Explain.

18. You are a nurse in an elementary school in a close-knit rural community and become aware of various medical and other problems. Which of the following do you report to the authorities? Explain your answers. You might want to research actual cases.

    a. A child who often has severe bruises and lacerations on the arms, legs, and buttocks. The child seems not to be under any stress and has a reputation for clumsiness. Weigh the consequences of not reporting a possible case of child abuse against those of being a false accuser.

    b. A child who brings no lunch to school and is always hungry. You know that the parents care for the child but have very little money. Yet the child may be apprehended and taken from them if you report this case.

    c. A child with a medical condition (spine curvature, poor eyesight or hearing) that is debilitating but not life-threatening but that the parents (a) cannot afford to have treated or (b) refuse to have treated for religious reasons.

d. A child who sings religious songs at school to relieve her stress, even though any mention of her religion in school facilities is forbidden so as not to offend others, and the law says violators can be apprehended by the authorities and if they are children, removed from their parents. Does it matter whether (a) your religion is the same as hers or different, (b) the girl's religion is the majority or a minority one in the jurisdiction, or (c) it was your child? Research an actual case and comment.

19. You are a hospital nurse with many years of experience, and now on duty with a doctor who is a recent medical school graduate. An emergency patient comes in and the doctor orders tests but omits one that you know ought to be and is normally done. Do you order the test, exceeding your authority, if (a) the doctor has by now gone home and cannot be reached or (b) you bring it to her attention but she dismisses your concern as unimportant?

20. Discuss the problems of medical diagnosis as they relate to cost, time, facilities, and the possibility of a malpractice suit.

21. What authority ought the state have to (a) permit, (b) require, or (c) forbid various medical procedures such as transfusions, surgeries, or vaccines? To what extent ought this to be done in defiance of, say, the religious or political beliefs of the patients, or their parents? Be specific and give an ethical argument to justify your conclusions.

22. Suppose that advanced medical technology made a fetus able to be maintained outside the womb from the moment of conception to the normal end of gestation.
    a. What effect, if any, would this have on the abortion debate?
    b. Should public funds pay to allow infertile couples to use this technology to have children?
    c. Should public funds pay for women to use this technology to avoid the problems of pregnancy?
    d. Should such technology be (a) required for all births and pregnancies or (b) forbidden as too hazardous?

23. The harmful effects of poisonous substances such as tobacco and alcohol are well documented. Given this, discuss the implications of

forbidding advertising of such products. Is the value of freedom more important than the value of deprecating the use of such products?

24. Which is preferable, to attempt to prevent trafficking in mind-altering drugs or to make such drugs legal and freely available and treat the consequences? There are ethical, medical, and economic issues here. You might start with alcohol and tobacco and go from there. Include a discussion of what should be done the tenth (or later) time a patient needs resuscitation from a drug overdose.

25. One way of reducing medical costs is to transfer some techniques and responsibilities from expensive doctors to other less-expensive medical personnel. Discuss the benefits and limitations of this from ethical, medical, and economic standpoints. In particular, consider the potential responsibilities of nurse practitioners, nurses, nurses' aides, orderlies, technicians, and other hospital or public health staff.

26. The text mentioned a potential advantage of colonizing space is the survival of humanity in the event of global nuclear conflict. Is this the case, or would such colonies themselves simply become additional targets? Would the existence of such colonies make wars more or less likely?

27. Research the use of frozen embryos in livestock breeding programs. Now consider their use in human reproduction. Suggest several situations in which they could be employed, then discuss the ethical, legal, and any other problems that arise from this technique. On balance, is this a useful and desirable technique?

28. Research and discuss the issue of patenting new life forms developed in the laboratory. What stand have the courts taken thus far? To what extent do you think new life forms ought to be patentable? Answer for plant, animal, and human-derived genetic material.

29. Research the use of animal organs (or human ones grown in an animal) in human transplant cases. What are the advantages and disadvantages of such work from a medical and ethical point of view?

30. Under what circumstances, and for what groups of people ought the law mandate periodic checks for the use of drugs? When the law itself does not so mandate, should employers do it? Consider issues of employee performance, safety, cost, risk, and ethics.

31. Some Canadian Aboriginals still make their living as trappers. In response to the concern of animal rights activists, Great Britain proposed legislation mandating the labelling of Canadian furs with a warning that the animals may have been caught in leg-hold traps. The intended effect of the law was the elimination of such trapping in Canada. Critics respond that a secondary effect would be increased unemployment among one of Canada's poorest groups. Discuss the ethics of this situation, giving particular attention to the relative rights of the trappers and the animals.

32. In the course of the discussion on scarce medical resources, the text made the statement: "Neither is it easy to argue that a woman has any fundamental right to bear children." Develop an argument for or against such a right. Can your argument be applied to support or deny (as the case may be) a parallel right to not bear children? Why or why not?

33. Which is a higher priority, and why—to spend public money on researching the causes of a sexually transmitted disease or to spend it on cancer research?

34. Determine how much money your government puts into research on prostate cancer and breast cancer. Now, what are the incidences of both in men and women, respectively? Do expenditures match? In what sense? Should they? Why or why not?

35. Which is more important, and why—space exploration, or poverty relief? Or, is there any link between spending on one and not the other?

36. Ought a state to permit (to encourage?) (to assist in?) the use of suicide to reduce medical costs and keep the population down? If you say "no," how do you deal with those who are terminally ill, in great pain, and costing the state large sums of money to stay alive? If you say "yes," how do you deal with the young and healthy who commit suicide and leave behind small children and a destitute spouse? In either situation, how would you deal with the case if the potential suicide were, say, a renowned cancer researcher on the verge of a significant breakthrough?

37. Research the contention that population pressures are the result of poverty and that raising the standard of living will eliminate these pressures.

38. Suppose that a government determines its territory has become overpopulated to the point where its people are at risk of starvation. Is an enforced birth control program justifiable? Is a war to gain more territory? Are there any other measures?

39. Suppose that a government determines its territory has become underpopulated to the point where its national identity is at risk of extinction. What measures if any can it legitimately take to increase its population?

40. Propose and defend against the alternatives a solution of your own for (a) the problem of medical scarcity and (b) population pressures on food supplies and living space.

41. Research cases such as those involving the building of dams, where infrastructure projects in one country affect its population positively, but those in another negatively. What factors go into the decision to proceed and why? Discuss the weighing of potential or possible effects versus those with known ones.

42. An air traveller from Europe to Japan stops in Canada to change planes, has a heart attack at the airport, and is rushed to hospital, where it is determined her heart is severely damaged and she needs an emergency transplant. A heart is available but was scheduled for another patient who is in non-emergency condition. Who gets the transplant and why? Canada has universal Medicare, but what if the traveller's country does not and the traveller has no insurance to cover it? Does it matter if the traveller can afford to pay the full cost, or cannot?

43. Birth tourism has become commonplace for hospitals on the West Coast of North America. Pregnant women from countries across the Pacific arrange to travel there to have their children, so they can obtain dual citizenship as a hedge against an uncertain future at home. The substantial cost is paid through the birth tourism travel agent, so the hospital and medical system do not lose any money. However, this puts a strain on the medical systems in the states and provinces affected by limiting their ability to serve the surrounding population. Should this practice be (a) encouraged as a money-making venture or (b) forbidden to conserve limited resources? Why?

44. A deadly pandemic rages, but a vaccine is developed and made freely available. However, an emergent conspiracy theory claiming

the disease is a fake and the vaccine merely a step toward total government control of the population, so many refuse to accept it, despite it being mandated by the government. An unvaccinated individual gets sick and does recover, but not before infecting several children for whom the vaccine is not yet tested and approved. One of the children dies, and the miscreant is charged with reckless endangerment causing death (also known as manslaughter, or third-degree murder in some jurisdictions). You are a member of the jury hearing the case. The prosecution argues that the defendant knew or should have known from the available science that the disease was real and the vaccine safe and effective, so his actions were akin to someone driving drunk and running over the child. The defense argues that the defendant was acting based on a reasonable and widely held belief, that could well be true and is therefore not criminally responsible for the child's death. Its lawyers suggest, without offering evidence, that the child died of something else, rejecting expert testimony establishing she died of the disease and was otherwise healthy. (a) In the jury room, how do you vote, and why? (b) Supposing that a guilty verdict is returned, what should the sentence be, and why?

45. The poorest in any country, especially if of a minority group, usually have impaired access to its medical system. What can be done to alleviate this inequity?

Bibliography

ACM Committee on Professional Ethics. *ACM Code of Ethics and Professional Conduct.* ACM, 2018.

Alcorn, Paul A. *Social Issues in Technology: A Format For Investigation (Fourth ed.).* Englewood Cliffs, NJ: Prentice-Hall, 2002.

Anglin, Gary J. *Instructional Technology: Past, Present, and Future (Third ed.).* Libraries Unlimited, 2010.

Anmoore, Louise. *Cloud Ethics: Algorithms and the Attributes of Ourselves and Others.* Duke University Press, 2020.

Appiah, K. and Anthony, Gutmann, Amy. *The Only Race is the Human Race.* The Journal of Blacks in Higher Education No. 19 (Spring, 1998), pp. 134-137.

Arden, Harvey. "The Fire That Never Dies." *National Geographic* 172, 3 (September 1987).

Asimov, Isaac and Frenkel, Karen A. *Robots: Machines in Man's Image.* New York: Harmony, 1985.

Baase, Sara and Henry, Timothy. *A Gift of Fire: Social, Legal, and Ethical Issues for Computers and the Internet (Fifth ed.).* Pearson, 2017.

Baecker, Ronald M. *Computers and Society: Modern Perspectives.* Oxford University Press, 2019.

Ballard, Edward Goodwin. *Man and Technology: Toward the Measurement of a Culture (Third ed.).* Pittsburgh: Duquesne University Press, 1980.

Barbour, Ian. *Religion And Science.* San Francisco, Harper Collins, 2013.

Barger, Robert N. *Computer Ethics: A Case Based Approach.* Cambridge University Press, 2008.

Barlow, Daniel Lenox. *Educational Psychology: The Teaching-Learning Process.* Chicago: Moody Press, 1985.

Barr, Donald. *Who Pushed Humpty Dumpty: Dilemmas in American Education Today.* New York: Atheneum, 1972.

Barraclough, Geoffrey. *Turning Points in World History.* London, England: Thames and Hudson, 1979.

Barrow, Robin. *Radical Education–A Critique of Freeschooling and Deschooling.* Routledge, 2014.

Barton, Len and Walker, Stephen (ed.). *Education and Social Change.* London: Croom Helm, 1985.

Bebbington, David. *Patterns in History.* Waco, Texas: Baylor University Press, 2018.

Bennett, Gaymon (ed.). *The Ethics of Biotechnology.* Routledge, 2022.

Berg, Ivan. *Education and Jobs: The Great Training Robbery.* New York: Praeger, 1970.

Berggren, W.A. and Van Couvering, John A. (eds.). *Catastrophies and Earth History: The New Uniformitarianism*. Princeton University Press, 1984.

Berman, P. *Debating PC: The Controversy over Political Correctness on College Campuses*. New York: Laurel, 1995.

Bibby, Reginald W. *Fragmented Gods: the Poverty and Potential of Religion in Canada*. Toronto: Irwin, 1987.

Bibby, Reginald W. *Unknown Gods: the Ongoing Story of Religion in Canada*. Toronto: Stoddart, 1993.

Bibby, Reginald W. *Restless Gods: the Renaissance of Religion in Canada*. Toronto: Stoddart, 2002.

Bibby, Reginald W. *Beyond the Gods and Back: Religion's Demise and Rise and Why It Matters*. Lethbridge: Project Canada, 2011.

Bibby, Reginald W. *Resilient Gods: Being Pro-Religious, Low Religious, or No Religious in Canada*. Toronto: Stoddart, 2017.

Biehler, Robert F. & Snowman, Jack. *Psychology Applied to Teaching (Sixth ed.)*. Boston: Houghton Mifflin, 1989.

Blaumer, Robert. *Alienation and Freedom: The Factory Worker and His Industry*. Chicago: University of Chicago Press, 1964.

Bloom, Allan. *The Closing of the American Mind: How Higher Education Has Failed Democracy and Impoverished the Souls of Today's Students*. New York: Simon and Schuster, 1987, 2012.

Bloom, Harold. *The Western Canon: The Books and School of the Ages*. New York: Riverhead, 1995, 2000.

Bowen, James. *A History of Western Education v1-3*. Routledge, 2003.

Bowers, C.A. *The Promise of Theory: Education and the Politics of Cultural Change*. New York: Longman, 1984.

Boylan, Michael (ed.). *Environmental Ethics (Third ed.)*. Wiley-Blackwell, 2022.

Braswell, George W. Jr. *Understanding World Religions*. Nashville: Broadman, 1983, 1994.

Braybrooke, David. *Ethics in the World of Business*. Totowa, NJ: Rowman and Littlefield, 1989.

Brophy, Donald (ed.). *Science and Faith in the 21st Century*. New York: Paulist Press, 1968.

Burke, James. *The Day the Universe Changed*. Boston: Little Brown, 1986.

Burkhardt, Margaret A., Nathaniel and Alvita K. *Ethics and Issues in Comtemporary Nursing (Fourth ed.)*. Delmar, 2019.

Burton, Emanuelle and Goldsmith, Judy, et.al. *Computing and Technology Ethics: Engaging Through Science Fiction*. MIT Press. 2023.

Bush, Ryan A. *Designing the Mind: The Principles of Psychitecture*. Independently published, 2021.

Butterfield, H. *The Origins of Modern Science 1300-1800*. New York: Macmillan, 1962, 1965.

Byars, Stephen M and Stanberry, Kurt, et al. *Business Ethics*. Oxford University Press 2019.

Byl, John. *God and Cosmos: A Christian View of Time, Space, and the Universe*. Banner of Truth Trust, 2001.

Cahn, Steven M.,and Shatz, David (eds.). *Contemporary Philosophy of Religion*. New York: Oxford University Press, 1982, 1999.

BIBLIOGRAPHY

Carman, John and Juergensmeyer, Mark (eds.) *Bibliography of Comparative Religious Ethics*. Cambridge: Cambridge University Press, 1991.

Cetron, Marvin and O'Toole, Thomas. *Encounters with the Future: a Forecast of Life Into the 21st. Century*. New York: McGraw Hill, 1982.

Chamberlain, Paul. *Can We Be Good Without God?: A Conversation About Truth, Morality, Culture and a Few Other Things That Matter*. IVP, 2002.

Chewning, Richard C., Eby, John W., and Roels, Shirley J. *Business Through the Eyes of Faith*. HarperOne, 1990.

Chittick, Donald E. *The Controversy: Roots of the Creation-Evolution Conflict*. Portland, OR: Multnomah Press, 1984.

Clarke, Arthur C. *Prophets of the Future* (Millenium ed.). London: Gollancz, 1999.

Coeckelbergh, Mark. *AI Ethics*. MIT Press, 2020.

Coeckelbergh, Mark. *Robot Ethics*. MIT Press, 2022.

Condrey, B. J. *The Possibility and Role of Supererogation in Evangelical Ethics*. Wipf and Stock, 2023.

Cowley, Robert (ed.). *What If?* Putnam, 1999.

Coysh, Joanne. *Human Rights in Education and the Politics of Knowledge*. Routledge, 2018.

Craft, Maurice (ed.). *Education and Cultural Pluralism*. Philadelphia: Falmer, 1984, Reprint: Routledge Library Editions 2017.

Cramer, John G. *Rejuvenation and the DNA Methylation Clock*. Analog, March-April 2021 p75–77.

Crane, Andrew and Matten, Dirk, et. al. *Business Ethics: Managing Corporate Citizenship and Sustainability in the Age of Globalization (fifth ed.)*. Oxford University Press 2019.

Dannenfeldt, Karl H. *The Church of the Renaissance and Reformation: Decline and Reform from 1300 to 1600*. St Louis, MO: Concordia, 1970, 1978.

DeGeorge, Richard T. *Business Ethics (Seventh ed.)*. Pearson, 2009.

DeGregori, Thomas R. *A Theory of Technology: Continuity and Change in Human Development*. Ames, Iowa: The Iowa State University Press, 1985.

DeMarco, Joseph P, Jones Gary E. and Daly, Barbara J. *Ethical and Legal Issues in Nursing*. Broadview, 2019.

Dembski, William and Kushiner, James(ed.). *Signs of Intelligence: Understanding Intelligent Design*. Brazos, 2001.

Dembski, William. *Intelligent Design: The Bridge Between Science and Theology*. Downers Grove, IL: InterVarsity Press, 2002.

Denning, Peter J. and Metcalfe, Robert M. *Beyond Calculation: The Next Fifty Years of Computing*. New York: Springer-Verlag, 1997.

de Raadt, J.D.R. *A New Management of Life*. Edwin Mellen, 1997.

Dershowitz, Alan. *Cancel Culture: The Latest Attack on Free Speech and Due Process*. Hot Books, 2020.

Dewey, John. *Experience & Education*. New York: Collier, 1968, Free Press Reprint ed. 1997.

Diamandis, Peter H. and Kotler, Steven. *The Future Is Faster Than You Think: How Converging Technologies Are Transforming Business, Industries, and Our Lives*. Simon & Schuster, 2020.

Dixon, Bernard. *What is Science for?* New York: Harper & Row, 1973.

Donaldson, Dwight Martin. *Studies in Muslim Ethics*. Hassel Street, 2021.

BIBLIOGRAPHY

Donaldson, Thomas, and Werhane, Patricia H. (eds.). *Ethical Issues in Business: A Philosophical Approach (Eighth ed.).* Pearson, 2007.

Downey, Deane, and Porter, Stanley (eds.) Sutcliffe, Richard J. (cont.). *Christian Worldview and the Academic Disciplines.* Hamilton: McMaster Divinity Press, 2009.

Drexler, K. Eric, and Peterson, Chris. *Nanotechnology.* Analog, (Mid-December, 1987): 48–60.

Drexler, K. Eric. *Engines of Creation: Challenges and Choices of the Last Technological Revolution.* Garden City, NY: Anchor, 1986.

Drexler, K. Eric. *Engines of Creation: The Coming Era of Nanotechnology.* Garden City, NY: Anchor, 1987.

Drexler, K. Eric. *Nanosystems, Molecular Machinery, Manufacturing and Computation.* Wiley, 1992.

Dubber, Markus and Pasquale, Frank. *Oxford Handbook of Ethics of AI.* Oxford University Press, 2021.

Durant, Will and Ariel. *The Lessons of History.* New York: Simon and Schuster, 1968, 2010.

Ellul, Jacques. *Money and Power.* Downers Grove, IL: InterVarsity Press, 1984.

Ellul, Jacques. *The Technological Society.* New York: Knopf, 1967, 1973.

Emberley, Peter C. and Newall, Waller R. *Bankrupt Education: The Decline of Liberal Education in Canada.* Toronto: University of Toronto Press, 1996.

Emberley, Peter C. *Zero Tolerance: Hot Button Politics in Canadian Universities.* Toronto: Penguin, 1996.

Evan, William M. and Manion, Mark. *Minding the Machines: Preventing Technological Disasters.* Prentice Hall, 2002.

Ezorsky, Gertrude (ed.). *Moral Rights in the Workplace.* New York: SUNY Press, 1972, 1987.

Fjermedal, Grant. *The Tomorrow Makers: A Brave New World of Living-Brain Machines.* New York: Macmillan, 1986, 1988.

Flynn, Michael F. *The Great Ptolemaic Smackdown,* Analog January/February 2013 p 14–27.

Flynn, Michael. *An Introduction to Psychohistory.* Analog April 1988 p 60–78 (Part 1) and May 1988 p38–64 (Part 2).

Fraley, Alger. *The Artificial Intelligence and Generative AI Bible: (5 in 1) The Most Updated and Complete Guide | From Understanding the Basics to Delving into GANs, NLP, Prompts, Deep Learning, and Ethics of AI.* AlgoRay, 2023.

Frankena, William K. *Perspectives on Morality.* South Bend, IN: University of Notre Dame Press, 1976.

Friedman, Thomas L. *The Lexus and the Olive Tree: Understanding Globalization (Second ed.).* Farrar, Straus and Giroux, 2000.

Garfield, Jay L. *Buddhist Ethics: A Philosophical Exploration.* Oxford University Press, 2021.

Geisler, Norman L. *Ethics: Alternatives and Issues.* Grand Rapids, MI: Zondervan, 1971.

Geisler, Norman. *Christian Ethics: Contemporary Issues and Options.* Baker Academic, 2010.

Gish, Duane T. *Evolution The Fossils Say NO!* San Diego: Creation—Life, 1973.

Glos, Raymond E. et al. *Business: Its Nature and Environment, An Introduction (Ninth ed.).* Cincinnati: South-Western, 1980.

BIBLIOGRAPHY

Granberg-Michaelson, Wesley (ed.). *Tending the Garden: Essays on the Gospel and the Earth*. Grand Rapids, MI: Eerdmans, 1987.

Green, Erin and Singh, Divya et. al. *AI Ethics and Higher Education: Good Practice and Guidance for Educators, Learners, and Institutions*. Globethics.net, 2022.

Green, Ronald M. *Religious Reason: The Rational and Moral Basis of Religious Belief*. New York: Oxford University Press, 1978.

Greer, Sandra C. *Elements of Ethics for Physical Scientists*. MIT Press, 2017.

Grenz, Stanley. *The Moral Quest: Foundations of Christian Ethics*. IVP Academic, 2000.

Grudem, Wayne. *Christian Ethics: An Introduction to Biblical Moral Reasoning*. Crossway, 2018.

Hall, Ernest L. *Robotics: A User-Friendly Introduction*. New York: CBS, 1985.

Hammer, Michael and Champy, James. *Reengineering the Corporation: A Manifesto for Business Revolution*. ˆHarper Collins, 1993, 1994.

Hammond, Phillip E. *The Sacred in a Secular Age: Toward Revision in the Scientific Study of Religion*. Berkely: University of California Press, 1985, 2022.

Hancock, Roger N. *Twentieth Century Ethics*. New York: Columbia University Press, 1974.

Hawkin, David J. *Christ and Modernity: Christian Self-Understanding in a Technological Age*. Waterloo, Ontario: Wilfred Laurier University Press, 1985, 2010.

Heimbach, Daniel R. *True Sexual Morality: Recovering Biblical Standards for a Culture in Crisis*. Crossway, 2004.

Henry, Carl F. H. *Christian Personal Ethics*. Baker, 1977.

Henson, H. Keith. *Memetics and the Modular Mind: Modelling the Development of Social Movements*. Analog, August 1987: p29–42.

Hill, Winifred F. *Learning: A Survey of Psychological Interpretations (Seventh ed.)* Pearson, 2001.

Hillerbrand, Hans J. *Men and Ideas in the Sixteenth Century (Sixth ed.)*. Waveland, 1984.

Hirsch, E.D. Jr. *Cultural Literacy: What Every American Needs to Know*. Boston: Houghton Mifflin, 1987.

Hodges, Henry. *Technology in the Ancient World*. New York: Knopf, 1970.

Hoffman, W. Michael, Frederick, Robert E., and Schwartz, Mark S. *Business Ethics: Readings and Cases in Corporate Morality (eds.) (Fifth ed.)*. Wiley-Blackwell, 2014.

Hofstadter, Douglas R. *Gödel, Escher, Bach: an Eternal Golden Braid*. New York: Basic Books, 1979.

Hollinger, Dennis. *Choosing the Good: Christian Ethics in a Complex World*. Baker Academic, 2002.

Holloway, Richard. *A Little History of Religion (Reprint ed.)*. Yale University Press, 2017.

Holmes, Arthur F. *All Truth is God's Truth*. Inter-Varsity, 1979.

Holmes, Arthur F. *The Idea of a Christian College*. Grand Rapids, MI: Eerdmans, 1987.

Hoogkaas, R. *Religion and the Rise of Modern Science*. Regent College, 2000.

Horton, John and Mendus, Susan (eds.) *Aspects of Toleration*. London: Methuen, 1985, 2013.

Hudson, W. D. *Modern Moral Philosophy (Second ed.)*. New York: St. Martins, 1983.

Hume, Robert E. *The Worlds Living Religions (rev. ed.)*. New York: Scribners, 1959.

Hummel, Charles E. *The Galileo Connection: Resolving Conflicts Between Science and the Bible*. Downers Grove, IL: InterVarsity, 1986, 1994.

Humphreys, Kenneth K. *What Every Engineer Should Know About Ethics*. Marcel Dekker, 1999.

BIBLIOGRAPHY

Inose, Hiroshi, and Pierce John R. *Information, Technology and Civilization*. New York: Freeman, 1984.

Jencks, Christopher and Riesman, David. *The Academic Revolution*. Transaction, 2001.

Jenkins, Clive, and Sherman, Barrie. *The Collapse of Work*. London: Eyre Methuen Ltd., 1979.

Feinberg, John and Paul. *Ethics for a Brave New World, (Second ed.)*. Crossway, 2010.

Fischler, Martin A. and Firschein, Oscar. *Intelligence: The Eye, the Brain, and the Computer*. Addison-Wesley, 1987.

Johnson, Phillip. *Evolution as Dogma: The Establishment of Naturalism*. Haughton, 1990.

Jones, David. *An Introduction to Biblical Ethics (B&H Studies in Christian Ethics)*. B and H Academic, 2015.

Kaku, Michio. *The Future of Humanity: Our Destiny in the Universe*. New York: Anchor, 2019.

Kaku, Michio. *The God Equation*. Doubleday, 2021.

Kaku, Michio. *Visions: How Science Will Revolutionize the 21st Century*. New York: Anchor, 1999.

Kaku, Michio. *Hyperspace: A Scientific Journey Through Parallel Universes, Time Warps, and the 10th Dimension*. Anchor, 1995.

Kallman, Ernest A. and Grillo, John P. *Ethical Decision Making and Information Technology: An Introduction with Cases (Second ed.)*. McGraw Hill, 1993, 1996.

Karier, Clarence J. *The Individual, Society, and Education*. University of Illinois Press, 1986.

Kelly, Northrup. *Legal Issues in Nursing*. St. Louis, MO: C.V. Mosby, 1987.

Kenny, Martin. *Biotechnology: The University-Industrial Complex (Rev. ed.)*. New Haven, CN: Yale University Press, 1988.

Kenyon, Kathleen M. *The Bible and Recent Archaeology*. Atlanta: John Knox, 1978.

King, Peter J. *The Western Canon of Classic Literature: "The Great Books of The Western World."* CreateSpace, 2016.

Klass, Morton and Hellman, Hal. *The Kinds of Mankind: An Introduction to Race and Racism*. Philadelphia: Lippincott, 1971.

Klemke, E.D. et al. (ed.) *Introductory Readings in the Philosophy of Science (Third ed.)*. Buffalo, NY: Prometheus, 1998.

Kline, Morris. *Why Johnny Can't Add: The Failure of the New Math*. New York: St. Martin's, 1973.

Knight, David. *The Age of Science*. New York: Blackwell, 1986.

Koertge, Noretta (ed.). *A House Built on Sand: Exposing Postmodernist Myths About Science*. Oxford University Press, 1998.

Kovalik, Dan. *Cancel This Book: The Progressive Case Against Cancel Culture*. Hot Books, 2021.

Kozol, Johnathan. *Death at an Early Age*. Bantam, 1968.

Kuhn, Thomas S. *The Structure of Scientific Revolutions: Vol 2 No 2 in The International Encyclopedia of Unified Science (Fourth ed.)*. Chicago: The University of Chicago Press, 2012.

Larson, Eric J. *The Myth of Artificial Intelligence: Why Computers Can't Think the Way We Do*. Harvard University Press, 2021.

Lencioni, Patrick M. *The Advantage: Why Organizational Health Trumps Everything Else in Business*. CreateSpace, 2016.

Levine, Arthur and Van Pelt, Scott J. *The Great Upheaval: Higher Education's Past, Present, and Uncertain Future.* Johns Hopkins University Press, 2021.

Lewis, C.S. *The Abolition of Man.* New York: Macmillan, 1953.

Lin, Patrick, Abney, Keith et al. *Robot Ethics: The Ethical and Social Implications of Robots.* MIT Press, 2014.

Lin, Patrick, Jenkins, Ryan et al. *Robot Ethics 2.0: From Autonomous Cars to Artificial intelligence.* Oxford University Press, 2019.

Ling, Trevor. *A History of Religion East and West.* London: Macmillan, 1968.

Litfin, Duane. *Conceiving the Christian College.* Eerdmans, 2004.

Lo, Thomas Y. and Chien, Paul K. et al. *Evolution and Intelligent Design in a Nutshell.* Discovery Institute, 2020.

Logstrup, Knud E. *The Ethical Demand.* Philadelphia: Fortress, 1971.

Lower, Arthur R.M. *A Pattern for History.* Toronto: McClelland and Stewart, 1978.

Lund, Erik, Phil, Mognes, and Slok, Johannes. *A History of European Ideas.* W. Glyn Jones, trans. Reading, MA: Addison-Wesley.

Martens, David. *Data Science Ethics: Concepts, Techniques, and Cautionary Tales.* Oxford University Press, 2022.

Martin, Robert C. *Clean Craftsmanship: Disciplines, Standards, and Ethics.* Addison-Wesley, 2021.

Mason, Stephen F. *A History of the Sciences (Rev. ed.).* New York: Collier, 1970.

Miller, Franklin and Wertheimer, Alan (eds.). *The Ethics of Consent: Theory and Practice.* Oxford University Press, 2009..

Minsky, Marvin. *The Emotion Machine: Commonsense Thinking, Artificial Intelligence, and the Future of the Human Mind.* New York: Simon & Schuster, 2007.

Minsky, Marvin. *The Society of Mind.* New York: Simon & Schuster, 1988.

Montagu, Ashley (ed.). *Science and Creationism.* Oxford: Oxford University Press, 1984, 1999.

Montgomery, John Warwick. *Human Rights and Human Dignity.* 1517 Publishing, 2019.

Montgomery, John Warwick. *The Shape of the Past: A Christian Response to Secular Philosophies of History.* Wipf and Stock, 2008.

More, Thomas. (tr. Turner, Paul) *Utopia.* Penguin Classics, 2003.

Morris, Henry M. (ed.). *Scientific Creationism.* New Leaf, 2012.

Morris, Henry M. *An Answer For Asimov.* in Impact #99 El Cajon, CA: Institute For Creation Research 1981.

Morris, Henry M. *Biblical Basis For Modern Science (Rev. ed.).* New Leaf, 2002.

Naisbitt, John and Aburdene, Patricia. *Megatrends 2000.* New York: Morrow, 1990.

Naisbitt, John and Aburdene, Patricia. *Re-inventing the Corporation.* Macdonald and Co., 1986.

Niebuhr, Reinhold. *Moral Man and Immoral Society: A Study in Ethics and Politics.* Must Have Books, 2021.

Nielsen, Kai. *Ethics Without God.* London: Pemberton, 1973.

Nyholm, Sven and Hales, Steven D. *This is Technology Ethics: An Introduction.* Wiley-Blackwell, 2023.

O'Donovan, Oliver. *Resurrection and Moral Order: An Outline for Evangelical Ethics (Rev. ed.).* Eerdmans, 1994.

Ohmae, Kenichi. *The End of the Nation State: The Rise of Regional Economies.* New York: Touchstone, 1996.

Orwell, George. *Nineteen eighty-four (Reprint ed.)* Harmondsworth, England: Penguin, 1964.
Owens, Virginia Stem. *And the Trees Clap Their Hands: Faith, Perception, and the New Physics.* Wipf and Stock, 2005.
Owens, Ernest. *The Case for Cancel Culture: How This Democratic Tool Works to Liberate Us All.* St. Martin's, 2023.
Pemberton, Prentiss L. and Finn, Daniel Rush. *Toward a Christian Economic Ethic: Stewardship and Social Power.* Minneapolis, MN: Winston, 1985.
Piel, Gerald. *The Age of Science.* Basic Books, 2001.
Plant, Raymond, et al (eds.) *Information Technology: the Public Issues (Fulbright Papers).* Manchester: Manchester University Press, 1988.
Popper, K. R. *The Logic of Scientific Discovery.* London: Hutchinson, 1959.
Price, J. Randall and House, H. Wayne. *Zondervan Handbook of Biblical Archaeology: A Book by Book Guide to Archaeological Discoveries Related to the Bible.* Zondervan Academic, 2017.
Quebedeau, Richard. *By What Authority: The Rise of Personality Cults in American Christianity.* San Fransisco: Harper & Row, 1982.
Quinn, Michael. *Ethics for the Information Age (Seventh ed.).* Pearson, 2016.
Powers, Thomas M. *Philosophy and Computing: Essays in Epistemology, Philosophy of Mind, Logic, and Ethics.* Springer, 2018.
Rees, Martin. *On the Future: Prospects for Humanity.* Princeton University Press, 2021.
Reid, W. Stanford (ed.). *The Reformation: Revival or Revolution.* New York: Holt, 1968.
Reigeluth, Charles M. (ed.). *Instructional Theories and Models Vol I-IV.* Routledge, 2009–2016.
Reynolds, George W. Ethics in Information Technology *(Sixth ed.).* Course Technology, 2018.
Robson, Gregory J., Tsou, Johathan Y. *Technology Ethics: A Philosophical Introduction and Readings.* Routledge, 2023.
Rogers, Glenn. *21st Century Ethics: An Introduction to Moral Philosophy.* Simpson and Brook, 2012.
Roszak, Theodore. *The Cult of Information: A Neo-Luddite Treatise on High-Tech, Artificial Intelligence, and the True Art of Thinking.* University of California Press, 1994.
Rowe, Christopher and Thompson, Jane. *People and Chips: The Human Implications of Information Technology (Second Ed..* McGraw Hill, 199.
Rybczynski, Witold. *Taming the Tiger: The Struggle to Control Technology.* Penguin, 1985.
Salzman, Marian. *The New Megatrends: Seeing Clearly in the Age of Disruption.* Currency, 2022.
Sandin, Robert T. *The Search for Excellence: The Christian College in an Age of Educational Competition.* Macon, GA: Mercer University Press, 1982.
Schaeffer, Francis A. *How Should We Then Live: The Rise and Decline of Western Thought and Culture.* Old Tappan, NJ: Fleming H. Revell, 1976, PB: Crossway 2022.
Schori, Katherine, Jefferts (cont.) and Wallace, Peter M. (ed.) *Faith and Science in the 21st Century: A Postmodern Primer for Youth and Adults.* Church, 2018.
Schuurman, Egbert. *Technology and the Future: A Philosophical Challenge.* Toronto: Wedge, 1980, PB: Paidela, 2000.
Scorer, C.G. *The Bible and Sex Ethics Today.* London: Tyndale, 1966.

Sherlock, Richard and Morrey, John D. (eds.). *Ethical Issues in Biotechnology.* Rowman and Littlefield, 2002.
Shermer, Michael. *The Borderlands of Science: Where Sense Meets Nonsense.* Oxford University Press, 2001.
Shuurman, Egbert. *Technology and the Future: A Philosophical Challenge.* Toronto: Wedge, 1980.
Sichel, Daniel E. *The Computer Revolution.* Brookings Institution, 1997.
Sieber, Ulrich. *The International Handbook on Computer Crime.* New York: Wiley, 1986.
Smaldino, Sharon E., Lowther, Deborah L. and Mims, Clif. *Instructional Technology and Media for Learning (Twelfth ed.).* Pearson, 2014.
Smith, A. E. Wilder. *The Creation of Life: A Cybernetic Approach to Evolution.* Wheaton, IL: Harold Shaw, 1970.
Smullyan, Raymond. *Forever Undecided: A Puzzle Guide to Gödel.* New York: Knopf, 1987.
Snow, C. P. *The Two Cultures: and A Second Look.* London: Cambridge University Press, 1963.
Snowman, Jack and McCowan, Rick. *Psychology Applied to Teaching (Fourteenth ed.).* Wadsworth 2014.
Sommerville, Margaret. *the Ethical Canary: Science, Society, and the Human Spirit.* Penguin, 2000.
Sowa, John F. *Knowledge Representation: Logical, Philosophical, and Computational Foundations.* New York: Brooks Cole. 2000.
Spencer, Nicholas. *Magisteria: The Entangled Histories of Science and Religion.* Oneworld Publications. 2023.
Sterling, William and Waite, Stephen. *Boomernomics: The Future of Your Money in the Upcoming Generational Warfare.* Ballentine, 1998.
Stine, George Harry. *The Hopeful Future.* Macmillan, 1983.
Swade, Doron. *The History of Computing: A Very Short Introduction.* Oxford University Press, 2022.
Sykes, Charles J. *Profscam: Professors and the Demise of Higher Education* Washington: Regnery, 1988.
Tavani, Herman T. *Ethics and Technology: Controversies, Questions, and Strategies for Ethical Computing (Fifth ed.).* Wiley, 2016.
Taylor, Richard. *Ethics, Faith and Reason.* Englewood Cliffs, NJ: Prentice-Hall, 1985.
Taylor, Richard. *Good and Evil: A New Direction.* Buffalo, NY: Prometheus, 1984.
Teich, Albert. *Technology and the Future (Twelfth ed.).* Wadsworth, 2012.
Thiroux, Jacques P. and Kraseman, Keith W. *Ethics: Theory and Practice (Eleventh ed.).* Pearson, 2014..
Tillyard, E. M. W. *The Elizabethan World Picture.* Harmondsworth, England: Penguin, 1966.
Toffler, Alvin and Heidi. *Creating a New Civilization: The Politics of the Third Wave.* Turner Pub, 1995.
Toffler, Alvin. *Previews and Premises (Rev. ed.).* Black Rose, 1999.
Toffler, Alvin. *The Third Wave.* New York: Morrow, 1980; Univ of Oklahoma Press, 1993.
Trefil, James S. *Space: Time: Infinity.* Pantheon, 1986.
van der Poel and Ibo, Royakkers, Lamber. *Ethics, Technology, and Engineering: An Introduction.* Wiley-Blackwell, 2023.

Walsh, Brian J. and Middleton, J. Richard. *The Transforming Vision: Shaping a Christian worldview*. Downers Grove, IL: InterVarsity, 1984, 2005.
Wekert, John. *Computer Ethics*. Routledge, 2019.
Weber, Max. *The Protestant Ethic and the Spirit of Capitalism*. New York: Scribner's, 1958.
Westin, Alan F. *Whistle Blowing! Loyalty and Dissent in the Corporation*. New York: McGraw-Hill, 1981.
Wicks, Andrew and Freeman, R., et al. *Business Ethics*. Pearson 2009.
Wiebe, Philip H. *Theism in an Age of Science*. University Press of America, 1988.
Wilcoxon, Allen, Remley, Theodore P., Gladding, Samuel T. and Huber, Charles H. *Ethical, Legal, and Professional Issues in the Practice of Marriage and Family Therapy (Fifth ed.)*. Pearson, 2013.
Wilson, Edward O. *Consilience: The Unity of Knowledge*. New York: Knopf, 1998.
Wolff, Johathan. *An Introduction to Political Philosophy (Fourth ed.)*. Oxford University Press, 2023.
Wright, Steven A. *Ethics, Law and Technology Adoption: Navigating Technology Adoption Challenges*. Independently published, 2023.

Web resources

Ethics:

The Ethics center for Engineering and Science https://www.cwru.edu/affil/wwwethics/index.htm.
The Institute for Business & Professional Ethics https://condor.depaul.edu/ethics/about.htm.
Bioethics Online Service https://www.mcw.edu/bioethics.

Technology and Social Issues:

Cranor, Lorrie. *Links to Sources of Computers and Society Information*. St. Louis: Washington University. (1997 10 17).
Kay, Charles D. *Computers, Ethics, and Society: Online Coursebook*. Spartanburg SC: Wofford College, Feb 10, 1997. (1997 10 17).
MacDonald, Chris . *Business Ethics Resources on WWW*. Vancouver: center for Applied Ethics, University of British Columbia. (1998 04 28).
Racism, Science, and Pseudo-Science. Proceedings of the symposium to examine pseudo-scientific theories invoked to justify racism and racial discrimination. Athens, 30 March to 3 April 1981. New York: UNESCO, 198.

Creation & Evolution:

Creation Research Society <https://www.creationresearch.org/> (Accessed 2023 06 20).
Talk Origins Archive: Exploring the Creation Evolution Controversy <https://www.talkorigins.org/> (Accessed 2023 06 20).
Biologos: God's Word, God's World <https://biologos.org/> (Accessed 2023 06 20).
PBS Evolution Site <https://www.pbs.org/wgbh/evolution/>.

Other:

Rick Sutcliffe's Fiction and non-Fiction Books. <https://www.arjaybooks.com> (Accessed 2024 08 05).
Rick Sutcliffe's Monthly Column on Technology and Related Issues <https://www.thenorthernspy.com/> (Accessed 2024 08 05).

www.ingramcontent.com/pod-product-compliance
Lightning Source LLC
Chambersburg PA
CBHW052047290426
44111CB00011B/1646